Knowledge-Based Systems and Legal Applications

This is volume 36 in the A.P.I.C. Series

General Editors: M.J.R. Shave *and* I.C. Wand

A complete list of titles in this series appears at the end of this volume

The A.P.I.C. Series
No 36

Knowledge-Based Systems and Legal Applications

edited by

T.J.M. BENCH-CAPON
Department of Computer Science, University of Liverpool, England

ACADEMIC PRESS

Harcourt Brace Jovanovich, Publishers
London San Diego New York Boston
Sydney Tokyo Toronto

ACADEMIC PRESS LIMITED
24/28 Oval Road,
London NW1 7DX

United States Edition published by
ACADEMIC PRESS INC.
San Diego, CA 92101

This book is printed on acid-free paper

British Library Cataloguing in Publication Data

is available

ISBN 0-12-086441-X

Printed and bound in Great Britain by
TJ Press Ltd., Padstow, Cornwall

CONTENTS

Preface vii

Biographical information xi

Part I - Context 1

1 The representation of law in computer programs 3
Marek Sergot

2 The opportunities of the DHSS Demonstrator project 69
Trevor Bench-Capon

Part II: Tasks 75

3 A support environment for adjudicators 77
Andrew Taylor

4 Support for the formulation of legislation 95
Andrew Taylor and Trevor Bench-Capon

5 Support for members of the public 115
Nigel Gilbert

6 Using a common knowledge base in several applications 129
Trevor Bench-Capon

Part III: Prototypes 137
7 The Local Office system 139
Justin Forder and Andrew Taylor
8 The Policy system 165
Graham Storrs
9 The Claimant Advice systems 183
Nigel Gilbert
10 Managing a large collaborative project 199
Charlie Portman

Part IV: Issues 209
11 Analysing texts for knowledge based systems 213
Elizabeth Cordingley
12 Knowledge representation for legal applications 245
Trevor Bench-Capon and Justin Forder
13 Mixed Initiative interaction 265
David Frohlich and Paul Luff
14 Group decision making 295
Graham Storrs
15 Organizational and social implications 309
Andrew Taylor

16 Conclusion 329
Trevor Bench-Capon

Bibliography 343
Index 365

PREFACE

INTRODUCTION

Artificial intelligence is by nature an experimental science, and the subfield of knowledge based systems applied to the legal domain is no exception to this general principle. The field has been stimulated by such notable experiments as McCarty's TAXMAN described in [McCarty 1977], Rissland's HYPO [Rissland and Ashley 1977] and the British Nationality Act experiment of Imperial College [Sergot *et al.* 1976]. Progress has been made through an implementation which serves to clarify the strengths and weaknesses of the underlying ideas, and by reflecting on the experience of implementing these ideas in a working system. Of course, it is not just the reflections of the experiment that are of value, but those of the wider community too. This book is intended to make available the experience gained, and some of the lessons learnt, from a substantial group of related experiments in the field of knowledge based systems and law performed in the Alvey–DHSS Demonstrator project. This project, which ran from 1984 to 1989, represented a remarkable opportunity for the performance of sustained experiments. The chapters in the book represent the reflections on the project of a number of people who participated in the project: some of their conclusions may differ, but they are grounded in a common experience.

The Alvey–DHSS Demonstrator project was a large Demonstrator Project, supported by the Alvey Directorate of the UK Department of Trade and Industry and the UK Science and Engineering Research

Council. The project collaborators were ICL, Logica, Imperial College, and the universities of Lancaster, Liverpool and Surrey. Additionally the Department of Health and Social Security (DHSS), assigned several members of staff to work full time on the project.

The book is organized into four parts. The first part contains some background material needed to put the remainder of the book into context. The second part concentrates of the tasks within the target organization that the project examined ways of supporting. Three distinct areas capable of being supported by KBS were identified, and prototype support systems were built for each of the three areas. An important lesson learnt from the Demonstrator project was that the nature of the task being supported has an all-pervasive influence on the nature of a system to support the task: it is simply not appropriate to build a system and hope that it may be used to support a whole range of users. The detailed teasing out of the distinctive needs of the various tasks was one of the major achievements of the Demonstrator. The third part gives details of the systems constructed in the Demonstrator. These systems are of interest in themselves, and the chapters also serve to give detail of the experimental grounding of the observations and general comments in the other chapters of the book. The final part is organized according to a number of issues which arise in the construction of a KBS in law. Thus there are chapters on knowledge analysis, knowledge representation, the nature of the interaction which such systems, co-operative working and the social and organizational implications of these kinds of system. Lastly, there is a concluding chapter in which I attempt to draw together some of the strands of the previous chapters to produce a framework for the discussion of KBS applied to the legal domain.

Thanks are due to all those who participated in the project and contributed to it in their various ways over its long life. These include Alison Adam, Jo Bird, Andy Bilbe, Sue Blackburn, Tim Bond, Simon Brooke, Julie Browne, Sarah Buckland, Chris Burton, Alan Bustany, Tony Chandler, Marcus Clarke, Carolyne Coleby, Andrew Coney, Betsy Cordingley, Jo Cove, Alan Cox, Leo Crossfield, Ann Currie, Jo Dartnall, Shashi Dave, Patrick Dawson, Paul Duffin, Gary Flood, Justin Forder, David Frolich, Chris Gardner, Nigel Gilbert, Dave Goodwin, Steve Green, Zhang Haiying, Michael Hardey, Ginny Hardy, Sandra Hillawi, Heather Hopkins, Steve Hopwood, Pam Hosking, Will Hounslow, Marina Jirotka, Kevin Johnstone, Simon Katz, Bernard Kelly, Mike Knox, Nick Lapham, Jacky Loh, Duncan Lowes, Angela Lucas, Paul Luff, J.O. Marks, Lil Masterman, Rosemary Mathams, George Matieson, Tony McEnery, Lynette Middleton, Alison Mill-Ingen, Hilary Minor, Steve Owsianka, Mick Pappas, Chris Penn, Martin Perret, Nick Perry, Phil Pettit, Sarah Pettit, Ian Pickup, Charlie Portman, Mark Reeder, Gwen Robinson, Peter Robinson, Tom Routen, Marek Sergot, Murray Shanahan, Graham Storrs, Andrew Taylor, Walton Teasdale, Chris

Thomas, Steve Timms, Peter Turner, Richard Turner, Julie Weaver, Kelvin Hall van der Werve, Mary Whittaker, David Wolstenholme and Graham Young. I would also like to thank my colleagues at Liverpool who helped with the preparation of this book, notably Paul Dunne and Ken Chan.

BIOGRAPHICAL INFORMATION

TREVOR BENCH-CAPON read philosophy and economics at St John's College Oxford, where he also took a D. Phil. He worked for six years at the Department of Health and Social Security in policy and computer branches where he helped to set up the Alvey DHSS Demonstrator project. He then went to Imperial College, London to contribute to the Demonstrator project and to research into logic programming applied to legislation. He has been a lecturer in computer science at the University of Liverpool since 1987.

ELIZABETH S. CORDINGLEY received a bachelors degree in physics in the USA and then obtained a masters degree in social research from the University of Surrey. Her research experience includes studies of computer use in local authority social services departments and she worked on the Alvey DHSS Demonstrator Project from July 1984 until its completion. Elizabeth is currently working as an executive engineer at BT Research Laboratory.

JUSTIN FORDER is a principal consultant at Logica Cambridge Ltd. On the Alvey DHSS Demonstrator he contributed to the policy and local office applications and the definition and design of the Toolkit. He is continuing to use lessons learned from the project in decision-support applications ranging from intelligence analysis to the design of safety-related systems.

DAVID FROHLICH graduated in Psychology at the University of Sheffield in 1980, and stayed on to complete a PhD in skill acquisition. His interests in human-environment interaction led him into the field of human-computer interaction. He worked for a Human Factors consultancy for one year from October 1983 before joining the Alvey DHSS Demonstrator Project as Research Psychologist on the Claimant Information Team at Surrey University. During his 5 years on this project he worked on a variety of tasks supporting the design of the Forms Helper and Advice System, including studies of paper and electronic form-filling, specification of human computer interactions, secondary analysis of advisory consultations, experiments on menu-based natural language interfaces, dialogue design, knowledge analysis and cooperative evaluation. He also held the post of Associate Lecturer at the University, and developed a course on human computer interaction in the Department of Electronic and Electrical Engineering. After leaving the Demonstrator Project in December 1989, David spent several months travelling abroad before taking up his present position as member of technical staff in the Advanced Information Management Department of Hewlett-Packard Laboratories, Bristol. is currently working at Hewlett Packard's research laboratory in Bristol.

NIGEL GILBERT is reader in sociology at the University of Surrey. He pioneered computer welfare benefit information systems for use by claimants with a prototype developed in 1980 and was one of the members of the Alvey DHSS Demonstrator project at its inception in 1984. He now leads the Social and Computer Sciences Research Group at the University of Surrey. His interests include the sociology of scientific knowledge, social mobility, artificial intelligence and human computer interaction. He has published five books and numerous papers on these topics.

PAUL LUFF was awarded a B Sc (Hons) in computer science at the University of York in 1983 since when he has been involved in research into computational linguistics, knowledge-based systems and human-computer interaction. In 1985 he joined the Claimant Information Systems Group of the Alvey DHSS Demonstrator project at the University of Surrey where he helped with the design and implementation of the interface and interaction components of two knowledge-based systems: the Forms Helper and the Advice System. Recently he has co-edited '*Computers and Conversation*' for Academic Press. At present, he is involved in research both at the University of Surrey and Cambridge EuroPARC.

CHARLIE PORTMAN joined Ferranti's computer department in 1954 after gaining a B. Eng at the University of Liverpool. He worked as a circuit engineer, a logic designer and a test programmer and led a drum commissioning team before taking responsibility for the Sirius project. He worked on the Ferranti Orion computer and took the first of these machines to Sweden in 1963. He later started development of the 1900 series machines at West Gorton, Manchester. In 1972 he set up and managed the software division for ICT which had responsibility for 1900 executive programs, test programs for both 1900 and the early 2900 machines, and the early 2900 supervisor program. Later roles in systems engineering and advanced development led to the task of managing the Alvey DHSS Large Scale Demonstrator for the Alvey Directorate of DTI. Currently Charlie is manager of the knowledge and requirements capture programme in ICL's Strategic Systems Service unit in Manchester and is project manager of the JFIT MAKE project.

MAREK SERGOT read mathematics at Trinity College, Cambridge and worked in mathematical modelling before joining the Logic Programming Group of the Department of Computing at Imperial College, London in 1979. He was appointed as a lecturer in 1985. His research interests centre on the use of logic for knowledge representation in artificial intelligence and deductive databases, with particular interest in application to legal and temporal reasoning.

GRAHAM STORRS is a senior consultant with Logica Cambridge, Ltd., a research and development centre for Logica worldwide. He works with the Human-Computer Interaction group which is responsible for a range of projects in the areas of intelligent training, intelligent front ends and HCI analysis and design methods. His present activities include leading a design team on a Civil Aviation Authority project developing a new front end for the Oceanic Air Traffic Control Centre, and the ASAM project, a research project into tool support for safety critical software development. Previous work in Logica has included the Alvey DHSS Demonstrator project, development of intelligent tutoring systems and HCI consultancy. His background has been in human factors consultancy, and in academic research into HCI and AI. His PhD work at the University of Surrey was in the field of cognitive psychology..

ANDREW TAYLOR read Philosophy at the University of Lancaster and Sheffield and did a Ph D in Information Systems at Lancaster. He worked for ICI as a management consultant before joining the the Department of Systems at the University of Lancaster. He worked on the Alvey DHSS Demonstrator throughout its life and has recently joined Linklater Payne.

PART I

CONTEXT

The majority of the chapters in this book describe work based on the Alvey DHSS Demonstrator project. The purpose of this part is to provide the context into which the project fitted: for research does not proceed in isolation, but is influenced both by what went before, and by contemporary developments. The first chapter, by Marek Sergot - a distinguished figure in the field of KBS and law, and who while not a full participant in the demonstrator project, had close links with it for much of its life - is an authoritative survey of a number of different approaches to the representation of law in computer systems. The second chapter, written by the Trevor Bench-Capon, sets out the opportunities that the demonstrator project presented; the scale and nature of the enterprise meant that these were quite different from those that had been afforded by any previous undertaking in the field.

CHAPTER 1

THE REPRESENTATION OF LAW IN COMPUTER PROGRAMS

Marek Sergot

1.1. INTRODUCTION

There is a substantial amount of literature concerned with the applications of computers to law. This chapter is a survey of those projects which have proposed or implemented representations of law in a form which can be processed by computer.

The survey is not primarily a catalogue of projects. I have tried to compare and contrast the various approaches that have been taken, and to indicate how they are related to one another. I have selected for detailed consideration certain projects, or groups of projects, which are representative of a particular approach. For each, I have given a basic description of the project and references to similar projects elsewhere. These descriptions are just abstracts. Concrete examples would of course make the descriptions more intelligible and self-contained, but space does not permit. In addition to the abstracts, I have added a commentary of my own. This commentary identifies the characteristic features of the approach represented and discusses the fundamental issues raised. The survey can be read in two ways: its main aim is to describe and compare the various approaches, but it can also be read as a catalogue of abstracts by ignoring the commentary included with each entry.

It is always dangerous to attempt a comparative survey, particularly in an area which has such a wide range of diverse approaches. Even though this survey makes no specific recommendations on relative strengths and weaknesses, it must be stressed that my commentaries

KNOWLEDGE-BASED SYSTEMS AND LEGAL APPLICATIONS. ISBN 0-12-086441-X express a personal opinion. I have not been able to discuss every aspect of every project. In omitting some detail, I may have misrepresented some projects unintentionally, or imposed an emphasis that the original investigators would not share. Definitive accounts of projects can only be obtained from the originators. I have included references to all the projects I mention.

1.1.1. The representation of law in computer programs

Many of the projects described in this survey are examples of what McCarty [1983a] has called legal analysis and planning systems. In very general terms, such a system allows the facts of a real or hypothetical case to be represented at some appropriate level of abstraction; it incorporates a representation of the law in one form or another; it is designed to 'apply' or 'match' this representation to the given facts; and it can thus determine what legal concepts and relationships would seem to hold and what legal consequences would seem to follow. As McCarty points out, this is the kind of system that most often comes to mind when computer-based legal consultation is referred to.

The description is over-simplified. In particular, the nature of the law is such that we can never say with certainty whether a legal concept does or does not apply in a given case. In all but exceptional circumstances, it is not computer programs but courts of law or other adjudicating authorities that decide such questions.

Though there are notable exceptions, most projects concerning the computer representation of law make use of artificial intelligence techniques. In such cases, it is common to speak of programs that can 'reason with the law'. References to legal expert systems are also common. In this survey I shall avoid referring to a program as an expert system. The term is now so imprecise that it has lost most of its meaning. Worse, the term 'expert systems' has many connotations, some of which are unacceptable in an area as sensitive as the law. For these reasons, I prefer to speak of computer programs that represent the law, and that can process, or execute, or 'reason with' these representations. Where I do use the term 'expert system' it refers specifically to a particular approach.

Representation of the law in computer programs is not a new idea. Loevinger [1949] and Mehl [1958], for example, anticipated many of the systems that are currently being implemented and proposed. And of course speculation on the possibility of mechanising parts of the legal process predates this by centuries. Similarly, some of the very earliest computer applications can be regarded as embodying a representation of law. Payroll systems, for example, perform calculations on salaries and make deductions as laid down by tax and related legislation. Indeed, many data processing applications are essentially (quasi) legal, in that they are designed to administer the rules and regulations that govern the running of an organization. The idea that many actual financial and administrative systems can be specified, first in terms of rules and regulations, and then in terms of the way these regulations are translated into information processing tasks, is the basic motivation behind Ronald Stamper's LEGOL project. LEGOL is examined in section 1.9 of this chapter.

Following Stamper, section 1.7.5 classifies administrative data-processing systems as programs that incorporate a representation of 'law', where this representation is not made explicit. It is freely admitted, of course, that a typical payroll system would not be classified by most commentators as a 'legal analysis system that can reason with tax law'. Nevertheless, there is no essential difference between a program that calculates how much tax to deduct from an employee's salary and a program that determines whether a legal concept (like 'taxpayer') should apply in the case of a given individual.

1.2. SCOPE OF THE SURVEY

There is a topic of direct relevance to this survey, which has a much longer tradition than computing or artificial intelligence. The role of logic in the law, and the logical analysis of law and legal reasoning, have always been central issues in jurisprudence and legal philosophy. Although I do not attempt a survey of writings on this topic, I have included some discussion because investigations into the logical analysis of law and legal reasoning are directly related to many current projects concerning the computer representation of law. Moreover, any representation of law in any form of symbolic logic can, in principle, be processed by computer.

Most applications of computers to law fall outside the scope of this survey. Many have nothing to do with representing the law: word processing, accounting, time-costing and time-recording, communication systems, court administration systems, and so on, are excluded from this survey. On computing applications in the law office generally, see for example [Bellord 1983], [Ruoff 1984]. Also excluded are those computer systems which store and retrieve legal documents. If this had to be justified, one could distinguish between the sources of law, such as statutes, codes, rules and regulations, case reports and legal textbooks, and the law itself, that which is actually applied by judges and lawyers and other legal practitioners. Document retrieval systems store and retrieve the sources of law. This survey is concerned instead with systems that attempt to go beyond the text itself, to represent and process the 'meaning' of legal documents. For an excellent survey of document retrieval systems in law, see [Bing 1984].

Document retrieval systems are excluded from the survey but they are not disregarded entirely. There is a body of work that attempts to enhance the functionality of document retrieval systems by incorporating a representation of the law to guide the retrieval process. Much of this work has been influenced by, and has influenced in turn, approaches more directly concerned with representing and reasoning with law. This work is covered in section 1.14. Lastly, some projects P, particularly those concerned with case law P, can be regarded as reasoning with representations of the law essentially for the purpose of identifying relevant legal sources.

There is also a small body of research on the use of artificial intelligence techniques to study the cognitive processes involved in legal reasoning. This work falls outside the scope of this survey. See [Kolodner *et al.* 1985] for an example.

1.2.1. Sources of information

No detailed comparative assessment of the leading projects in this area has been published to my knowledge, though several useful surveys and digests are available.

Many of the supplementary references for this paper were taken from an extensive bibliography and collection of abstracts compiled by Biagioli and Fameli [1987], and from the bibliography in Richard Susskind's doctoral thesis and book [Susskind 1986a]. The survey in Anne Gardner's doctoral thesis [1984] is also recommended.

A concise account of some early projects is provided by [Cook *et al.* 1981] in which the investigators of six projects summarize their work. A general article by Thorne McCarty [1983a] from the same period describes several potential types of application and is a good introduction to the area.

In 1979, a meeting on computers and law held in Swansea was attended by most of the leading researchers in the field. The collection of papers that resulted from that meeting provides good accounts of many important projects [Niblett 1980]. IDG (Istituto per la Documentazione Giuridica) in Florence has organized a series of conferences (proceedings include [Ciampi 1982], [Martino 1982] and [Martino and Socci 1986]) and publishes a periodical *Informatica e Diritto*. Conferences were held at the University of Houston in 1984 and 1985 (proceedings in [Walter 1985, 1988]). Lastly, in addition to the numerous conferences and workshops that now take place regularly, there is an established series of International Conferences on Artificial Intelligence and Law. The first was held in Boston in 1987, the second in Vancouver in 1989 and the third will take place in Oxford in 1991. The proceedings of these conferences give an up-to-date account of many current projects and an excellent source of information on projects which have had to be omitted from this survey.

1.2.2. Structure of the survey

The main part of the chapter comprises the survey of projects and approaches. The abstract provided with each entry can be understood without reading the attached commentary.

It is the issues discussed in the commentary which determine the order in which projects appear in the survey. The commentaries grow progressively smaller because many of the issues will have arisen already. The commentaries in the first two entries are the longest since they must introduce the most fundamental questions that apply to any attempt at representing law in a computer program. This would have been the case whatever order had been chosen.

Because projects are not listed in chronological order, the next section provides a brief historical overview to give some impression of the scope and development of the field.

1.3. HISTORICAL OVERVIEW

The computational formalisms that are used to represent and process the law in computer programs can take many forms, not excluding conventional programming languages. It is artificial intelligence techniques, however, which are normally associated with projects in this area.

The first serious proposal for research into the application of artificial intelligence techniques to law was made by Buchanan (who was involved in the DENDRAL project) and Headrick, of Stanford Law School [Buchanan and Headrick 1970]. Several important and influential projects in the area were initiated around this time, the best-known and most sustained of which is Thorne McCarty's TAXMAN project, begun in 1972 and still continuing. McCarty, whose aims are primarily theoretical, has been investigating several fundamental questions of legal reasoning, particularly in his later work on TAXMAN II. He takes as his experimental domain the area of corporate tax law in the USA. McCarty's most recent work has been on components of a language for legal discourse, a logical formalism and a set of underlying fundamental concepts which together will provide what is essentially a theory of practical reasoning. In this survey McCarty's work is presented in two separate sections: the early work on TAXMAN I appears in section 1.12, while TAXMAN II and the Language for Legal Discourse are described in section 1.16.

Also in the early 1970s Jeffrey Meldman began a study at MIT in the torts of assault and battery. Meldman's PhD thesis, completed in 1975, presents the design of a system which attempts to combine reasoning by rules with reasoning from decisions in individual previous cases. Meldman's system was later partially implemented by King in 1976. Anne Gardner's doctoral thesis, completed in 1984 at Stanford University, also attempted to combine reasoning by rules (derived from statutes) with reasoning from previous cases. Central to Gardner's work is the treatment of legal questions to which there is no immediate answer, and the attempt to identify which aspects of a case are 'hard' and which are 'easy'. Gardner's work is grouped here with Meldman's since it can usefully be regarded as an extension and elaboration of that approach. These two projects are described in section 1.15.

The program JUDITH [Popp and Schlink 1975], which treats part of the German Civil Code, also dates from this period though it is not described further in this survey.

Ronald Stamper's LEGOL project also began in the 1970s. The main aim of the LEGOL project was to develop a methodology for the analysis of administrative systems in terms of the rules and regulations that govern an organization, and the information processing tasks to which these regulations give rise. Because of the central role of rules and regulations, and because Stamper took legislation as his main source of experimental material, LEGOL can quite properly be regarded as an investigation into the computer representation of (typically, statute) law. LEGOL appears in section 1.9.

Other influential early projects include Carole Hafner's LIRS system, a system to improve the performance of document retrieval systems, Jim Sprowl's ABF, a language designed for computer-aided drafting of legal documents, and CCLIPS (Civil Code Legal Information Processing System), an attempt at a 'scientific codification' of parts of the Louisiana Civil Code, conducted by Cary deBessonet and George Cross. LIRS and CCLIPS are described in section 1.13. ABF appears in section 1.8.1.

Two institutions have been notably active in the general field of computers and law since at least the beginning of the 1970s. These are the Norwegian Research Centre for Computers and Law (NRCCL) at the University of Oslo, and the Istituto per la Documentazione Giuridica (IDG) in Florence. References to some of the projects conducted at these institutions are given in the text.

There are three more projects which are described in some detail in this survey. The first is Waterman and Peterson's work on legal expert systems (section 1.5.1). There is no imprecision in applying the term 'expert system' to Waterman and Peterson's work. The second is the use of logic programming for applications in law, pioneered by Sergot and Kowalski at Imperial College, London and now used quite extensively elsewhere (section 1.10). This work has been conducted since approximately 1980 and is obviously the approach with which I am most familiar. The third is Rissland and Ashley's HYPO project, generally regarded as the most intensive and developed of the work on case-based reasoning specifically (section 1.17).

The 1980s have seen an explosion of projects and proposals P: too many to attempt even a full list of references. (See the proceedings of the various conferences mentioned earlier.) I have included brief descriptions of some representative examples, but I do not wish to imply that those I have omitted are in any way less worthy or significant. It was not possible to give a full and fair survey of all the recent work. There are no doubt important projects which I have had to overlook, and I apologize for this in advance.

1.4. POSSIBLE CLASSIFICATIONS AND ISSUES ARISING

Most of the literature on computer applications to law concerns the retrieval of legal documents. Even when this is discarded, a bewildering range of approaches remains.

Different projects address different aspects of the law and different activities within the overall legal process (such as drafting of legislation, document preparation, administration of the law, and legal reasoning in general). Projects differ in the methodologies they adopt and in their choice of computational technique. Most importantly perhaps, projects differ in their aims and objectives. Some projects have aims that are primarily practical. These projects attempt to provide computer programs, constructed by whatever means are convenient, to give useful assistance in the everyday practice or administration of law. There are other projects which see in the law an ideal domain in which to apply techniques developed elsewhere, typically in artificial intelligence. And there are projects whose aims are essentially theoretical, where the primary concern is to cast light on the nature of law and on the processes involved in legal reasoning.

It seems clear that some kind of classification is required. This section considers some of the possible ways of organizing the projects into general categories, but its purpose is not to identify any particular classification. None is ideal. The real purpose of this section is to give a general description of the different approaches that have been taken, and to introduce the concepts and terminology that are encountered in the literature. It is also a means of beginning a recurrent discussion of what it means for a computer program to represent the law: a theme which is taken up again in the commentaries that follow.

1.4.1. Classification by activity

One possible classification is by the particular activity within the overall legal process that a given project is designed to support. Litigation and the resolution of legal disputes ('judging') are only one small fragment of the everyday practice of law. Other activities include the design and drafting of legislation, the drafting of other documents (like contracts and wills and various notices), routine administrative tasks (like the preparation and processing of claims for benefits), and general giving of advice. The list is not intended to be exhaustive. Not all of these tasks need engage the services of a lawyer. Many will be undertaken by officials of government and other agencies, or members of advice giving organizations. Classification by activity does not seem to be very appropriate: While some of the projects I have mentioned are designed to support one particular activity (Sprowl's system helps with the drafting of legal documents, for example), most are not. In any case, legal analysis and planning systems, which are by far the most common type of system proposed, could be used in practical systems to support any of the activities mentioned.

1.4.2. Classification by computational formalism

An obvious and common classification of projects is to look at the computational formalism adopted. Stressing the choice of computational formalism, however, distracts attention from more fundamental issues. It stresses how a particular approach has been implemented, rather than its objectives and the assumptions that underlie it. Many of the approaches that have been proposed can be re-implemented straightforwardly in a different computational formalism. Some examples are provided later. Similarly, many quite different approaches are sometimes grouped together, simply because they happen to have been implemented in a particular programming language. In particular, projects which have used PROLOG as an implementation language are often treated as instances of a single approach even though they are actually quite different in nature. (This is what Susskind [1986a] does in his classification.)

1.4.3. Distinguishing between statutes and case law

A standard and much better classification distinguishes systems that reason by rules derived from statutes (and other written rules and regulations) and systems that attempt to reason from the decisions of previous cases.

Although this is a reasonable distinction, I believe it is a mistake to rely on it too much. It can give the false impression that reasoning from the decisions of previous cases is only relevant to systems of law with a strong common law tradition, like the English and American systems of law, which rely to a great extent on case law and a formal doctrine of precedent (*stare decisis*). Reasoning from the decisions of previous cases seems less applicable in systems of law which are based on civil codes, where the significance of previous cases is given less emphasis.

Of course, reasoning from the decisions of previous cases is particularly appropriate for application to common law systems, because there many human activities are not governed by statute, but by previous cases. A formal notion of precedent in common law systems obliges judges to decide new cases in the same way that similar cases were decided in the past.

But the presence of a statute can never entirely eliminate the need to reason with the decisions of previous cases. This holds as much for civil code systems as it does for systems with a common law tradition. There will always be circumstances where the application of a statute is open to doubt: where there is a dispute about the specific meaning of a phrase or section; where a statute includes an element of discretion and there is a dispute about whether the discretion should be applied in a given case; where it can be argued that there are unstated but clearly intended exceptions to a statute; where two otherwise clear statutes both apply to the facts of a given case but lead to different conclusions; where a statute conflicts with more general laws or legal principles (such as a constitution); or simply where the rigid application of a statute would lead to undesirable or ridiculous results.

In such circumstances, a dispute can arise which is resolved by presenting arguments for both sides before a court of law (or some other adjudicating authority). It would be nonsensical, in any system of law, if the same arguments had to be repeated every time a similar dispute arose. All systems of law have some mechanism for recording the decisions of a court. It is only by reference to these past decisions that unnecessary duplication of argument, and the possibility of inconsistency, can be reduced. The decisions taken in previous cases always have to be considered: in systems of law with a common law tradition because there is a formal doctrine of precedent; in other systems of law because there is a natural concern for fairness and consistency which demands that similar cases be decided in a similar way. In practice, legal disputes are resolved in exactly the same way in both types of legal system, though there may be a difference in the way that arguments are presented and in the way that previous cases are brought to the court's attention.

Because the meaning of a statute is open to question, it is open to judicial manipulation also. Another objection to distinguishing too much between systems that represent statutes and systems that represent case law is that the distinction can be very misleading. It can give the false impression that there exists some essential difference between reasoning with statutes and reasoning with past cases. In particular, it can give the false impression that reasoning with statutes is mechanical and certain in its outcome, in a way that reasoning with cases is not. Clearly, statutes will normally provide fewer opportunities for imaginative interpretation, since most are designed to provide relatively precise statements of their intended meaning. Clearly, some statutes are more open to interpretation than others. But even with statutes an element of uncertainty always remains.

1.4.4. Open texture

At this point I introduce the notion of open texture, for this is a term which is frequently encountered in the literature, and is the main concern of many of the projects to be discussed.

In any new case we cannot say with certainty what its outcome will be. Statutes and case law may provide good guidelines, but it is always possible that a court will decide otherwise. We know whether a given legal concept applies to cases which have been decided by a court. But we have no way of determining with certainty whether a given legal concept holds in a new case, except by taking the case before a court. Until the case has been decided in court, there is no fact of the matter. Legal concepts are therefore only 'pointwise defined' and are said to exhibit open texture: a legal concept has a precise definition only for those cases which have been decided by a court at the appropriate level of authority; there is no precise definition of the concept for cases which have still to come to court.

Vague and discretionary concepts in law are most obviously open textured. But even legal concepts which appear to be precisely defined in a statute or civil code exhibit open texture. For however precise a definition might seem, it is always possible that a court will decide to take a different interpretation of the statute, or decide there is some good reason why the statute should not be applied in a new case.

The notion of open texture has its origins in the philosophy of language, but it is in jurisprudence that this notion has been most useful. The legal philosopher who is most often quoted in this connection is Hart, who argues that legal concepts are incurably open textured [Hart 1961]. Hart's views, though persuasive and very influential, have not been universally accepted. Dworkin [1967], for example, argues that there is no open texture in law, because any case, no matter how abstruse, can be decided by the proper process of legal reasoning and argumentation. These are philosophically interesting positions, but the debate seems to have no practical significance. There is no dispute about what processes a court should use in coming to its decision. In practice, the concepts of law are incurably open textured (if you follow Hart) or behave as if they were incurably open textured (if you follow Dworkin, say). Open texture is one, fairly standard way of characterizing the fundamental uncertainty in law, which is eliminated only when a case comes to court and a definitive decision is given.

1.4.5. Fixed interpretations of the law

A classification of projects which distinguishes between statutes and case law is not ideal, partly because it can suggest that one is fundamentally more certain in its outcome than the other, and partly because some projects attempt to reason with both sources of law. I think that a better classification would distinguish between systems that represent a single, fixed interpretation of the legal sources constructed in advance, and systems which attempt to be more flexible in their interpretation of the original sources.

The distinction can be made clearer if we take the following, simplified model of what is involved in determining whether a legal concept applies in a given case:

1. Identify relevant facts.
2. Construct legal rule from relevant legal sources.
3. Apply relevant legal rule to relevant facts.

The stages are not distinct, of course, but are bound together inextricably. In order to determine what are the relevant facts, we must first have some idea of what legal rules are relevant and where we can find them. Further, we would normally be interested in identifying those legal rules which apply to the facts in a particular way, for example in a way that is most favourable to the interests of a client; and once a suitable legal rule is identified and ready to be applied, this will in turn determine what facts in a case are relevant.

I am making no claim, therefore, for the accuracy of the simplified model. Its purpose is merely to provide a basis for classifying projects into various categories. Further, 'legal rule' here is not limited to 'rule of law' in any strict sense, but is intended to encompass anything at all that might be deemed relevant. I include in this even the judge's personality or what he ate for breakfast or the opinion of his six-year-old daughter if these are considered to have a bearing on the outcome of a given case.

Examined in terms of this simple model, most of the projects to be considered simplify matters still further. They assume, or rather pretend, that 'the relevant sources of law' have been identified and that legal rules have been constructed from them. That is, they incorporate a single, fixed representation of the law constructed in advance, and they concentrate on applying this fixed representation to a variety of fact situations.

It is true that most of these systems consider only statutes and other explicitly written rules and regulations. If a fixed representation is to be of much practical value, then there must be some reasonable consensus that the representation is an accurate model of the law. There is less doubt about the accuracy of a model based on certain kinds of statute than one based on sources of law which are more open to alternative interpretation, or where there is some doubt about which legal sources are relevant.

Further, the majority of projects to be considered implement a form of deductive reasoning with rules, and these rules are usually derived from statutes. Computational techniques for mechanising deductive reasoning are relatively well understood While applying the provisions of a statute can often be seen as deduction, to a first approximation at least, reasoning with cases is harder. Reasoning with cases resembles inductive or analogical inference more than it does deduction (though this does not imply that such reasoning is non-logical). Reasoning with cases (or statutes which are open to many different interpretations) cannot be approximated realistically by identifying all the relevant legal sources and deciding in advance how they should be interpreted and applied. Identifying previous relevant cases and interpreting the significance of their decisions according to the context of a new case is where the essential problem lies, and a system which eliminates this aspect altogether is of little or no value.

It should be noted that no project to my knowledge has attempted to reason directly with the sources of law. Reasoning directly with the sources of law would require a computer program that could understand natural language at a level of sophistication that is well beyond the capabilities of any system that could be constructed in the foreseeable future (or ever). Those projects which attempt to reason with case law must still devise some suitable abstraction and representation of the original sources, but one which is flexible enough to allow some of the interpretation to be delayed and only undertaken by the system as the context of a new case requires. What characterizes case-based reasoning is the need to leave part of the interpretation of sources to the system itself, but successful techniques for this could equally be applied to statute law as well.

1.5. MODELS OF LEGAL EXPERTISE

This section describes two systems developed by Don Waterman and Mark Peterson (LDS and SAL), Robert Michaelsen's TAXADVISOR system, and Philip Capper and Richard Susskind's Latent Damage System. All of them are examples of legal expert systems, in the strictest meaning of that term. Waterman and Peterson's approach will be examined in most detail. Their systems are unusual in that they attempt to address all aspects of the legal decision-making process.

1.5.1. Waterman and Peterson

The Legal Decision making System (LDS) is a system developed by Don Waterman and Mark Peterson which addresses the problem of settling product liability cases [Waterman and Peterson 1980, 1981, 1984; Peterson and Waterman 1985; see also Cook *et al.* 1981]. Given such a case, the system determines the defendant's liability, and then calculates the value of the case, which is the amount that would be acceptable to all parties as a fair settlement of the case.

The knowledge represented in LDS is both of a formal kind based on legal authority (legislation and case law) and of an informal kind such as the strategies used by lawyers and claims adjusters in practice, for example in proving a product defective. The value of the case is determined by analysing the effects of the loss (what type of damage was caused); the probability of establishing the defendant's liability; the percentage of the plaintiff's responsibility in causing the damage; the characteristics of the case, based on such considerations as the ability of the lawyers and the personal characteristics of the parties; and the context, which includes such elements as the strategy, timing and type of claim made by the plaintiff. LDS is a rule-based system implemented in ROSIE [Waterman *et al.* 1979].

LDS differs from systems which seek to perform legal analysis. Waterman and Peterson's aim in LDS is to model legal skill and expertise. Their primary goal is to develop (rule-based) models of the actual decision making processes of lawyers and claims adjusters in product liability litigation. In the case of LDS, the intention is to use these models to study the effect of changes in legal doctrine (what the relevant statutes and cases are taken to mean) on settlement strategies and practices. In order to do this, they modify the rules and note the effect on the operation of the model when applied to a body of selected test cases. This kind of analysis is undertaken to provide insights that might suggest useful changes in legal doctrine and practice. As Waterman and Peterson [1980] have remarked, their system could also be used as an expert advisor in product liability cases with very little modification.

The characteristic feature of Waterman and Peterson's work is the range of different kinds of knowledge which their systems employ. This feature is again evident in another example of their approach.

SAL — System for Asbestos Litigation — is intended to assist lawyers and claims adjusters in evaluating claims relating to asbestos exposure [Waterman *et al.*, 1986]. It is currently limited to a single illness (asbestosis) and to only one class of plaintiff (technicians whose job it is to install asbestos insulation). SAL provides an estimate of the sum to be paid in order to reach a rapid settlement of litigation. Again, the knowledge employed concerns the loss incurred, the defendant's liability, the plaintiff's responsibility, and other features of the case such as the personal characteristics of the parties in litigation and the ability of the lawyers. SAL too is implemented in ROSIE.

1.5.2. Commentary

Waterman and Peterson's aim is to model how the law is actually used in practice in settling certain types of case (product liability). The skill and expertise of an expert lawyer obviously involves more than the ability to read legal documents. Consequently, Waterman and Peterson's systems have to represent not only the relevant sources of law but also how the law is used, and all kinds of other factors which can influence the outcome of a case.

In addition to rules derived from statutes and case law, Waterman and Peterson's systems must represent generally accepted practice (such as that reasonable and proper compensation for pain and suffering is normally taken to be three times the medical expenses incurred in certain types of case). This type of knowledge should not be confused with case law. It has no legal authority (it could not be cited in a court of law) but represents only empirical observations of what generally seems to happen in practice.

These systems must also contain a model of the way that an expert lawyer makes use of this knowledge of the law. They have to represent the strategies and practices that are used by lawyers and claims adjusters in preparing cases of this kind. They also have to represent, for example, a knowledge of what kind of evidence is needed to establish some given point, and be able to estimate the likelihood that this evidence will prove sufficient. This might depend on subjective criteria like deciding how physically attractive the plaintiff is.

In order to model accurately what actually happens in practice, Waterman and Peterson's systems must represent the influence of various extra-legal factors on the outcome of a case. A lawyer will want to estimate (and exploit if he can) such things as the timing of various stages in the case, the personalities of the parties involved, the abilities of the lawyers, and perhaps even the personality and known prejudices of the judge before whom the case is likely to be heard if ever it comes to court. A project to simulate the subjective decision-making processes of judges who deal with particular kinds of serious crime in the USA is being conducted by Bain [1984].

I have begun this survey of projects with Waterman and Peterson's work because theirs illustrates best the number of other considerations, besides the law itself, which go towards determining the outcome of a real case. Most other projects do not address all the aspects involved in reaching a legal decision. They focus on one aspect of the whole, and address only that. It follows that other approaches cannot, by themselves, be used to determine or predict the outcome of a case. They are intended to assist in the analysis of a legal problem.

The need generally for the kinds of informal 'legal' knowledge contained in Waterman and Peterson's systems is fairly clear from common sense. It is instructive, however, to refer to the massive amount of jurisprudential literature devoted to this topic. Richard Susskind [1986a] has published a detailed and extensive account of jurisprudential material relevant to the computer representation of law. Susskind cites Lord Denning in this context:

The reading of books in libraries — or the attending of lectures by

> professors — gives you only a blurred and incomplete picture. In order to understand what the law is all about, you must see it working in practice.
>
> [*The Family Story*. Butterworths, London, 1983, p 93]

Susskind then goes on to say (references omitted):

> The second piece of evidence that suggests academic legal knowledge is insufficient for legal problem-solving can be drawn from our jurisprudential sources: in the writings of the American Legal Realists, and in works of social jurisprudence. If there is a central theme to American Realism at all, it is that judges do not come to their decisions solely on the basis of law-statements. One group of realists — 'rule skeptics', according to Jerome Frank and now to common jurisprudential usage — alleged that those putative legal rules articulated in judicial decisions, that is, those 'paper rules', 'pseudo rules', 'accepted rules' or 'verbally formulated rules' were of no use in assisting the lawyer in the important job of predicting judicial decisions. For that task, they argued, it was necessary to divine the 'real rules' or 'latent rules' which they maintained were discoverable from patterns in judicial behaviour. The arch rule sceptic, Llewellyn, in fact suggested that these real rules would be more suitably designated 'the practices of the courts', for he maintained that the law was 'what I officials do about disputes'. While the rule sceptics have been criticised widely and convincingly, when their (often intentionally) extravagant claims are stripped of their excess, and confined to hard cases, one residual thesis is now generally espoused by theorists and practitioners alike. That thesis is that in advising clients on difficult questions of law, lawyers must look beyond law-statements, and seek to predict court decisions. When this is done regularly, general trends emerge and informal rules encapsulating these regularities are deployed (often subconsciously, no doubt). A contemporary analytical jurisprudent, Harris, has reaffirmed the importance for legal scientists of acknowledging social phenomena and social rules beyond the law-statements (but has questioned their status as law).

Another passage from Susskind neatly summarizes two extreme views of the legal decision-making process:

> Frank suggests that we reject the formula 'R x F = D' which he asks us to accept as a shorthand representation of the notion that legal rules can be applied by the judge to the facts of a case resulting in the mechanical production of a decision. In its stead he offers a replacement formula 'S x P = D' ('S' being the stimuli that affect the judge and 'P', his personality).

Both views summed up by Frank's two equations are extreme. Certainly no-one could think that legal disputes are resolved by mechanically applying a legal rule to the facts of a case. This is evident from common sense, or from the jurisprudential literature, or from examining the many different kinds of knowledge that Waterman and Peterson employ in their 'real' expert systems. The other extreme position, that legal cases are never settled by routine means, or that 'paper rules' are not relevant to the resolution of legal disputes, is not tenable either. Again, this is evident from common-sense or from the jurisprudential literature. Susskind's jurisprudential enquiry is particularly relevant: much of it is devoted to establishing the circumstances in which the equation R x F = D does accurately summarize the legal decision-making process. This discussion will be taken up again in the next section.

1.5.3. TAXADVISOR

The TAXADVISOR system was constructed by Robert Michaelson in his doctoral research at the University of Illinois [Michaelsen 1982, 1984; Michaelsen and Michie 1983]. TAXADVISOR is designed to assist lawyers with tax planning for clients with large estates (valued at more than $175,000). The system, implemented in EMYCIN, collects data about clients and makes planning recommendations and suggestions for organizing their estates. Entering into life insurance contracts and retirement schemes, making wealth transfers, gifts, purchases and wills are all things which can improve the client's tax position. TAXADVISOR is concerned particularly with the strategic planning aspects of this problem, rather than with the analysis of facts to determine tax results. It is imagined that the tax effects of any recommendations would be calculated by a more conventional program.

The knowledge represented in TAXADVISOR comes primarily from lawyers' experience and the strategies they use, especially the criteria that experts use to guide them in formulating financial plans. Michaelsen notes that for cases which fit the special area treated, validation by several practising accountants indicated that about two-thirds of TAXADVISOR's recommendations were identical to those the experts would have made, while the remaining one-third were different but were still acceptable planning options.

TAXADVISOR belongs in this section because it is another example of a system that has concentrated on modelling, not so much the law itself, but rather how a knowledge of the law is actually used in practice.

1.5.4. Latent Damage System

Phillip Capper and Richard Susskind have implemented an expert system which advises legal professionals on the application of the UK's Latent Damage Act 1986. Unusually, this system is published commercially, distributed as a package of disks together with an accompanying book describing its development and explaining in detail what users can and cannot expect of the system [Capper and Susskind 1988].

The Latent Damage System addresses the difficult issues relating to the time within which a claimant may begin proceedings in the law of negligence if the loss or damage is discovered some time after its occurrence (hence 'latent' damage). The Latent Damage Act 1986 was passed to deal specifically with such questions, but it cannot be understood without an extensive knowledge of tort, contract and product liability law within which it operates.

In operation and computational techniques employed, Capper and Susskind's system resembles a 'text animator' or computer-aided instruction (CAI) program more than it does an expert system that computes by inference over some explicit representation of knowledge. The computational details are not as important, however, as the nature of the knowledge that the system contains.

Capper and Susskind's system is an example of a legal expert system of a different kind from those considered so far. It is an expert system because it incorporates Capper's expert analysis of the implications of the Act and how its provisions should be applied to the solution of practical problems. It differs from the other expert systems in this section in that it does not seek to represent what actually happens in legal practice (Waterman and Peterson) and it does not try to simulate an expert's advice-giving behaviour (Michaelsen).

Capper and Susskind's system might have been classified with other approaches, especially the algorithmic representations of law described in the next section. These too incorporate an analysis of how a piece of legislation can be applied to a problem P presumably an expert's analysis if the system is to have much practical value. But I have put Capper and Susskind's system in this section because of the exceptional range of additional legal knowledge it contains beyond a representation of what is actually said in the Act.

1.5.5. Questions raised

Most approaches to the computer representation of law restrict attention to a form of legal analysis which resembles R x F = D. The main question to be raised after looking at the approaches described in this section is whether there is any benefit, practical or theoretical, in neglecting 'social stimuli' and 'personalities' and representing only 'paper rules' of law. This question is examined after a number of specific examples have been described.

1.6. ALGORITHMIC REPRESENTATIONS OF LAW

This section describes a class of systems, all of which represent some fragment of the law by means of an algorithmic programming language (often BASIC) or a formalism, like flowcharts, which can be directly implemented in such a language. These systems normally operate by presenting a series of pre-programmed questions to the user. The answers given by the user determine what additional questions must be asked, until the program has enough information to compute and display 'its' analysis.

1.7. Algorithmic programs

The examples cited most often of this approach are a series of programs implemented by Robert Hellawell treating aspects of tax legislation. These programs are CORPTAX [Hellawell 1980], CHOOSE [Hellawell 1981] and SEARCH [Hellawell 1982]. All are implemented in BASIC. Bellord [1980] has also implemented a similar program in BASIC to represent a section of the UK's tax legislation.

Programs such as Hellawell's are often classified as a simple kind of legal analysis system (see, for example, [McCarty 1983a]). Typically, it is the limitations of the approach that are stressed in order to provide some motivation for adopting artificial intelligence techniques for similar purposes. As Hellawell points out, the difficulty in writing such a program lies in analysing the legislation to such a level of detail that it can be cast into the required form. It is necessary for the author to anticipate all possible answers to all questions, and all possible interactions among these answers, and then to provide an explicit branch within the program for every combination of answers. In effect, what Hellawell is describing is the construction of a flowchart where the answers to questions determine which branch of the flowchart is followed.

1.7.1. Flowcharts

The idea that one can better understand the intended effects of a complicated statute by constructing a flowchart is a natural one. In a text intended primarily for lawyers, Twining and Miers [1982] propose flowcharts as a practical aid to understanding, and applying, the provisions of a complex statute. (This suggestion appears in the first edition of the book by Twining and Miers, and not in the second edition which is the reference given here.) Many explanatory leaflets and booklets make use of flowcharts too. And if one can construct a flowchart to represent the application of some statute or set of regulations, then it is sometimes worth the extra effort of mechanizing the flowchart by means of a simple program. This is precisely what Hellawell and Bellord have done in constructing their programs. It is also the method normally used to produce the simple tax calculators and other advisory programs that can be purchased in bookshops and department stores for use on micro-computers.

1.7.2. Decision nets

A recent example of the attraction of flowcharts is provided by the DataLex project [Greenleaf *et al.* 1987] where they play a fundamental role. This project has been developing a programming shell LES (derived from Legal Expert System) for building applications in law. A central module in LES allows a lawyer to construct what the authors call decision nets or decision networks. These decision nets constitute the main component of most LES applications. Since they are executed by an 'inference mechanism consisting of the explicit interconnections between the modules which are activated by responses supplied by the end user', they seem to correspond exactly to what I have called flowcharts. The LES shell translates decision nets into a C program which is then compiled to produce an executable program. There are other modules in the LES shell to cope with case law and text retrieval. The case law component of LES is sketched very briefly in section 1.17.1 on case-based reasoning.

1.7.3. Commentary

The programs by Hellawell and Bellord, the flowcharts advocated by Twining and Miers, and the decision nets used in the DataLex project, represent legal provisions implicitly. A statute or some other piece of legislation is represented by an algorithm which is designed to apply the statute's provisions to the facts of a given case in a certain, very specific way. Because of the direct correspondence between a flowchart and a program which can implement it, I shall regard flowcharts as a type of computational formalism, whether or not the algorithms they express are 'executed' by a human agent or a computer. There are three points that have to be made about the use of this type of computational formalism for representing the law.

Firstly, there is the difficulty noted by Hellawell (and Bellord) of designing the algorithm itself. Legal provisions are seldom expressed as detailed algorithms, and the task of converting even a small fragment of legislation into this form can be so daunting that it becomes practically impossible. Experience with other techniques (following sections) demonstrates that the difficulty of the task can be significantly reduced by choosing a more appropriate, higher-level, non-algorithmic computational formalism. The use of a rule-based programming language, for example, would be a natural and obvious choice. It would allow the resulting representation to resemble more closely the structure of the original text. And it would reduce the need to design a specific algorithm, since this would largely become the responsibility of the program executor. Several projects in which rule-based and other high-level programming techniques have been used are described in the next section. The authors of the DataLex project, incidentally, argue just the opposite: that flowcharts can have significant practical advantages over rule-based techniques, particularly where the representations are to be constructed by a lawyer [Greenleaf *et al.* 1987].

Secondly, algorithmic representations of law are typically very poor as regards their transparency. An algorithm for applying a piece of legislation to the facts of a given case specifies one particular way of using the legislation. Its structure will normally not resemble the structure of the legislation it applies. The alternative is to construct an explicit representation of the legislation and describe separately procedures to apply it. Again, higher-level computational formalisms are better suited to achieving this separation.

The third point, and one that is seldom mentioned, is that to devise a suitable algorithm, one must first decide what the legislation is to be used for. If one looks at a piece of legislation, it is immediately clear that there are many purposes for which the legislation is passed. A statute, for example, may define a legal concept in more or less precise terms, but it will also include many different types of provision, describing for example how the statute affects other related legislation, or specifying the penalties that will be incurred if its provisions are transgressed, or setting out general requirements for the procedures to be used in its administration. Even an apparently simple statement like 'claimants must submit applications before 1 January' can be read in many different ways. The statement tells a claimant how much time he has to prepare his application. It helps the administration to determine whether an application should be rejected. It could even be used by a lawyer in arguments about the meaning of 'valid claim' or 'submitted' in other areas of law.

It should be clear, then, that one cannot begin to devise an algorithm to apply legal provisions without determining first its intended purpose and by whom it will be used. I do not want to give the impression that determining the intended purpose of a computer program that represents the law is a major practical problem. In practice, one approaches the construction of a program (or algorithm or flowchart) with an intended use in mind. This is implicitly assumed by Twining and Miers, for example. I wanted to make the point here, where the question is fairly clear, rather than when discussing higher-level, non-algorithmic computational formalisms where the same point arises but is rather less obvious.

1.7.4. Data-processing applications

There is very little difference between a program like Hellawell's CORPTAX and a typical data-processing application such as a payroll system. In both cases, analysis involves the construction of detailed algorithms to apply the appropriate legislation: sections of tax statutes in the case of CORPTAX, other rules and regulations in the case of a data-processing system (tax legislation in the case of a payroll system also). Implementation is the task of expressing these algorithms in a suitable programming language. In both cases, the resulting programs execute an algorithm which applies the provisions of a statute or a set of regulations to the facts of a given case. In CORPTAX many of these facts are obtained by asking the user questions as the algorithm is executed. In a typical data-processing application, these facts would normally be determined in advance and stored in a file or database. Data-processing systems are normally used to process many cases one after the other, and might have to generate various documents and files in addition. But the basic processing task in both types of program is essentially the same. Hellawell and Bellord use BASIC to express their algorithm. Data-processing systems often use COBOL.

Many of the limitations of Hellawell's CORPTAX, and programs constructed by similar means, can be traced to the use of inappropriate computational formalisms. Higher-level programming techniques can ease the task of representing the relevant legislation, and will usually improve the transparency of the resulting program. It can be argued that these alternative techniques would improve conventional data-processing systems also. Data-processing applications could be implemented with explicit representations of the regulations they administer, and analysed and specified in terms of these regulations from the outset. As mentioned earlier, the central role of rules and regulations in data-processing applications is due to Ronald Stamper, and provides one of the main motivations for his LEGOL project, described in section 1.9.

1.7.5. Limitations

Later sections describe projects which have constructed legal analysis programs based on explicit representations of the law, in a variety of computational formalisms. It is important to draw attention first to the nature of the legal knowledge that is typically represented. This question is as relevant to the algorithmic representations of law discussed in this section as it is to those alternative representations described later.

All the programs described in this section, Hellawell's and Bellord's tax analysis programs, conventional data-processing programs, the flowcharts suggested by Twining and Miers, and the decision nets of DataLex, represent a single, fixed interpretation of the legal sources on which they are based. In all these examples it is assumed that the author will be able to identify the relevant legal sources, and extract from them an unambiguous (though not necessarily precise) reading of what legal rules are currently in force.

The previous section emphasized the range of factors, beyond a knowledge of the formal sources of law, that can influence the outcome of a legal case. In principle, there is no reason why an algorithmic representation of the law could not encompass the effects of 'stimuli' and 'personalities' as well as 'paper rules', but in practice algorithmic representations of law are largely used for modelling the effects of 'paper rules' (decided upon and fixed in advance).

It follows that such programs are necessarily limited. They cannot address every aspect of the legal decision-making process, and they simplify even those aspects which they can address. One should not conclude immediately that such programs can have no practical, or theoretical, value. If a legal case falls at first sight within the provisions of a particular statute, then sooner or later it will be necessary to examine the effects of applying the statute, even if this is only part of a wider analysis that takes other factors into consideration as well. And if the statute is complex, then drawing up a flowchart or executing an algorithm might be a useful practical aid in this examination. (This is precisely what Twining and Miers have in mind when they suggest that flowcharts can be useful. This suggestion appears in a book whose main theme is that legal rules are not fixed, but have to be applied with flexibility and a proper regard for other considerations if nonsensical conclusions are to be avoided.) A suggestion that fixed 'paper rule' representations can be useful in analysing how a statute applies to a given case does not imply there is no need to consider other factors as well. Such programs are intended to help in the analysis of a case, by temporarily disregarding the influence of all other factors that might have a bearing on the outcome. They are normally constructed for use on their own, but they might well be incorporated as components of a much bigger representation, as in Michaelsen's TAXADVISOR system where one (unimplemented) module is used to calculate tax liabilities as required by the more 'expert' parts of the system.

A question to consider is whether these 'paper rule' representations could be used not just as aids in legal analysis, but also to take legal decisions themselves, autonomously.

It was remarked in the introduction that litigation and the resolution of legal disputes account for a tiny fragment of the activities that take place every day within the law. In the day to day practice of law, most tasks are routine. They are performed by mechanically applying what is generally accepted to be 'the law'. Here, Frank's R x F = D equation is a reasonably accurate summary of how the law is actually used.

There are many different schools of thought in legal philosophy and the jurisprudential literature is dominated by arguments over the true nature of law and legal reasoning. But the fact that most everyday legal problems are solved by applying Frank's R x F = D equation has not gone unnoticed. Susskind [1986a; see also 1986b] points out in his jurisprudential enquiry that what legal philosophers argue about most is the processes by which difficult legal problems are, or should be, resolved. It is hard legal problems which interest legal philosophers and which account for the bulk of writings on jurisprudence. But there is a general consensus, in every school of legal philosophy, that easy cases are solved every day by simply applying generally recognized legal rules to the facts of the case. Susskind's extensive research has established that there is this consensus. It would surely be surprising if there were not.

In the light of this discussion, data-processing systems apply legal or quasi-legal provisions in a routine and mechanical fashion. Since they decide cases autonomously, it follows that they are based on the implicit assumption that all the cases to be processed will be easy. Few people would regard the introduction of a computerized payroll system as an infringement of civil liberties, even though the payroll system automatically deducts tax contributions and other payments in accordance with tax and related legislation. This is because the task is mundane and routine, and all the cases are easy.

It does not follow that all routine and mundane tasks within the law could be similarly automated. There are very few areas of the law where it is possible to assume that every case which arises will be an easy case. Consequently, there are very few areas of law where it is acceptable or feasible to introduce computer programs that will decide cases autonomously. Almost without exception, computer programs can only be used to help in the analysis of legal problems. And it must be stressed that every single point I have just made applies whatever computational formalism is used to represent the law.

Of course all of this begs a fundamental question, since it is not at all clear what 'easy' and 'hard' mean exactly. Jurisprudence gives little practical guidance. Some suggested heuristics for how a computer program might determine whether a given legal case is easy or hard are be examined in section 1.15.2 where the work of Anne Gardner is described.

Most descriptions of legal analysis programs (of whatever kind) do not state explicitly the assumptions on which these programs are based or the purposes for which they are intended. This has led to occasional misunderstandings.

1.7.6. Criticisms

Philip Leith [1986a] has argued for the rejection of legal 'expert systems' that represent only 'paper rules'. In a modified version of the same paper he concentrates his attack on the use of logic programming techniques specifically [Leith 1986b]. However, many of these criticisms apply equally to the approaches described in this section, and the questions Leith raises are, therefore, examined here.

Leith's central contention is that basing a computer system on 'paper rules' alone is equivalent to claiming that legal problems are resolved by mechanically applying 'clear legal rules'. As Leith points out, such rules are fictional: there is more to legal decision-making than applying the R x F = D equation, because the sources of law support different interpretations, and are subject to unstated exceptions, and are open to judicial manipulation, and because there are many other factors which need to be considered besides legal rules. Leith concludes that to consider only the effects of 'paper rules' is tantamount to a fundamental misunderstanding of the true nature of law.

One interpretation of Leith's argument is that any system which represents only 'paper rules' simplifies the law to such an unacceptable extent that the system has little or no value in legal analysis. This criticism would apply whatever computational formalism were employed. But it is surely well established, by observing common legal practice and by examining the jurisprudential literature, that simplified 'paper rule' representations can have legitimate and valuable uses, and that there are occasions when R x F = D is an accurate model of how the law operates.

A weaker interpretation of Leith's argument is more tenable. The programs we have been discussing simplify the legal decision-making process. While the authors of such a system may be fully aware that their programs can address only one aspect of a complete legal analysis, it is not necessarily the case that the users of these programs will be aware of these limitations too. In other words, there is a danger that users will overestimate the value of the analysis they obtain from such a program. When Twining and Miers suggest that flowcharts can help in analysing a set of legal provisions, they presumably imagine that such a flowchart will be constructed by a lawyer for his own personal use. But the user of a computer program will often not be its author.

Leith has directed his attack at 'expert systems' and logic programs. An interpretation of Leith's argument, and possibly the one he intended, is that this danger is substantially increased when a legal analysis program is labelled 'expert system' by its authors or its users, or when its conclusions are referred to as 'logical consequences'. If this is Leith's point then he is surely right. While there is always a danger that users of computer programs will place too much confidence in the output they obtain, it is very much easier to be seduced by a program which is sold (metaphorically or literally) as an 'expert system' or whose conclusions are advertised as 'logical consequences'. I referred in the introduction to unacceptable connotations of the term 'expert system' and this is just such an instance. 'Logic consequence' is a technical term with a very precise meaning but even technical terms can be used irresponsibly.

Where I would disagree with Leith is in his implied suggestion that many accounts of work in this area refuse to acknowledge the limitations of their approach, either intentionally or out of ignorance of the true nature of law. Certainly there have been instances where 'legal expert systems' have been released commercially with an irresponsible lack of concern for accuracy (see [Susskind 1987] for a discussion). However, the general impression is that investigators of projects to construct representations of law (in whatever form) are aware that their systems are limited to addressing one aspect of legal analysis out of many. Most of the longer descriptions of projects begin with some discussion on the nature of law (and this paper is no exception). Shorter reports often omit this background material, presumably because the authors have wanted to report on details of their programs, and have assumed that other investigators in the field share their objectives and presuppositions.

Leith's criticisms serve to underline the importance of making users aware of the limitations of the programs they use. This will always involve explaining to users what a program can and cannot do, and what aspects of legal analysis it is designed to support. But it also means that programs which can make explicit the assumptions on which their conclusions are based are generally to be preferred to programs which cannot. A major disadvantage of the algorithmic approaches described in this section is their lack of transparency. They tend to bury their representations of law in the procedures which manipulate them. Other computational formalisms are better suited to separating out the underlying representation of the law and keeping this explicit. Some projects that have employed these alternative formalisms are described next.

1.8. EXPLICIT REPRESENTATIONS OF LAW

The algorithmic approaches described in the previous section construct implicit representations of the law which are buried in the procedures that apply them. This section gives examples of projects which have used computational formalisms that enable an explicit representation of the law to be separated from the procedures that apply it. There are two main motivations for employing this kind of formalism: to ease the task of constructing the representation itself, and to provide a system which allows its representation to be assessed for accuracy and which can provide some justification for the conclusions it produces.

The two types of formalism described in this section are rule-based formalisms of various kinds, and the use of procedural PROLOG. (I explain the difference below.) Semantic networks and frame-based representations have also been used, though much less frequently. Some examples are given in later sections.

1.8.1. Rule-based formalisms

The law resembles a set of rules more than it does a set of detailed algorithms, and it is not surprising that many attempts to construct computer representations of law have employed rule-based formalisms. This is an innocuous remark but it needs some clarification because there is an unfortunate ambiguity that has caused some confusion.

The term 'rule-based model of the law' can have different meanings in different contexts. 'Rule-based' can refer to the law or it can refer to the chosen computational formalism, or to both. One can choose to view the law as a set of 'rules' but represent these 'rules' in some non-rule-based computational formalism. Twining and Miers' flowcharts are an example. Similarly, one can choose not to view the law as 'rules' but still employ a rule-based computational formalism for representational purposes. Waterman and Peterson's expert systems can be regarded as an example of this.

Some commentators have fallen into the trap of assuming that using a rule-based computational formalism for representation purposes implies that the authors belong to some — possibly very extreme — school of jurisprudence. Criticisms of the computational formalism are tangled up with accusations of jurisprudential naivety. This section is concerned with the use of rule-based computational formalisms.

There are so many projects that have used rule-based formalisms to represent law that I cannot give a comprehensive list of references. I give only a selection of some early examples.

Waterman and Peterson's systems implemented in ROSIE, and Michaelsen's TAXADVISOR implemented in EMYCIN have already been discussed in some detail (section 1.5).

Philip Leith has used a production system of his own design [Leith 1983] to construct ELI [Leith 1982], a system which treats part of the UK's Social Security legislation.

Duncan and Elizabeth MacRae have implemented a system to advise tax lawyers and accountants on section 74 of the US Internal Revenue Code which deals with prizes and awards [MacRae 1985a, 1985b; MacRae and MacRae 1985]. This system is implemented in PROLOG. It should not be confused, however, with projects that have used PROLOG as a representation language or with the approach described later under the heading 'Representing law as logic programs'. The representation language used in the MacRaes' system is a propositional rule language of their own design. PROLOG is used only to implement the inference mechanism. An important feature of the MacRaes' system is the emphasis they have given to interface and control issues. The system is designed to be used by someone who is already an expert in the domain. The MacRaes have been concerned particularly with developing an interface which gives their expert users control over the execution of the system, by directing search away from areas which are felt to be irrelevant or redundant.

David Gold and Richard Susskind collaborated on an interdisciplinary project (computing and jurisprudence) which developed a rule-based language for representing certain kinds of law [Gold 1987; Gold and Susskind 1986; see also Susskind 1986a]. Gold and Susskind have illustrated the use of this language with an example based on the law of divorce in Scotland. Susskind [1987] also describes a number of practical systems which are being built by him and others with other rule-based programming tools.

Another system which is sometimes classified in this general category is Jim Sprowl's ABF processor [Sprowl 1979, 1980; see also Cook *et al.* 1981]. This system was designed for the computer generation of legal documents, but as McCarty [1983a] points out it could be used for building legal analysis programs as well. The ABF system is a kind of word-processor, where the programmer specifies in the ABF language how fragments of text together with data obtained from the user are to be inserted into the document being generated. The document specification can include expressions constructed from arithmetical operators and keywords like AND, IF, OR and NOT. The ABF processor evaluates these expressions when they are encountered during document generation. But the programmer is allowed to include his own terms in these expressions too, which he defines by means of IF/THEN and IFF expressions. When the ABF processor encounters a term defined by the programmer, it evaluates its truth value by working backwards from conclusion to conditions through the definition. Since these definitions can be of arbitrary complexity, the ABF processor could be used as a backward chaining interpreter for propositional rules. (Although I have seen Sprowl's ABF processor referred to as a rule-based system on several occasions, I am not aware that it has been used in practice for anything other than document generation.)

There are many other projects described in this survey that employ rule-based formalisms to build representations of law. The main ones are LEGOL, the logic programming projects, LEX, ESPLEX, and Gardner's doctoral project. TAXMAN I used a frame-based formalism and Meldman used semantic networks. In both of these cases, the system can be reconstructed easily in terms of rules. These projects are not included in this section because they are all described separately in more detail later.

The programming language PROLOG can also be regarded as a rule-based formalism. I have separated out descriptions of the use of PROLOG because there are some specific comments that I want to make about this.

1.8.2. Procedural PROLOG

Several projects have used (procedural) PROLOG as a representation language. Dean Schlobohm [1985] has written a PROLOG program which helps to analyse the rules dealing with 'constructive ownership of stock' in section 318(a) of the US Internal Revenue Code. David Sherman [1986, 1987] has implemented a large PROLOG program which models the Income Tax Act of Canada.

Section 1.10 of this chapter is devoted to the applications of logic programming to law. In order to understand why the projects in this section have been listed in a separate category, it is necessary to appreciate the difference between procedural PROLOG programs and declarative logic programs (which can be executed by PROLOG but which can be executed in other ways as well).

The programming language PROLOG is based on logic, specifically on a subset of first-order logic which I shall call 'extended definite clauses' in this survey. These are logical implications of the form A<PW where A is an atomic conclusion and W is any expression of first-order logic expressing a set of sufficient conditions for the conclusion A to hold. A set of such clauses has a declarative meaning which is quite independent of any computational uses it might have.

One way to use PROLOG is to take a set of extended definite clauses, rewrite them in PROLOG syntax, and then execute the result as a PROLOG program. But not every PROLOG program is a set of extended definite clauses written in PROLOG syntax, and not every PROLOG program can be given a coherent declarative reading. This is because PROLOG includes a number of language features which are nothing to do with logic. A PROLOG program which makes use of these features has a procedural reading only. It cannot be understood independently of its behaviour inside a machine. The projects described in this section have used PROLOG, not as a way of executing declarative representations expressed in logic, but as a procedural programming language in its own right.

Schlobohm's program illustrates this procedural usage of PROLOG most clearly. The program operates by asking the user to supply the facts it needs to reach a conclusion. The program statements mix conditions which express legal rules with procedure calls to generate the required dialogue and specify which way the computation should proceed next. In this respect Schlobohm's program is very similar to Hellawell's CORPTAX. Schlobohm states explicitly the order in which questions should be asked, anticipates all possible answers, and specifies which branch of the computation is followed for every possible answer. PROLOG execution of these statements gives the required behaviour. The program cannot be read declaratively, and would not behave correctly with a different execution strategy.

Schlobohm has included in his program the ability to explain its current line of reasoning and its final conclusions. These features are implemented by maintaining a trace of the reasoning as the computation proceeds. As with the generation of dialogues, routines which add to the trace are explicitly programmed wherever they are required.

Schlobohm's program is written to execute an algorithm that applies the Internal Revenue Code's provisions in a very specific way. It could quite properly be grouped with the algorithmic approaches described in the previous section. Nevertheless, although Schlobohm's program does not entirely separate its representation of the law from the procedures which apply it, the program does bear some resemblance to the structure of the original legislation. It is fairly easy to identify those parts of the program which express legal rules and in this respect it differs from the approaches in the previous section.

Schlobohm's description of his program includes a full listing of the PROLOG code. Some PROLOG statements correspond directly to sections of the Internal Revenue Code. Others would correspond directly if they did not contain procedure calls to generate dialogues and to affect program behaviour. It is fairly straightforward to extract from the listing a set of extended definite clauses which represent the selected fragment of the Internal Revenue Code. Once extracted, there are several ways this declarative representation could be used. One way would be to execute the representation using an interpreter that automatically generates requests for the facts that it needs and that automatically constructs traces to justify its conclusions. This would be a system with the same functionality as Schlobohm's program, but based on an explicit, declarative representation of the Internal Revenue Code in logic, rather than an implicit, procedural representation in PROLOG. This alternative approach is described in more detail in section 1.10 on logic programming representations.

While Schlobohm's program could be grouped with the algorithmic approaches in the previous section, Sherman's PROLOG model of the Income Tax Act of Canada could be included, with minor modifications, in the section on declarative logic programming representations. Sherman envisages that a user of his program will describe the facts of his case in a supplementary PROLOG database before the consultation begins. Except to produce occasional output, the PROLOG statements do not contain calls to dialogue generation routines. The program does not construct a trace of its reasoning. Consequently, Sherman's program does not rely on PROLOG's extra-logical features to anything like the same extent as Schlobohm's. Nevertheless, Sherman has written his program to be executed in PROLOG. He has relied on PROLOG's specific execution strategy, and occasionally he has used PROLOG's extra-logical features to obtain the program behaviour that he wants. His program would not behave correctly if it were executed in any other way. Again, it would appear from the listings supplied that a declarative representation expressed in logic could be extracted from Sherman's program without too much difficulty.

1.8.3. Commentary

The various approaches described in this section make use of relatively high-level computational formalisms to separate explicit representations of the law from the procedures and inference mechanisms that apply them to the analysis of legal problems. Many of the considerations brought up in the previous section apply to the use of these alternative approaches as well. All of the approaches and programs described in this section represent a single, fixed interpretation of the legal sources on which they are based. By the same arguments that were put forward earlier, the programs in this section are similarly not intended to solve legal problems autonomously (except in the very special circumstances which allow them to be used as data-processing systems and administrative systems for other 'routine' tasks). The perceived advantages of these higher-level formalisms is that they can ease the task of representing a fragment of the law, and that these resulting representations can be made relatively transparent. Both are a direct consequence of separating the representations from the procedures that apply them. Many of these points have already been addressed, and are well documented anyway in the literature on expert systems.

To balance these observations a little, I refer to my earlier remark that the authors of the DataLex project argue against the use of rule-based formalisms. Our experience with production rules led to the observation that the lawyers who were attempting to define rules were actually drawing decision nets first and then writing the rules from them [Greenleaf *et al.* 1987]

Lastly, apart from the system designed by Gold (and perhaps also Leith's) all of the systems described until now have employed general-purpose formalisms that can be applied equally to domains outside the law. A question to consider is whether legal applications impose requirements that can only be satisfied by a formalism specifically designed for representing law. The next section describes Ronald Stamper's LEGOL project which developed a computer language that is both rule-based and specifically designed for representing certain kinds of law.

1.9. LEGOL AND NORMA

The LEGOL project was conducted by Ronald Stamper at the London School of Economics from the middle of the 1970s [Stamper 1976, 1977, 1979, 1980; see also Cook *et al.* 1981]. Though LEGOL itself has now finished, Stamper — now at the University of Twente — has continued the same line of investigation and is currently developing a formalism called NORMA [Stamper 1986].

1.9.1. Description

The original motivation for the LEGOL project was to develop improved techniques for the analysis and specification of data-processing systems, and administrative systems more generally. Many such systems are based on legislation and other rules and regulations that govern organizations, and are designed to translate the requirements of these rules and regulations into information processing tasks to be performed by humans and computers. Consequently, a central concern of the LEGOL project was the development of formal languages with the power to express these rules and regulations precisely. Since Stamper takes legislation as his experimental domain, LEGOL and the later work on NORMA can be regarded as investigations into computational techniques for representing legislation.

As some of its practical outputs, the LEGOL project developed several dialects of a language, each with its interpreter, which were capable of expressing an increasing variety of rules. These languages were applied to various examples including such areas as social security legislation, the law of intestate succession, degree regulations, order processing, and tax regulations [Stamper *et al.* 1982].

The LEGOL language (in its executable dialects) was conceived as an extended relational algebra with special operators for handling time [Jones *et al.* 1979]. The language could be used to simulate the effects of legal provisions by executing a set of LEGOL rules which defined new relations by means of expressions of the relational algebra. Some versions of the language provided a set of conventional program control structures in addition: sequencing of rules, if-then-else branches, and iteration [Jones 1980]. Computation proceeded by executing the control structures and evaluating expressions of the algebra. A number of (unimplemented) extensions were also proposed to enable the language to handle such concepts as purpose, right, duty, judgement, privilege and liability [Stamper 1980].

These are some of the practical outputs of the LEGOL project, but it must be stressed that Stamper's main objectives are primarily theoretical: to address fundamental semantic questions, and to develop a methodology for analysing and representing legislation based on these. In the case of LEGOL, the representation of a fragment of legislation was guided by an 'epistemological semantic model' [Stamper 1979] which was used to identify the entities, concepts and relationships present in the legislation. The semantic model was intended to ensure that a sensible correspondence exists between data structures and what they represent. A methodology for analyzing problems for the application of LEGOL, based on Stamper's semantic model, is described in [Stamper *et al.* 1982].

The emphasis on semantics continues in Stamper's more recent work on NORMA. Stamper has long maintained that the classical approach to the semantics of (predicate) logic and other formal languages is inadequate for application to law, and has argued that alternative theories of meaning need to be adopted. See [Stamper 1989] for a summary of these arguments. For NORMA, Stamper has proposed a semantics which relates all signs — including the symbols used in the representational formalism — directly to the notions of agent, intention and behaviour [Stamper 1986].

1.9.2. Commentary

Because the executable versions of the LEGOL language were based on relational algebra, it is fairly straightforward to reinterpret LEGOL rules and control structures in logic programming terms [Sergot 1980]. This translation suggests an alternative way of computing with LEGOL rules. It frees the LEGOL language from the need to be embedded within an algorithmic programming language; and if the LEGOL rules are executed backwards as in PROLOG, it allows recursion to be expressed directly, a feature missing from the original LEGOL algebra. It also means that a set of LEGOL rules can be used for purposes other than simulating the effects of legal provisions. (This type of reconstruction is reminiscent of developments in the relational database field. An alternative way of allowing recursion to be expressed in LEGOL would be to introduce the kind of transitive closure operator that relational algebras often now include.)

A translation of LEGOL rules into logic programming form gives an alternative way of executing these rules but it does not address any of the fundamental issues investigated in the LEGOL project. It is the methodology by which these rules are identified and constructed, and the underlying semantic model especially, that are the central concerns of Stamper's work on LEGOL and NORMA.

The motivation for some kind of systematic methodology for analysing and representing legislation is easy enough to understand, but it is impossible to comment in detail on Stamper's semantic proposals here. Most approaches to the computer representation of law have paid little or no attention to (formal) semantics. To the extent that others have addressed semantics at all — I am thinking particularly of the use of logic programming techniques and McCarty's work on TAXMAN and the Language for Legal Discourse — they have simply taken the standard semantics of the logical formalism adopted or presented their own variant in traditional style. Stamper argues that such approaches to semantics are inadequate. In doing so he is questioning some of the most fundamental notions in the theory of formal languages and the philosophy of language generally. Clearly it is not possible to undertake a detailed discussion here.

1.10. REPRESENTING LAW AS LOGIC PROGRAMS

This section describes a general approach: the construction of declarative representations of law using some convenient form of symbolic logic, and the execution of these representations by automated theorem-provers, potentially for a variety of different purposes. This approach is most closely associated with Sergot and Kowalski at Imperial College, London.

1.10.1. General description

In this general approach, the law is modelled by a set of logic sentences (an axiomatic theory) which represent some chosen unambiguous interpretation of the selected legal sources. ('Axioms' is the correct tech nical term for these sentences but used informally it has connotations which are not intended and which might lead to misunderstanding; 'explicit assumptions' would be a reasonably accurate informal alternative.) In principle, there is again no reason why case law and other 'stimuli' that influence judges' decisions should not be represented. In practice, most applications of the approach have incorporated representations constructed from statutes only (for precisely the same reasons that most other projects have concentrated on statutes also). An automated theorem-prover is used to derive useful consequences of the representation. For example, if the facts of a given case are described by a supplementary database and added to the representation, the theorem-prover can be used to determine the consequences of 'applying' the law to the facts of the case. The law is 'applied' to facts by deduction. This method can be used to construct systems with the same capabilities as the programs described in earlier sections. Specific examples of applications are given below. A detailed account of the approach is provided in [Sergot 1985a]. See also [Sergot 1985b; Sergot *et al.* 1986a; Kowalski and Sergot 1987, 1990].

In theory, it is possible to use any form of symbolic logic as the representational formalism as long as it has an automatable deductive system. But for many kinds of simple provisions encountered in legislation, the most practical and convenient choice of logic is the subset of first-order logic which earlier I called extended definite clauses (the form of logic on which the programming language PROLOG is based). Recall that these clauses are implications of the form A <P W where A is an atomic conclusion and W is any expression of first order logic stating sufficient conditions for conclusion A to hold. Sergot [1985a] argues that

many kinds of legislation are essentially definitional in nature, and that extended definite clauses provide a simple and natural formal language for expressing such definitions precisely.

For practical application, the easiest way of implementing the required theorem-prover is simply to execute the representation using PROLOG. This just involves rewriting the clauses in PROLOG syntax and then executing the result as a PROLOG program. At Imperial College most applications have been implemented in APES [Hammond and Sergot 1983, 1984] which is an augmented form of PROLOG. APES, like PROLOG, works backwards from conclusions to conditions, and has the same fixed execution strategy.

There are two main ways in which APES 'augments' PROLOG: it constructs proofs of all its conclusions, which can be examined during the computation or when a final conclusion is reached; and it incorporates an implementation of 'Query-the-User', a declarative model of input-output for logic programs [Sergot 1983]. The 'Query-the-User' module in APES automatically generates requests for any missing information that is required and checks and stores the answers supplied by the user. More sophisticated versions of 'Query-the-User' allow users to omit answers to questions, either because they do not know or because they do not want to provide an answer. Conclusions derived in such circumstances are conditional: they are qualified by conditions which remain to be decided. All conclusions, whether conditional or not, are logical consequences of the axioms that represent the law and any information provided by the user.

Executing a declarative representation of the law in a system such as APES gives a program with roughly the same functionality as the legal analysis programs described in previous sections. Indeed, it provides a means of implementing programs with extended capabilities: the proof generation mechanism provides a means of justifying the analysis obtained in terms of the original legislation; and the possibility of deriving conditional analyses is a feature which is normally not provided by legal analysis programs (but see the description of Gardner's system in section 1.15.2).

The 'Query-the-User' mechanism is not an essential component in all applications. Two alternative types of application can be mentioned in particular. Firstly, it is possible in certain circumstances to describe the facts of specific cases in a supplementary database in advance, instead of requesting them as the need arises during computation. This gives a system which corresponds to the behaviour of typical data-processing applications (and applications implemented in LEGOL). Secondly, there is the possibility of deriving consequences of a more general nature, with potential application in the drafting of legislation (discussed in section 11).

1.10.2. Examples

The approach has been applied to a number of sizeable fragments of legislation. The best-known example is a representation of the British Nationality Act 1981 constructed during the summer of 1983 [Sergot *et al.* 1986a, 1986b]. When executed in APES, this representation can be used to determine, for example, whether a given individual is a British citizen according to the provisions of the Act. (In the light of previous discussions, it is hardly necessary to add that the program cannot be used to decide such questions autonomously. The program can help only in analysing the implications of a single interpretation of the Act, and it ignores the effect of all other factors that might also have to be taken into account in deciding a real case.) This exercise was undertaken as a feasibility study whose purpose was to demonstrate that the approach could be applied to a substantial piece of real legislation.

Other examples are provided by a series of MSc projects undertaken at Imperial College: those incorporating realistically sized fragments of legislation include a subset of the UK Immigration Act 1971 [Suphamongkhon 1984], regulations for government grants to industry [Lowes 1984], pension regulations with associated tax legislation [Chan 1984], landlord and tenant legislation [Stathis 1987], stock exchange regulations [Lakhani 1988] and the law of patents [Roberts 1988]. Bill Sharpe [1984, 1985] describes an attempt to represent Statutory Sick Pay legislation in the UK. Alan Hustler [1982] has used similar techniques to represent rules relating to the tort of assault and battery. Hustler's system is mentioned again in section 1.15.1 where the work of Meldman is described. Peter Hammond [1983] at Imperial College has used APES in a system which advises on the entitlement of individuals to one of the Social Security benefits available in the UK. Hammond's system is not typical because it seeks to represent, not the formal sources of law but the practical experience of an expert in this area of law. In this respect, Hammond's system could be classified with Capper and Susskind's Latent Damage System (section 1.5.4), though it differs in operation and does not compare in depth and range of knowledge represented.

Another example constructed at Imperial College is based on a substantial part of the UK's social security legislation [Bench-Capon *et al.* 1987]. This exercise was undertaken specifically to investigate the problems that arise when large scale representations of this type are attempted. Here additional difficulties are introduced simply by the size and complexity of the source legislation. In this example, the legislation is contained in one main act, supplemented by ten sets of regulations, it has undergone considerable revision and amendment, and it interacts with many other laws.

Examples of recent projects elsewhere include the IRI-Project at the University of Bologna which is addressing environmental law [Pattaro *et al.* 1989], and a project at the Government of India's Department of Electronics which currently has two main applications: one deals with import and export regulations [Bajaj *et al.* 1989a] and the other with pension regulations [Bajaj *et al.* 1989b].

Apparently logic programming techniques have been adopted by several commercial organizations, mostly in Europe. The only published account I am aware of is ENIDATA's PROLEG system [Andretta *et al.* 1988].

1.10.3. Commentary

The general approach described in section 1.10.1 must be contrasted with the use of procedural PROLOG. The emphasis here is on constructing declarative representations. Practical programs can be built with these representations by executing them in systems such as APES. This gives a program with the same functionality as, for example, Schlobohm's tax advisor mentioned in section 1.8.2, but without sacrificing the declarative nature of the representation. A declarative representation has important practical properties. Firstly, it allows the same representation to be executed with different control strategies. A program which reasons forwards from data to new conclusions is more appropriate in some practical applications. Another possibility is to provide a system which gives an expert user control over its execution, along the lines of the mixed-initiative system implemented by the MacRaes (mentioned earlier). Other possibilities are described briefly in [Kowalski and Sergot 1990; Bench-Capon *et al.* 1987]. Secondly, a declarative representation means that 'explanations' of reasoning generated by the program are not merely traces of computation but logical proofs of any conclusions reached. The practical importance of proofs is stressed in [Sergot 1985a]. Thirdly, a declarative representation can be used for many different purposes. Of particular interest, and enormous potential significance, is the use of declarative representations of law as aids in the drafting of legislation itself. This type of application is discussed in section 1.11.

Executing a set of extended definite clauses in PROLOG or in APES is a simple, efficient way to implement the deductive reasoning that 'applies' the representation to the facts of a real or hypothetical case. But is is only appropriate in certain (well-defined) circumstances, because of the way that PROLOG (and APES) treat negated conditions in clauses. PROLOG (and APES) interpret negation as 'negation by failure' — not B holds when all ways of proving B fail (in finite time). Negation by failure has intuitive appeal and is very efficient, but it is only justified by the assumption that sufficient conditions are actually necessary conditions as well. In other words it assumes that 'if' really means 'if and only if' throughout. Sergot [1985a] argues that this reading of negation (or 'if' as 'if and only if') is often appropriate and often corresponds to how one expects legislation to be read. However, there are clearly numerous occasions when this reading of negation is unwarranted ot unacceptable. In such cases, extended definite clauses are not expressive enough and PROLOG (and APES) do not provide an adequate theorem-prover. Something more sophisticated must be used instead. Kowalski [1989] proposes some other treatments of negation, to complement negation by failure or to replace it when its use cannot be justified. An overview of other developments and extensions is provided in section 1.10.4.

The process by which most of the examples in section 1.10.2 have been constructed contrasts directly with the kind of systematic methodology that Stamper is seeking to develop in LEGOL and NORMA (section 1.9). In the case of the British Nationality Act, for example, one way to read and use the provisions is as a definition of British citizenship, but there are many other possible uses of the same legislation, some of which are not related to notion of British citizenship at all (to support arguments about possible meanings of the term 'father' in some other piece of legislation, for example). Once some overall goal is identified, such as a desire to model the conditions which define British citizenship, the representation proceeds by expressing in precise terms whatever concepts are defined in the legislation. Concepts which are left undefined in the legislation become the primitive, atomic concepts of the representation. In this way, all vague concepts (and other phrases such as references to other legislation) become the responsibility of the user. If the representation is executed in a system like APES, then the user will be asked to decide whether such a concept holds in the given case. If he refuses to answer then any conclusion reached by the system will be qualified by the conditions that were left undecided.

Note that there is no constraint — and no guidance — on what should be taken as the primitive concepts of the representation. It would obviously be preferable if some more systematic method of analysis could be devised, but projects such as LEGOL have not yet developed methodologies to the level where much assistance can be given in the representation of a sizeable fragment of legislation. This remark is based on practical experience, and not on any theoretical objection to the methodologies which have been proposed, in LEGOL or elsewhere. The question of which, and what kind of, primitive concepts to include in a representation is discussed further when McCarty's TAXMAN is introduced (section 1.12) and again in section 1.13.4.

Logic programming techniques have been applied almost exclusively to what Sergot [1985a] calls 'definitional law' — a fragment of law which is either a definition of some legal concept (like 'British citizen') or which can be taken to be a definition for practical purposes. An important simplifying feature of this type of law is that the distinction between ideality (what ought to be the case) and actuality (what is the case) does not arise or can be ignored. There are some parts of law, however, which are more accurately modelled as a set of norms of conduct and where the distinction between ideality and actuality is fundamental. The logical analysis of this distinction is the province of deontic logic — the logic of prohibition, permission and obligation. Discussion of the possible role of deontic logic in computer representation of law is delayed until section 1.16.2 which is concerned with this topic (presented in the context of McCarty's work on TAXMAN).

Lastly, note that the representations described in this section again express a single interpretation of the legal sources on which they are based. A possible approach which could relax this requirement is outlined in [Sergot 1985a]. [Bench-Capon and Sergot 1985] address the representation of open textured concepts specifically.

1.10.4. Developments and extensions

Section 1.8.3 raised the question of whether special-purpose formalisms are required for legal applications. Of course, the systems that are used to execute representations of law would normally be expected to provide a range of additional facilities P such as the ability to store and examine the original source texts P that make them better suited to legal applications, but I am referring here to the representational formalism itself. Experience with examples like those in section 1.10.2 would suggest that general-purpose formalisms are adequate, at least for representing the simplest kinds of 'definitional' legislation. But it is also true that various extensions are desirable, both to make the formalism more convenient and more expressive.

Kowalski [1989] presents proposals for treating negation, and general rules and exceptions specifically, to replace or complement negation by failure where this is inadequate or inconvenient. Bench-Capon [1989a] discusses possible treatments of counterfactual conditionals, which are a very common form of linguistic device in legislative texts, especially where the texts have undergone substantial revision and amendment. More generally, Routen [1989] shows how introducing additional metalevels of description can yield representations that are richer in content and more closely resemble the structure of the original source texts.

One motivation for these various extensions is that sentences in a typical legislative text vary in their character. Some state definitions of legal concepts in more or less precise terms. Others express norms of conduct. Still others describe how other parts of the text should be read, or state exceptions and modifications to general rules appearing elsewhere. The list is not exhaustive. It would clearly be desirable to attempt some kind of classification, perhaps developing a particular construct or set of constructs for each type. [Bench-Capon *et al.* 1987] and [Routen 1989] make some specific suggestions along these lines.

The need for such extensions is particularly apparent when large scale representations are undertaken. For example, just the frequent and heavy use of cross-references can cause severe practical difficulties. In [Bench-Capon *et al.* 1987] it is suggested that large scale representations can benefit from constructing first a data base which describes the structure of the regulations, to be used as an aid later during construction of the representation proper. Humphreys [1988] and Roy-Burman [1988] develop this idea further.

A closely related project outside the logic programming context is the ANAPHORA project [Studnicki *et al.* 1982a, 1982b] whose objective is to develop an automated method for resolving various kinds of cross-references in legislative texts. A systematic classification of the sentence types and linguistic devices most commonly encountered in legislation is a central component of this work.

In addition to 'definitional law' and norms of conduct it is possible to distinguish 'procedural law' — procedures laid down to govern the administration of some other area of law. The representation of procedural law has received comparatively little attention. The only attempts (of which I am aware) to address procedural law specifically is an object-oriented system to simulate the law of patents in Japan [Nitta *et al.* 1986; also Nitta 1985] and an investigation by Roberts [1988] on the application of logic programming techniques to the corresponding area of law in the UK.

Most of the language extensions mentioned above are motivated by linguistic devices and other constructs occurring in legislative texts. The basic representational language could also be extended to provide direct support for concepts and modalities that arise frequently in legal applications. The event calculus [Kowalski and Sergot 1986] for example can be regarded as such an extension for dealing specifically with events, change and time. Extensions to deal with the deontic concepts (section 1.16.2) would be another example.

McCarty's recent work on a language for legal discourse (section 1.16.3) has the objective of providing a range of such features in an integrated framework. The next section describes part of this language, its intuitionistic logic programming core.

1.10.5. McCarty's Language for Legal Discourse

An overview of McCarty's Language for Legal Discourse is presented in section 1.16.3 of this survey. I have included part of its description here because its core is an intuitionistic logic variant of the general approach summarized in section 1.10.1.

McCarty has argued that intuitionistic rather than classical logic should be taken as the basis for a representational formalism for law. The motives are partly the usual ones for preferring intuitionistic to classical logic P to avoid the paradoxes of classical (material) implication and to provide a formal system that better captures our intuitive understanding of 'if' (and 'not'). In this case, McCarty also finds the model theory for intuitionistic logic particularly convenient for integrating the semantics of other components of his language into a single framework. The semantics and proof procedure for McCarty's intuitionistic logic programming are presented in [McCarty 1988a, 1988b]. [McCarty 1988c] discusses the treatment of defaults in this system.

Syntactically, McCarty's intuitionistic logic programs are also sets of extended definite clauses A <P W. When W is a conjunction of atomic conditions (or empty) McCarty's intuitionistic logic programming and classical logic programming coincide. The difference lies in the treatment of implications and negations occurring inside the conditions W.

There is much more to the Language for Legal Discourse than its intuitionistic logic core. A range of additional language features will support the representation of various basic, common sense concepts. A brief description of these other components appears in section 1.16.3.

The LEX project (next section) can be regarded as another variation on the general approach of section 1.10.1.

1.10.6. The LEX project

The LEX project is a collaborative research project between the University of Tbingen and the IBM Scientific Centre in Heidelberg [Jones 1986; Haft *et al.* 1987]. The project is developing two kinds of application: a consultation system, which gives legal advice to lawyers and helps them to prepare a case (what I have been calling a legal analysis program); and an intelligent tutor, a computer-assisted instruction system based on a representation of legal knowledge. The project is taking traffic law regulations in the German penal code as its main experimental domain.

The LEX project has emphasized the declarative nature of its representations, and the use of automated theorem-proving techniques to execute these representations in practical applications. In this respect, the project shares the motivation and many of the presuppositions of the approach described in section 1.10.1. The LEX project, however, developed from research into natural language interfaces to relational databases. It differs from the approach described in the previous section in its continuing concern with natural language issues. It differs too in its specific choice of representational formalism and theorem-proving technique.

The representational formalism adopted in the LEX project is a language based on first-order predicate logic with some additional syntactic features, whose formulas are called discourse representation structures [Gunthner *et al.* 1986]. This in turn is based on the Discourse Representation Theory of Kamp [1981]. LEX provides a general-purpose parser for German, and a mechanism which transforms the parser's results into this representational formalism [Gunthner & Lehmann 1984]. As in the approaches of section 1.10.1, the basic inference mechanism is deduction. But instead of a more standard theorem-prover based on resolution, LEX employs a theorem-prover based on tableau calculus. This is implemented in such a way that discourse representation structures, first-order formulae and PROLOG predicates are treated uniformly [Schunfeld 1985]. In these respects, the LEX project can be regarded as an interesting and sophisticated variation on the general approach described in section 1.10.1.

1.11. THE DRAFTING OF LEGISLATION

This section is concerned with the use of symbolic logic to aid the process of drafting legislation (and other legal documents). The topic falls within the scope of this paper because it involves the representation of legislation in logic. In principle, any such representation can be processed by computer. The topic is also closely related to the use of logic programming techniques in law, and indeed provides a class of potential applications for these techniques. Further, the work of Layman Allen, which is described in this section, has had a major influence on many projects concerned with the computer representation of law.

I am not suggesting there are no other computer aids that could be applied to the drafting of legislation. For example, there are many commercial systems that are used already to help with the drafting of standard legal documents like contracts and wills. But these systems are essentially modified word-processors that only deal with the wording and appearance of a legal document. They do not store its 'content' or 'meaning' and I have therefore excluded them. (The idea of basing a legal document generator on a representation of what the document 'says' as well as how it 'looks' has been suggested from time to time. There are some on-going projects along these lines but I know of no published descriptions.)

1.11.1. Allen's normalized form

An early paper by Layman Allen [1957] recommended the use of symbolic logic as a practical tool for analysing and potentially simplifying the structure of complex legal documents. Allen is now most closely associated with his proposals for a normalized form for legal documents [Allen 1980, 1982]. Allen's normalized form is designed to improve the precision of legal documents by eliminating unintended ambiguities P not the use of vague terms, which are a necessary and desirable feature in legal documents, but accidental syntactic ambiguities. Simple examples of syntactic ambiguities are constructs like 'A and B or C' where there is confusion over the intended way this expression should be bracketed, the use of 'if' when 'if and only if' is intended, the common usage in English where 'and' might mean disjunction and 'or' might mean conjunction, and so on. For example, Allen points out how many different meanings an apparently precise connective like 'unless' can have.

Allen's normalized form is based on a disciplined use of the propositional connectives (AND, OR, NOT, IF, IFF), and includes a number of syntactic conventions (such as conventional numbering schemes and standard ways to indent subsections). The intention is not that the draftsman should be forced to eliminate all imprecision from documents, but that there should be a method of expression that allows him to be precise when something precise is what he wants to say.

Allen's normalized form has had some influence on the way that legislation is drafted, particularly in some parts of the USA. Gray [1985] describes the experience of enacting a statute drafted in normalized form, and some of the practical difficulties that were encountered. Allen and Saxon [1985] have developed computer programs to assist with the normalization of legal documents. 'Normalization' refers to the process of identifying syntactic ambiguities present in a document, determining which of the possible meanings is intended, and translating the original text into a form which supports only the meaning intended.

Allen and Saxon [1986] have also recommended that legal provisions should be analyzed in terms of the 'Hohfeldian concepts' (right, duty, privilege, etc). These concepts are commonly referred to by this name in recognition of early work by Hohfeld [1913, 1917]. See also the discussion on conceptual models in section 1.13.4.

1.11.2. Commentary

The only computer-aided drafting tools based on Allen's recommendations (of which I am aware) are the normalization aids referred to earlier. These help to translate a document into normalized form, but they do not attempt to proceed beyond this, to process the resulting representations further.

The normalization aids produce a set of expressions which can be regarded as a representation of a legal document or a piece of legislation in propositional logic. Such a representation could be processed by computer, to derive various useful consequences of it. As Allen suggests in his early paper [Allen 1957], a computer program could be used to simplify the structure of legal documents in much the same way that they are used to simplify the structure of combinatorial circuits in electrical engineering. A natural development of this suggestion is to use theorem-provers to derive more general consequences of the representation, to help in predicting the effects of legislation and determining whether it is likely to meet its intended aims. It has often been pointed out that the ability to test out the effect of modifications on a library of test cases and stereotypical situations could be of substantial benefit in drafting or amending legislation. But I am referring also to the derivation of more general consequences, to test whether a draft has a particular desired property (that all women between 16 and 60 years of age are entitled to receive some benefit, for example). There would seem to be no theoretical obstacle to providing theorem-proving systems to aid in the drafting of legislation. As far as I know, no such system has ever been used in practice.

There is a related project which is investigating the use of theorem-proving methods, not for the drafting of legislation, but to help at the pre-drafting stage in the formulation of policy [Bench-Capon 1987]. This work is addressing directly the problem of predicting whether a piece of legislation will achieve its intended aims, or whether, through interaction with other legislation or because of unanticipated socio-economic effects, it will cause unintended and undesirable side-effects. This work is clearly very ambitious and still at a preliminary stage. The paper by Trevor Bench-Capon gives a number of real examples and shows how they might be treated with the help of such a system.

1.12. TAXMAN I

The best-known and most sustained project on the application of artificial intelligence techniques to law is Thorne McCarty's TAXMAN project which began in 1972. This section describes McCarty's early work on TAXMAN, now referred to as TAXMAN I [McCarty 1977, 1980c; Sridharan 1978a; McCarty and Sridharan 1980; see also Cook *et al.* 1981]. The later work on TAXMAN II and McCarty's recent proposals for a language for legal discourse are described separately in section 1.16.

McCarty has often contrasted the 'deep conceptual' model underlying the TAXMAN system with the representations that are incorporated in simple legal analysis programs (like Hellawell's CORPTAX program). This issue is examined in this section. TAXMAN II addresses specifically the representation of open textured concepts and reasoning with the deontic concepts (obligation, permission and prohibition).

1.12.1. Description

McCarty's aims in the TAXMAN project are primarily theoretical. He has described TAXMAN as 'an experiment in the application of artificial intelligence techniques to the study of legal reasoning and legal argumentation'. The experimental domain chosen for this investigation is US corporate tax law.

The US Internal Revenue Code classifies certain corporate transactions as tax-free reorganizations (of type B, C or D). The TAXMAN I system was constructed to represent the statutory rules and concepts which define these reorganizations. When the facts of a given corporate transaction are described in the TAXMAN formalism, the system can apply its definitions to determine whether the transaction would be classified as a tax-free reorganization. TAXMAN I was originally implemented in a version of micro-PLANNER [Sussman, *et al.* 1971]. Subsequently TAXMAN I (and TAXMAN II) were implemented in AIMDS — a frame-based system [Sridharan 1978b], [Sridharan 1980].

Representation in TAXMAN begins by constructing a model of the underlying legal domain. For corporate tax law, the domain will contain 'objects' like corporations, individuals, stocks, shares, securities, transactions, etc. Each class of object is described by a template: a particular object will be represented by a template instance, which can be viewed as a collection of assertions describing the object's properties (name, address, size, etc). The domain is further described by a system of relations which express the possible relationships between objects. The facts of a particular case are described by a set of template instances and the relations between them. Legal concepts defined by the statute (like 'tax-free reorganization') are also represented by templates (though normally these contain variables which can be instantiated to have particular values). The statutory rules which define these concepts are represented by logical templates, a term which is intended to suggest the way that templates for the high-level concepts are 'matched' to the lower-level fact descriptions during the analysis of a case.

McCarty [1983a] contrasts the structured representation of the TAXMAN domain with the unstructured questions that a program like Hellawell's CORPTAX might ask: does TP and family actually own 50% or more (in value) of the stock of a corporation which is a partner in a partnership which owns Redcorp stock? In CORPTAX (section 1.7.4), this is just a portion of text which is not broken down into its constituent parts. It is not connected in any way to other portions of text that mention 'stock' or 'ownership' or 'corporation'. Conceptually, McCarty suggests, this means that the underlying primitive concepts of CORPTAX are concepts like TTP and family actually own 50% or more (in value) of the stock of a corporation which is a partner in a partnership which owns Redcorp 'stock'. This he contrasts with TAXMAN's representation, which is constructed from much more basic primitives like 'stock' and 'ownership' and where the relationships between these primitives are made explicit.

For future reference, it is also worth summarizing here McCarty's reasons for choosing a 'technical' domain like corporate tax law rather than some 'simpler' legal domain.

> [It] is tempting to start with the 'simplest' possible legal issues, such as the subject matter of the first-year law school courses. But these cases are 'simple' for law students primarily because they draw upon ordinary human experience, and this is precisely what makes them

> so difficult for an artificial intelligence system. I Paradoxically, the cases that are most tractable for an artificial intelligence system are those cases, usually involving commercial and corporate matters, which a lawyer finds most complex. There is a simple reason why this is so. I Because of their technical complexity, the legal rules at the top levels of this conceptual hierarchy are difficult for most lawyers to comprehend, but this would be no obstacle for an artificial intelligence system. The commercial abstractions, in fact, are artificial and formal systems themselves, drained of much of the content of the ordinary world.
>
> [McCarty 1980b]

What McCarty is referring to here, of course, is the difficulty of representing common sense in a computer program, and a number of projects to be described later would seem to confirm his analysis. Yet it is important not to misunderstand what McCarty is getting at. The artificial worlds of commerce and taxation eliminate some of the problems of dealing with the ordinary world, but they are still filled with open textured concepts whose (technical) meanings shift and evolve as new cases are decided. The representation of open textured concepts is a main theme in McCarty's work on TAXMAN II.

1.12.2. Commentary

There are two main points to be made about the TAXMAN I system: the nature of the analysis that the system performs; and the significance that McCarty attaches to the choice of primitive concepts, and the use of adjectives like 'deep' and 'structured' in this context.

It is very straightforward to reconstruct the TAXMAN I system in logical terms. Template instances correspond to sets of assertions about an individual object together with an object-oriented indexing scheme, exactly as in the now familiar reconstruction of frames as 'bundles of assertions'. See for example [Hayes 1979] and [Charniak and McDermott 1985]. (The reconstruction of frames as 'bundles of assertions' is criticized because it overlooks one of the fundamental motivations for frames, which is to deal with concepts — stereotypes or 'natural kinds' — that do not admit definition in terms of precise necessary and sufficient conditions. But the reconstruction of TAXMAN I's templates as 'bundles of assertions' is accurate. The attempt to deal with stereotypes and imprecisely defined concepts is what characterizes McCarty's later work on TAXMAN II.)

If this reconstruction is carried out, then logical templates can be viewed as 'if and only if' definitions. As McCarty [1983a] points out, the matching of a logical template to the facts of a case for the purpose of recognizing whether a higher-level concept holds can be viewed as reasoning backwards from the conclusion of the defining rule to its conditions. TAXMAN's use of templates (bundles of assertions) is convenient for the kinds of object it manipulates, but the inference mechanism employed in TAXMAN (TAXMAN I) is deduction. TAXMAN (I) can be reconstructed straightforwardly as a logic program. (It can also be reconstructed in the spirit of the 'event calculus' [Kowalski and Sergot 1986] which would treat transactions and reorganizations as primitive concepts rather than describing them indirectly in terms of transitions between states.) In this respect, TAXMAN I might even be classified as an example of logic programming applied to the representation of law (except of course that it pre-dates that particular technique). Note that TAXMAN I, like all the systems considered so far, represents only a single, fixed interpretation of the legal sources on which it is based. TAXMAN II can be regarded as an attempt to remove this restriction.

The significance of TAXMAN's 'deep' and 'structured' conceptual model of the underlying legal domain is more difficult to explain. What McCarty is addressing is the question of what one should take as the primitive concepts in terms of which everything else is represented. In the area of corporate tax law, a natural set of such primitives would include such concepts as 'stock' and 'corporation' and some representation of how they relate to one another; by comparison taking TTP and family actually own 50% or more (in value) of the stock of a corporation which is a partner in a partnership which owns Redcorp 'stock' as a primitive concept just seems wrong.

In order to understand a piece of legislation, it is clearly necessary to understand something of the domain in which it operates. A program needs this too, and it can be argued that an explicit representation of some part of the underlying domain is just as important as an explicit representation of what the legislation itself expresses. I think this is why McCarty emphasizes the nature of the conceptual model in the TAXMAN representation. I think 'deep' and 'structured' are used here as relative terms: TAXMAN I's representation is 'deep' and 'structured' when compared with CORPTAX's which is 'shallow' and 'unstructured'. (The adjective 'deep' can have other meanings. Some of these are pointed out in section 1.13.4.)

It seems clear that 'deep' representations are preferable to 'shallow' but I want to make an additional remark about what seems to happen in practice. If one considers an example like the representation of the British Nationality Act referred to in section 1.10.2, one sees that undefined and therefore primitive predicates like 'was found abandoned as a newborn infant in the UK' often appear in the representation. These 'hyphenated predicates' are just like the unstructured questions produced by CORPTAX (and indeed in a system like APES they generate exactly this type of question). This might suggest that the underlying conceptual model for the British Nationality Act representation is shallow in the same way that CORPTAX's is shallow. This is not necessarily so.

In TAXMAN-like terms, the conceptual model for the British Nationality Act representation contains objects like persons, places and times, and relationships like 'parent of', 'date of birth' and 'settled in' between them. It is easy to imagine how such facts about a given individual could be 'bundled together' as template instances in TAXMAN. As argued in [Sergot 1985a], however, it is not realistic to construct 'deep' representations of concepts like 'was found abandoned as a new-born infant in the UK' in terms of something more primitive. It is difficult to imagine what the representation of such a concept would look like. In any case, it might turn out later that the concept has a technical meaning in law because it is precisely defined somewhere else.

The need for primitive (undefined) 'hyphenated predicates' arises when one attempts to construct a representation of a sizeable fragment of legislation. I would guess, without any supporting evidence, that the reason McCarty was able to construct a representation of the TAXMAN statutes without relying at all on 'hyphenated predicates' is because the system represents a tiny and fairly well-contained fragment of the US Internal Revenue Code. It could be that CORPTAX generates unstructured questions because of features in the legislation it represents, and not only because the underlying conceptual model is 'shallow' nor because of the inadequacy of the computational techniques employed. None of this is to argue that McCarty is wrong to stress the importance of choosing reasonable primitive concepts and making explicit the relationships between them. Even in systems which rely on querying the user for all facts about a given case, the absence of a conceptual model of the underlying domain manifests itself in a number of unacceptable ways (such as the generation of meaningless dialogues). [Sergot 1985a] discusses these issues in more detail. See also [Bench-Capon 1989b].

There are several projects which can be classified with McCarty's TAXMAN I in that they too have placed particular emphasis on conceptual models of the domain in which a set of legal rules is applied. Some of these projects have been very influential in the development of the field. Examples are given in the next section.

1.13. CONCEPTUAL MODELS AND DOCUMENT RETRIEVAL

Two projects described in this section have attempted to improve the performance of document retrieval systems by incorporating a conceptual model of the underlying legal domain. The two projects are Carole Hafner's doctoral project at the University of Michigan [Hafner 1978, 1981; see also Cook *et al.* 1981], and the CCLIPS project conducted by Cary deBessonet and George Cross at the Louisiana Law Institute (see references below). Although document retrieval systems are outside the scope of this survey, both of these projects have influenced the computer representation of law. Both are examples of what McCarty [1983a] and others have called conceptual retrieval systems.

The motivation for conceptual retrieval systems is clear. The automated retrieval of legal texts from large databases of documents was one of the earliest applications of computing to law, and commercial systems such as LEXIS and WESTLAW are now familiar to many legal practitioners. Bing [1984] has compiled a good survey of legal document retrieval systems. Currently, document retrieval systems use text searches that are specified by Boolean combinations of keywords, but the limitations of this technique have been pointed out by many researchers (see for example [Bing 1986]). It has long been established that retrieval based on the meaning and content of documents would be far more appropriate. Conceptual retrieval systems attempt to store and retrieve documents using an index based on a conceptual model of the particular legal domain.

I have also included in this section a brief description of the ESPLEX project conducted at the Istituto per la Documentazione Giuridica (IDG) in Florence. Although this project does not address conceptual retrieval specifically, it has placed considerable emphasis on conceptual models of the underlying legal domain. It also allows me to make additional remarks on the different things that a conceptual model could contain.

1.13.1. Hafner

Conceptual retrieval has been illustrated by Hafner in a system that stores and retrieves documents related to parts of the US Uniform Commercial Code [Hafner 1978, 1981; see also Cook *et al.* 1981]. This legislation governs 'negotiable instruments' such as cheques and notes. Working with a conceptual model of the situations that typically occur in negotiable instruments law, Hafner constructed a database containing about two hundred cases and two hundred subsections of the code. The conceptual model allows the system to retrieve relevant documents even if none of the terms specified in the query appear in the document. For example, a request for occurrences of 'an unauthorized signature on a draft' would retrieve a document where the term 'a forged endorsement of a check' is mentioned. An account of Hafner's more recent work is given in [Hafner 1987].

Hafner's system illustrates the potential of conceptual retrieval, but practical implementations remain to be investigated and built. As Hafner points out, the conceptual analysis of a legal document involves a massive amount of work and poses a major practical obstacle. Furthermore, Bing [1987] has pointed out the need to investigate the assumption that conceptual retrieval really will improve on the performance of standard document retrieval systems. He has begun an interesting experiment at

NRCCL in Oslo to test out the practical benefits of conceptual retrieval, by constructing a retrieval system for Norwegian pension legislation based on a very simple and easily constructed conceptual model of the domain. His idea is to take as the conceptual model simply whatever propositions are obtained by translating the legislation according to Allen's normalization process (section 1.11.1).

1.13.2. CCLIPS

The CCLIPS (Civil Code Legal Information Processing System) project of Cary deBessonet and George Cross began at the end of 1970's. Its aim is to build a conceptual model of several sections of the Louisiana Civil Code dealing with contract law. (Louisiana is one of the few States with a legal system based on civil codes rather than common law.) One of the main purposes of the project is to clarify the structure of the Civil Code itself. An additional purpose, once the conceptual model has been formulated, is to experiment with alternative designs for a conceptual retrieval system. [deBessonet 1980, 1982, 1983, 1984; deBessonet and Cross 1985, 1986; Cross and deBessonet 1985a, 1985b]

The formulation of the conceptual model, which deBessonet and Cross call 'scientific codification', is heavily influenced by Allen's normalization process. Legal rules in the model are represented essentially in the form of propositional rules. These rules in turn are expressed in terms of abstract primitive objects and abstract primitive actions resembling those of Schank's conceptual dependency theory [Schank and Rieger 1974]. The intention is to capture the 'deep' semantic structure of the objects and actions that are encountered in the domain of contract law. The representation language is called Atomically Normalized Form (ANF) (and the representations constructed in it Analytical Legal Databases). The representations are intended to support the conceptual retrieval of legal information, but the system can also generate inferences. The facts of a case can be described in the ANF language in terms of the underlying conceptual model, and the rules can then be applied to this representation to determine legal consequences.

Note that deBessonet and Cross seem to use 'deep' in a different sense to McCarty's in TAXMAN I. The representation in CCLIPS is 'deep' in the same way that Schank's representation of verbs like 'sell' is 'deep' when it is expressed in terms of abstract primitive actions like 'abstract transfer of possession', 'transfer of physical location' or 'movement of body part'.

1.13.3. ESPLEX

The ESPLEX system [Biagioli *et al.* 1987] is being developed as part of the Automated Analysis of Legislation project which has been conducted at the Istituto per la Documentazione Giuridica (IDG) in Florence since 1981. ESPLEX combines the use of logic for the representation of rules embodied in legislation with the use of frames and semantic networks to model the general legal concepts that are required to understand the legislation. The experimental domain for the project is the law relating to agricultural tenancies, part of the law of contracts. A main objective of the ESPLEX project is to develop a methodology for the analysis of legislation which takes into account the different kinds of sentences and concepts contained in legal rules. The implementation language used is PROLOG.

Work in the general field of computers and law has been conducted at IDG since (at least) the early 1970s. Abstracts and references to other projects are provided in Biagioli and Fameli's bibliography [Biagioli and Fameli 1987].

1.13.4. Commentary

In TAXMAN I, CCLIPS, Hafner's LIRS, ESPLEX (and LEGOL and NORMA) there is emphasis on the underlying conceptual model and on the choice of primitives in terms of which the representation is constructed. All of these conceptual models are 'deep', but in quite different senses of the word. In later projects (notably TAXMAN II and the Language for Legal Discourse) 'deep' can be applied in a different sense still.

The conceptual model in TAXMAN I contains primitives like 'corporation' and 'ownership' and various relationships between them. Hafner's is like this too. This is 'deep' compared with, say CORPTAX, but it could be made 'deeper', and in many different ways. One possibility is to follow CCLIPS and attempt to reduce everything to some set of very primitive 'Schankian' concepts. Another is to follow Allen and Saxon's recommendations ([Allen and Saxon 1986] and section 1.11.1) and think in terms of the Hohfeldian concepts of 'right' and 'privilege' and 'duty' etc. Thus, 'ownership' could be expressed as some package of Hohfeldian concepts which capture something of what 'ownership' means. For the Language for Legal Discourse (section 1.16.3), McCarty proposes another specific set of useful primitive concepts. With NORMA (section 1.9), Stamper has proposed thinking in terms of agent, intention and behaviour. All of these are candidates for a set of primitive concepts. All of them would yield a 'deep' conceptual model. I am making no comment on their relative merits. My intention is simply to point out how many different kinds of deep conceptual model there can be.

In some countries, the academic legal tradition is to account for or describe some area of law in terms of an underlying normative or ethical or sociological theory. Here, something like 'contract' might be regarded as a particular kind of 'social interaction' (say) and elements of contract law would be explained in terms of how social interactions must work for moral, ethical or pragmatic reasons (whatever). In English and American legal circles, the tradition seems to be more empirical, by which I mean that there is little emphasis on presenting underlying theories of law or society to account for why cases have been decided in the way that they have. These different traditions could also be reflected in what an underlying conceptual model has in it.

As a concrete example, consider 'deep' representations of 'borrowers must return books to the library by the date due'. I might wish to reduce a verb like 'return' to some combination of abstract primitives like 'abstract transfer of possession' and 'transfer of physical location'. Or 'book' could be represented as a particular kind of 'communication medium' or as a particular kind of 'library resource'. Or I might want to concentrate on the modality 'must' and express what this means in terms of deontic or Hohfeldian concepts. If I were a sociologist I might want to view the regulation in terms of primitives like 'administrative convenience' or 'anti-social behaviour'. As a very extreme example, I might simply choose to assert that the library is a bourgeois institution.

All of these options are possible and all have their uses. All of them are 'deep' in some sense of the word.

I stress again that my intention is only to draw attention to the many different kinds of conceptual model there can be.

1.14. SYSTEMS THAT COMBINE STATUTES AND CASE LAW

All of the systems described so far are based on a model of the law that represents one fixed interpretation of the legal sources. (And for the reasons explained in the introduction, they have largely concentrated on statutes). They have avoided the problems of reasoning with concepts with several possible meanings either by approximating, or by passing responsibility to the user. I have mentioned only in passing the possibility of removing this limitation. Even though one of the main aims of the work by Waterman and Peterson has been to investigate the effects of other models, this has required altering the rules in the model explicitly. At any one time, their model of the law is fixed. Other systems have taken a similar line.

The projects which are described in the rest of the chapter have attempted to reason with representations of law that do not embody a single, fixed interpretation of the legal sources. These systems cannot rely completely on inference which is purely deductive (or which can be viewed as an implementation of deduction). Many of them are investigating the nature of legal reasoning itself. Others are primarily concerned with developing practical aids, normally to help in the analysis of legal problems which are primarily governed by case law.

This section describes two early projects which have attempted to combine reasoning by rules with reasoning from the decisions of previous cases. Both were conducted as doctoral projects. They are Jeffrey Meldman's study in the tort of assault and battery [Meldman 1975, 1977; see also Cook *et al.* 1981], and Anne Gardner's treatment of offer and acceptance in contract law [Gardner 1983, 1984, 1985]. As mentioned in the historical overview, they can usefully be considered together. Other projects investigating techniques for reasoning with case law are described separately in sections 1.15 and 1.16.

1.15. Meldman

Jeffrey Meldman, in his doctoral project at MIT, designed a system to perform a 'simple kind of legal analysis' on cases involving assault and battery [Meldman 1975, 1977; see also Cook *et al.* 1981]. The analysis was based on a (tiny) fictitious body of legal sources *Corpus Juris Mechanicum* (CJM) extracted from a standard textbook on tort by Prosser. The sources comprised a collection of 'legal doctrines' and a set of cases and their decisions. Both were to be represented in the same way, in a kind of semantic network. The user would present a semantic network describing some hypothetical set of facts and the system would determine the extent to which these facts 'fell within legal doctrines by syllogism' (applied its rules to the facts by deduction) or 'near to these doctrines by analogy'. (Meldman was careful to stress that his system supported a very simplified form of analogy.) During this process, the system would ask the user for any additional facts that it needed to perform the analysis. It would then report its conclusions, justified by reference to the legal sources in CJM.

Meldman's system was designed to be executed by a system called OWL [Szolovits *et al.* 1977], though it was never implemented. Later, a program based on Meldman's design was implemented by King [1976] who placed more emphasis on reasoning by analogy than Meldman had done originally.

There are three main features that characterize Meldman's system: the nature of the legal sources represented, the choice of representational formalism, and the general approach to legal analysis and the treatment of case law specifically.

A standard text like Prosser's on tort has a special status in (English and American) common law systems. It presents the author's commentary and personal analysis of some area of law, and therefore is only a secondary source of law; but eventually it is referred to so extensively and takes on such authority that it becomes effectively the definitive source in its particular area. It contains a collection of the most important decided cases, organized by what the author has identified as broad general principles or rules, or what Meldman calls 'legal doctrines'. These general doctrines account for how most cases have been decided; but there are also references to cases which seem to be exceptions and to cases which contain some unusual feature that the general doctrines cannot capture. Because of the authority that such a text eventually accumulates, its doctrines can be regarded as having almost the status of legislation (though they are not as detailed as typical statutes). Meldman's *Corpus Juris Mechanicum* (CJM) re-creates this type of legal source, containing a few general doctrines together with a set of decided cases that supplement them. (In CJM all the cases provide some additional detail rather than exceptions to the general doctrines.) Meldman's system would work in exactly the same way for statutes supplemented by case law.

Meldman's design uses a kind of semantic network to represent the sources and a 'matching' operation to perform the analysis of a new case at hand. However, it is fairly straightforward to recast this representation in more familiar rule-based form. The following account is in terms of rules rather than the original semantic networks, but it preserves all the essential features.

Some of the rules in Meldman's system represent the general doctrines of the CJM. When the facts of the case to be analysed match all the conditions of a rule, the rule is applied by deduction and the case falls within a legal doctrine by 'syllogism'. This part of the processing is standard. It is the treatment of the individual cases that needs more explanation.

For individual cases, Meldman's approach is to view the decision in a previous case as evidence for the existence of a detailed but still general rule of law. This model of reasoning with case law is supported explicitly by the system: the decision in a previous case is represented as the general rule which corresponds to what is often referred to as the *ratio decidendi* of the case. (There are usually several general rules which can be extracted from a single case: in Meldman's system there is only one.) Judges rarely state the *ratio decidendi* of a case in explicit and precise terms; normally the *ratio decidendi* has to be reconstructed by someone else from the judicial arguments used to justify the decision. It should be clear that there is consequently severe doubt over what is or what was intended to be the *ratio decidendi* in a given case. Indeed, arguments over the meaning of a legal concept can often be reduced to disputes over what the *ratio decidendi* of a previous case should be taken to be. In Meldman's system the rule expressing the decision of a case is constructed explicitly by him.

The *ratio decidendi* of every decided case in CJM is represented in exactly the same way as the general legal doctrines. So now, if the facts of a new case are identical to those in some previous one, then the corresponding *ratio decidendi* is applied by deduction (by 'syllogism') like any other rule. Since this is not likely to happen very often, Meldman has an additional 'analogy' mechanism to deal with cases which do not match exactly.

Meldman's analogy mechanism is based on a hierarchical classification of the concepts represented in his system. When the facts of a case do not match exactly the conditions of a rule in the system (expressing either an established legal doctrine or the *ratio decidendi* of a previous case), Meldman's system uses its classification of concepts to provide an extended notion of 'matching'. A fact in a given case is considered to 'match' a condition in a rule when they are both instances of a more general concept in the hierarchy. Thus 'kick' and 'hit' would match because they are both instances of the more general concept 'violent physical contact'. In this way, the facts of a new case can be subsumed by the *ratio decidendi* of a previous, similar case. (Note that the analogy mechanism also applies to rules representing general doctrines. Since these have conditions that are already rather abstract the analogy mechanism is seldom invoked for them.)

Meldman stresses that his mechanism provides only a very simplified form of analogy. (In fact it corresponds to what is sometimes called 'first-order generalization' [Reynolds 1970]). Ashley [1985] has compiled a survey of research in artificial intelligence on reasoning by analogy and discussed the applicability of these techniques to applications in law. See also [Kedar-Cabelli 1984].

Schild [1989] describes a quite different way of using the general doctrines that appear in a text like Prosser's P not as deductive rules in a legal analysis program, but as a way of organizing the storage of case reports and bringing the user's attention to possibly relevant instances. In what seems to have been a small student exercise, Hustler [1982] implemented a logic program based on Meldman's extracts from Prosser; he did not attempt to reconstruct Meldman's semantic network representation directly and he ignored the analogy mechanism altogether.

1.15.1. Commentary

Meldman's early system anticipated many of the features of current legal analysis programs. The treatment of general doctrines (where others have statutes) is fairly standard. It is the treatment of individual cases that needs most comment.

Meldman's approach, to represent a case by a single rule expressing its *ratio decidendi*, has very severe limitations. (These criticisms are intended to highlight the limitations of the approach, and not as attack on Meldman's work.)

Firstly, there is the problem of determining what should be taken as the *ratio decidendi*. As remarked earlier, this is the source of many legal disputes because the *ratio decidendi* of a case is very rarely stated explicitly. One could argue that in principle extracting a general rule from the decision of a case is no more difficult than determining how the provisions of a statute should be construed. But it must be clear that the significance of decisions in previous cases is much more open to other interpretations than the relatively precise statements which appear in statutes and other legislation. (That is one reason that statutes are passed.)

Secondly, as Meldman acknowledges, his simplified form of analogy ('first-order generalization') is quite inadequate for what he intends. It is important to be clear why.

Case law allows great scope for generalization. If a statute mentions the term 'car' explicitly it would be difficult to argue that the term 'car' was used by the draftsman to mean 'motor vehicle of any kind'. Suppose, however, that a case arises where a car is driven deliberately through a window and it is decided that the driver should pay for the damage. If later a truck is driven deliberately to cause similar damage, it could reasonably be argued that the previous decision should be followed, because the judge in the previous case intended 'motor vehicle of any kind' though he explicitly mentioned 'car' in his judgement. It is this type of reasoning that Meldman's analogy mechanism is attempting to simulate and — depending of course on what is in the hierarchy — it works in this example. But the mechanism is much too simple to be useful. As a single example, suppose that another case arises where a car is driven deliberately through a window. Suppose a lawyer argues that a passenger should pay for the damages since the judge in the previous case meant 'any occupant of the car' though he specifically mentioned 'driver'. Common sense suggests that such an argument is unlikely to succeed; in Meldman's system it would succeed if both passenger and driver are instances of the more general concept 'occupant'. Of course, this could be avoided by adding more detail to the *ratio decidendi* that is stored. But this is not a practical solution either. When do we stop adding additional detail to the cases that are stored?

Lastly, when a new case exactly matches the facts of an old case in Meldman's system, the mechanism is simply to apply the rule in the old case directly. This too is an over-simplification. It is always possible to argue that the decision of a previous case should not be followed, because the new case has extra features not present in the old case. It must be stressed that exactly the same thing can arise if the rule applied to the facts of a new case is derived from statutes. For it is also possible to argue that the statute should be construed differently by pointing to special features in the case and arguing that these could not have been anticipated. When the represented facts of a new case are identical to those of an old case, Meldman's system behaves exactly like one which incorporates a single, fixed interpretation of the law. The reason that Meldman's system is unlikely to produce a useful analysis in such circumstances is due entirely to the difficulty of extracting a general rule or *ratio decidendi* and finding some reasonable consensus that the rule accurately expresses what the case is taken to mean in practice. Finding some reasonable consensus about the meaning of a set of statutory provisions is very much easier (though of course there are many exceptions).

When dealing with statutes (or even very well-established common law 'doctrines') it is sometimes possible to pretend that a new case has a definite answer and still obtain a useful analysis (if the statute is complex and detailed, for example). But case law is so open to different interpretations, and the significance of any individual case is so dependent on context, that it is unrealistic to think that a program can yield a definite answer, or should even attempt to do so. I think the limitations of Meldman's system come essentially from this. A discernible trend in other approaches to the treatment of case law and open texture more generally has been to concentrate on producing an analysis of possible solutions, rather than seeking a definite 'right' answer. As a first example, the next section presents Anne Gardner's approach to the treatment of open texture.

1.15.2. Gardner

The main aim of Anne Gardner's doctoral project [Gardner 1983, 1984, 1985] was to address directly the treatment of open texture and thus the use of case-based reasoning to complement reasoning with statutes. A central feature is her attempt to construct a system that can identify which parts of a case are 'easy' and which involve the resolution of 'hard' legal questions. The system was intended to perform at a level of sophistication where it could analyse examination questions. The problem domain is the law of contracts, and specifically offer and acceptance, a concept which is defined mostly by case law. The significance of examination questions lies in the type of analysis that is required to answer them. Given some hypothetical state of affairs, a candidate is expected not to dwell on the trivial but to recognize where the important legal questions arise (the 'issues') and discuss their effect on the possible outcome of the case. It is this 'issue spotting' ability that Gardner was attempting to simulate in her program. Gardner's system is implemented in MRS [Genesereth *et al.* 1984].

In describing Gardner's system it is again useful to separate the component which applies relatively clear rules (normally derived from statutes) from that part which specifically addresses reasoning with case law. In addition to the 'relatively clear rules' which provide definitions for technical legal concepts, Gardner's system contains rules expressing common-sense definitions of non-technical concepts (CSK rules). A concept can have both a technical and a non-technical definition: in such cases the technical definition is normally preferred.

The feature of Gardner's work which most distinguishes it from previous approaches is her emphasis that most legal questions do not have a single 'right' answer (until they have been decided in court). Her system is designed to provide various analyses leading to alternative possible outcomes. Gardner describes a mechanism which produces as output a tree of all the solutions which can be reached for a given case. Branches in this tree are introduced by the presence of open textured concepts which cannot be decided definitely one way or the other. An alternative way to view this mechanism is in terms of a standard deductive system which determines whether a legal concept holds by reasoning backwards with the rule that defines it. This system does not attempt to determine whether conditions involving open textured concepts are satisfied. Instead, such conditions become qualifications on the final conclusion reached. Gardner's tree of possible solutions corresponds to a set of conditional answers, where each answer is qualified by the open textured conditions that remain to be determined. (A mechanism that produces such sets of conditional answers can be implemented straightforwardly by modifying a standard refutation theorem prover. Alternatively, Gordon [1989] has suggested using an ATMS [deKleer 1986] for the same purpose.)

In practice, not all occurrences of open textured concepts are 'hard' to resolve. (If they were then everything would be an 'issue' which is clearly not the case.) The other main component of Gardner's system attempts to determine which of the open textured conditions are 'hard' (the 'issues') and which are 'easy'. To capture the notion of 'hard', Gardner allows a concept to be defined by several different rules which are marked as competing. When the system encounters a condition which has several competing definitions, every competing rule must be tried. If the choice of rule makes a difference to the outcome (the rules do not agree in their conclusions) then there is a 'hard' legal question and the condition becomes one of the qualifications on the final conclusion reached. If all the competing rules agree, then the condition is taken as decided and does not become a qualification on the final conclusion. Gardner suggested a number of other heuristics that could be used in addition to distinguish 'hard' from 'easy' conditions. (Again, my account of Gardner's system simplifies the original presentation but preserves the essential features.)

Gardner also proposed an extension to allow her system to generate competing arguments for the different ways that 'hard' questions could be decided. The generation of arguments both for and against a legal conclusion is also a feature of several other approaches to case-based reasoning described in later sections.

1.15.3. Commentary

Both Meldman and Gardner chose very difficult areas of law as their experimental domains. Assault and battery and offer and acceptance are both areas of law that rely less on a detailed knowledge of technicalities than they do on the need to apply common-sense. As McCarty points out (section 1.12.1), it is the representation of the required common sense that make these apparently 'simple' areas of law among the most difficult to address computationally; and P partly with hindsight P he cites assault and battery and offer and acceptance as specific examples of law that could be expected to cause most representational problems.

Gardner's project placed a great deal of emphasis on the treatment of common-sense. The CSK rules in her system are an example of this concern, but the whole work is largely dominated by consideration of the common-sense required to understand the notion of offer and acceptance. For example, a central concern in offer and acceptance is whether a particular form of words does or does not constitute an offer, and whether the form of the reply signals acceptance. Does a letter which mentions the price of an item constitute an offer to sell at this price? Is there a difference if the letter arrives in direct reply to an enquiry? Does it matter whether the reply is sent in a telegram rather than a letter? These are some of the questions which Gardner addressed in her project. She devoted a great deal of effort to devising a method of representation based on Searle's theories of speech acts. In my opinion, all this distracted attention from the fundamental aims of her project which were to address aspects of legal reasoning rather than very difficult issues more directly concerned with the comprehension of natural language.

Others have also argued for the generation of alternative, conditional solutions to account for the presence of undecided open-textured concepts (see for example section 1.10.1 on logic programming techniques and [Sergot 1985a]), but no one else has stressed this as much as Gardner. Neither has anyone else addressed directly how to distinguish 'hard' questions from 'easy' ones. Gardner's motivation was essentially to simulate aspects of legal reasoning in an artificial intelligence approach, but the question has important practical considerations too. Without some such distinction all open textured concepts are 'hard' and the trees of conditional analyses become unusably bushy. I think this is the most interesting part of Gardner's work and I think it is a great pity that she did not devote more attention to it in her account of the work.

1.16. TAXMAN II AND LANGUAGE FOR LEGAL DISCOURSE

McCarty's TAXMAN project was introduced in section 1.12, which described the early part of this work (TAXMAN I). The TAXMAN I system can be viewed as an implementation of deductive reasoning by rules which are expressed in terms of a structured representation of the underlying domain. TAXMAN II builds on this earlier work.

There are two main lines of investigation which McCarty has been pursuing in TAXMAN II. The first addresses specifically the treatment of open texture. It proposes a structure called prototypes-plus-deformations, to be incorporated as an extension to the logical templates framework used in TAXMAN I. The other part of TAXMAN II is the development of a version of deontic logic (the logic of obligation, permission and prohibition).

McCarty's most recent work has been on components of a language for legal discourse. This work is described in section 1.16.3.

1.16.1. Prototypes plus deformations

Although the domain in which TAXMAN operates is the largely artificial one of objects like corporations, stocks and transactions, the meaning of these concepts is as subject to change as that of concepts in any other area of law. McCarty has been investigating treatments of open texture and the representation of 'evolving systems of legal concepts' since the late 1970s (at that time in collaboration with Sridharan) [McCarty 1980c; see also Cook *et al.* 1981]. The primary goal of this work has been theoretical, to cast light on the nature of legal reasoning. These investigations led McCarty and Sridharan to propose a 'computational theory of legal argument' based on the representation of concepts in structures called prototypes-plus-deformations [McCarty and Sridharan 1981, 1982]. See also [McCarty 1989b].

The prototype-plus-deformations structure is based on the idea that a legal concept whose meaning has evolved with the accumulation of case law can be represented in terms of a structure with three components.

1. There is an invariant 'core' which expresses necessary but not sufficient conditions for the concept to hold. This component can be optional.
2. There is a set of exemplars each of which matches some but not all instances of the concept.
3. There is a set of transformations which express the relationship between the exemplars by stating how one exemplar can be mapped into another.

The resolution of a legal question, in other words deciding whether an open textured concept does or does not apply to the facts of a new case, involves argumentation. In the prototypes-plus-deformation model, to support a claim or hypothesis that the concept holds for a new case, it is necessary to demonstrate how a coherent representation of the concept can be constructed in the prototype-plus-deformation framework in such a way that the new case is included. A 'coherent' representation is one in which a sequence of allowed transformations maps the new case into one for which the concept is decided. This process might generate hypothetical cases where there is agreement whether the concept holds. Legal argumentation is adversarial in nature: it would be up to an opponent to construct another representation of the concept in which the new case is decided differently, which accounts better for the known cases where the concept is decided.

McCarty has shown how some of the arguments that were used by senior judges in key cases concerning the concept of 'taxable income' can be reconstructed in this model [McCarty 1980a, 1982; see also Brody 1980].

I find it difficult to assess McCarty's proposal for prototypes-plus-deformations. Though some specific examples are given, the prototype-plus-deformation model is still rather vague and has not been described in sufficient detail to evaluate its adequacy or its intended uses (in my opinion). Some aspects of McCarty's model of legal argumentation can be reconstructed in logical terms P the transformations associated with a concept are applied to the new case to generate a hypothesis for a definition of the concept, and then this hypothesis is tested for consistency with decided cases. This reconstruction would provide an alternative account of the judicial arguments considered by McCarty, but I am unsure to what extent this reconstruction would accurately reflect McCarty's intention. Similarly, it is unclear (to me) whether McCarty is suggesting that all legal argumentation can be reconstructed in terms of the prototype-plus-deformation model, or whether this is intended to account only for certain common but specific patterns of legal argument.

1.16.2. Permissions and obligations

The nature of the legal knowledge in the corporate tax domain of TAXMAN has led McCarty to investigate the representation of the deontic concepts, and reasoning with the concepts of permission and obligation particularly. In the course of these investigations McCarty has proposed a system of deontic logic [McCarty 1983b, 1986]. McCarty's deontic logic is unusual, in that from the outset he has given consideration to its suitability for computation.

There is a substantial amount of literature devoted to deontic logic, though very few of the logics proposed have addressed computational issues. One exception is Belzer's system 3-D [Loewer and Belzer 1983; Belzer 1986a], who has discussed its implementation in PROLOG [Belzer 1986b, 1987]. Belzer's logic is also interesting because it is designed to address defeasible reasoning (the derivation of conclusions which may have to be withdrawn if new information is made available). Defeasible reasoning is a central research issue in its own right, for all applications of artificial intelligence. An interesting discussion on the relationship between obligation and permission, with special reference to McCarty's logic, is given by Jones [1987]. Standard references to deontic and related logics include the texts by Castaneda [1975], Hilpinen [1971], Rescher [1966], Smith [1976] and von Wright [1963]. See also [Jones and Prin 1985, 1986] for an example of a recent approach. The early work by Hohfeld [1913, 1917] is also closely related.

The role of deontic logic in the computer representation of law has received comparatively little serious attention. (See [Sergot 1985a], [Bench-Capon 1989b], [Jones 1989] and of course McCarty for some discussion.)

As a practical matter, the occurrence of deontic modalities in legislative texts can often be ignored or approximated adequately. But not always. Representation and reasoning with the deontic concepts must be addressed to deal adequately with some parts of law. Indeed it can be argued that to ignore the distinction between ideality (what ought to be the case) and actuality (what is the case), and to ignore deontic reasoning, is to ignore one of the most essential features of legislative language and legal reasoning. There is also an extreme position which deserves some comment.

Because all law can be regarded as a set of norms, and because legislative language contains many occurrences of deontic modalities, it is sometimes suggested that some form of deontic logic is indispensable for the adequate representation of law. Some proposals for incorporating deontic logic in a representation language for law seem to assume that there are only technical obstacles to be overcome — there is the problem of deciding which particular version of deontic logic is most appropriate, and there is the problem of automating deduction in this logic with reasonable efficiency. But these proposals do not question where deontic reasoning is present in legal reasoning or when it is required for an adequate computer representation of law.

McCarty's position — which happens to coincide with my own — has been clearly stated. Deontic modalities are encountered in legislation and the need for reasoning with the deontic concepts does arise in legal analysis and problem solving. But deontic concepts have no extraordinary status in this respect: they are one instance of a whole range of modalities and concepts that deserve attention too.

McCarty's most recent work on his Language for Legal Discourse subsumes his work on deontic logic and addresses some of these other concepts within one general framework. This work is described in the next section.

1.16.3. Language for Legal Discourse

McCarty's proposal for a Language for Legal Discourse consolidates his work on TAXMAN and sets objectives for future developments.

He present the basic idea very succinctly: There are many common sense categories underlying the representation of a legal problem domain: space, time, mass, action, permission, obligation, causation, purpose, intention, knowledge, belief, and so on. The idea is to select a small set of these common sense categories, the ones that are most appropriate for a particular legal application, and then develop a knowledge representation language that faithfully mirrors the structure of this set [McCarty 1989a].

The core of McCarty's Language for Legal Discourse is his intuitionistic logic programming language [McCarty 1988a, 1988b], whose elements were summarized in section 1.10.5. This core is to be extended to provide a range of integrated language constructs that support directly representation of some of the common sense categories mentioned above. As an initial set of such 'building blocks' McCarty identifies sorts and subsorts, count terms and mass terms, defaults, prototypes and deformations, time, events and actions, and permissions and obligations [McCarty 1989a]. Some of these components already exist or can be integrated from McCarty's earlier work. Others are the subject of future developments.

Although some elements of it will emerge in the short term, McCarty's Language for Legal Discourse is clearly a very ambitious and long term research plan — what he is describing is essentially a substantial part of a complete computational theory of practical reasoning.

1.17. CASE-BASED REASONING

The main part of this section (1.17.2) describes HYPO, part of a project on case-based reasoning conducted by Edwina Rissland and Kevin Ashley at the University of Massachussets. Section 1.17.3 provides some very brief descriptions of other work on cased-based reasoning and references to related proposals. Other approaches to case-based reasoning covered by this survey appear in sections 1.14 and 1.15.

It is easiest to explain the operation of HYPO by considering first a simplified version of its retrieval mechanisms. I do this in section 1.17.1 This allows me to present a simple and common scheme for storing and retrieving cases, with references to two specific examples of this type (the case law component of DataLex and the SARA system). HYPO itself is described in section 1.17.2.

1.17.1. Retrieval from a database of examples

A simple and practical approach that has been suggested for dealing with case law is to construct a database of examples together with the decision in each case. The examples are either stereotypical cases, or real cases that have been decided. When presented with a new case for decision the system will attempt to match the case under consideration with the cases in its database to extract those which appear to be most similar. Some method of describing cases at an appropriate level of abstraction is obviously required, together with a matching algorithm for measuring 'similarity'.

If attention is restricted to some specific open textured concept, then it is sometimes possible to draw up a list of factors that are taken into account when a case involving this concept is decided. Every case in the database would be stored with a list of those factors which applied to it. (Of course the list would have to be large enough and flexible enough to capture all the possible variations, and therein lies a major potential problem.) A matching algorithm is now required to measure the 'similarity' of cases in terms of these factors. The simplest proposals would associate some kind of weight with each factor as a means of indicating which features of an example were considered to be most relevant in determining a decision in its case. In this sort of scheme the matching algorithm calculates a weighted sum and the examples with scores above some threshold are taken to be the most 'similar'. More sophisticated matching algorithms which take other factors into account could of course be devised. (See [Bench-Capon and Sergot 1985] for further discussion.)

This is roughly the approach that has been taken to the treatment of case law in the DataLex project (section 1.7.3). In DataLex, 'legally significant parameters' correspond to what I have called 'factors' and the matching algorithm is based on measures of similarity and statistical analysis [Greenleaf *et al.* 1987].

In some respects, this is also the approach that was taken in the SARA system, though the function of SARA was not to retrieve similar cases but to assist in the analysis of cases governed by discretionary rules. SARA was developed as a demonstration prototype at the Norwegian Research Centre for Computers and Law (NRCCL). The user would describe a new case in terms of factors that would influence its decision, and SARA would indicate the estimated 'weight' or importance of each factor calculated by comparison with the factors that had influenced past decisions stored in its database [Bing 1980].

1.17.2. HYPO

HYPO [Ashley and Rissland 1986, 1987, 1988; Rissland and Ashley 1987, 1989; Rissland 1989; Ashley 1987, 1989] is based on Rissland's earlier work on reasoning from examples [Rissland & Soloway 1980; Rissland 1983; Rissland, Valcarce & Ashley 1984] and the structure of arguments [Rissland 1984, 1985a, 1985b]. See also [Mendelson 1989] for a case study.

Ashley and Rissland's approach involves both the retrieval of relevant legal sources (cases) and the use of these in the construction of legal arguments. Ashley and Rissland leave the actual decision-making to the user of the system: the function of their system is to generate arguments to assist in reaching a decision. HYPO operates in the domain of trade secrets law.

The retrieval component of Ashley and Rissland's HYPO is a sophisticated elaboration of the basic idea sketched in the previous section. The most serious limitation of that simple scheme is that a case must be described in terms of abstract 'factors': the major part of analysing a case is determining what the relevant factors are. In an attempt to overcome this limitation, HYPO maintains a library of dimensions, each one of which, in the first instance, corresponds roughly to one of the 'factors' that determine the outcome of a case. In addition, each of HYPO's dimensions contains a set of conditions which specifies when the dimension applies in a given case. These conditions are expressed in terms of factual predicates which are used to describe a case. Given a case described with factual predicates, HYPO's case-analysis module can thus determine which of the dimensions in its library apply to the facts of the case. In fact, to provide a more detailed analysis, HYPO's case-module also determines which of the dimensions in the library nearly apply to the facts of the case. This is implemented by a similar mechanism: each dimension in HYPO also contains a set of conditions which specify when the dimension nearly applies. Given a new case, the case-analysis module constructs the list of dimensions that apply and that nearly apply to the facts. This list of applicable and 'near miss' dimensions is then matched against the cases in the database to extract those which are similar. The matching cases are ordered (in a lattice) from most-on-point to least-on-point.

This simplified description only accounts for HYPO's retrieval process. The other main component in HYPO uses the set of retrieved cases to construct the skeleton of a legal argument, in which cases are cited for and against a particular decision in the new case. The structure of this argument is determined by the cases which have been extracted and their relative ordering. The argument includes references to cases which could be cited as counterarguments, and also provides citations that could counter the counterarguments. The argument might be further refined by the addition of hypothetical cases [Rissland 1984, 1985a]. Hypothetical cases are generated by a set of heuristics which suggest what kind of hypothetical case might be useful in an argument, and by another component stored in each dimension.

1.17.3. Related research

In certain respects the basic operation of HYPO, and its motivation, resembles a treatment of open texture proposed by Bench-Capon and Sergot [1985] which uses sets of conflicting rules to generate arguments for and against a particular decision (also reminiscent of Gardner's work described in section 1.15.3). Bench-Capon and Sergot's proposal is very preliminary and the structure of the arguments it could generate does not compare with the sophistication of those produced by HYPO but it would be immensely interesting (and challenging) to investigate whether HYPO could be reconstructed in logical terms along these lines.

Any treatment of open texture must recognise the adversarial nature of reasoning in law. All the proposed treatments of open texture described in this survey have stressed the generation of arguments. There have been several recent proposals to base future investigations on the work of philosophers like Toulmin who have been studying the structure of arguments [Toulmin 1958, 1972; Toulmin *et al.* 1979]. See for example [Dick 1987] and [Marshall 1989]. Perelman's work in jurisprudence is also closely related [Perelman 1963; Perelman and Olbrechts-Tyteca 1969]. See also [Branting 1989] for a different approach to dealing with precedents.

In addition to projects already described, there seems to be (surprisingly) little research on the use of artificial intelligence techniques to model argumentation. But see [Birnbaum *et al.* 1980], [McGuire *et al.* 1981], [Birnbaum 1982] and [Dyer and Flowers 1985].

CHAPTER 2

THE OPPORTUNITIES OF THE DHSS DEMONSTRATOR PROJECT

Trevor Bench-Capon

2.1. THE ALVEY DHSS DEMONSTRATOR PROJECT

The Alvey-DHSS Demonstrator project was a large Demonstrator project, supported by the Alvey Directorate of the UK Department of Trade and Industry and the UK Science and Engineering Research Council. The project collaborators were ICL, Logica, Imperial College, and the Universities of Lancaster, Liverpool and Surrey. Additionally the Department of Health and Social Security (DHSS), assigned several members of staff to work full time on the project. The project was intended to investigate the potential for the application of KBS techniques to large legislation based organisations, of which the DHSS — later to become the Department of Social Security (DSS) — provides a prime example, being responsible for the administration of Welfare benefits in the UK. The project afforded unique opportunities for the exploration of the application of KBS to law, and in this chapter I summarize some of these distinctive opportunities, and the implications they had for the project.

2.1.1. Size of the project

The chief feature which distinguished the Demonstrator project from anything that had previously been attempted in this area was its sheer size, in terms both of its duration and of the number of people involved. Because it lasted for a long time — five years as against the two or three years which is the more typical duration for such a project — it was possible to have a very substantial initial period of exploration before

KNOWLEDGE-BASED SYSTEMS AND
LEGAL APPLICATIONS. ISBN 0-12-086441-X

commencing to develop the 'final' demonstration systems. The primary advantage of this was that design commitments could be deferred. There was no pressure to adopt an existing model for the systems as would be the case were it necessary to produce a demonstrable system in a shorter time, so that the needs of the applications could be determined and taken fully into account in the design of the systems. Moreover, the time scale meant that there was substantial scope to revise some of the original conceptions: the shifting emphases of the various applications through the course of the project is described in the chapters of Part III. It was also a very large project in terms of the number of people involved: around sixty-five over its life, and at any given time there would be some thirty or more people working on it. This again contrasts with the typical situation in KBS in law where projects are carried out either by individuals or by small teams. Not only did the resource available make possible a more ambitious conception in terms of the scale of the implementation that would be produced and the size of the knowledge bases that could be developed, but also whereas a small project is inevitably shaped by the personal skills and ideas of the people involved, the diversity of viewpoints and changing composition of the Demonstrator team meant that the the backgrounds and inclinations of particular individuals were less critical.

2.1.2. Interdisciplinary nature of the project

The number of people working on the project meant that it would inevitably have an inter-disciplinary flavour. The commitment of the project to interdisciplinary research, however, went much deeper than this. Of the academic collaborators, two, Imperial College and the University of Liverpool, were computer science departments, but the University of Lancaster was represented by the department of systems and the University of Surrey by the sociology department. The presence of these two unusual inputs had valuable consequences: the department of systems was able to contribute effectively to the organizational and 'business case' issues relating to the various systems, and the sociologists were uniquely well placed to determine the needs of the claimant users — a diverse and hard to find group — and to evaluate the effectiveness of the systems produced for use by this sort of user. The skills of both these groups of people, which might appear a luxury in a smaller project, were thus of vital importance in orientating the systems to the tasks they would perform in practice. Moreover, the team members had an unusually wide spread of educational backgrounds ranging from mathematics to philosophy through psychology and engineering. This again contrasts favourably with the range of backgrounds that might be found in a small team; typically we find there a collaboration between a computer scientist and a lawyer. One, perhaps surprising, feature of the composition of the team was that there were so few members with a legal background — although there were project members with first degrees in law there were no practising lawyers or academic law departments involved. This was perhaps offset by the fact that qualified lawyers only rarely get involved in social security: adjudication and the first level of appeal are carried out by lay people, and it is only at the highest level of appeal that qualified legal representation is used.

2.2. A CONCERTED APPROACH TO A VARIETY OF APPLICATIONS

Perhaps the greatest benefit of the size of the project was that it enabled several different areas of application to be pursued within the framework of a common project. In a small project there must inevitably be a focus on a specific area, and so there can be no scope to explore the relationship between various applications that may exist in an organization. This is a practical concern of the highest importance since it must be recognised that any large organization which has a use for a range of knowledge based systems will want a co-ordinated approach to their use. While small scale pilots and experimental systems can be developed piecemeal, the routine and practical exploitation of the techniques will require that the various developments cohere as much as possible. The scale of the Demonstrator meant that consideration could be given to the range of needs of the whole organization With this in mind the project operated by constructing several applications to support different areas of the organisation's activities, so as to gain insight as to how, in a real implementation, KBS might be produced in such a way as to allow the various systems within an organization to be mutually supportive. This approach also allowed comparison between the various applications to be made: one important question for KBS and law is the extent to which the nature of the task which the KBS is designed to support determines the nature of the KBS. Where a project is producing only a single system it is extremely difficult to get a handle on the answer to this question, but members of the Demonstrator, several of whom were engaged in producing more than one of the applications, or in producing tools to support several applications, were very well placed to see just what sort of impact the task had on the system. Thus the project was able to supply a reasoned basis for consideration of how the nature of the area of application affected the nature of the supporting KBS: where it was strictly necessary for the applications to diverge as well what parts could be shared.

2.3. BREADTH OF REMIT

The remit of the Demonstrator was to investigate the potential for the application of KBS techniques to the work of large legislation based organizations. This remit is notable both for its breadth and its practical focus. Most projects in KBS and law have set out with the intention of tackling a specific problem in the field, such as the HYPO project of Rissland and Ashley [1987], which attempted to find a way of reasoning with cases; or of trying out a particular approach to the field, as in the British Nationality Act work of Sergot *et al.* [1986], which attempted to show what could be done with a literal formalization of a fragment of legislation; or to produce a system related to a particular piece of law, as in the Latent Damage Advisor of Capper and Susskind [1988]. The Demonstrator, in contrast, had no commitment to any particular approach or area of law, and so could allow itself to be driven by what would be useful to the customer organization. This put an emphasis on the target users of the applications which is often absent from projects which are more problem orientated, and so ensured that the *need* for the systems produced and their role in the organization was always high on the agenda. This resulted in placing great emphasis on the development of a clear notion of the nature of the support environment that would be required by the different sorts of users, the fruits of which are described in the chapters of Part II.

2.4. CLOSENESS OF THE CUSTOMER ORGANIZATION

Another important feature of the Demonstrator project was the very close relationship that existed with the customer organization. The DHSS was involved as an integral part of the project from the outset. The individuals assigned to work on the project were in the main drawn from the computing branches of DHSS: their function was not to act as experts themselves, but to represent the Department, and to make available the correct people in the organization as and when expertise or information was needed. This approach meant firstly that the project was in no way constrained by the expertise made available to it: had particular experts been assigned to the project, the particular nature of expertise may have tended to force the project to take a particular direction. Secondly, it meant that there was less danger of experts becoming 'socialised' into the project and hence over-committed to its success: the experts could rather always maintain a distance — and a healthy scepticism about its objectives. As well as domain experts the project could also talk to, and take account of the views of, the people who ran the Department up to a fairly senior level. This helped to give an appreciation of the organizational needs, which again sharpened the practical focus. For a system to be a practical proposition, it is not sufficient for it to be a technical success: it must also play a beneficial role in the organization as a whole.

2.5. SIZE OF THE APPLICATIONS

A great deal of the effort involved in constructing a KBS needs to be put into developing the knowledge base. Where the project is small, and its main focus is on the functionality of the system — the ways in which the KBS will be manipulated and used — the temptation is to keep the knowledge base as small as is consonant with providing a reasonable test of the ideas of the project. Typically, therefore, even quite significant projects have incorporated knowledge bases which are small relative to the size of the knowledge base that would be needed in a practical application. The problem with using knowledge bases of a restricted size is that the process of constructing the knowledge base and the techniques that can be used to manipulate it, do not necessarily scale up when the knowledge base is of the sort of size necessary to support a truly practical application. This point applies of course to all areas of computer developments: techniques which can be used to construct small programs become inadequate when applied to very large programs — hence the whole enterprise of software engineering. The resources available to the Demonstrator meant that a serious attempt could be made to build sizeable knowledge bases — and, indeed, the exploration of difficulties involved in large scale developments were a key concern of the project. This led to an appreciation of the software engineering aspects of the problem found on few other projects.

Another aspect of software engineering which sprang from the size of the applications was a rather clearer separation between programmers and designers than is possible on many smaller projects. In a small project a single person often originates the initial idea, designs the system and writes the code. In consequence the three stages often blur together and compromises between them are not clearly identified. In the Demonstrator project, there was always a pressing need to communicate ideas to other members of the team and when moving from design to implementation, to write a specification which the implementor (who was typically a professional programmer rather than an AI researcher) could follow when implementing the system. Of course, changes were made to the specification during the implementation process, but again these needed to be thoroughly discussed and recorded. The result was a much clearer perception of what was being implemented, and code that can measure up to industrial standards.

2.6. SUMMARY

The above sections outline some of the advantages and opportunities that the Demonstrator provided, but the size of the project did have some negative influences as well. A project of this size, particularly when it is distributed across a number of different sites carries with it a substantial overhead in terms of administration, communication and co-ordination. The implications of this are discussed in Chapter 10. Also the very diversity in background, interests and focus which was a major strength of the project, also meant there was no clear, single, vision of the systems that should be produced. Whatever the balance of advantage, the fact remains that the Demonstrator provided a unique context in which to tackle the problems of AI and law. The remaining chapters represent the extent to which the opportunities were grasped.

PART II

TASKS

If we consider people whose work is related to law, we can see that they are engaged in a variety of tasks. In the legal system as a whole, judges, barristers solicitors and their clients all have different parts to play. Inside DHSS there are people who are responsible for formulating and justifying legislation, others who apply the law in particular cases, and others, not necessarily employed by the Department, who advise people on what they may be entitled to claim. All of these people may ultimately deal with the same legislation, but they exhibit very different skills. A policy maker may not be able to adjudicate cases effectively, an adjudicator may not be the best person to advise you on benefit entitlement, and an advice worker may lack the attributes of a policy maker. The question therefore arises as to what extent the tasks which a KBS is designed to support influences the design of the system. At one extreme, perhaps implied by Sergot *et al.* [1986], is the view that since all these tasks are grounded on legislation a single executable formalization of the legislation could serve to support all of them. A less extreme position, expressed in [Bench-Capon *et al.* 1987], is that support systems for the various areas would have a common core, but require individual elaboration in order to be useful. At the other extreme it might be argued that the differences in the expertise required for the different tasks inevitably necessitate completely separate systems. Certainly the nature of the support that is required is very different, and this may well have deep implications for the knowledge to be represented, and the way in which it is represented.

In this part, therefore, there are three discussions of the different tasks related to legislation that formed the basis of prototype systems in the demonstrator project. These tasks are thought to be generic, and applicable in one way or another to any piece of legislation. For all laws are made, giving rise to the policy task, all laws are applied, and so require adjudicators, and it is desirable that all laws should be understood by those to whom they apply, so that they can regulate their behaviour appropriately. The first chapter, by Andrew Taylor, who was responsible for determining the requirements for both the system for adjudicators and the system for policy makers, discusses the nature of a support environment for adjudicators. This is a crucial task, since it is the obvious area to provide support for a large legislation based organisation such as DHSS. The nature of the environment described is significantly different from the kind of consultative expert system which is usually proposed as a model for this kind of support. The second chapter by Andrew Taylor and Trevor Bench-Capon, who as well as being closely involved with the policy application throughout the project, began his working life in a DHSS policy branch, describes the nature of system to support policy makers. Again the demands made on such a system mean that it must have radically different properties from a standard KBS. The third chapter, by Nigel Gilbert, who led the team working on information systems for the public, discusses the nature of their requirements; whilst these are perhaps the closest to a standard consultative expert system, there are again important differences. Consideration of the requirements of the three areas of application as explained here should dispel any idea that it is possible to build a system which can offer impartial support across the whole range of tasks. The final chapter, by Trevor Bench-Capon, returns to the question of whether it is possible for the different types of system to share a common knowledge base. The discussion is focused on a small and simplified example which despite its triviality serves to point to places where divergence is necessary.

The conclusions of these chapters show that there is a good deal more to a legal KBS than law, and that it is important to identify clearly the task at which the system is to be directed before starting to build it. Too often in experimental systems this practical focus has been lacking. The task is important because it determines the functionality required from the system and the information that can be expected from the user of the system, and this should have a pervasive effect on what is represented and how it is represented.

CHAPTER 3

A SUPPORT ENVIRONMENT FOR ADJUDICATORS

Andrew Taylor

Existing work on knowledge based systems and law has proved, in the main, to be still quite distant from the support requirements of specific decision makers. Firstly, the dominant emphasis has been on the capabilities of systems which support a particular style or form of reasoning rather than with the needs for a complex, highly focused and integrated environment of support which a serious working system would require. There has been important work into case based reasoning, logical modelling of legislation and representation of 'expert legal knowledge', which has recently acknowledged that they represent complementary techniques any of which in isolation is inadequate. Unfortunately, this work has generally failed to address how these various capabilities need to be combined and integrated to support specific decision making tasks. Secondly, the intellectual grounding of the work has concentrated on the issues of jurisprudence and abstractions of legal reasoning rather than on the less pure, even 'messier', but in a pragmatic sense more relevant issues arising from socio-legal studies.

Lastly, where real systems have been developed, there has been a tendency to design them with 'non-specific' uses, almost as an alternative to publishing a book. This assumes, however, that the differences in requirements of specific users either do not matter or could be accommodated with 'add-on' facilities.

The local office demonstrator presented an unusual opportunity to:

1. Consider the specific requirements of a complex decision making

KNOWLEDGE-BASED SYSTEMS AND
LEGAL APPLICATIONS. ISBN 0-12-086441-X

environment; not least by highlighting the inadequacies of existing general or straightforward capabilities.

2. Design an integrated and highly focused system with appropriate interaction capabilities.
3. Study the complex organizational and social aspects of such a support system.

This chapter attempts to extract some general lessons from this work concerning the potential for developing any support environment for adjudicators. Firstly, it will consider the question of what a support system for adjudicators should be aiming to achieve (and what it should be aiming to avoid). Secondly, it will characterize our conclusions on what general support is required for the adjudication task. It concludes with a consideration of some of the issues which still need to be resolved.

3.1. ADJUDICATION, ADJUDICATORS AND SOCIAL SECURITY

Decisions on entitlement to benefit are made by officers appointed by the secretary of state. Historically, decisions on entitlement to non-contributory benefits were taken by DHSS staff who had substantial powers of discretion in their decision making but whose decisions could be appealed against to an independent appeal body. Since 1980 all entitlement decisions have been the responsibility of adjudication officers. These officers are responsible for their own decisions though nominally acting in law under the general supervision of the chief adjudication officer. The 1980 reforms removed much of the discretion in the supplementary benefits system — making the adjudication officers task primarily one of applying the, admittedly complex, law to the facts.

The task of an adjudication officer may appear no different from other decision processes which are tightly controlled by regulations (eg. in financial or insurance services). For our work, however, the particular features of adjudication proved to be fundamental for the design of relevant support.

The distinguishing feature of legal adjudication is that, for a decision to be adjudicatory, certain procedural restraints must be placed on the decision maker. In particular:

1. They need to provide reasoned arguments and justifications for their decisions.
2. They should be demonstrably impartial and independent.
3. The exercise of their remaining discretion, in the interpretation of conditions, should be within the tenets of administrative law.

To help them with the complexities of the legislation and its application, the adjudication officers are provided with guidance in the form of the Adjudication Officer's Guide (AOG). While not being bound by this guidance they are encouraged to take it into consideration when arriving at their decisions.

In practice these ideals of adjudication have frequently been called into question. Firstly, there is the issue of the status of the AOG. For the most part it is uncommon for the adjudication officer to decide contrary to the recommendations it includes — unless they have limited access to the guidance itself. The guidance is therefore in danger of becoming what has been called quasi-legislation. Secondly, there is the problem of routinization whereby officers inevitably evolve standard ways of interpreting rules and handling ordinary cases.

> Bureaucratic behaviour is of necessity determined by routine since the average officer cannot know all the rules and does not have time to determine what course the rules set for every claim. In fact routinisation is one of the virtues of bureaucracy for it contributes to reliability, continuity, efficiency and impartiality. [Cranston 1985]

One problem of this, however, is that it can lead to a tendency to ignore the complexity of particular cases. Equally, it might take some time for changes in the rules to work their way through to day to day practice.

Thirdly, and by far the major constraint, there are administrative and practical pressures on the maintenance of adjudication standards. In the area of income support alone there are over one hundred thousand officers assessing in excess of five million claims per year. Many offices have difficulty in retaining suitably qualified staff. The training they receive comprises twenty-six weeks initial training followed by three weeks extra training which concentrates on their role as adjudicators and the law. It is unusual for them to have any prior legal training. The legislative conditions they have to apply are large in number and in some areas particularly complex:

> The Statutes on Social Security are necessarily complex: because they have to cover the whole range of human activities and human wants. The Regulations are necessarily detailed because they have to provide so many different benefits in so many different circumstances. [Denning 1986]

In addition to these problems of scale there are issues arising from the organisational control of adjudication. Adjudication officers will only spend a proportion of their time carrying out this adjudication role. For the rest of their time they are responsible to the manager of the local office. In situations of pressure on case loads, maintaining a clear distinction between these two roles must be difficult.

One result of these constraints is that the quality of adjudication has generally been considered to be far from adequate. In the annual report of the chief adjudication officer, rates for decisions on Supplementary Benefit adjudication which raised comments from monitoring staff were on average 35% and in some aspects as high as 70% [ARCA 1988]. In an environment where the volume of claims is high and there is an urgent priority to respond to these claims quickly, issues of quality have tended to take a secondary role to issues of effective administration. It has also been difficult to establish how quality could be improved.

3.2. AIMS OF AN ADJUDICATION SUPPORT SYSTEM

The primary aim of the local office demonstrator was to show how knowledge based decision support tools could assist with the quality (as opposed to the cost or speed) of the decision making and associated service in adjudication of benefits. There were a number of motivations for this. The existing computerization programme of the Department of Social Security was directly concerned with issues of cost effectiveness and administrative aspects of benefit processing — highlighting the need for any parallel experimental work to address the remaining issues of quality. The capabilities of knowledge based systems seem more appropriate for addressing such issues of quality. Lastly, the work was explicitly directed at the support and enhancement of human decision-making processes rather than at their replacement or diminishment.

Such a commitment to 'quality' of adjudication did not take us far in establishing aims for the system, however. Firstly, such a commitment implicitly assumes knowledge of what it is that is 'wrong' in current practice — and what causes underlie these mistakes. We therefore needed to establish the criteria for quality and the sources of mistakes in adjudication. Secondly, it was necessary to understand the constraints on achieving improvements in quality.

Lastly, it was important to consider the other complementary, or possibly competing, objectives additional to that of quality of adjudication.

The pervasive complexity of statutory conditions within the social security Acts and Regulations is both intimidating and a source of confusion for those outsiders looking at the process of Social Security adjudication and considering how it could be supported. Equally, the conceptual uncertainties introduced by the 'open texture' of legislation presents the possibility of considerable difficulties arising with the interpretation of specific conditions. It is not surprising, therefore, that a typical conception of the support requirements is to provide a system which not only explicitly simplifies the identification and application of appropriate legal rules but also presents specific case guidance on the interpretation of specific open textured conditions.

Unfortunately, it is frequently the case that observers of a decision-making context develop strong conceptions of what they believe the decision-makers will find problematic and error prone while the actual problems of these decision-makers are quite different. One reason for this, of course, is that the decision makers are trained and acquire experience which overcomes the specific problems of novices — it would be foolish, for example, to characterize the main problem of motorists as being the manipulation of gear changes and general car handling, rather than the drivers perception of the behaviour of other road users. It was essential, therefore, to investigate the actual problems and sources of error in adjudication rather than work on our own assumptions.

One approach we took to identifying problems was to examine the reports of the social security commissioners who, in addition to ruling on specific appeals which are referred to them also comment on the quality of earlier decisions on cases. Additionally, the Department of Social Security has its own body of expertise in the form of the office of the chief adjudication officer which annually produces a report on the quality of decisions and makes recommendations about ways of improving this quality. From these sources it became apparent that the majority of complaints concerning quality related to failure to consider all the appropriate evidence concerning a case, and inadequate explanation or justification of the original decision. Following such evidence it was appropriate to include support for the collection of evidence and the processes of argumentation and justification supporting the decision making.

Already, therefore, we had four sub-goals concerning improvement in quality:

1. Support with identification and application of rules.
2. Support with case reasoning, interpretation and open texture.
3. Support with consideration of relevant evidence.
4. Support for explanation and justification of decisions.

One immediate problem, then, was to establish how we should choose between these subgoals in terms of priorities and to establish the extent to which they were conflicting. A straightforward approach might have been to ask users, develop small and separate prototype systems for each of the goals and then progress these separate systems incrementally. Our concern was that this would lead to inadequate and unintegrated systems. Instead we adopted a 'holistic' approach to developing a support environment. Before we could start to address the four issues and their relative priority, we had to recognize that the results of problems with the adjudication process cannot be equated with the causes; thus the application of wrong rules could be resulting from ignorance of the conditions and their logical relationships or from misinterpretation of facts of the case. Failure to consider relevant evidence could be resulting from ignorance of the conditions which required such evidence or made it relevant, and so forth. It was necessary, therefore, to consider the more specific tasks of the adjudication officers and to identify which of these tasks were considered problematic and why. This analysis and its implications are described further in the section.

Justifying support requirements solely on the basis of a conceptual analysis of problems assumes that the factors influencing adjudication quality are predominantly rational. In contrast, however, the practical issues of the amount of time available for adjudicating cases, the frequency of changes in the conditions and problems with keeping up to date with these, the political and administrative pressures on the decision making process, and the lack of experience of certain adjudication officers, all combine to create problems and requirements over and above those associated with the logic of the decision making task. We therefore needed to consider the overall organizational context of the decision making, in particular with regard to the constraints it imposes, and establish any additional aims relevant for the organization as it stands. Such an approach effectively acknowledged that the specific requirements of social security adjudication differ not only from other decision making in law but from other adjudicatory decision making, (for example, by Inland Revenue officers).

Following this approach, five objectives were identified: for more details and explanation, see, Taylor [1988].

1. Quality of legal decision making — with the system supporting the correct and consistent application of legal conditions, and attempting to ensure that the Adjudication Officer considers all the relevant information relating to a case.
2. Training — that by using the system the adjudication officer would become more skilled and develop an improved understanding of the legal conditions.
3. Level of service — with the system supporting the development of well-argued and justified decisions with better explanations and information being provided to claimants, and support in the development of better quality submissions to appeal tribunals;
4. Monitoring — providing facilities whereby decisions can be monitored either by those responsible for guiding and supporting adjudication officers in their decision making, or by policy makers interested in the number of claimants for particular benefits;
5. Flexibility — illustrating the potential for improvement in the speed and effectiveness of implementing changes in the regulations and having these applied by local office staff.

The challenge we faced was to address all of these issues in our design.

3.3. SUPPORT REQUIREMENTS

Establishing appropriate objectives for an adjudication officer support environment proved a difficult task. Identifying the support requirements was equally difficult. The general approach taken was to identify the tasks carried out by adjudication officers, establish the problems they found with detailed aspects of these tasks and then identify support mechanisms which would help with these problematic aspects while being appropriate for achieving the overall aims of the system. This was pursued through analysis of cases and legislation plus interviews with local office staff, training staff, management and, in particular the monitoring and OCAO staff.

The difficulty lay in the fact that, while many individuals were able to contribute to the analysis of requirements, members of the user organization were generally unable to articulate what their tasks were, were frequently unaware of the real nature of specific problems they faced, and were all ignorant of the possibilities which the technology could offer in terms of support. One example of this was when an adjudication officer expressed the belief that a system which gave him access to his previous decisions would be extremely useful — 'I often think that I had a case like this a few weeks ago and would like to shortcut by seeing what I did last time'.

In response to such comments, staff at OCAO were concerned that this would succeed in perpetuating poor quality decisions — 'the chances are the decision was wrong in the first place so we don't want it carrying over again'.

In this sense it is arguable that many adjudication officers have wrong conceptions about their tasks, its associated problems and the appropriateness of certain support. In effect they cannot, particularly in view of the high error rate in decision making, be taken as authoritative or reliable sources of requirements. Such a situation was made more difficult by the fact that the differing perspectives of other authorities led to conflicting views on what would count as appropriate support. It was therefore necessary to develop hypotheses as to what the adjudication officers tasks involved, to develop support systems and then to seek evaluations and comments from users, which would be used as a base of critiques of both the system and the understanding of requirements. This analysis was approached in two ways. Firstly by the relatively straightforward analysis of sources along with their role, purpose and structures; secondly, through the more difficult detailed analysis of adjudication officers' tasks.

3.3.1. Sources

The adjudication officer is presented with four categories of source material to help them arrive at their decision: legislation, case law, claim data and evidence, and official departmental guidance.

The main legislation is the Social Security Act 1986 and the income support (General Regulations) 1987. It would be dangerous to assume, however, that for the purposes of an Income Support decision the legislative sources are clearly defined in scope. Parts of the legislation are irrelevant to the precise content of a particular case, being concerned with the empowering of the adjudication officer and the definition of appropriate procedure.

Many specific details of an income support case will require reference to totally separate legislation: e.g. the Trustee Act 1925 on contingent interests in capital; the Social Security (Mariners Benefits) Act 1975 on share fishermen. In terms of supporting the adjudication officer, the structure of the legislation is also particularly important. To a large extent the legislation follows the topics which need to be decided for an income support assessment to be completed:

1. Establishing the validity of a claim (i.e. that the application has been made correctly, by someone who is in an appropriate position to make a claim).
2. Ensuring that the major conditions of entitlement for income support are met (e.g. residence in UK, age conditions, etc.).
3. Establishing the membership of the family being claimed for and the roles of the individuals within it.
4. Assessment of the family's requirements (applicable amounts) and resources (capital, income, and other resources).
5. Determination of how much Income Support should be paid, by what means, and from what date.

The assessment of applicable amounts, capital and income are large, complex topics of which only a small fraction is likely to be used in any given case. Generally they are structured according to subsets of types of applicable amount, capital, etc. Certain types of case therefore invoke specific conditions within the general structure. For example, 'self-employed' or 'business cases' raise particular entitlement issues as to whether, if the claimant is claiming on the basis of being unemployed, they are actually available for work or still running a business; the subsequent assessment of capital raises issues of the value of business assets, etc. Certain types of case cut across this structure, however. For example, special rules apply to all topics for the treatment of people involved in a trade dispute.

Case law is available mainly to the adjudication officer in the form of commissioner's decisions. These are categorided as 'reported' and 'unreported'. Copies of all reported decisions are distributed to local offices for the use of adjudication officers. Bound versions are maintained, arranged in historical order. Social security case law is similar to other case law in terms of its technical language and specialized style. Although it may be an over-simplification, a distinction can be made between cases that expound a general principle and therefore have a widespread impact and those which give detailed consideration to the facts of the case, and are distinguished from other similar cases. In other instances, a case may be significant in that it expands or explains the meaning of certain words — sometimes this explanation may take the form of a 'rule' which clarifies or illustrates a term, at other times it may be a more general discussion of a term or phrase. Some case law is not directly concerned with the features of a claimant's circumstances and the applicability of the statutes to them, but rather with the procedures followed by the adjudication officer and the Department, including the adequacy and role of evidence used to arrive at the decision. Social security decisions are also, of course, bound by other case law where this is relevant — particularly cases from administrative law and rulings from the European Court.

It is too early for many cases on income support decisions to have been heard by the Commissioners, although other case law for social security benefits is applicable where common concepts are used. Many benefits include such common or closely related topics: e.g. 'living together as husband and wife', 'incapacity for work', 'residence in the UK'. In general, case law is most frequently used by adjudication officers in order to clarify and help interpret specific clauses in the regulations. As a result, with the exception of certain general areas (such as 'living together' cases where special training is provided), usually only a very small number of cases are relevant to the decision. It is therefore untypical of adjudication officers to be overwhelmed with a large number of potentially relevant cases as may arise in other areas of law. Equally, the general rules and principles from case law are more often incorporated into the overall guidance, training and support of adjudication officers. Nonetheless, adjudication officers are presented with the common problems of not being able to find the relevant case law, finding difficulty in establishing whether a case is still applicable (or has been overturned by another decision or by changes in the legislation), being unaware of the relevance of case law outside of their own benefit area, and having insufficient experience and skill in how to use case law in helping to decide a case. Some help is provided in finding relevant case law by indexes of commissioners' decisions. A number of different indexes are available, some produced by the training organization, others produced by local offices. An indexed digest of social security case law decisions, providing excerpts from case law, was produced in *Neligan's Digest* [Neligan 1986]. This is now only used to a limited degree, with adjudication officers depending instead on the Adjudication Officer's Guide (AOG) to notify them of, and give them references to, relevant case law.

The guidance provided to adjudication officers is intended to address many of the complexities in identifying and applying the relevant legislation and case law. Much of the guidance involves a restructuring of the conditions of the regulations so that for certain types of case, and certain recurring problems, the procedural sequence of steps in the assessment are made clearer and more accessible. Similarly, it contains 'pointers' to other relevant areas (for example, para 25005: 'In no circumstances can a person under the age of 16 be entitled to IS; where such a person has a child see AOG Part 26'). This means that the AOG inevitably contains a certain amount of repetition. The guidance also contains explications of tacit conditions: for example, implications of the scope of applicability of the legislative conditions and their interrelationship, or 'common sense' rules (for example para 25301: 'A claimant is to be treated as available for employment if: 1. None of the circumstances apply to him in which a claimant is not to be treated as available for employment; and...'. Similarly, para 25184: 'The termination/ interruption of employment under the remunerative work exclusion should not apply to the self-employed person'.)

One of the major features of the guidance, however, is the assistance that it offers with the interpretation of vaguely defined statutory conditions. The style in which this is presented ranges from quasi rules imposing a restrictive interpretation, to general discussions of the factors which should be taken into account, often illustrated with a hypothetical case. Frequently the AOG presents lists of circumstances in which conditions will and will not be satisfied; (for example, para 26046: circumstances in which absences (from the household; Appendix D) should be treated as temporary, includes a list of temporary absences amongst which are:

1. A partner goes away to look for work.
2. A partner goes away to look after a sick relative.
3. A partner goes away for a period of convalescence.
4. A family has been evicted and are being accommodated separately.)

The important point, however, is that the guidance only has the status of advising the adjudication officer and cannot be considered as defining how they should decide cases. These factors help to explain the unacceptability of the suggestion that the contents of the AOG should be turned into rules within a knowledge based system. Not only would it be inappropriate to represent the large part of the contents of the AOG as rules, but even if some appropriate representation were possible, the AOG does not have the status necessary for it to be applied by a system to the circumstances of the claimant.

Lastly, there is the claim data itself. The main, and certainly initial, body of this is on the claim form. In fact there are different claim forms corresponding to the different reasons why a claim may be being made. These include separate claim forms for students, pensioners, unemployed, and people Involved in a trade dispute. The advantage of different forms is that necessary information can be collected early on, thereby limiting the need for subsequent time consuming questioning of the claimant. It cannot be assumed, however, that the claimant has filled in the right form — or even that the person claiming is the appropriate member of the household to be claiming. Similarly, as the case is being assessed, many circumstances arise where additional information may be required. Sometimes this may be of a nature whereby a written request can be sent to the claimant or some other party. In other cases interviews or visits may be required. The status of the information and evidence is often important. Certain facts have to be assumed unless there is reason to believe otherwise. Generally, the statement of the claimant is taken as acceptable. In specific cases, however, verification of the information is required.

3.3.2. Tasks

It is common to distinguish the application of clear rules, and calculation of arithmetic values, from the aspects which incorporate interpretation. This is to adopt a perspective which is predominantly implementation based: how hard is it to computerize these decision making processes? It is clear, however, that it is dangerous to try to separate the treatment of hard and easy cases in practice — not least because until a case is finished it is difficult to be sure which category it falls into. Equally, it is naive to believe that certain types of decision involve exclusively 'rule based reasoning' while others use exclusively 'case-based reasoning'. From a human decision making perspective the tasks of the adjudication officer more naturally fall into the categories of identifying relevant entitlement rules, interpreting the facts of the case and deciding how to apply the rules, working through the sequence of decisions defined by the rules for these facts, and justifying the overall decision. The importance of these tasks is that complexities derive from the rules, from the facts of the case, and in particular from the matching of these two.

In terms of the rules, there is an apparently overwhelming quantity of explicit, complex rules which need to be adhered to. There are two types of complexity which derive directly from these rules. Domain complexity typically arises when there is a large number of rules, when the set of rules include obscure or rarely used conditions, or when the relationship between rules, and the effects they have on each other, is complex. Domain complexity can lead to situations where a rule is forgotten, or where it cannot be found. It can also lead to the misapplication of rules or application of the wrong rule. Lastly, it can lead to situations where the interactions between rules, for example where one rule overrides another or changes the way in which it should be applied, are inappropriately handled. Procedural complexity arises when there is a process to go through which may be inherently straightforward but which involves a complex sequence of steps. This complexity may be due to many subprocedures, which can often lead to excessive memory loads. Equally, it may require the involvement of more than one individual. Alternatively it may just be poorly specified and difficult to comprehend.

In principle, procedural complexity can be controlled by the methodical and carefully recorded working through of the relevant rules. Domain complexity is more difficult to resolve. In particular it is not sufficient just to have all the rules available; the problem is finding the right rule or knowing what to look for and how to look for it. The situation with problems of domain complexity is analogous to looking for a book in a large library when you are not sure that it exists, you do not know what it is called, you do not know who wrote it, and you certainly do not know how to find it. Significantly, however, you know what it contains and would recognize when you had found the right book.

These types of complexity are manifest throughout the income support assessment process. For example, the determination of membership of the family can involve a number of issues around the question of whether a child is to be treated as a dependent of the claimant. Firstly, it is necessary to establish who precisely is the claimant. Secondly, it is necessary to establish who is to be considered normally responsible for the child. Thirdly, it is necessary to consider whether the current circumstances of the child's residence imply that the normal criteria of responsibility for the child temporarily do not hold. Answers to earlier questions not only determine which subset of further questions may be relevant but, more importantly, establish whom these subsequent questions should be asked of. The point about the answers to these questions is that they need to be recalled later in the assessment, for example when assessing the value of dependant's capital.

In practice, a common source of error is a failure to realize that certain conditions have changed. This is one aspect where the experienced adjudication officers may be more susceptible to error, believing that they know the rules while the more inexperienced adjudication officers will refer continually to the guidance and legislation.

It is not clear, however, that these problems deriving exclusively from the rules themselves are the major or most frequent sources of problem to the trained or skilled legal decision maker. The set of issues most frequently arising for this class of decision maker are those relating to what can be called 'problems of categorization'. Pursuing the earlier analogy even further, it would be like finding half a dozen books which all seemed potentially relevant and not knowing which was the best. Categorization problems arise because of the necessity to interpret and apply a limited number of rules to a wide variety of specific and often unique circumstances. They can present themselves in a number of ways:

1. There can be a disagreement or uncertainty about what the facts behind a case were or how they should be described.
2. The case may be an example of an extraordinary contingency not obviously covered by any rule, or lying on the borderline of the rule, leading to doubt as to whether the rule should cover the situation under decision.

3. Doubt as to what meaning, if any, is implied by the words used in the rule, which in some circumstances may be exacerbated by the existence of past authoritative interpretations which conflict or are unsatisfactory.
4. More than one rule can be seen to apply to a particular circumstance and determining which rule is to be considered decisive may be difficult. [Twining and Miers 1982].

Obvious problems of interpretation arise throughout income support assessment.

Deciding on the 'living together' cases is an obvious example. In such cases, the adjudication officer has no necessary or sufficient conditions which will decide the case one way or another. Instead there are a number of factors which need to be considered together.

> R(G) 2/72 To decide whether a widow is co-habiting as a man's wife it is necessary to look at the whole picture. Important elements to be considered include living together in a house and habitually sharing a bed, being the parents of a child which she was expecting when he came to live with her, having sexual intercourse and the pooling of financial resources.

These general principles are further supported with case law which give detailed consideration to the facts of a case.

> R(SB) 30/83 The claimant lived with his fiancee in rented accommodation during university vacations. The fiancee lived separately from him during term time. Then she lived in a bed-sitting room near the university. She received a local authority student grant. The Commissioner considered in some detail the meaning of 'living together as man and wife' in the above context and he held that the claimant and his fiancee were an 'unmarried couple' for the purposes of the Resources Regulations 1980 even during term time; that the fiancee's grant should be taken into account as part of the claimant's resources, but the outgoings in respect of the fiancee's bed-sitting room were not part of the claimant's requirements.

The most important point about these categorization problems, however, is that they do not just arise at the level of individual rules but often permeate, and are dependent upon, the whole approach towards a case and the question of what the decision maker is trying to establish. This gives them a general significance and scope of impact which is often difficult to identify and assess.

Firstly, it is clear that adjudication officers, as all decision makers tend to, work with what can best be called 'classifications' of a case. This classification process involves deciding, or at least hypothesizing, what are the key features of the case, what legislation is invoked, what evidence is relevant, and how it should be progressed. Within the working environment it is common to hear cases referred to as a 'trade disputes' case or a 'business' case. The impact of this classification is to identify particular issues which require closer consideration before the case can be completed. Adoption of an incorrect classification can mean at best wasted effort in pursuing irrelevant facts, at worst the neglecting of relevant facts of the case or the application of inappropriate conditions. While the specific details of the process in social security adjudication are particular to that environment, similar processes arise within any legal context — when a commercial client asks a firm of solicitors to handle a transaction one of the first requirements on the solicitor is to identify the set of issues, relevant legislation and any additional information they require. It is necessary, therefore, to consider how these classifications structure the component tasks in the decision making and how they could be used to integrate the support facilities.

Secondly, we have to be concerned with the interrelationship between factual information and the legal conditions. This relationship arises in a number of different ways. On the one hand, it is necessary to select conditions relevant to the facts of a case. On the other hand, the conditions determine additional facts which need to be established before a decision can be made. The assessment of capital conditions is a good example of this type of problem. The general question with assessing capital is whether the capital it to be disregarded or taken into account for the purposes of the assessment, and if it is to be considered then what value should be assigned to it. Examples are given of capital which is to be disregarded, including property (the claimant's main residence), personal belongings, and certain types of savings. One example of disregarded savings is 'sums set aside for home improvements' — on the condition that this has not been held for a period of more than six months. Unfortunately it is unlikely that a claimant will declare that they have a 'sum set aside for home improvement which is disregarded capital for the purposes of IS assessment'. It is more likely that they will describe the amount in terms of their 'real world' categories (e.g. a loan from the council to repair a roof, but which they have not been able to spend yet). The task of the adjudication officer is to recognize the 'real world' descriptions of the claimant as falling within the scope of the 'legislative' descriptions used in the regulations. The point is that the legal categories are structured according to types of 'disregarded' and 'non-disregarded' capital, whereas the real world categories are more likely to be structured according to broader concepts of types of capital, e.g. property vs. money and savings, with the latter breaking down into cash in hand, arrears of benefit, lump sums received, money not accessible, etc. The matching of these two alternative structurings is likely only to arise at the vary detailed levels of description. The adjudication officer, therefore, needs support in the process of describing the real world facts.

Lastly, the need to justify the decision implies that throughout the decision-making process certain obligations to record information and factors considered must be satisfied. This is important for notifying the claimant of the reasons for the decision. It is more important for those cases where an appeal is made and the original decision has to be reconsidered. It is particularly important when the conditions invoke terms such as 'in the opinion of the adjudication officer' or 'reasonable'.

The discussion throughout this section has concentrated on the conceptual issues in the task of the adjudication officer. It was mentioned in the previous section, however, that the practical, personal and contextual elements of the task were, perhaps, more important. The relevance of these aspects, however, was seen to lie in general requirements about the form, rather than the content, of the support given to adjudication officers. Adjudication is like many other sophisticated decision-making tasks in that it involves many different types of decision-making, it is carried out by people with different skills, it has to respond to different degrees of 'completeness' in the information which is available. These factors combine to the extent where, if we look at a decision-maker tackling any single case or topic they will:

1. Call on a variety of knowledge sources and try a number of different approaches to the case before deciding which is the best.
2. Do it differently from how someone else with different experience and 'memory' might have done it — even though they may end up with precisely the same answer.
3. Do it different next time.

Our conclusion was that the user of any suitable support system must be able to control the sequence in which they addressed certain issues in the assessment and the use of the system must be efficient in terms of not constraining the user to pursue unnecessary tasks. In addition, however, the system must constrain the user not to make mistakes in terms of contravening the Regulations, working with inconsistent or contradictory conclusions, or attempting to complete a case having failed to consider all the relevant information and conditions. The way in which these requirements were made more specific and reconciled with the objectives of the overall system, are discussed further in Chapter 7.

3.4. OUTSTANDING PROBLEMS AND CONCLUSIONS

This chapter has attempted to describe the issues concerning the development of objectives and requirements for an adjudication support system in social security. Some important questions are still outstanding, however. They all centre around the question 'even when we have provided this integrated range of capabilities, then how should the various components be used?' The problem originates both in the uncertainty over the precise policy objectives of an eventual system and in the essential indeterminacy of the effects and appropriate bounds of use of this technology.

Policy decisions concerning the administration of benefits are currently made on the basis of a delicate balance of political and social interests, combined with an understanding and acknowledgement of the practical (both administrative and financial) constraints involved in operating an adjudication process. Introduction of a support system could obviously change the balance as to what it is practically feasible to do. More specific and directed advice to adjudication officer's, wider and more detailed consideration of case law decisions and the consideration of potentially exceptional features in the case would all be possible, and could contribute to improvements in the quality of adjudication. Alternatively, it may be decided that the system should concentrate more directly on improving the speed and efficiency of handling claims and less on the quality of adjudication. This decision is not simply a choice between quality and financial cost — the overheads involved in appeals resulting from not getting the decision right in the first place, the training costs of maintaining appropriately qualified staff and the support costs in terms of disseminating guidance, are all considerable.

More specific decisions are required on the roles and responsibilities of the adjudication officers. The system could be seen as having a deskilling effect on staff; equally it could slow down the decision-making of experienced staff by requiring them to go through a lengthy interaction when they know what the decision should be earlier on. There is already debate within the Department about the level of authority which is empowered to decide on certain adjudication issues. Certain issues are already deemed to be decidable by lower-level staff. Introduction of computerized support raises the possibility of reallocating such responsibilities, possibly assigning a higher proportion of decisions to lower-level staff. This inevitably raises questions as to the acceptability/desirability of such changes, but also of the assumptions built into the design of the system and whether these would allow for different users. The system would present additional capabilities for monitoring the quality of decision making, but monitoring may have additional connotations of excessive control. What level of monitoring is necessary, acceptable or feasible? Lastly, what would be the effect on the legal independence of the adjudication officer? Would the system constrain their discretionary powers and in what senses would this be acceptable (how far should the powers allow an adjudication officer to be wrong in their decision making?)

Similar issues arise concerning the status of the knowledge base. This obviously has to address questions of the correctness and validity of the knowledge. It is not sufficient, however, that the knowledge be correct — it must be demonstrably correct. This implies that procedures are in place to ensure its evaluation and maintenance. It is current policy that the *Adjudication Officer's Guide* is publicly available. To what extent could it be argued that the introduction of a knowledge based support system unbalanced the availability of information? Would the potential for improved flexibility in updating the conditions, and indeed of implementing new policy, have an effect on the way in which benefits policy developed?

One of the problems in establishing any specific policy objectives is that there exist many groups within the DSS who have different concerns with and responsibilities for adjudication officer decision making. The management of the decision making is carried out in local and regional offices. The regional directorate is responsible for the administration of the regional and local organization including training, operational aspects of adjudication and issues of administrative efficiency. Policy divisions are responsible for the overall effects of the social security system and ensuring adequate responsiveness to political requirements and decisions — they include branches specifically responsible for individual benefits and one branch responsible for adjudication policy issues. Finally, the office of the chief adjudication officer is responsible for the guidance used by adjudication officers and for monitoring the standard of legal decision making to ensure the legal correctness and impartiality of the system. It is not possible to take one of these groups in isolation, or indeed to consider adjudication officers as the primary 'user' in terms of establishing objectives and evaluation criteria. Instead it is necessary to balance all of the perspectives and their corresponding requirements.

The issue of the indeterminacy of the effects of the system only serves to complicate these decisions further. Again, the question of the scope and form of the knowledge base must be a particular focus for these questions.

One problem with the selection of appropriate legislation is its interconnectivity and need for cross-references. No set of statutes exists in complete independence of other areas of law, and consequently, a decision on any one issue may involve aspects of a wide variety of disparate legal conditions. What are the implications of making the wrong choices? If important parts of legislation are omitted from the system then there may be exceptional cases where the wrong conditions are applied, or where there is merely insufficient support for the adjucation officer in understanding what they should do. This, of course, may lead to incorrect decisions. If inappropriate legislation is included, or included in an unsuitable form, this may cause the adjudication officer to err in law; the alternative to this is that the system may involve the user in a tedious and frequently irrelevant interaction. Whereas those responsible for producing the current support (i.e. the published guidance) have developed a style they believe to be appropriate for the support of the assessment task, new skills will have to be developed for employing these new mechanisms.

It is not even clear that an empirical evaluation of the use and effectiveness of a system or its components would help to resolve these questions. The problem with empirical testing is that it depends upon a test environment which artificially excludes certain variables. Our problem is that it is not possible to predict which factors of the organization may have what effects when using the system. The setting up of an experimental situation, therefore, may fail to inform us at all about the actual effects of a fully operational system.

Our only solution is to conclude that the indeterminacy of many aspects of the technology is not really something we should be attempting to design away. The problem arises from looking for a system which will solve all of these problems when what is really required is a new set of processes for adjudication which make use of systems. The basic difficulty is that although there are people who can design and implement systems, there are few people who are able to design such organizational processes. Perhaps, then, the dangers identified by the project will be ignored and systems built without concern for these questions.

This may be one of the most important conclusions of the project for other work in KBS in law. The project presented a unique opportunity to investigate the practical realities and complexities involved with a sophisticated support environment for adjudication. In the process it highlighted the inadequacies of most work in KBS support for law in the way in which it seems to trivialize or severely underestimate the subtlety and sophistication of the task being supported — or believes that this subtlety does not impinge on the success and usefulness of the resulting systems. The local office demonstrator continually highlighted that these factors do matter and that careful and substantial work is required to even give a chance of developing an acceptable system. It would be encouraging if a similar realism and concern about the effects of the systems could be adopted as an important topic for any development of KBS in law. Perhaps, however, the first stage in this should be the realization that 'law', given its complex and widely varied manifestations, can be a dangerously vague and misleadingly uninformative heading under which to study KBS applications.

CHAPTER 4

SUPPORT FOR THE FORMULATION OF LEGISLATION

Andrew Taylor and Trevor Bench-Capon

4.1. INTRODUCTION

The majority of knowledge based systems developed for the legal domain have been intended to support the application of legislation to the facts of a given case. They may be intended for use by the adjudicator, or by a party to the case, or the targeted user may be unspecified, but they take the law as something that is essentially fixed and unchanging while the case is under consideration. But laws are not fixed; they are made to achieve certain aims and will be amended if they fail to achieve those aims, or if the aims themselves change. This opens up the possibility of a different kind of legal KBS which is aimed at those who are charged with deciding what the law should be. This origins of this kind of system may be traced back to Layman Allen, who in [Allen 1957] advocated the use of logic for the clarification of legislation, both when drafting and when interpreting it. Originally, Allen saw the benefits from the use of logic as independent of computerisation, but subsequently he has done considerable work, e.g. [Allen and Saxon 1987], on creating computer aids for the logical normalization of legislation. Moreover, with the advent of interest in producing executable formalizations of law, there has been a further impetus to develop a system to assist with the formulation of legislation. Outside of the DHSS Demonstrator, assistance has normally been seen as being provided by a conventional formalization of legislation through which hypothetical cases could be fed to provide guidance as to the likely consequences of the legislation. This sort of suggestion is made

KNOWLEDGE-BASED SYSTEMS AND
LEGAL APPLICATIONS. ISBN 0-12-086441-X

in [Sergot *et al.* 1986], and underlies some work done within the ESPLEX project, an overview of which, may be found in [Biagoli *et al.* 1987]. Some of the difficulties in straightforwardly using an expert system designed to apply the law in this way were explained in [Bench-Capon 1987]. These result from some of the distinctive characteristics of reasoning about legislation with a view to changing it, most notably that it is classes of people, not individuals, that are being considered, so that the cases cannot, even in principle, be specified to the level of detail which is typically required by an adjudication-oriented system, and because, in sharp contrast to adjudication systems, there is no clear direction to the reasoning, so that the question 'what are the characteristics of someone over pensionable age?' is as likely to be asked as 'is someone with these characteristics of pensionable age?'. An assessment system, designed to answer the second sort of question, may not support answers to the first kind of question.

The potential of a system for policy support is significant: the cost of mistakes at this point of the legislative process, both in terms of the tangible cost of correcting them when they come to light, and in terms of the intangible costs of social confusion, hardship and inequity that can result from them, is so enormous that even a small improvement would be very cost effective. The problems which arise in such a context are also significant from an AI perspective, and are often of a quite different character from those which occur in the more typical legislative applications. We shall mention four here.

Firstly, the problems of producing and using a formalization of legislation are at their sharpest here, since the legislation is part of the subject matter of this system: whereas an adjudication-oriented system can, if necessary, have recourse to an ad hoc workaround, provided that the system gives the correct answer, such a technique may be highly misleading in a system supporting formulation. Secondly, the problems here are natural ones for treatment using constraints rather than more simple-minded application of rules: constraint programming is becoming increasingly important, and this area can give an exploration of its potential. Thirdly, it offers an opportunity to explore a style of reasoning not encountered in other traditional AI application areas. Fourthly, the policy process involves many tasks and there are significant challenges in producing an integration of the various tools that the system must provide into a usable system, especially one which must be used in a group working environment. The area, therefore, has considerable interest for the AI specialist as well as as having practical potential.

In this chapter we discuss the nature of the policy task, and the types of knowledge that need to be represented to support the task indicate a number of specific areas where support could be provided by KBS, and discuss what the nature of the KBS that could fulfil this role might be. We shall then go on to discuss some of the problems that arise in this area.

4.2. POLICY MAKERS AND WHAT THEY DO

A major role of the UK government departments is to advise ministers and other government officials regarding changes in policy and the development of new legislation to achieve these policy objectives. This work is carried out by the policy divisions, staffed by senior civil servants. The work centres around the formulation of new policy — which typically takes many years to develop and implement. Policy divisions also have a responsibility for providing explanations of the existing policy to any other government officials or members of the general public who may require this information. Such queries often arise in the form of parliamentary questions put to the minister, or government, through the House of Commons.

One of the problems in describing what policy makers do is that there is no clear consensus on what the process involves. In particular there is the danger of adopting an 'over-rational' account of the policy process. In fact, policy making is 'an extremely complex process without beginning or end, and whose boundaries remain most uncertain. Somehow a complex set of forces together produces effects called "policies".' In order to identify the genuine potential of KBS support for policy it is necessary to impose boundaries on the scope of the support in such a way that it is relevant for the environment within which policy is carried out and for the conceptual tasks which actually require support.

4.2.1. The policy environment.

The environment within which policy is developed is the result of a complex interaction between, on the one hand, certain structural, historical, almost 'objective' features of the policy process and, on the other, the cultural, personal and 'idiosyncratic' characteristics of the policy makers themselves. Among the structural aspects there are four major factors.

Firstly, the policy divisions are not themselves responsible for decision-making: all decisions are made by the government minister based on the advice of the policy divisions. The policy worker is responsible for producing submissions to ministers which outline the options available along with various evaluations of these options. Secondly, the staff in the policy divisions are typically generalists, requiring a breadth of understanding of the whole of the policy and legislation, drawing on the services of expert statisticians, solicitors or economic advisers as and when they need. Partly in order to maintain this general appreciation, a policy worker will typically be moved onto another area of policy work within three to four years. Thirdly, policy development has to be seen as a group decision process, with any proposals for change needing the involvement of those policy workers responsible for any of the areas which may be affected by the proposed changes, an aspect which is discussed in detail in Chapter 14. In a broader sense, it is also subject to the opinions, and even prejudices, of the interested parties outside the government department who may be lobbying for, or resisting change. Lastly, it is worth noting that one of the major criteria in the evaluation of policy is the avoidance of 'overlooking' or failing adequately to follow though the implications of a new item of policy — whether in terms of its material effects or simply in terms of the arguments and reactions in which it results.

It is perhaps also useful to note certain characteristics of social welfare policy which makes it particularly complex. Social security benefits are intended to support the whole range of welfare needs that people may have. The range of attributes of people which may be interesting to the social security policy maker is therefore extreme. 'The Statutes on Social Security are necessarily complex: because they have to provide so many different benefits in so many different circumstances.' Historically there have been many changes in the commitment to differing principles of social welfare, the social and political expectations from the policies and the different approaches to the implementation of policies (particularly in terms of the codification in legislation). This has further complicated an already inherently complex set of issues and policies.

These structural features are one source of the complexity in trying to understand and support the policy process; the cultural features are, perhaps, even more complex.

The culture within policy divisions in UK government departments is one of the more unusual, idiosyncratic and, to an outsider, perplexing features of the British political process. Policy makers include people of high intellectual qualification who take great pride in the creativity, relevance and persuasiveness of their ideas and (sometimes an even greater concern with) the form and quality of their presentation. They include people who are enthusiastic about the potential of technology and others who are reluctant to see its introduction, being content with well-established traditions and procedures.

The skills of the policy maker are essentially untaught, being acquired through exposure to the complexities of the task and by the support and example of more senior policy staff. The policy task itself requires co-operative, creative and analytical skills which are adaptive to rapidly changing situations. Within such an environment it is not surprising that the styles and working methods are diverse.

In all cases the requirements of particular ministers are of first priority and the results of the policy process must satisfy such external expectations along with other, more objective, criteria of adequacy. The process itself, however, is subject to considerable variety. Some of this variety arises from differences in the character of individual policy staff.

Other forms of variety arise from external factors. For certain policy problems their starting point is the evaluation of a number of obvious, if not predefined options; for others it is the working up of arguments and counter arguments for and against a solution already favoured by the Minister. Moreover, the life cycle of policy development means that in many cases a policy problem takes more the form of a review of existing policy than a new policy development. This variety in the character of policy is influenced by factors such as the particular government in office, together with its time in office and current political standing.

These factors can be responsible for the sometimes extreme shifts in context — from periods of more radical and innovative policy changes affecting benefit structures through to the more conservative tidying up of policy for certain classes of people.

These variations help to explain the different opinions about what is 'typical policy'. It was particularly noticeable how social security policy varied in style over the period 1983-1989 — from the maintenance of an 'old' supplementary benefit with identifiable anomalies, through the wide reaching consideration of options and major consultation of the reviews, to the current, predominantly defensive, justification and minor amendments to the new scheme of income support.

The implication of this is that the policy process cannot be seen as a prescribed set of tasks with a typical start or end, or with recurring, pre-established criteria of appropriateness. On the other hand, we do believe that within this fluid environment there is a consistent and uniform set of processes which act as conceptual components in the policy task and which are drawn upon and combined by policy staff to achieve their specific purposes.

4.2.2. Conceptual components of the policy task.

In a simple sense the policy process can be seen as being directed towards the development or amending of legislation in order to remove anomalies and inequities, and/or to achieve certain political goals. Even with this simple conception it is important to distinguish between the process of policy formulation and that of drafting legislation. It is the role of the solicitors within the government department to draft the legislation; the policy maker's role is to specify the aims which the legislation should help to achieve, and the general means by which these aims should be achieved. Looked at in this way, the task of policy formulation can be seen as following a number of stages including:

1. Verification that an issue/problem exists.
2. Clarification of the origin and character of the issue.
3. Identification of ways of resolving the issues.
4. Articulation of candidate 'options'.

5. Exploration of consequences of options and assessment of implications.
6. Specification of requirements for legal changes to draftsmen.

The problem with this view of policy, which formed the basis of the early prototypes of the DHSS Demonstrator described in Chapter 8, (and expounded in [Bench-Capon 1987]) is, fundamentally, its 'goal-oriented' perspective of 'problems' and their 'solutions'. In practice, policy is much more concerned with a continual cycle of argument development with changing political priorities and expedience being applied to a complex network of welfare benefit provisions. Policy 'issues' are seldom solved: they are rather recycled and temporarily resolved until they resurface as important concerns at a later date. It is therefore inappropriate to adopt any model which assumes that the process of forming policy has a beginning, a middle and an end. In contrast, therefore, our analysis of the major concerns and activities of policy staff led to the conclusion that it is the process of argumentation that is central to policy. Throughout the various policy activities, the construction, development and presentation of arguments is a common strand or unifying theme.

To understand the role of the arguments it is necessary to establish whom they are for and whose interests they represent, where the policy and the arguments originated from and the perspectives which explain why the issues have become important, and the expectations in terms of what is expected to be achieved by the policy work — when will it be seen to have been resolved? In addition it is necessary to consider the scope and boundary of the policy arguments, their status and their 'currency' in terms of their relevance at this time, plus the context and the relation to other arguments and areas of policy.

The policy argumentation process is thereby characterized by its flexibility and its relative indeterminacy. It is an essentially dynamic process where elements which had previously been established can be revised or redefined, it involves collective argument and debate, and the problems which it is trying to address will typically continue to exist for many years — emerging in different circumstances and with different characteristics, but still representing the same underlying problems. Although policy decisions have to be made, the underlying policy issues are seldom fully resolved.

This more subtle and dynamic view of policy does not invalidate the notion of KBS support which assists with the processes of issue clarification, option specification, implication assessment, etc., as characterized by the earlier model. What is does imply is that the support system needs to be embedded within a wider set of argumentation support capabilities. Similarly, the uses of the KBS facilities are likely to be open and exploratory rather than narrowly focused on well-defined problems.

Our wider model of the policy process is therefore based on three components each covering different aspects of the overall policy process, but which are dynamically linked and in effect developed in parallel with each other. The three components are:

1. Defining the context of the argument — in which the policy makers lay out the situation as they see it now, identifying the major issues and possibly including initial thoughts on potential changes.
2. Developing detailed arguments — where the specific issues and options identified in the first stage are considered in more detail, developing arguments and counterarguments for particular changes.
3. Rationalisation and commitment — where the policy makers evaluate the suggestions, comments and alternative options directed at them by their colleagues and reform the arguments to appear in what they consider to be the most appropriate light.

Any of these three may involve reference to specific issues, options and their implications, at varying degrees of precision. In turn, they impose additional requirements in terms of:

1. Explanation of the problem or issue in terms of the previous policy commitments and the importance of any particular policy aims in determining the earlier course of the policy.
2. Policy justification in terms of presenting the strongest arguments to support the chosen policy.

4.2.3. Types of knowledge used in policy

The explicit knowledge used by policy makers (i.e. that over and above the tacit knowledge about the policy process and acceptable procedures acquired through experience, and the 'ordinary knowledge' of the world) has a variety and extensiveness which it is difficult to characterize in any simple structured way. In general, however, the knowledge relates to the following three questions:

1. What are the political aims, priorities and expectations, and what associated constraints do they imply?
2. What are the needs of the priority client groups?
3. What Policy actions are possible/feasible?

Knowledge associated with the first of these centres around existing and planned political commitments, the particular aims and priorities of ministers, financial constraints and the characteristics of the priority client groups which give them this priority. Mistakes associated with errors in this knowledge would result in the proposal of inappropriate options to the minister and thereby a failure in the essential objective of the policy process. The knowledge involved necessarily extends across all areas of policy while being focused on the particular benefit and area under consideration.

Knowledge associated with the second includes both the socio-economic information and the knowledge of legal conditions and their application to the classes of 'real world' individual. Socio-economic factors include statistical information from surveys or the Department's own sources. They are particularly important in identifying the cost implications of any policy options. Knowledge of the legal conditions is necessary in order to identify and understand potential traps, whereby people who ought to be entitled to benefit are excluded by some anomaly or conflict of legislative conditions, as well as helping to appreciate the particular treatment of types of person within the existing legislative provisions.

Knowledge of the third type includes:

1. The mechanisms made available by the legislative framework, including the feasibility of targeting the policy to the high priority groups while minimising the unintended knock-on effects, the feasibility of operationalising the legislation within the administrative structure, and the enabling powers provided by the legislation defining what actions the secretary of state can and cannot perform.
2. Administrative and operational possibilities, along with the associated costs of implementing the administration of the policy, and including the knowledge of procedures required for approving and committing resources to a policy (e.g. its passing by advisory and parliamentary committees).
3. Theories of cause and effect in terms of the efficacy of certain actions (e.g. whether the raising of a benefit rate by a certain percentage will affect the take up rate for that benefit).

This variety of knowledge required by the policy process is not the only source of complexity. The scope of the knowledge required, in terms of its breadth, depth and completeness can be similarly intimidating. In terms of the breadth of knowledge required, any individual policy maker with direct responsibility for an item of policy development will usually have responsibilities covering a limited group of policy issues, with emphasis on one body of legislation — for example, housing benefits or disability benefits. Frequently, however, any policy development will raise issues which extend beyond this boundary having potential impact on other benefits and so on the work of other policy staff. In a significant number of cases, this boundary extends across government departments and sometimes raises additional issues concerning European legislation. In principle, therefore, the policy maker has to be concerned with aspects of the whole of the legislation emanating from his own department, potentially that of other departments, and, where applicable, that of the European Community.

Turning to the depth of knowledge required, the major concern of the policy maker is again with the general concepts of the legislation rather than with its application in specific instances. This implies that their concern is for the most part with the Acts and Regulations rather than with the detail of interpretation and application, or with the considerable detail of case law from appeal commissioners. In contrast to this general rule, however, the policy maker will often be required to understand or predict how the legislation will be applied in order to be able to assess its implications as to whether or not specific types of people will be entitled to benefit, and to respond to particular landmark decisions. This is particularly important where the match between the legal concepts and the attributes of real people do not have an obvious or clear correspondence. In a rather smaller number of potentially more important instances, the policy maker will need to make predictions or assumptions about how an item of legislation will be treated in appeal, in order to know whether the policy will achieve its desired consequences — or more directly to assess whether the legislation achieves the policy intent. In principle, again, the policy maker should have access to and an understanding of the guidance used by those applying the legislation to specific cases, and to the case law rulings which determine how the legislation is to be applied.

Lastly, the analysis of policy makers needs to be as exhaustive as can be achieved in terms of considering every possible perspective and/or outcome of a policy development. One reason for this is the severe potential political impact of even the smallest number of publicised cases of unfair treatment. Equally important are the scales of cost resulting from failures to limit the targeting of benefits, whereby many millions of pounds can be misdirected. The implication is that, again in principle, the policy maker is expected to consider all permutations and implications of the policy with a high degree of completeness.

According to these considerations it appears that the task of the policy maker is impossible in terms of the scope of the knowledge they are required to apply. It is, however, unrealistic to believe that all of this 'possible relevant knowledge' is actively considered by policy staff as part of their routine work. This would be totally impracticable, particularly given the limited time-scales for responding to ministerial requests and the general burden of work they have to carry out. In fact, the policy process is carried out within the time and resource constraints by means of:

1. Individual policy makers having a 'wide but shallow' general knowledge of the overall legislative conditions and their significance combined with a 'narrow but deep' knowledge of the particular area within which they are working.
2. The group process involving potentially interested colleagues in reviewing the recommendations in order to identify areas of knock on effects or overlaps/inconsistencies in policy, thereby extending

both the range of deep knowledge applied, and the number of perspectives taken on the problem.

3. The experience and 'potential problem spotting' skills of the established senior policy staff who can establish when a particular aspect of the policy deserves closer analysis and investigation.

In general, therefore, the policy process is not concerned with details of individual cases and how they are handled, nor with the precise operationalisation of the statutory conditions. It has to be acknowledged, however, that in practice many problems are not identified until the policy has been implemented and therefore subsequently has to be revised. An improvement to this situation seems to depend upon an increase in the factors considered and thereby the knowledge used in the policy process.

4.2.4. Potential Benefits.

The requirement for a system to support policy, and the associated benefits of such a system, ultimately derive from the expectations and priorities from the policy process; and the constraints which face policy staff in their existing environment. The expectations and priorities have their origin in the political nature of the policy task. One of the primary expectations of policy is that it should have considered all of the issues with implications for, and possible counterarguments to, a particular policy line. This is not to say that there has to be a conclusive rebuttal for any counterargument; just that the proposer of the policy should be prepared for the counterargument and have some response. Another is that there is a strong requirement to avoid inconsistency in the explanation or justification of a policy. Potential benefits of a system then, depend on its ability to identify otherwise 'unthought-of' issues and any potential inconsistencies in explanations.

In terms of removing constraints, the policy process differs from more traditional application areas in that the scale of the activity is relatively small. The potential for supporting policy therefore derives not from factors of scale but rather from issues associated with the sophistication and significance of the policy process. The constraints on policy development are agreed to originate in four features of the policy process.

1. *The unbounded, indeterminate, unstructured nature of policy issues* Policy is an extreme example of what have been called "wicked" problems [Rittel and Webber 1973]. Particular features of such problems include the following. There are intangible objectives, often with unclear conceptions as to what precisely is required from the policy. There are competing conceptions about the nature and source of the problems. Decisions have to be made on the basis of inadequate information. The effects of any option are indeterminate, and subsequent changes to accommodate unforeseeable effects can

cause tensions between these changes and the original philosophy.

2. *The inherent complexity of the policy task* The variety of elements which need to be considered, including all the options and their implications, quickly become extremely complex in terms of their links. Possible knock-on effects make it difficult to manage all these elements and in particular make it difficult for any single individual to understand all of the necessary elements. Implementation of policy has to take account of all the required procedural tasks and ensure that they are planned according to a realistic timetable. At the same time all of this complexity builds a high dependence for a particular item of policy on the key individual involved. This can lead to problems if there is a high turnover of staff.
3. *The number of relevant interest groups* Policy needs to consider, and where possible accommodate, the opinions and expectations of a wide range of interests. Equally it is dependent on other groups for the provision of information and the implementation of policy. This process is exacerbated by the lack of a common language for describing issues and options. The presentation of policy in an appropriate form for particular audiences is one of the major tasks of the policy staff. This needs to take account of the key criticisms which may be used against the policy and may also lead to adapting of the options.
4. *Timescales* The fact that a policy evolves and develops over significant periods of time gives added importance to the ability to retrieve earlier material and to ensure consistency and accuracy of current information. However, time constraints mean that the recording of key events, options considered and assumptions may be given a low priority, with little information actually recorded. The fact that during policy development priorities may change quickly, plus the major pressures for rapid implementation of policy, can lead to significant time and resource constraints in amending and presenting the new policy. In contrast with these long-term developments of policy, there is a continual pressure on resources required to answer questions and respond to minister's short-term demands.

In the face of these general constraints the justification for policy support is agreed, by members of a committee charged with evaluating the Demonstrator prototype and the majority of policy staff interviewed, to lie in its potential for:

1. Reducing the effort required to develop and particularly to revise the policy.
2. Providing a quicker, clearer and more complete response to those concerned.
3. Minimising the occurrence of oversights or confusions.

4. Avoiding 'reinvention of the wheel'.

4.3. POSSIBILITIES FOR KBS SUPPORT

The general requirement for support of policy will probably concentrate on the capturing of assumptions, facts, aims and decisions which take place during the development of new policy, and the retrieval and analysis of this information for subsequent amendments and additional policy. The particular potential for KBS support of policy lies with a system which could complement this overall process with capabilities that would identify potential issues, problems or inconsistencies and check assumptions — typically in terms of the qualitative effects of particular actions.

4.3.1. Issue verification

A policy maker may be alerted to the existence of an issue in a variety of ways. Very often this will be through some complaint, in the form of letter to the Department or a parliamentary question or a press article, about the operation of the system, although it can also arise internally, from concerns of policy makers themselves with the effectiveness of the current provisions, for example. In essence, however, an issue only has significance if the context which argues that it is a concern is accepted. The first task will therefore be to see whether these complaints and concerns are well-founded. Suppose that someone complains that they do not receive a retirement pension even though they are over pensionable age. This is not in itself a problem since age is not the only condition for receipt of retirement pension: a person must also have paid the relevant contributions and be retired. These conditions, of which the complainant may be unaware, represent real policy goals, and there is thus no issue, unless these goals have ceased to be important. Thus given a description of a class of people and a claimed benefit that should accrue to this class, the policy maker must find out whether it really does fail to accrue, and if so why it fails so to do. If it fails for still valid reasons, the issue is resolved. KBS can support this activity by demonstrating that the claimed consequences of the description do occur, and providing the reasons that they occur, at the first level in terms of other features of members of the class and the pertinent legislation, and at a second level in terms of the thinking and goals which underlie this legislation.

Something being accepted as an issue depends then on acceptance of the assumptions underlying it (that the facts described are accurate; that the types of individual of concern are in fact treated as they are claimed to be; that the problem is one of policy and not, say, of errors in procedure) and adherence to priorities or existing policies which make it appropriate or consistent to accept the issue. KBS can assist in teasing out these assumptions.

4.3.2. Issue clarification

Sometimes a genuine problem does exist, so that there is an issue of policy; for example, there may be a group of people who were intended to benefit from a provision who, in practice, fail to benefit from it. It is necessary to clarify which aspects of the current policy are the major factors in generating the issues of concern. Moreover, it is also necessary to establish the boundary of the issue — whether it affects other areas of policy, perhaps even relating to other government departments, and whether it is a specific, localized issue or part of a generic problem extending throughout the policies. In the example of a mistargeting of benefit, this means determining exactly who it is that forms the group intended to receive, but not receiving, the benefit, and explaining why the legislation fails to meet their case. The individual complainants may differ widely in their circumstances, but there will be some common factor which explains why they fall into the problem category. It is the identification of this common factor which enables the policy maker to see precisely who it is that is suffering from the defects in the legislation, and to explain why this is so.

Sometimes the issue may develop because some of the underlying theories that were used in the original design of the legislation are not correct. Suppose that there was no retirement condition on retirement pension, perhaps because there had been a theory which said that no one would work if they could receive a pension, or perhaps because there had been a theory that no one over pensionable age would be able to retain a job. This would mean that some people in full time work over pensionable age would be able additionally to claim a retirement pension. This is in conflict with the aim that such a pension should be payable only to those people without a job, and the legislation would be defective. Given a conflict between the theories and the fact that there are people over pensionable age who are in full time employment, the theory must be modified. Once the theory is modified or abandoned, it becomes clear that some extra condition analogous to the retirement condition is required to enable the legislation to achieve its desired aim.

At this stage exploration of a model of the legislation within a KBS can help to identify those features which distinguish the group giving rise to concern, as so produce a more precise characterization of that group. The better the characterisation of the problem group involved, the better the understanding of the mechanics of the problem, the more focused the search for a remedy, and, it is to be hoped, the better the solution.

4.4. Issue Explanation

Having considered the issue and its implications, a policy-maker may adopt a line of 'explaining away' the issue — arguing perhaps that there is no alternative or that in spite of undesirable consequences the existing policy is required because of the overall beneficial effects. In this situation they need to present their formulation of the problems and issues in such a way as to emphasize the positive features and limit the concerns with the negative aspects.

More generally, policy makers always have to understand as clearly as possible why the existing policy is the way it is — what was the original intent and with what objectives. Here we would look to KBS to support the construction of these arguments against the background of the issue as clarified along the lines of the previous section. When a precise description has been produced, the explanation of the problem in terms of the parts of the legislation which lie at the root of the issue, and how the problems arise is facilitated. Two levels of explanation may be involved; one in terms of the interaction between the various components of the model of legislation, and the other in terms of the justification for these features of the model, that is in terms of the goals they are supposed to achieve.

4.4.1. Option Generation

If it is decided that the problem requires amendment of legislation, the next step is to decide what can be done to cure the problem. Usually there will be several different ways of amending the legislation to reach a state where the problem no longer occurs. The retirement condition in the example mentioned when discussing issue verification above, could be expressed in a variety of ways; any work at all might be made a disqualification, or else an hourly limit on work done could be imposed, or else the pension could be reduced in accordance with earnings in a variety of ways, pound for pound, with a cut-off at a certain earnings threshold, or by a certain proportion of earnings. The policy maker should at this point generate as many candidate solutions as his ingenuity will allow. It is important that policy makers are seen to have considered all possible options and not simply adopted the most immediate and obvious course of action. Even where particular options are infeasible or inconsistent with existing policy, it is important to consider why they should be rejected rather than reject them without consideration.

Couched in knowledge base terms, generating an option can be seen as choosing rules to delete, amend or add which will mean that a description of the target group will provide necessary and sufficient conditions for possession of the desired feature. Often this will be impossible, and different options will approximate to this ideal to different degrees and in in different ways. Using a logical model, the support given for option generation will comprise explanation of the mechanics of the problem, together with the means of determining the extent to which an option achieves the desired result. Where it falls short it will provide an explanation of its deficiencies. In a more ambitious system it would, however, be possible to incorporate elements of knowledge based planning which would call on information as to the generic types of option available to policy makers to provide additional support.

4.4.2. Option evaluation and solution verification

The acceptability of a particular policy option needs to be assessed against the plurality of policy aims — for example targeting the needs of priority client groups, or administrative practicality. Particular care is required in analysing the implications and knock-on effects of selected policies. This analysis ideally needs to be exhaustive in the sense that it traps all of the implications associated with the option so that arguments can be developed for and against the option.

Within the framework of a KBS this might be done by using the logical model to explore the consequences of the various solutions, so as to arrive at the good and bad points of each. Some will have to be rejected because they have consequences which conflict with other aims. As an example, if there were an aim to remove the need for means testing for benefits in the case of the elderly, then the retirement condition could not be made to depend on earnings. Other solutions may generate other problems because of an interaction with other pieces of legislation. Some of these knock-on effects may be subtle and hard to find, and support for their identification is highly desirable. Some solutions may be better that others on grounds of cost or administrative simplicity. All these consequences need to be weighed by the policy maker, but, of course, the consequences need to be identified before they can be weighed.

The policy maker will now submit a proposal to the government ministers, setting out several options for changes that would eradicate the problem, together with a recommendation based on the advantages and disadvantages of the various options. The minister will select one option, which the policy maker will be expected to put into practice.

4.4.3. Solution specification

When a policy maker has decided what he wants to do about a problem he must pass his instructions on to legally qualified people to draft the legislative changes which will give effect to the solution. Currently this is, perforce, done in natural language and two kinds of problem may arise. It may first be that the solution has not been fully specified, and the looseness of natural language allows this to be concealed. Secondly, it may be that the ambiguity inherent in natural language leads to unnoticed misunderstandings between the policy maker and his drafter. Since the natural specification output from a KBS will be in the form of a well specified formal language, both of these difficulties should be ameliorated.

4.4.4. Policy justification

It is not surprising that once a particular policy has been adopted, the policy staff are responsible for presenting it in the most convincing and beneficial light. It is not uncommon for particular policies to have perceived beneficial implications which were not a concern of the original policy formulation at all but help to strengthen the argument in its favour. The presentation of the solution, to ministers, parliament and the public, needs to be in the form of arguments rather than the conventional, proof trace style, output form associated with typical KBS. This requires an entirely different kind of KBS from an adjudication oriented system, but will be a vital part of providing support to policy makers.

4.5. NATURE OF KBS TO PROVIDE THIS SUPPORT

The previous section gave a variety of areas where KBS could provide valuable support to the policy maker in the various stages of the policy making task. In this section we will discuss the kinds of demand that are made on a KBS which would be able to contribute this support: in so doing the differences between such a system an an adjudication oriented system will become very clear.

4.5.1. Reasoning about classes not cases

When a case is presented to an assessment system, all the properties associated with the case can, in principle at least, be decided in a determinate fashion. This may be as a result of observation, or as the result of a legal decision on the basis of evidence. The point is that all questions have a determinate answer. In considering a policy issue, however, there is no possibility of such complete specification, since we are reasoning with a class of people, not an individual, and the specification of the class will necessarily leave the values of certain features undetermined. What is at issue here is the constraints imposed on features by membership of that class. Determining this is quite different from executing a formalization of the constraints as they apply to an individual, and there will need to be corresponding differences in the nature of a KBS to support such reasoning. We believe that what is required here is not the model generation approach that assessment systems naturally fall into, but rather a constraint-based approach. The approach adopted in the DHSS Demonstrator project is more fully discussed in Chapters 8 and 12.

4.5.2. Lack of specified goals

When building an assessment system there is a clear idea as to what questions it will help to decide. Typically legal concepts such as 'pensionable age' will be defined in terms of factual predicates such as 'age'. Predicates in such a system can therefore be divided in to those to be deduced by the system and those to be supplied by the user as facts. This rigidity is inapplicable to a system to support policy. It is as likely that it will be necessary to deduce the factual features that a person falling under some legal concept must have as to decide whether a given set of factual features suffice to confer title to the legal concept. Therefore the task orientation which tends to be built into an assessment system needs to be absent from the representation to be used by a policy supporting KBS.

Moreover, there is likely to be no well specified goal even when a user brings the system to bear on a particular problem. The user of a policy system is not posing a question, but rather exploring the consequences of a situation. This again makes the consultative model around which most assessment systems are based inappropriate.

4.5.3. Integrating the facilities of a policy system

As was said in section 4.2.1, the policy process is not a prescribed set of tasks with a defined start and end. While there will be activities within a policy task which can be supported by KBS, the order in which, and the extent to which, these activities will be pursued will vary from issue to issue. A policy KBS will thus comprise a set of tools supporting these diverse activities, and poses challenging questions as to how these can be integrated into a coherent and usable system. A first attempt at the integration of facilities for manipulating a logical model and facilities for constructing arguments was made in the Demonstrator prototype P3 described in Chapter 8.

4.5.4. Correctness of a policy KBS

Current consideration of policy issues often involves trawling a large number of people for comment, the idea being to identify as many opinions as possible. One use of a KBS in policy would be for it to be used in a similar way, to generate and stimulate further possibilities that might be overlooked in a trawl. Such a system would need to reason in a rather different way from an assessment system which is designed to help its user answer a specific question, and where it is important that any answer it may produce is correct. The policy KBS would, in contrast, need to go on where an assessment system would stop, making any necessary assumptions that it needs to do this. This may of course lead to conclusions that will on consideration be rejected, but provided the assumptions are explicit then this is not harmful, and the consideration may itself be valuable. What is important is that nothing is overlooked, so that the potential for surprises after implementation is minimized.

4.6. PROBLEMS

The major problems in providing KBS support for policy must result from in richness and fluidity of the policy task and the culture of the organization of that task.

4.6.1. Ownership of problem parts

Policy is not a task which is carried out by one individual, applying his own knowledge, but involves a complex interaction between various parties. In terms of some of the possible support capabilities we have considered, it is unclear who, precisely, owns the requirement and therefore at whom the system should be directed. One example of this is the degree to which the policy maker or the drafting solicitor is responsible for checking the effectiveness and implications of the proposed legislative changes. In principle, policy makers should ask for legislation to produce specified goals rather than suggesting specific changes to regulations, yet lawyers cannot be responsible for checking the political acceptability of all the implications of certain regulations. Because of the essential inseparability of the legal and policy issues in the evaluation of whether regulations achieve the political aims, it is difficult to establish whether the policy maker or the solicitor should be the primary focus for support.

4.6.2. Usability and dependability

The sophistication and inherent complexity of the KBS capabilities required to support policy inevitably lead to issues of usability of the resulting system. This is made worse by the fact that policy staff are unable to commit any major time and effort to acquiring the necessary expertise to use such a system. Lastly, within such an environment it would be essential that the user knows when, and how far, to trust the system in terms of being able to understand the limitations of any results it produces. This requires that they be able to use and understand the knowledge base editing facilities and the structure and content of the knowledge base itself.

4.6.3. Lack of criteria for assessing policy success

Systems are typically evaluated and justified on the basis of the contribution which they make to the effectiveness and efficiency of the task they are supporting. Unfortunately, within the policy environment it is not a straightforward task to assess such a contribution. Policy work seldom involves a clearly defined end-product; often the conception of what is acceptable changes throughout the development of the policy. Time and resource constraints imply that the best is done in the time available, with a continuing balance of risk against effort being maintained as the work progresses.

4.6.4. Scoping of policy problems

Perhaps one of the most difficult outstanding issues is whether and how the system could be used in either a focused or general way. At various stages throughout the policy process the policy maker will want to make either very cursory, general queries to check the overall structure of a problem and its general implications or very detailed and exhaustive analyses of all the specific implications of a policy. Between these two extremes are all the permutations of depth and breadth of analysis. For such a task it would be unacceptable to have a system which produced excessive detail of all possible implications for any query. Equally, it is unreasonable to expect the users of the system to revise their formulation of queries in order to achieve the desired effects. The solution probably lies in what is generally called a 'problem structuring' of the knowledge base and queries, whereby the policy maker can flexibly constrain the scope of the knowledge over which inferences are carried out. How such problem structuring could be achieved is still an open question.

4.7. CONCLUSION

In this chapter we have tried to describe a novel area for the application of KBS techniques to a legislation based domain. Our discussion is firmly based in the experience of working on the various policy demonstrators described in Chapter 8. The conclusion is that such an area poses novel challenges for KBS, and that any KBS developed to support this kind of work will be significantly different, both in its construction and style from that found in other legal areas. The area is worth pursuing both because it offers opportunities for exploring distinctive and complex problem-solving behaviour of highly intelligent people, and because there are also great potential practical benefits from the use of such a system. Nor should it be thought that the application of a system of this type would be confined to government departments. Any administrative organization is concerned with the production of policy, and although the details of the process are likely to differ, the general style of system and the KBS techniques required will be capable of being transferred. This chapter then is not about presenting solutions, but about delineating an interesting area for the application of KBS techniques, and offering a warning against an over-simplistic approach.

CHAPTER 5

SUPPORT FOR MEMBERS OF THE PUBLIC

Nigel Gilbert

As other chapters in this volume have explained, knowledge-based systems have great potential *within* legislation-oriented organizations. But rather less attention has been paid to the possibilities of making such systems available as resources for the *customer* of organisations. Two of the demonstrators developed by the project were prototypes of systems intended to show how knowledge based systems could assist members of the public in their dealings with the Department of Social Security: the 'Forms Helper' and the 'Advice System'. This chapter will describe the objectives and the design of these two demonstrators. Firstly, however, it is important to review the reasons why building systems intended for the customers or clients of an organization is worthwhile.

5.1. KNOWLEDGE BASED SYSTEMS FOR CUSTOMERS

Designing knowledge based systems which the public can use successfully is a challenge requiring great attention to the details of the interface. One cannot expect the public to undergo training courses, read manuals or even pay much attention to on-line help. Many of those who do succeed in using the system for the first time will have forgotten how it works by the time they come to it again. Thus designing for public use immediately raises the question of 'usability' in perhaps its most extreme form. If it were possible to formulate successful design techniques for this audience, the same techniques might also be valuable for other, more experienced classes of user, especially where training is expensive

KNOWLEDGE-BASED SYSTEMS AND
LEGAL APPLICATIONS. ISBN 0-12-086441-X

or users cannot find the time to learn how to operate the computer.

Developing systems for public use can therefore bring technical returns in promoting the development of better interfaces. There can also be commercial returns. The services offered by many large organizations are complex and have to be fitted to the particular needs of the customer. For example, many financial institutions are now offering a very wide range of saving and investment plans and are selling them on the basis that one will suit the specific needs of the client. But how is the client to discover which of the offerings is the best for him or her? The conventional approach is to have highly trained salespeople or agents who ascertain the client's circumstances and make recommendations about the best plan to purchase. However, there are several problems with this approach and financial institutions are becoming well aware of them. From the organization's point of view, maintaining a highly trained salesforce is very expensive. Doing business through agents results in a loss of control over the delivery of services and is costly in terms of commission. From the customer's point of view, having to deal with a salesperson can be intimidating, and raises the suspicion that the investment they are being sold may not be the best but the one for which the salesperson receives the highest commission.

This problem about how to communicate effectively with clients and customers is not confined to financial institutions, although the dilemmas they face are particularly clear. Many government departments have to deal with what is essentially the same problem, of offering many complex services to a public which needs help with selecting the right one, and in general they have not been particularly successful in overcoming it [Cordingley and Gilbert, 1987]. The Department of Social Security (DSS), for example, has been criticized for over forty years for the poor quality of information provision to its clients. Sometimes this criticism has been unfair, but generally the DSS has had a problem in conveying the details of the very complex social security system to those who need to know.

The contribution that knowledge based systems can make is that they can provide the kind of personalized, detailed information that clients require, at modest cost. Clients could explore options with the computer, which would act as a indefinitely patient and knowledgeable advisor, indicating the decisions which have to be made to arrive at the correct choice of service [Gilbert, 1988b]. Paradoxically, the machine can provide personalized advice, impersonally. Once a selection has been made by the client, the system could automatically arrange for the service to be delivered. For example, a knowledge based system for public use, sited in a bank or building society branch, could be used by an intending saver to select the appropriate savings plan for their own situation. When the customer had made a choice, the necessary administration could be completed automatically by the system sending an order to the bank's central computer. In fact, trial systems of this kind have already been installed in some banks in the USA.

5.2. KNOWLEDGE BASED SYSTEMS FOR SOCIAL SECURITY CLAIMANTS

Knowledge based systems thus have a contribution to make to organizations in helping them provide a range of complex services more cheaply and more easily. But the gains are not all one-sided. These systems can also be valuable for the customers. This is most clearly seen in the context of large legislative organizations like the DSS, where failure to understand the social security system can lead to people with low incomes being even further disadvantaged [Gilbert, 1985a].

The extent to which there is a problem in disseminating information about social security can be gauged in part from the rates of take-up of benefit (the ratio of the number of people actually claiming a benefit to the number eligible). Take up rates are politically sensitive information and are released by the DSS at infrequent and irregular intervals. Moreover, the reliability of some of the data can be called into question because of the difficulty of assessing the denominator of the ratio (the number of people eligible for benefit). Nevertheless, it is clear that the take-up rates for the important means-tested benefits are very much less than 100%. For example, the latest available figures show that in 1985-6, 52% of those eligible for family income supplement did not receive it and that the corresponding figure for housing benefit was 22% and for supplementary benefit was 16% [DSS, 1989]. Family income supplement was replaced by family credit in 1988 and initial estimates show a take-up rate of 49% for this new benefit. The rate for Income Support, which replaced Supplementary Benefit in 1988, has not yet been published. In contrast, almost all those eligible for non-means tested benefits, such as the state retirement pension and child benefit, do claim their entitlement.

Take up rates of less than 100% are a matter of social policy concern because means-tested benefits are targeted at the very poorest families. Those who are eligible, but not receiving benefit, are therefore existing on incomes below the level which the state believes is the acceptable minimum. While the effect of a low take-up is to reduce state expenditure by substantial amounts (£310 million in housing benefit was unclaimed in 1984), rationing benefits by relying on low take-up is a very inequitable procedure. Those who have most difficulty in dealing with state bureaucracies, whose circumstances are least stable and who have least social support tend to be those who are not getting the benefits to which they are eligible. No reasonable welfare policy would intentionally provide less financial assistance to this group than to others who are already better off.

Several reasons have been put forward to explain the low take-up of means-tested benefits. The regulations governing eligibility and the amount of award of means-tested benefits are complex and, not surprisingly, claimants have a poor grasp of the rules. Thus, the vast majority are not able to assess their own eligibility unaided. The only sure way of determining entitlement is to claim and then wait for the DSS to make a decision. However, the process of claiming is itself seen as difficult and threatening, involving the completion of lengthy forms asking complex questions about claimants' personal circumstances.

There have been several studies of the process through which claimants pass in making a claim [Kerr, 1982], [Corden 1982], [Buckland and Dawson 1989]. Buckland and Dawson argue that claiming a benefit is not the result of a simple choice about whether or not to claim, but the outcome of a complex sequence of decisions which depend on the circumstances of the household in which the claimant lives and the history of other claims made previously or concurrently. They present a model of the claiming process which distinguishes five stages in the 'life cycle' of a claim: conception, preparation, assessment, transmission of outcome and routine claiming. Reaching the final routine claiming stage depends on successfully navigating through each of the earlier stages. A consequence is that to improve take-up rates it is not sufficient merely to provide information to potential claimants about the benefits they might be eligible for. This would only aid them in the initial conception stage. It is also necessary to provide assistance at each of the subsequent stages.

There is considerable evidence to show that claimants are not at present obtaining advice and information when they need it. For example, studies by Berthoud [1984] and Howe [1985] highlight the degree to which the DSS's own staff fail to provide appropriate advice to claimants. Berthoud's study found that less than one-third of those who asked for a single payment grant reported that they had received any explanation of the rules governing the award of these grants either in writing or verbally. Howe's observation of seventy-five DSS local office staff/claimant interviews demonstrates how interviews are used mainly to collect information rather than to impart it. In this situation, claimants turn to three main sources of help [Dawson *et al.* 1990]. Firstly, the Department of Social Security publishes a range of leaflets which set out the main features of the benefits and show which are most applicable to particular groups of people. However, these leaflets are inevitably general in nature and cannot offer information specific to the reader's own situation. Consequently, in order to be comprehensive, the information appears complicated. Secondly, voluntary agencies, such as the Citizens' Advice Bureaux, welfare rights groups and local authority social services departments, provide individualized advice about benefits to clients. However, these agencies are already over-stretched and claimants have to go specially to seek out their advice. Thirdly, neighbours, relatives and friends can provide information either directly or indirectly through recounting their own experiences. However, this advice can be seriously misleading when the informant has only a partial view of the regulations determining the award of benefit.

How could knowledge based systems help in this situation? This was the question a team of researchers based at the University of Surrey asked in 1984. Over the following five years, several surveys and experiments were carried out culminating in the design, construction and evaluation of two systems: one to help in providing information and advice about social security benefits throughout the claiming process, the 'Advice System', and one to help in completing application forms to claim benefits, the 'Forms Helper'.

5.3. THE FORMS HELPER

5.3.1. User requirements

The purpose of an application form is to manage a transaction between the applicant and an organization in a standardized, and therefore easily administered, way. In the case of social security application forms, the transaction is between a claimant and the DSS. The transaction is intended to obtain standardized information from applicants whose circumstances are anything but standard. The form must be designed long before any application is made and it must cater for all variations in circumstances. In practice, this means that most forms have a branching structure with some questions being intended to be answered by only some of the respondents. The need for administrative processing of the completed forms means that from the organization's point of view there are advantages in restricting form-fillers' answers to one of a small number of options, thus forcing the respondent to reply in terms which immediately imply corresponding administrative action.

Many of the difficulties encountered by form-fillers stem from these aspects of forms. For instance, their branching structure leads to navigational obstacles if the respondent fails to notice the cues about which questions to answer next [Frohlich 1986, 1987]. The provision of a limited range of answer options requires the form-filler to engage in what may be the difficult task of fitting their circumstances into one of the supplied categories. Form-fillers are not likely to be aware of the organizational implications of giving particular answers and thus may find it difficult to judge matters such as the precision of the answer required or the way in which they are supposed to represent answers on the form. For example, if asked when they left their last job, respondents may not be clear whether the exact date of leaving is required, nor whether the date of leaving is the last date they attended the workplace or the last date for which they were paid.

These problems are exacerbated by the fact that there is usually no-one thought to be prepared and available to help with filling in social security forms (in fact, both the DSS and Citizens' Advice Bureaux offer assistance, but only a very small percentage of claimants make use of it, possibly because of the inaccessibility of these sources of help). In addition, there are difficulties which are specially pronounced in the case of DSS forms. Because of the complexity of many of the benefits, a great deal of rather detailed information is required from claimants and so the application forms are very long (twenty-two pages in the case of the application form for income support) and often have very complicated branching structures.

5.3.2. Computer assistance

An interactive computer system can help with many of theform-filling problems, even if it cannot remove them entirely. For example, with respect to the problem of routing through a form to answer only those questions which are relevant to the respondent's circumstances, the computer can selectively present questions on the basis of previous answers. Other questions can remain hidden from sight. With respect to the problem of understanding questions and the import of different answers, the computer can display explanatory material appropriate to the question at hand, either automatically or on request from the user. The computer can provide sample answers to indicate the precision and format required. And the computer can do some preliminary checking of the answers that the form-filler gives to ensure consistency and to restore some of the interactivity which is so lacking in a printed form.

The Forms Helper was designed to show how this support for form-fillers might be provided in practice. Although the prototype was constructed for the DSS form used to claim income support, the design is such that it could be used to support any of a very wide range of forms. It is especially suited to those which, like the income support form, are available for the public to complete, are filled in only once or infrequently by any one individual, and are lengthy and involve complex routing. One area of application which will serve as an illustration of the possibilities is Customs and Excise. In 1988, the EEC introduced the Single Administrative Document which is required to accompany all goods exported across Common Market borders. This document is a form which many small firms find forbidding to complete. The Forms Helper could be of great assistance. A rather different example is the Post Office. The Forms Helper could provide an improvement to the service offered to Post Office customers by including electronic copies of all the forms at present obtainable over the counter, so that not only would blanks always be available immediately, but also help could be given in completing forms.

For the demonstration, it was assumed that the user population would consist of claimants of income support or individuals acting on their behalf. It was also assumed that users were able to operate the computer, were sufficiently literate to be able to understand simple English and were willing to learn how to use the system. Those who were not capable in any of these ways could enlist the support of a friend or relative to help them. These assumptions still allow for a very heterogeneous population varying greatly in their knowledge of computers, of social security and their previous experience with the Forms Helper. The differences between users were accommodated by providing facilities commensurate with the needs of the 'worst case' users which could be by-passed if not required. The system offers sufficient support with individual questions to help users with no previous knowledge of social security regulations and procedures. This can be avoided by those who are confident about how to respond. Similarly, for first time users with no familiarity with computers, help is available on how to operate the system at all points in the interaction [Frohlich *et al.* 1985].

The Forms Helper was implemented on a Xerox 1186 personal workstation [Gilbert *et al.* in press]. It is intended to be sited in some convenient public place such as a library, advice centre or DSS local office in a location which affords privacy of use. The interaction begins with the user selecting the particular form he or she wishes to complete from a number on offer covering the different benefits. The outcome is a fully or partially completed form which could be printed out on paper or stored in computer-readable format.

The Forms Helper program is designed as a 'shell' to which knowledge about any particular form can be added in order to provide support for that form, without having to change the program itself in any way. There are five parts to the specification of a new form for the Forms Helper: a database which indicates the static appearance of the form, including the wording and positions of all the questions; a set of help texts for the various kinds of support; a set of 'routing rules' which are used to compute the next recommended question on the basis of the layout of the form and the answers that the user has given; a set of rules which are used to perform consistency checks of the user's answers; and a grammar which defines the formats of recognizable dates, numbers and money sums.

5.3.3. The electronic form

It is a well-established finding that people form conceptual models of interactive systems and that these are used to explain the way the system appears to work and to predict the effect of control actions on it. This has important consequences for system design, since it suggests that systems which behave according to a consistent and familiar conceptual model will be easier to understand and operate than those which do not.

The design adopted for the Forms Helper encourages users to think of the system as an 'electronic form'. Other designs, such as displaying one question at a time, or developing an iconic interface, were considered, but there were several advantages in adopting the electronic form model. The idea of a form and its properties are likely to be familiar to users, reducing the learning required. Users will come with the expectation of having to fill in a form and therefore the conceptual model will be easily recognized. And the scope of the system is evident from the model. For example, users are unlikely to expect the system to do more for them than conveying a claim to the organization; they will not expect it to act as their advocate or advisor.

Having a conceptual model is an advantage for the designer as well as the user: it proposes a style of interaction and suggests the appearance and properties of the objects displayed on the screen [Frohlich and Luff, 1989]. Nevertheless, the model serves only as a partial explanation of the interface. There are properties of paper forms which were intentionally avoided in designing the Forms Helper (e.g. the fact that a paper form includes explicit routing instructions whenever the next question to be answered is not the next on the form). Some properties of paper forms could not easily be reproduced even if they were desirable (e.g. the possibility of 'pencilling in' trial answers). And the fact that the electronic form is implemented on a computer enables it to have some desirable properties which go beyond what is possible with paper.

For example, the Forms Helper controls the display of questions on the form by only showing those on the current 'page' when it becomes clear that they are relevant for the particular user. Typically, the first question on the page is a filter question, for instance a question asking about whether the form-filler rents their home. If this question is answered in the affirmative, further questions about details of the rental arrangements appear on the page below the filter question. If the respondent does not rent, these questions remain hidden. As the user works through the form, pages are added, covering up previous, completed pages. An index at the side of the screen allows users to return to previously visited pages to examine or amend their answers.

Another way in which the electronic form differs from a paper form is that the areas for users' answers start by being just large enough for a normal answer. As users enter more information, the areas are automatically extended, moving later questions out of the way if necessary. Thus there is never the problem of not having enough room to provide a full answer.

The effect is that of a growing form showing only questions relevant to the individual user. The form-filler's attention is directed by the system to the next appropriate question, at or near the advancing front of the form. This scheme largely removes the problem which many users experience in managing paper forms, that of navigating their way through a complex branching structure. It also enables the system to present questions in their context, surrounded by other related questions. This is in itself a powerful clue about the intention of the question and the kind of answer which is appropriate.

Although users are always guided to the question which the system considers should be answered next, they can override this recommendation and take control. In this respect, the design allows 'mixed initiative', that is, either the system or the user can control the interaction as appropriate (see Chapter 13). Users obtain the initiative by moving the cursor back to any previous question or forwards to any visible question lower down on the current page. This gives them the opportunity to change or check answers to previous questions and to omit answering some questions on their first pass through the form. Taking the initiative carries with it the danger that a user could become 'lost', but the Forms Helper avoids this by returning the cursor to the next relevant question in sequence each time the user has input an answer.

5.3.4. Electronic help and support

One way in which the electronic form is visibly different from its paper counterpart is in its provision of help and support. When the system recommends or the user selects a question for which there is supporting information, a panel of notes and explanations is displayed next to the question. All the notes, instructions and explanations which appear on the paper form have been moved to these panels which appear only as they are needed. This means that the electronically displayed form is relatively uncluttered and the user's attention is directed to the immediately relevant material. The effect is rather like a running commentary on the import of the questions as the user moves through them.

In addition to material related to the question, the user is also offered the chance to request three kinds of further help. First, there is procedural help on the mechanics of entering an answer on the electronic form. Secondly, for many questions there are example answers. Thirdly, there are rephrasings of the questions if the user is unsure of the meaning of any of the terms in the question. All this material is available to form-fillers as they answer the question. For some questions, there is further help which appears only when an answer has been provided. This additional information informs the user about the consequences of the answer. For example, there are some responses which mean that the form-filler is rendered ineligible for benefit and if the user selects one of these, they are told immediately.

Some questions request answers which are expected to have a specific structure, for example, answers consisting of a date or a sum of money. There are advantages to the processing organization if such answers are presented in a standard format. The Forms Helper therefore includes the capability of 'parsing' certain kinds of answer, including dates, numbers and sums of money. This decomposes the user's answer into parts and reassembles it into a standard format. The parser is driven by a grammar which allows a very wide range of formats to be understood (for example, a date may be entered as 20th March 1989, or 20/3/89 or 3/20/89 or 20-3-89 or in a variety of other styles). If the parser is not able to make sense of the input, the user is given examples of the standard format and asked to re-enter the answer.

At the beginning of the interaction, the user is presented with a 'training form', intended to help with learning about the mechanics of filling in an electronic form. The training form begins with a section explaining the use of the mouse, describes the types of question and how to provide answers (typing into text boxes or 'ticking' boxes by pressing the mouse button while the cursor is over a small square tick box) and gives practice at deleting mistakes and amending answers. It also explains how to complete a session, either midway through to obtain a partially completed form, or at the end of the form.

5.4. THE ADVICE SYSTEM

While the Forms Helper is intended to help claimants at the point of lodging a claim, the Advice System aims to give support throughout the claiming process. It provides advice and information about many aspects of claiming, including not only assessments of eligibility, but also information about the procedures to be followed in making a claim, advice about the possibility of appeals against unfavourable decisions, information about the benefit system and social security in general, and so on. Like most expert systems, the Advice System can be divided into a knowledge base with associated inference engine, and a user interface [Gilbert *et al.* 1990]. In fact, there are several knowledge bases in the system. One contains information on the five major social security benefits, child benefit, one parent benefit, income support, family credit, and housing benefit. Another contains knowledge about DSS procedures [Gilbert and Jirotka 1990]. Two other knowledge bases are associated with the part of the system concerned with interacting with the user.

5.4.1. Representing knowledge about regulations and procedures

The knowledge bases concerned with social security regulations and procedures may be divided conceptually into three 'levels' and four 'kinds' [Gilbert 1987b]. The case level includes knowledge specific to the particular situation of the user under consideration, the domain level includes domain knowledge about social security regulations and procedures and the theory level concerns knowledge about domain knowledge, that is knowledge about why the social security system is organized as it is. The four kinds of knowledge which are distinguished are: taxonomic, knowledge about entities and their relationships, for example, the benefits themselves and how they interrelate; formal, analytic knowledge about relationships between entities' attributes, primarily the rules concerning eligibility and assessment of benefit; contingent, synthetic knowledge about causal and temporal relationships, which in the case of the Advice System consists of knowledge about procedures for claiming and appealing benefits; and control, knowledge about the system itself and its inferencing, that is the system's knowledge about the deductions it has made.

These three levels and four kinds may be cross-classified to yield twelve types of knowledge which can be manipulated in various ways to provide a full range of answers to questions about social security. Because some types of knowledge can be used to provide several sorts of answer, there are not twelve, but seventeen significantly different sorts of question to which the the system can provide an answer. For example, the Advice System can give answers to straightforward questions about whether the user is entitled to a particular benefit. But it can also answer questions about why the user is entitled to this benefit, what the regulations determining eligibility are, what the policy objectives of those regulations are, what procedures need to be followed to claim the benefit, what kind of benefit this one is, what other benefits the user might be eligible for, and so on. Conventional advisory expert systems are able to produce a few of these sorts of answer, but the remaining ones are not usually supported because the knowledge needed to generate them is either missing from the system or is 'compiled away' and inaccessible to the inference mechanism and answer generator.

5.4.2. A conceptual model for the Advice System

The choice of an appropriate conceptual model for the system was important in designing the user interface and the course of the interaction with the user. A number of possibilities were considered. Any kind of iconic or graphical interface is ruled out by the difficulty of representing graphically the complex and abstract concepts which are inevitably involved in social security (for example, 'income', 'weekly rent' and being 'responsible for a child'). The user interface has, of course, to be appropriate for users with no prior training. This rules out any form of command-driven interface (because users cannot be required to learn a command language). Natural language has been proposed as the most obvious and easiest medium for communicating with computer systems, including knowledge based systems (e.g. [Boguraev 1985]). This suggested a design based on the idea of a conversation or consultation with an advisor. The conversation would be conducted through textual, rather than verbal interactions, but would nevertheless be a recognizable as a conversation, with conversational openings and closings, and questions and answers from both system and user.

Although a natural language interface has great merits, no existing natural language understanding system can cope with every input a user might give it — they all are confined to (quite narrow) domains. This means that users normally have to learn what they can say and how they should express it before they can interact with the system effectively. However, natural language interfaces do have the strong advantage of great expressive power which it would be a shame to lose. The solution which has been adopted is to provide a menu-driven interface which allows the user to compose, in restricted natural language, any of the statements or questions which the system is capable of understanding.

The user interface consists of three parts: a scrolling dialogue window on the left of the screen in which all the input and output is displayed; a set of three buttons at the bottom right of the screen; and an area on the right of the screen in which menus are displayed by the system. The menus enable users to construct utterances for their side of the conversation. The buttons enable the user to request a rephrasing of a system utterance, to ask the system for a justification of its reasoning and to demand an immediate termination of the interaction (an 'emergency exit').

Unlike the majority of current user interface management systems, which limit the interaction possibilities to predetermined routes through a network of options, the interaction design for the Advice System is based on the idea of 'local management'. Each utterance, whether from the system or the user, is constrained only by the immediately preceding conversational context. Constraints on the next conversational turn are imposed by a set of 'interaction rules' derived from the analysis of human conversations. This component of the Advice System is described in more detail in Chapter 9.

As a consequence of this design, the user of the Advice System can obtain a wide range of types of information by asking questions during a dialogue in which the initiative passes back and forth between the user and the system. The dialogue allows the user to explore topics in whatever way seems best, mirroring spoken discourse, where generally conversations are not preplanned but proceed from 'one thing to another'. The intention is to provide a system which supports a style of advice giving where although both the content and the structure of the dialogue respond directly to the individual moment-to-moment utterances of the participants, extended interactions are coherent and cumulative, yielding advice and explanations that are built from individual conversational turns. Whether this objective has been achieved can only be determined by trials with users (see Chapter 9).

5.5. CONCLUSIONS

The two systems which have been reviewed in this chapter have been designed for use by clients of the DSS to help them claim social security benefits. But the software has been constructed in a way which allows them to be applied in many other domains. Both systems consist of a 'shell' and a set of knowledge bases. The shells are knowledge-free programs which provide sets of resources to the system builder. They work in conjunction with knowledge bases that are constructed specially for the particular application, in this case social security. For example, to develop an Advice System to provide advice about choosing between various savings plans, one would need to rebuild the knowledge bases, but one would not need to change the program itself.

These systems can thus be considered not just as programs to help people with claiming means-tested social security benefits but also in a wider sense, as prototypes systems designed for enhancing communications across institutional boundaries between clients and large, legislation-based organizations. The systems embody several general principles which are important for this kind of application. Firstly, both support 'mixed initiative', allowing both the user and the system to take control as appropriate. Mixed initiative is significant for client-organization communication because of the need in these circumstances for a negotiation between the two parties. The customer comes with some prior set of requirements; the organization with some set of services which can be supplied. The purpose of the system is to support the negotiation of a resolution of any differences between the customer's requirements and what the organization can supply.

The element of negotiation in the interchange between client and organization is also the basis of the second general principle embodied in the two systems: that they use the knowledge built into them in order to translate the users' views of their needs into the vocabulary of the organization, and vice versa. This is most clearly seen in the Forms Helper, but the Advice System can also be considered to be 'translating' concepts like eligibility for a benefit, which are meaningful to the organization, into specific queries expressed in terms that are meaningful to the user.

The third principle which the systems demonstrate is that users need to find a conceptual model of a system in order to use it effectively. Both the systems have been designed with a specific conceptual model in mind, and this has contributed to their ease of use. The models — of an electronic form for the Forms Helper and of a conversation for the Advice System — are based on existing modes of communication with which potential users can be expected to be already familiar.

These principles have emerged from, and have guided the design decisions which were made to construct the two systems. The evaluations described in Chapter 9 suggest that the principles have led to the development of prototypes which do demonstrate the effectiveness of knowledge based systems for assisting communication over organizational boundaries. The evidence is that the public could use the systems in their present form to help with claiming social security, and that they would be welcomed and be popular. However, whether these systems or their descendants are actually put into use by the DSS depends inevitably not only on the quality of their design, but on political decisions which have yet to be taken.

5.6. ACKNOWLEDGEMENTS

The Forms Helper and the Advice System were designed and built by Sarah Buckland, Betsy Cordingley, Leo Crossfield, Shashi Dave, Patrick Dawson, David Frohlich, Nigel Gilbert, David Goodwin, Michael Hardey, Marina Jirotka, Kevin Johnstone, Alison Mill-Ingen, Hilary Minor, Paul Luff, Mike Pappas, Nick Perry and Peter Robinson over the period 1984 to 1989.

CHAPTER 6

USING A COMMON KNOWLEDGE BASE IN SEVERAL APPLICATIONS

Trevor Bench-Capon

6.1. INTRODUCTION

In this chapter I discuss some of the considerations which relate to sharing a common knowledge base (KB) across several applications. I begin with an example which is sufficiently small to comprehend in its entirety; considering how we might go about building systems in this limited domain will reveal a number of powerful reasons for expecting substantial divergence between the knowledge bases for different applications, even when the domain is the same. This in turn highlights the importance of considering the task when constructing a KB.

6.2. An example

Suppose we were building three systems relating to the parish relief law of a fictional parish in Elizabethan England: one to assist in the processing of claims for relief; one to advise people wishing to claim such relief; and one to assist the parish in formulating policy on parish relief. The legislation relevant is:

> Any person shall be provided with parish relief if he apply to a beadle of the parish, and in the opinion of that beadle he is deserving of such relief.

Case in law is sparse since there are no systems of appeal and the only recourse of the disgruntled is to apply for a writ of mandemus to quash the decision.

KNOWLEDGE-BASED SYSTEMS AND
LEGAL APPLICATIONS. ISBN 0-12-086441-X

Two such applications for mandemus have been made. In the first it was held that relief was not payable to John Goodbody because he was a sturdy vagabond who could make his own shift ('make one's own shift' is an archaic phrase used by judges to mean 'provide for oneself'). In the second, relief was granted to Mistress Quickly, a widow the judge holding that of all people widows and orphans were most deserving of relief.

Following these decisions, instructions have been issued to beadles saying that they are not to grant relief to men of good health under the age of 65, nor to married women, nor to single women of good health under the age of 60, nor to anyone under the age of 14 with a living parent. Also that widows should be granted relief as should anyone with a certificate of unsturdiness from a registered physician, and a child under the age of 14 without a living parent.

Note that the guidance is intended to subsume the case law, and that the word 'orphans' as used in the judgement on the Quickly case has been interpreted as meaning a person without living parents under the age of 14. Some age limit is clearly needed, but the decision itself gives no help here, so the operationalization of the concept must be achieved through the guidance.

We begin to build our expert system by formalizing the legislation.

```
_Person is ProvidedWithParishRelief iff
    _Someone is ABeadle
    and
    _Person AppliesTo _Someone
    and
    _Someone ThinksDeserving _Person.
```

Note that terms beginning with '_' are variables. This formalization could be transformed into executable PROLOG, as:

```
PF1 ProvidedWithParishRelief(X):-

            IsABeadle(Y), AppliesTo(Y,X) ,
            ThinksDeserving(X,Y).
```

The rest of the formal examples are all given in PROLOG.

Now we could use this system both as a beadle to assess an application and as a potential claimant to get information. The system would be of some utility, but it would be limited; a claimant would learn that he would have to apply to a beadle and convince him that he was deserving, and the assessor would learn that he was empowered to decide the application if he was a beadle, and would have his attention directed the precise question on which he had to reach a judgement. Of course, the claimant would not have any indication of whether his application would succeed and the assessor would have no help in judging the merit of the applicant.

The policy team could also use the system to answer a variety of complaints. For example, if someone complained that Joe thought they were deserving and yet they did not get relief, the problem could quickly be spotted: Joe is not a beadle.

So far all three systems have a common KB. But it is unlikely that we would want the users to have the system as it stands. At a minimum we would provide an interface. A minimal interface might be:

I1 ShouldIGiveReliefTo(X):- ProvidedWithParishRelief(X).

for the assessment system and

I2 CanIGetRelief(X):- ProvidedWithParishRelief(X).

for the advice system. We might also wish to include some kind of thesaurus-type information to handle vocabulary differences between the assessors and the assessed. If the interface is knowledge-based, therefore, differences in the target users will necessitate differences in the KB.

Now we may formalize the case law.

```
CL1 ThinksDeserving(X,Y):- KnownDeserving(Y)) .
CL2 ThinksDeserving(X,Y):-
            not(KnownUndeserving(Y)) ,
            LooksDeservingTo(X,Y).

CL3 KnownDeserving(Y) :- widow(Y).
CL4 KnownDeserving(Y) :- orphan(Y).
CL5 KnownUndeserving(Y):-CanMakeOwnShift(Y).
CL6 CanMakeOwnShift(Y):-Sturdy(Y),Vagabond(Y).
```

Now we must formalize the guidance. Some parts will already be latent in the case law, and some will not. Consider the guidance again this time with the additional information which could be elicited from the author of the guidance, explaining the justification for each bit of guidance. The justifications are appended in brackets.

Do not relieve:

NR1 men of good health under the age of 65 (justified because such people can make their own shift; all sturdy vagabonds will be in this category)

NR2 married women (as they can look to their husbands for support)

NR3 single women of good health under the age of 60 (as they can make their own shift or marry as the fancy takes them)

NR4 anyone under the age of 14 with a living parent (as they can look to their parents for support)

Relieve:

R1 widows (the Quickly case)

R2 anyone with a certificate of unsturdiness from a registered physician (as they cannot make their own shift)

R3 children under the age of 14 without a living parent (an interpretation of orphan)

We may now formalize these provisions in a way which hooks it into the case law. In some cases, like R1 this will be the same as what we provided for the case law; in others we must extend it, and perhaps make use of the information provided in the justifications as well.

```
G1  CanMakeOwnShift(Y):- Male(Y),Age(Y,A),
    A < 65,Health(Y,good).
G2  CanMakeOwnShift(Y):- Female(Y),Age(Y,A),
    A < 60,Health(Y,good).
G3  orphan(Y):-Age(Y,A), A <14,not ( parent(Y,X),living(X)).
G4  LooksDeservingTo(X,Y):-DeemedDeserving(Y).
G5  LooksDeservingTo(X,Y):- not (DeemedUndeserving(Y)),
    JudgedDeservingBy(X,Y).
G6  DeemedDeserving(Y):- HasCertificateOfUnsturdiness(Y,C),
    IssuedBy(C,P),RegisteredPhysician(P).
G7  DeemedUndeserving(Y):-Female(Y),Married(Y).
G8  DeemedUndeserving(Y):-Age(Y,A),A<14,parent(Y,X),living(X).
```

Some of these clauses (CL1, CL2, G4 and G5) are not formalizations of anything to be found in the case law and guidance themselves but are required to represent the way in which these things are used in the assessment of a case. These kinds of thing can again be viewed as representing task knowledge, although this particular task — that of interpreting case law and guidance — may play a part in more than one application.

Now again we could simply use this KB as the basis for both expert systems, adding in I1 or I2 as appropriate. However, we could do more. The assessment system will only be invoked when an application is made and so there is no need for the assessment system to ask if application has been made. We could either simply modify the relevant clause in the assessment system, but if we have commonality as a goal we will want to add instead a clause ensuring that the goal is satisfied.

There are other things we might want to add to both systems. A list of beadles and registered physicians, for example. So far we have kept fairly closely to the aim of a common KB, but the systems, while not useless, are not as useful as they might be.

Suppose that we have on a database a number of records about the population of the form:

marriages with fields for man, woman, date.

births with fields for name, sex, date, father and mother

deaths with fields for name and date.

Now the assessment system would want to make use of this information, since it is a good way of getting validated information not readily available to people doing the assessment. Thus we would want the assessment system to include a number of rules which would allow use to be made of this information.

So we add some suitable clauses to access the database:

```
DB1   male(X):-born(X,D,boy,F,M).
DB2   female(X):-born(X,D,girl,F,M).
DB3   age(X,A):-born(X,D,S,F,M), thisYear(Y), A is Y - D.
DB4   widow(X):-married(X,Y,D),died(Y,D),not(married(X,Z,D2),
      D2>D.
DB5   married(X):-married(X,Y,D), not(died(Y,D2).
DB6   living(X):-born(X,D,S,F,M),not(died(X,D2)).
DB7   parent(X,Y):-born(X,D,S,Y,M).
DB8   parent(X,Y):-born(X,D,S,F,X).
```

It is less clear, however, that we will want to do this for the advice system. Firstly, it may be the case that there are practical difficulties in making these data available to the public. Alternatively, given that this sort of information is readily available to the claimant, we may prefer simply to ask the claimant for the information rather than accessing the remote database. If either is the case then the assessment system will need this part of the KB representing knowledge about how to use the database and the advice system will not. In the case where the information is held on several different databases, a system which is supposed to access them will need additional knowledge as to what is where. It may even be that the reliability of various sources is something that needs to be reasoned about.

6.2.1. Discussion of the example

So far we have noted some possible practical difficulties in using common knowledge bases, but there are a number of other things that we will need to consider, and which start to point to a necessary divergence.

The way we formalized the case law in terms of the guidance was subject to some interpretation, and it may be that the interpretation required for the advice system is not adequately reflected in the formalization motivated by the assessment system. Thus the advisors may wish to test the interpretation of the Quickly case by encouraging parentless 16 year olds to claim the benefit. By using the system as it stands such claims would be discouraged; it may be, therefore, that we will want different versions of these rules in the two systems.

Next it will be noted that the advice system does not in fact offer much in the way of advice. A useful advice system would need to tell its users where they might find beadles to apply to, and how they should make their application. None of this would be useful to the assessment system.

A clear case of this concerns the unsturdiness certificate. The assessment system is not at all interested in how such certificates are obtained, nor what the criteria of issue are. A claimant, on the other hand, would be interested in this information. Thus addresses of physicians, standard criteria employed by physicians to determine whether they should issue such certificates, and perhaps even information on which physicians are soft touches would all be valuable to the claimant. If, for example, the lack of at least one limb was required to obtain a certificate the claimant would want to know this so as to avoid wasting his time; but it would be of no interest to an assessor.

Additionally, the advice system might want to give advice on how to present a case to the beadle, for example instructing him to cough a lot to indicate the his health is not good. This might well be of interest to the assesment system, but the advisors would be reluctant to have it available to the assessors.

All of these things are paralleled in the assessment system. The beadle will want to know what he should do on granting relief; which money chest to go to, who should be informed, and so on. None of this is of interest to the advice system.

Instructions to find frauds parallel the advice on case presentation. Beadles may be instructed to wash the faces of the apparently pallid to detect the use of make up. This would be useful to the advice system, but the authorities would be reluctant to release it.

Thus the assessment and the advice systems will contain a common core based on the legislation and the guidance. But, particularly in the case of guidance deriving from case law, the two systems may diverge since there is no compulsion on the advisors to follow the interpretation represented by the guidance; further it is possible that in practice the guidance and justifications for it may not be available to the builders of the advice system. Moreover, the two systems will contain advice and procedures relevant to their users but of no interest to the users of the other systems, or which the owners of the information will not wish to make available to users of the other systems. There is no way in which this information can be derived from a common knowledge base. Lastly, given differences in the practical situations in which the two systems are to be used, there may well be differences in the way in which we wish to collect information, as in the questions of age and sex mentioned above.

Let us now return to the policy system to be used by the parish council. This will introduce an extensive set of new factors. The policy-makers will want the formalization represented in the full logical fashion so that they can conclude that anyone provided with relief has applied to a beadle, for example. Secondly, they will want an explicit representation of the case law as that expands and develops the meaning of the laws which they manipulate. They will need a formalization of the guidance, but this formalization needs to contain the additional information that this is guidance not law. Thus it is a fact that married women cannot get relief, but this obtains not as a theorem provable from the legislation but as a consequence of the guidance being followed. Thus if they encounter a case of a married woman in receipt of relief, they need to know that this unsatisfactory situation has arisen not as a defect of the law, which would then require amendment, but as a consequence of the guidance not being adhered to, which will require a different sort of action. This means that for the policy system it is essential that the rules be annotated to show their provenance. This is of little interest to the assessment system and of less interest to the advice system. This in turn means that we have to choose between including redundant information in the latter two systems, or having a specialized rule base for the policy application.

Further, there will need to be information available to the policy system which has no role at all in the other systems. For example, to decide whether changes should be made, and what these changes should be, the system would need to have a variety of statistics available on demography and how many people were starving. Also it would need models of what people needed and what would satisfy these needs. It would need to know about the political aims and constraints on their actions. It would need to know about financial constraints so that it could cost changes. None of this would need to appear in either of the other systems.

Conclusions

Working through the above example illustrated the following points:

1. There is a core KB which is common to all three applications. This could be used as a KB for any of the applications but it would give a system of limited use.
2. There are classes of knowledge which are relevant to only one system; procedures, practical advice and statistics providing examples. They are required by the systems to make them usable, and cannot be discounted. It is an open question as to what proportion of the system's required knowledge falls into this class, but one would suspect the proportion to be high, and for it to be the knowledge which is most difficult to obtain and the make or break component

for the success of the application.

3. There will be classes of knowledge, like the database example, which could be common but for practical or aesthetic reasons is better kept distinct.
4. There will be classes of knowledge where the content is debatable, like the case law interpretation. In such cases the owners of the systems might insist on different KBs.
5. There are classes of knowledge, such as that relating to fraud, which would be useful to more than one system but the owner would refuse to allow its inclusion in the other systems.
6. Different users will have different information available to them. A claimant will know if he is ill, an adjudicator will require a certificate. The KB may need to be organized differently in the two cases so that any questions asked to the user will take these differences into account.
7. The systems will require different interfaces; while this might be expressible as part of the KB it is probably best factored out for the discussion of common KBs.
8. Similar considerations may apply to the inference engines to applied, for example so as to generate different sorts of explanation.
9. Sometimes there is a tension between writing a rule in a way so as to be appropriate to one application or another. This may cause us to write either different rules, or a common rule to transform into different forms for the two applications, or may give rise to some redundancy or inefficiency in one or both of the applications.

6.2.2. Summary

In our applications there will be scope for sharing some of the knowledge particularly that deriving from legislation, case law and guidance. It should not be assumed, however, that this will simply be a question of writing for one application and then porting it to the others. Sharing will only be fruitful if it is written to take account of the needs that will be imposed by the other application. On the other hand, much of the knowledge will be local to a particular application, especially but not exclusively where task knowledge is required, and this is likely to be harder to obtain and be that part which makes the applications interesting and hence successful. The common knowledge is a *sine qua non* for all the systems, but it is the customized knowledge that gives the systems their point and their usefulness.

PART III

PROTOTYPES

Part of the value of the contributions to this book is that they are firmly grounded in the experience of building systems in the areas they describe. The authors both look back on their experience and look forward to what they would do given the benefit of this experience. It is therefore important to detail exactly what were the systems that were built, and it is the function of the chapters in this part to provide this information.

Before the Demonstrator project started there was a period of feasibility study in which a variety of areas for KBS support for DHSS were considered. In the early days of the project itself, teams were set up to pursue five of these areas. One team looked at support for the formulation of legislation, and they produced a series of prototypes, known collectively as the 'policy application'. This series of prototypes is described in the chapter by Graham Storrs, who led the policy team during the second half of the project. This was a particularly challenging application, since there were no existing systems to serve as models. In a real sense this work defines a new area for KBS in law.

A second team, based at the University of Surrey, was charged with looking at how KBS could support members of the public. In the first half of the project they developed a system capable of assisting a claimant to complete a claim form — a necessary but often difficult stage in the claiming process. In the second half they developed a system to advise people on what they could claim and how to go about it. The chapter by Nigel Gilbert, who led this team throughout the project, describes both these systems.

The other three teams were examining ways of supporting staff who adjudicate on claims to benefit. One team looked at supplementary benefit, which was chosen because it had associated with it a large number of rules, which it was thought could, once identified, be applied in a relatively straightforward fashion. This strand was meant, therefore, to explore problems associated with a very large knowledge base. A second team focused on mobility allowance and in particular the interpretation of the condition that a claimant be 'unable, or virtually unable, to walk'. It was felt that this was a highly judgemental decision, and this would therefore give scope for examining them problem associated with the application of open-textured concepts. The third team were to look at issues associated with training adjudicators. As the project developed, however, two things happened. Firstly, and outside of the projects control, supplementary benefit was replaced by a benefit called income support. Although the fundamental intention of the two benefits was the same, there were considerable changes to be accommodated. Secondly, it became clear that the simplistic division into a benefit with many rules which were easy to apply, and a benefit with few rules requiring a high degree of sophistication to interpret, was not a good reflection of the true situation. All legal adjudication contains elements of both kinds of decision-making. It was therefore decided to merger these two strands into what became known as the Local Office Demonstrator. This is described in the chapter by Justin Forder, who led this team from the time that this merge took place. The training strand was dropped at this time: it was felt that KBS tutoring systems pose their own problems, which were not best pursued within the Demonstrator project framework.

The final chapter, written by Charlie Portman, who was the project manager, describes some of the problems and challenges involved in running a large project whose members are drawn from different cultures and who are dispersed around the country. Given that collaboration between industrialists and academics is currently seen as a model for research projects, his experience is worth consideration by anyone who may become involved in such a project. Also the nature of collaboration had some impact on the types of system that were ultimately produced, and it is therefore helpful to be aware of this influence.

All of the prototype systems produced in the project are interesting examples of sustained experiments in KBS and the law, and shed light on the aspects of that field that they addressed. They are also interesting as examples of the way in which collaborative projects work, and as such collaboration is likely to be necessary to move such legal KBS forward from research into actual use, this experience should not be disregarded.

CHAPTER 7

THE LOCAL OFFICE SYSTEM

Justin Forder and Andrew Taylor

7.1. INTRODUCTION

The requirements laid out in Chapter 3, relate to the Local Office Demonstrator (LOD). The LOD is intended to demonstrate the potential for knowledge-based systems and advanced user interface technology to provide decision support to adjudication officers assessing claims for welfare benefits. The LOD combines the essential aims of the project's original supplementary benefit, mobility allowance and training applications. It provides support for decisions based on large volumes of complex legislation, where many of the conditions rely on the user's interpretation, with guidance from manuals and previous decisions. The same support environment is intended to serve the needs of skilled and less-skilled users: it constrains all its users to be consistent and thorough, while allowing skilled users to use their knowledge of the legislation and the support system to 'home in' quickly on crucial issues in cases. This flexibility, coupled with free access to on-line manuals of primary and secondary legislation, is intended to allow use in a training rule.

The evolution of understanding of requirements and technical approaches for the LOD occupied most of the five-year lifespan of the project. The last six months of the project contained a 'breakthrough' in convergence between requirements and design, followed by a rapid implementation of the system framework, knowledge base, and user interface, and a swift evaluation by Department of Social Security staff. Even now, we still believe that the approach taken in this final prototype is unique

KNOWLEDGE-BASED SYSTEMS AND
LEGAL APPLICATIONS. ISBN 0-12-086441-X

and valuable. In particular, it provided a natural and unforced integration of a variety of support capabilities, an integration which allowed different users, with different skills, to use the system in a manner most appropriate for their needs.

This chapter describes the evolution and final form (LOD3) of the Local Office Demonstrator. Starting with the objectives as seen at the outset of the project, we follow the path leading to LOD3, highlighting some of the lessons learnt along the way. The later part of the chapter contains a description and evaluation of LOD3 itself.

7.2. EARLY OBJECTIVES

The project proposal identified the following potential benefits of using knowledge-based systems in Department of Health and Social Security work. The project proposal identified a key problem in Department of Health and Social Security welfare benefits administration: Most of the DHSS areas for which demonstrations are proposed currently present difficulties because, although the rules exist and are carefully laid down in a large body of legislation, there are difficulties relating to the size of that legislation; and further the rules are in many cases difficult to apply, requiring judgement or interpretation in their application.

Use of knowledge based techniques rather than conventional data processing techniques allows solutions to following problems:

1. Applying and keeping up to date a large and complex rule-base.
2. Checking consistency and completeness of application of the rules.
3. Handling incomplete and uncertain information.
4. Handling erroneous information.
5. User characterization (i.e. modifying the response of a system according the the nature of the person using it).
6. Explaining how decisions have been arrived at.
7. The modelling of the effect of changes in the legislation.

The broad aims of the Department's operational strategy can be summarised as:

1. To improve operational efficiency.
2. To improve the quality of service to the public.
3. To modernize and improve the work of the staff.

Each of these objectives was addressed in turn:

Taking one DHSS area alone, that of supplementary benefit, staff are currently handling some seven million claims per year and producing twenty-eight million instruments for payment (mostly manually), and dealing with 92,000 appeals. Using these more sophisticated tools they would be able to offer a more efficient service, for example by enabling legislation changes to be incorporated much more quickly and at less cost.

The benefits to the DHSS outlined above are themselves potential benefits to claimants, in that claims and their processing could be dealt with more efficiently and with a better degree of explanation of decisions. This will lead to an increased level of claimant satisfaction with the DHSS, and to a reduction in the number of cases which go to appeal.

Involvement of staff at the beginning — in the development and evaluation of new technologies — will give them earlier awareness and allow for their views to be reflected in the application of advanced technologies. The use of such technologies could lead to:

1. The embodiment of knowledge and judgement in systems that aid in operations.
2. Improved training.
3. A widening of work experience.
4. Relief from boring, routine tasks.
5. Concentration on non-routine, more interesting and rewarding tasks.

7.3. INITIAL AREAS OF INVESTIGATION

Early in the project, separate application teams addressed 'procedural' and 'judgemental' decision support, in the respective areas of supplementary benefit and mobility allowance assessment. Supplementary benefit assessment involved a large number of decisions, most of which were, when taken in isolation, straightforward. Difficulties arose from the large number of interrelated rules. Mobility allowance, in contrast, rested on a single decision involving a great deal of human judgement, taking into account a substantial body of case law. A third team investigated the possible user of computer-based training systems for DHSS staff.

The supplementary benefit application produced two major prototypes. The first had a form-based interface which displayed various fields, corresponding to those on the claim form, for completion by the adjudicator. On the basis of this, a second form comprising entitlement details would be completed. The key question was seen as determining which fields from the claim form were relevant to the claim, so as to minimise the amount of information that needed to be transferred in order to make a decision. The system was underpinned by a set of production rules. These rules were first examined to see which fields were known to be relevant to the decision, as disclosed by backward chaining from overall entitlement. As the form was completed, the same rules were used forwards, drawing conclusions from the information as it was entered.

The prototype was implemented on a very small rule base: problems with it were seen as the amount of information that the adjudicator would need to transfer from the claim form to the computer form, and the lack of flexibility inherent in the application of rules to the case. For these reasons a second style of prototype was developed.

This second prototype focused on the completion of the A14, the worksheet completed by an adjudicator in the course of his adjudication. For the purposes of this system it was assumed that the information from the claim form would be available to the system before adjudication commenced, together with some other information existing on current records pertaining to the claimant.

This prototype was built around a display of the A14 worksheet. The assessment task required that each box on this form be completed so that it could be used to structure the task.

In some cases it would be possible to complete the boxes on the basis of information on the claim form, but in others the user would need to exercise judgement based on the law, on case law, or on the guidance in the adjudicators' manual. The prototype backward chained from the final box on the form (representing the amount of benefit awarded), highlighting boxes which would need completion before this box could be determined. At each step in the chain the user was presented with a number of methods of completing the particular box under consideration: he could invoke the system rules, examine parts of the manual or legislation concerning this field, examine relevant fields on the claim form, browse relevant past cases, use a default value (to cover incomplete information) or simply supply a value himself (if he felt able to reach a decision on the basis of his browsing).

The structure of the A14 was used to bring structure to the task, and the prototype emphasized the variety of sources used by the user in the course of the assessment, and made the relevant parts of these sources available to the user at each step of the assessment. The prototype suffered from having a very stilted user interface and from placing the onus on the user to spot issues and call up the necessary guidance. These deficiencies seemed to have important implications for future styles of KBS support.

The mobility allowance application produced two prototypes addressing different aspects of judgemental decision making.

One presented the decision making graphically via the traversal of a decision tree. The other represented cases using frames; this representation was used in a matching process to retrieve past cases which had been the subject of leading decisions relevant to the current case. Matching criteria were associated with individual 'paradigms' from past cases, rather than being globally prespecified or specified by the user. The scope of support was very limited, only addressing the requirement for help with specific judgements, and providing no help with the wider issues involved in a given case.

7.4. THE LOCAL OFFICE APPLICATION

By the midpoint of the project, when a review of progress against objectives was carried out, it was apparent that certain of the supplementary benefit decisions involved judgement and case law in the same way as the mobility allowance decision. There were both practical motives and conceptual justifications which led us to merge the two areas into a local office application (aimed at providing decision support to adjudication officers in DHSS local offices), working on the assessment of Supplementary Benefit and its planned successor, income support. Practically, resources were scarce and had been unevenly distributed. Conceptually, our analysis during the first eighteen months of the project raised some concerns that the separation of three demonstrations, when considered from the perspective of the user requirement, was over-simplistic and essentially misdirected. It became clear that it was dangerous to try to separate the treatment of *hard* and *easy* cases — not least because until a case is finished it is difficult to be sure what kind of case it is. Furthermore, the encoding of a large number of legal rules within a traditional knowledge based system did not obviously satisfy an existing need amongst DHSS staff — there was far greater concern with identifying which of the known rules would be applicable for a particular case, how those rules should be interpreted, what additional information was necessary before a decision could safely be arrived at. Lastly, it was questionable whether the training task could really be separated from the decision making process — it proved to be essential to support the development of staff during their decision making activities, rather than in a separate training environment. The emphasis on training was therefore changed; rather than continuing to examine specialized computer-based training systems, the potential for the decision-support systems themselves to have a training rule was to be investigated, so this, too, became an aspect of the local office application.

An initial analysis of requirements for the local office application focussed on trying to establish what support was required, based on what people found difficult and what the technology was capable of doing. The first consideration, therefore, was: who were the users, and what did they do? The introduction to the resulting report made the following statments.

The local office system would require three distinct groups of user if it were to be used operationally. Two of these (what we are referring to as the LOII users and the LOI users) would be involved in the actual operation of the system for carrying out assessments, the third (the OCAO user) would be responsible for the creation, validation and maintenance of the knowledge base. These user roles match closely with the current division of task within the DHSS.

The claimant details would probably be entered into the system by a clerical assistant. Additional claimant information would be accessed from existing databases. The task of making a claim assessment would be controlled by an LOII. The system and the LOII would 'negotiate' and 'critique each other' over problematic aspects of the case. Once these issues had been resolved the system would complete the straightforward aspects of the assessment, presenting its conclusions (at a level of detail as required by the user) for the LOII to assess and approve. Many of the decisions required to make an assessment can currently be carried out by the LOII, some of the more complex or interpretative issues, however, can only be decided by the more senior LOI. As these issues frequently require a greater degree of judgement additional facilities will be provided for the LOI user, particularly in the suggesting of analogous cases, which it would be inappropriate to make available to the LOII user. Lastly the assessment has to be authorized by an LOI who will need to be able to examine not only the final assessment but also any key assumptions or decisions made during the assessment process. If an appeal is made by a claimant, the local office case is prepared by the appeals officer (who is always an LOI) and checked at the regional office. Support should be available from the system for the preparation of such appeal submissions, particularly in being able to retrieve, re-analyse and re-present the arguments involved in the original assessment.

7.5. SETTING THE SCOPE OF PROTOTYPES

Given this revised and expanded perception of the requirements, a series of prototypes of increasing scope and ambition had to be planned. The scope of a given prototype could be restricted, with respect to the full system, in a variety of ways:

1. Subset of users.
2. Subset of tasks.
3. Subset of types of case handled.
4. Subset of issues within a case handled.
5. Subset of intended user-interface facilities.

Initial top-down analysis of a variety of source material (the Act, Regulations and Adjudication Officer's Guide) revealed a common underlying structure. This structure was introduced in the Act, and elaborated into detail in the Regulations. The structure was also reflected in that of the adjudication officer's guide, while being elaborated still further to contain guidance on interpretation of terms in the legislation.

We regarded the structure as an unfolding of the overall decisions about entitlement to benefit, and (if entitled) the appropriate amount of benefit, into 'topics' and 'subtopics' (etc.), each of which might or might not need to be investigated, according to the circumstances of the case. Each topic or subtopic was seen as a possible task component, with associated rules and guidance needing to be held in the system's knowledge base, and corresponding user interface components (e.g. forms). This gave us a powerful and flexible way of controlling the system scope, by exposing the correlation between components of the task, content of the knowledge base, and user interfacing requirements. supplementary benefit and its successor, income support, are both 'safety net' benefits, aimed at ensuring that families are provided with sufficient resources to meet their essential requirements. As such, these benefits are generally seen as defining the 'poverty line'.

A claim for benefit has to be made on an approved form, and the form has to be properly filled in. Entitlement depends on a variety of conditions, only one of which (a limit on permitted capital) involves assessment of resources. No assessment of requirements is needed to determine entitlement. The requirements do, however, depend on the make-up of the family, and there are rules concerning who is to be or is not to be considered a member of the family. Other (non-family) members of the household are also of interest, as they are assumed to contribute to the family's resources. Income and capital for the family are assessed, as is an 'applicable amount' representing the family's requirements. Capital over a certain threshold (but below the level where it prevents entitlement) is converted to an equivalent income. The amount of benefit paid is the family's applicable amount minus the family's income (so long as this result is positive).

This (simplified) account shows how 'real world' information about the circumstances of people is transformed into a 'legal view' of who to consider and how to treat them. A legal view of their requirements and resources is developed, and used to arrive at the amount of benefit to be paid. Figure 7.1 shows the 'topics' involved, the kinds of data being used or generated, and the main dependencies between them. Again, this is considerably simplified with regard to the legislation itself.

7.6. LOCAL OFFICE DEMONSTRATOR 1 (LOD1)

LOD1 demonstrated possible support for LOII users in the assessment of capital as required by supplementary benefit. A second version of LOD1 used the equivalent rules for income support; the draft regulations for income support had become available during LOD1 development. The key factors relating to quality of decision making in this type of task were seen as:

1. Awareness of relevant conditions.
2. Application of correct sets of conditions.
3. Correct interpretation or application of conditions.

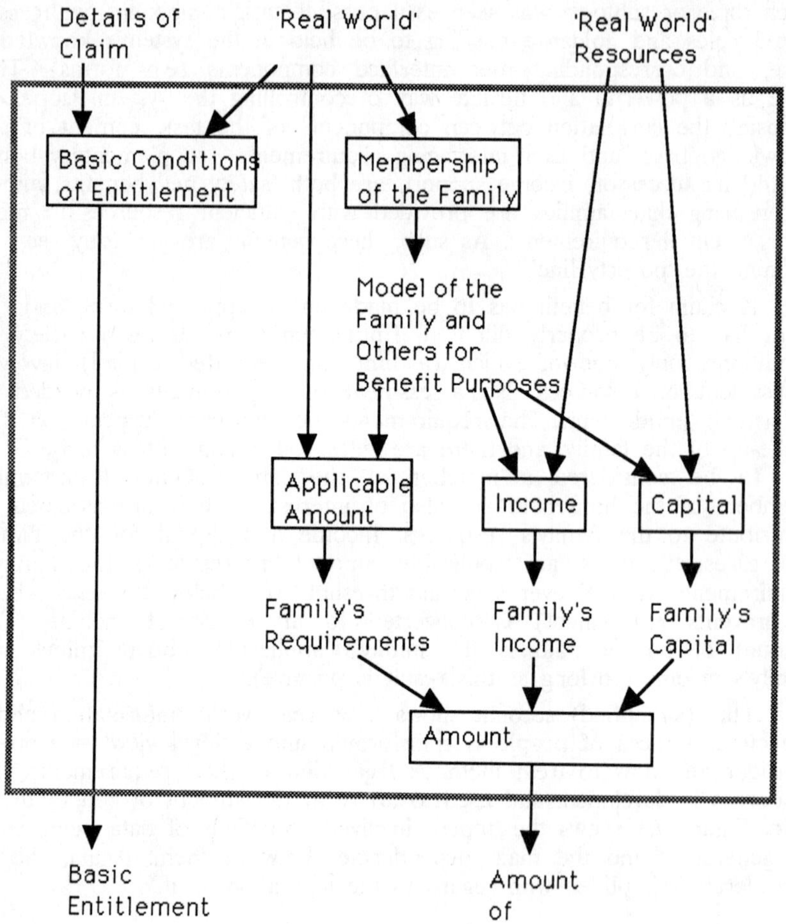

Figure 7.1

4. Sufficient information on a case to make the correct decision.

The specific objective of LOD1 was to support the identification and application of relevant rules to the case data.

Capital assessment involves determining how each item of a family member's capital should be regarded for the purposes of benefit assessment. An important part of the legal conditions relating to capital is concerned with determining whether an item of capital is to be 'disregarded' or partly disregarded, and what overall value should therefore be assigned to a claimant's capital. The problem is seen as being one not so much concerned with finding the legal conditions as with describing the real world facts of the case in such a way that the relevant legal conditions can be established.

LOD1 presented its user with a tree of 'real world' categories of capital item (e.g. building society accounts, home improvement grants), presented as a succession of connected menus. The user selected whatever he or she believed to be the most appropriate description of each given item of capital; additional guidance on the distinctions between the categories was available if required.

Once the user had chosen a category for the capital item, the system provided an input form for entry of relevant details of the item (i.e. those details required by the rules in the system to determine how to handle a capital item in this category).

Whenever the discretion or judgement of the adjudication officer is required (e.g. to say why a grant given for a particular purpose had not yet been spent, and whether or not this was seen as being 'reasonable'), the system requested and recorded a justification of their decision. A 'review' facility was provided, allowing the total capital sum to be taken into account and the total capital sum disregarded to be called up at any time. For each of these amounts, a detailed explanation could be produced, naming the individual items involved and giving a plain English equivalent of the Toolkit rule used to allocate each one.

The key features of LOD1 were that:

1. It would help with the identification of unusual legal conditions with which the user might be unfamiliar.
2. It would oblige the user to record all the justifications and additional information, giving the potential for better explanations to claimants and also helping in the event of an appeal being made.
3. It presented a potential flexibility in changing the legal conditions and ensuring that all users would be using the most up-to-date conditions.

On the other hand, it was acknowledged that there were some important limitations with the LOD1 system. In particular:

1. The system only supported one feature of the overall assessment process, and gave no context for using the results of this stage or for identifying when the support provided by LOD1 would be used.
2. Many decisions in an assessment involve different types of problem with different requirements for support, for example involving procedural complexities.
3. Other decisions impact on the assessment of capital, and vice versa;

for example it is important to distinguish between capital owned by dependents and that owned by the claimant or the claimant's partner, and some kinds of income need to be treated as if they were capital.

These limitations encouraged us to concentrate our work for the second prototype on the requirements for supporting the handling of a case.

7.7. LOCAL OFFICE DEMONSTRATOR 2 (LOD2)

LOD2 was to concentrate on the assessment of new claims while recording sufficient data about the assessment to enable facilities for reviewing assessments and preparing appeal submissions to be added later. Assessment would start with pre-input case data, and end with rejection of the claim or with a 'payment panel' giving the amount, means, and start date of payment.

The assessment task was seen as consisting of:

1. Checking that the claim has been properly made.
2. Identifying the type of case, and its associated problems.
3. Identifying the 'topics' that will need attention during the detailed assessment.
4. Choosing a sensible order in which to handle the topics.
5. Handling the topics.
6. Combining and summarizing the findings and completing the case assessment.

Decisions were seen as involving the selection of appropriate rules by ascribing some feature of the case to a specific legal category, as in LOD1, but also:

1. The (relatively) straightforward application of 'clear rules' (i.e. rules whose conditions do not require interpretation).
2. The (human) interpretation of legal conditions.
3. A sequence of procedures or decisions, depending on the results of earlier decisions.

The interaction was to involve guidance from the system, decision by the user, and the processing of straightforward results of decisions by the system. The user would identify the type of case and the problems associated with it. The system contained its own 'classification rules' which would be applied to the data. The system would ask for clarification if its classification rules gave different conclusions from those given by the user. The user would be guided by the system through the detailed conditions involved in assessing the given case — the system would contain 'planning' rules allowing it to recommend an order for handling the necessary topics. Relevant textual or case-related guidance was to be easily accessible when a condition requiring interpretation was being dealt with. The user had to be free to change his or her mind at any time about earlier inputs. The system was to help the user to keep track of the whole assessment process — the user is responsible for the outcome of the assessment, so must understand all aspects of it, including those performed by the system. If the user encountered problems in handling some part of a case, he or she was to be able to mark it for the attention of a reviewer, handle it in whatever way seemed best, and carry on with the rest of the assessment. Different styles of interaction were required to support the following types of task:

1. Starting up the system, selecting a case to work on, possibly going on to another case, and closing down the system after working on a case or series of cases.
2. Handling a case, including validating the case data, identifying problems associated with the case, finding and ordering relevant assessment topics, selecting each topic for handling, reviewing the overall result and closing the case.
3. Arriving at a decision based on the answers to sequences of questions, possibly presented in groups on forms, where the answers at a given stage in the interaction help to determine what questions will be asked next, and where the ordering is also based on the user's need to see some coherence in the interaction (we referred to this style as a 'structured dialogue').
4. Classifying items (as in LOD1) where the selection of a 'real world' class for an item leads to a request (by a form or a series of questions) for the detailed data needed to determine the treatment of such an item.
5. Retrieving relevant case-related information as guidance on the interpretation of a condition.
6. Retrieving textual guidance on the interpretation of a condition.

LOD2 demonstrated styles of interaction for all of these subtasks except (3) ('structured dialogue').

An icon representing the system expanded into a login dialogue box. After successful login, the user was presented with a menu of his or her cases. Selecting a case led into the case handling screen, containing a window holding case data, a window for results of assessments, windows for guidance and 'system help', and a working area. Icons at the side of the screen gave access to on-line legislation, guidance and procedures.

The user could browse through the case data using buttons beside the case data window to access sections corresponding to the sections of the claim form. On request, he or she could proceed to a classification stage, where a form allowed potential problem areas to be marked. Guidance was available for each potential problem area on the form, and justifications could be added to chosen items. When satisfied with his or her entries, the user could compare notes with the system; any differences in opinion about potential problem areas needed to be resolved or justified by the user before handling of the assessment could proceed further.

The system then used the classification first to derive a list of topics needing to be handled, and then to present them in a menu in the preferred sequence.

This menu of new topics was presented in the working area; when the user selected a topic it would take over the working area of the screen, and when the user suspended or completed the handling of the topic he or she would be returned to the new topic menu, with the topic that had just been worked on moved to a 'suspended' or 'completed' menu as appropriate. Completion of all necessary topics gave access to a final assessment display, with fields for the main conclusions in the case. The user was permitted to override the values in the final assessment, so long as a justification was given. Authorization of the final assessment would lead to the 'payment panel' containing the amount, date and means of benefit payment. The only topic fully implemented in LOD2 was capital, as implemented in LOD1. To allow demonstration of the retrieval of case-related guidance, some conditions in the classification form led to a case retrieval facility modelled on that of the mobility allowance application.

While the implementation of LOD2 appeared to make advances on LOD1 in terms of embedding specific support within an overall handling of a case, LOD2 was a disappointment to those involved in its specification and implementation. The interaction supported by LOD2 appeared unnatural and forced, in a number of ways:

1. Users were being required to go through a fixed preliminary stage of classification, whereas in practice their classifications would tend to emerge as they progressed through the case.
2. The general heading of 'classification' actually covered a range of separate issues, including:
   (a) the identification of ways of quickly resolving a case;
   (b) highlighting of potential 'problems' which require specific attention;
   (c) declaration of features of the case which have 'pervasive' implications (e.g. claimant involved in a trade dispute, or student).

   LOD2, however did not distinguish between these.
3. The number, and level of precision, of the classifications appeared 'arbitrary'.
4. The style of support raised concerns about its effect on users with

different levels of skill and the requirement for fast paths through the interaction.

5. The system required prior input of claim data; this raised questions about the status of data input by clerical staff, and made it likely that large amounts of data would be input unnecessarily.

Overall, we had the feeling that something was deeply wrong with the system, but had not yet got to the root of the problem. We were, by then, well into the final year of the project — if anything radical was to be done, it would have to be done quickly.

7.8. LOCAL OFFICE DEMONSTRATOR 3 (LOD3)

While LOD2 was being developed, its designers had been faced with a long list of demanding requirements. It was not clear whether some of these requirements could be met at all, how well others could be met, or whether some of the requirements conflicted with others. A literal reading of the requirements had led to a view of the system as having many parts, and strongly modal behaviour. This, coupled with the daunting nature of the list overall, had led to a rather piecemeal approach being taken to the design and construction of LOD2.

While LOD2 was never completed, and what there was of it had arrived late, it fulfilled the intention of a 'prototype' in giving a concrete basis for discussion between 'requirement owners' and designers. It gave a very clear indication that we were on the wrong track, and would have to reconsider our earlier intention to use LOD2 as a 'shell' within which we could scale up the domain knowledge and detailed user interface to produce LOD3. Some time was spent re-evaluating and prioritizing requirements. The following list was produced in early October 1988:

1. Needed throughout the system:
   (a) data input by user, validated by system;
   (b) access to explanations in terms of the legislation used;
   (c) ability to work on a claim with incomplete information;
   (d) system prompts for information should make it clear why the information is needed;
   (e) on-line browsable manuals and legislation;
   (f) on-line help with use of system (e.g. input formats);
   (g) support for the styles of subtask as described for LOD2;
   (h) support for appeals submissions (in terms of ability to review the working of a completed case, retrieving explanations in terms of the legislation used, possibly with the additional ability to select and assemble standard pieces of text together with parts of the explanation and case data within a standard textual

framework, and some word-processing capability to allow editing of the resulting draft).

2. Some demonstrable examples required:
   (a) 'fast paths' — fast ways of using the system for experienced users;
   (b) unsolicited help — warnings or guidance provided spontaneously by the system;
   (c) generation of requests for additional information;
   (d) support for review of assessments, including highlighting of places where the user has overruled the system;
   (e) 'comments box' on final assessment, flagging any unusual features of the case.
3. Nice to have if possible:
   (a) support tailorable for users of different skill levels;
   (b) blocking of 'fast paths' where legislation has recently changed;
   (c) multiple levels of detail available in explanations;
   (d) discrimination between assumed/told/verified status of input data;
   (e) support for OCAO and policy monitoring (selective retrieval of cases having particular characteristics for review).

At a meeting held shortly after this list was produced, we realized that we had been making a fundamental error in placing individual 'requirements', such as these, above simplicity and coherence of design. Instead of continuing to try to satisfy as many of the existing 'requirements' as possible, we now chose to see how much of the spirit of the requirements could be captured in a simple, coherent system. Within a few weeks a radically different approach to case handling had been sketched out and agreed between designers, implementors and requirement owners.

The project manager and stakeholders were reluctant to endorse such a dramatic change of course so late in the day, but accepted our advice that it was necessary, would reduce the amount of work to be done in the short time left, and would result in a better system.

7.9. THE REQUIREMENTS AS FINALLY SEEN FOR LOD3

The design of the Local Office Demonstrator now focussed on the provision of a support environment providing a set of complementary capabilities, combined and presented to satisfy a small set of key principles. These were:

1. The user would be responsible for all of the decisions declared to the system.

2. The system would keep a faithful record of the user's decisions, would infer straightforward implications of the user's decisions, and would prevent entry of inconsistent data.
4. The user would decide on the order in which to address issues, within constraints imposed by the system.

These constraints would relate to simple dependencies between topics and input data (e.g. a topic covering the details of the claimant's partner could only be accessed after the claimant had been declared to have a partner):

1. The system would help users to keep track of where they were in the overall assessment, why they were there, what they had done and what they still had to do.
2. Any relevant guidance would be easily available to the user.
3. The system would ensure that the case was not regarded as complete until all relevant issues had been examined and all relevant decisions had been made.

The model of control, then, was that the system should not 'decide' anything at all, but simply provide guidance and carry out straightforward inferences and arithmetic. What the system would do was to oblige the adjudication officer to enter all the required evidence, and prevent the adjudication officer from completing a case until a minimum set of acceptable criteria had been satisfied.

The interaction thus involved the system providing hurdles or legal constraints which the adjudication officer had to satisfy before the decision could be considered as 'completed', while providing all of the guidance relevant in helping the adjudication officer towards satisfying these constraints. It assumed that the skilled adjudication officer would know how to work through the interaction in the quickest manner possible, only being required to enter the justifications for decisions which they would have been obliged to provide anyway. Inexperienced adjudication officers, or ones dealing with issues outside their knowledge would be 'slowed down' by the system and forced to follow through the details of the guidance and the rules. This, we believe, would have the desired training effect through usage of the system.

7.10. THE DESIGN OF LOD3

The user interface of LOD3 was redefined, almost from scratch, in a (largely successful) attempt to remove problems that had been encountered with the user interface of LOD2. This resulted in a design in which 'fast paths', support for users of different skill levels, and choices concerning what data (if any) should be pre-input, were all catered for adequately in the normal mode of operation of the system, rather than needing additional facilities to support them.

The approach to classification/recognition of problems in the case was also simplified and spread uniformly through the system, rather than having a 'stage' of interaction dedicated to it.

The new approach allowed the handling of the case to develop into detail in a hierarchical manner, and gave the user control over the order of doing things at each level of development.

While review of previous cases and preparation of appeal submissions were not directly supported by the system, it kept a record of all aspects of the decision-making needed for these purposes, and a printed summary of each case could be produced. Cases were selected for handling from a menu, as for LOD2. A case could be saved at any stage in its assessment, and reopened later for further work. This could allow (for example) one user to input basic data, another user to do the assessment, and a third to review the case.

The left-hand side of the screen (Figure 7.2) was used for the assessment. The LOD2 concept of a 'topic' was generalized to operate at multiple levels of detail — the case was taken as the top-level topic, with basic data about the case being gathered on a form. Second-level topics were automatically generated to fit the case, and these in turn would perform some combination of data-gathering and decision-making, which could give rise to further subtopics.

Each topic had a summary area, titled with the topic's name and containing key conclusions from the topic, extending across the left-hand side of the screen. As work was done on the topic, important conclusions would appear, possibly accompanied by explanatory text, in the topic's summary area. Beneath the summary area was a 'subtopic bar', containing named icons for the topic's subtopics, if any. These would appear as and when work on the topic indicated that they needed to be investigated.

Beneath the subtopic bar was the 'working area' for the topic — this might be a form, or a 'classification' window supporting the kind of interaction provided by LOD1, or a 'structured dialogue' window (described below).

This arrangement was nested to reflect the topic hierarchy; the 'case' topic had its title bar immediately below a prompt area at the top of the screen, and its subtopics would open over its working area (so that the icons in its subtopic bar remained in view). As a result, the user could always see the titles, summaries and subtopic icons for the current topic, its siblings, and all higher topics on the current branch of the topic hierarchy.

Moving from one topic to another just involved moving the pointer to the relevant topic icon and clicking the mouse button. Inputs could be changed, simply by going back to the relevant place and entering a new value.

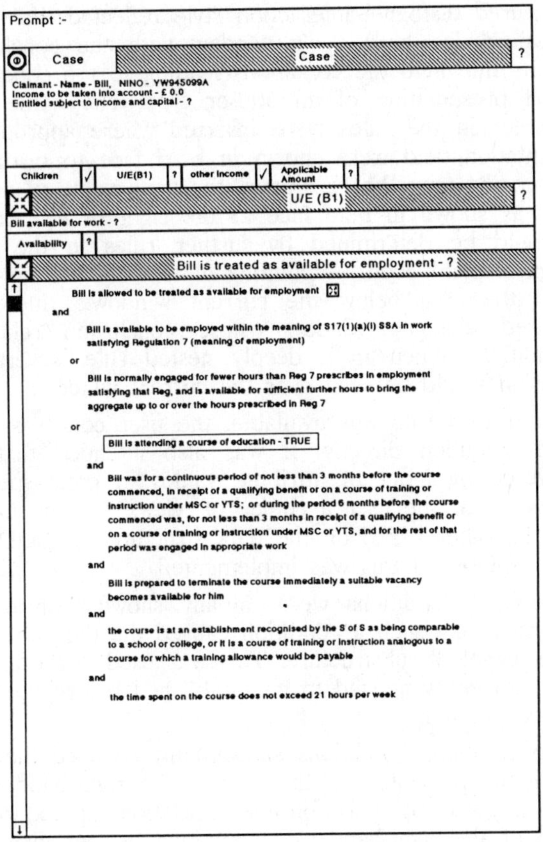

Figure 7.2

At any level, a topic was not regarded as complete until all necessary inputs had been given for it and all its subtopics had been similarly completed. Completion of a topic was indicated by a tick in its icon and in its title bar — incomplete topics had a question mark in these places.

Important items in a topic's summary might propagate up into the summary of the parent topic — so as work on a case progrésed, information would gradually move up into the top-level summary area. It was intended that explanations would be accessed by pointing at summary items and clicking the mouse button — a window containing a textual representation of the rules used in deriving the item (similar to the explanations in LOD1 and LOD2) would then appear to the right of the summary area. Unfortunately, there was not time for this facility to be implemented.

The 'structured dialogue' interaction style reflected the structures of rules in the knowledge base — a window with the conclusion to be determined as its title held the conditions leading to the conclusion as an indented textual presentation of an and-or tree. The names of entities bound to variables in the rules were inserted where appropriate in the textual representation, and were shown in bold face to distinguish them from the surrounding text. Where known, the truth value of any condition or conclusion was shown in bold face to the right of it. Any condition whose truth could be determined by further rules in the system was marked with an 'expand' icon — pointing at this and clicking the mouse button overlaid the area below the current window's title bar with a further structured dialogue window whose conclusion related to the 'expanded' condition. When in a deeply nested rule, several levels of pending conclusion would be seen over the current window.

Where no further rule was available, the user could assert or deny the truth of a condition directly. It was also intended that conditions might be answered by input of attribute values in entity-specific forms. This would have given the user a choice of 'views' — one based on the rule structure, the other based on the data structure. In LOD3, however, only one small example of this was implemented.

Some 'enabling' conditions were initially shown with *and...* underneath them — satisfying such a condition caused the the *and...* to 'unfold' showing all the 'enabled' substructure. This was used, for example, where the existence of an entity needed to be established before questions could sensibly be asked about it.

The use of enabling conditions substantially reduced the number of irrelevant conditions presented to the user. The right-hand side of the screen (Figure 7.3) was used for on-line legislation, procedures and guidance. The top of the right-hand side contained buttons giving access to the Act, the Regulations and the Adjudication Officer's Guide. These could be used at any time (whether a case is being handled or not) to 'open' the requested reference material on the screen. The body of the requested document, formatted as in its paper version, was displayed in a scrolling window in the upper two-thirds of the right half of the screen, and a window containing a contents list for the document occupied the lower third. The contents list was presented hierarchically, using indentation; the user could 'fold' or 'unfold' items in the contents list by clicking on icons next to them, and could cause the scrolling window holding the body of the document to jump to a desired item by clicking on the item's entry in the contents list.

Input fields on forms, and propositions in structured dialogue, could have relevant textual or case-related guidance directly linked to them — asking for guidance (using a dedicated function key) when such a field or proposition was selected would open the Adjudication Officer's Guide at the correct place, or, for case-related guidance, bring up a list of one-line descriptions of cases; pointing at any of these and clicking the mouse button would then bring up the full text relating to that case.

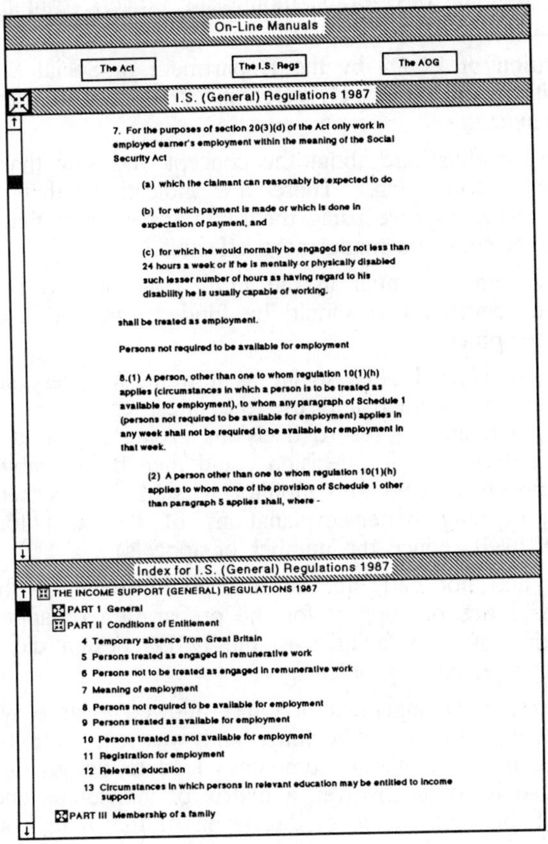

Figure 7.3

7.11. EVALUATION OF LOD3

The project had originally planned to carry out a study of the decision-making environment and the attitudes towards technology in DSS local offices. This would have provided a context and possibly a benchmark for evaluation of the eventual LO demonstrator. Unfortunately, the project was not able to achieve access to the local offices and so the proposed study had to be abandoned. At a later date, however, a number of adjudication officers were interviewed in six local offices around the country, and their reactions to the proposed developments were elicited and analysed. The most sustained and significant effort in evaluation was carried out with a variety of headquarters and monitoring staff, including policy, OCAO, regional directorate, monitoring officers, training personnel and central management staff.

An evaluation of LOD3 by the Department of Social Security itself took place in its model office at Preston in early 1989; the report on this evaluation concluded:

> Users were enthusiastic about the concept and saw that a valuable product was developing. There are indications that adjudication standards might improve using the LOD system and that monitoring arrangements could be made more effective.
>
> Users saw some potential in the LOD concept and recommended that further development should be funded and end users involved in this development.

From our point of view, LOD3, so far as it went, was very successful. It obliged the user to consider and use the latest conditions, to consider every relevant point, and to record decisions properly. Full details of the case, evidence and reasons for decision could then be available for future reference by appeals officers and monitoring staff. The system also had potential for producing better explanations of decisions for claimants (which might in itself reduce the number of appeals).

While we had not had time to incorporate most of the intended explanation capabilities or support for the preparation of appeals submissions, the addition of such facilities to the LOD3 design did not appear to present serious technical problems.

The hierarchical arrangement of topics allowed a large system to be developed without being overwhelming, and was easy for the user to navigate around. It did, however, sometimes lead to design difficulties, as much of the case handling involved a matrix of individuals and their circumstances, and the best choice of dimension of this matrix along which to separate topics seemed to vary between different parts of the system.

More work was needed on 'structured dialogue', as it did not yet support all the Toolkit rule constructs. More generally, whereas we had devoted much attention to maintainability and flexibility of the knowledge base, it was clear by the end of the project that any product based on the LOD design would need an HCI definition language in addition to the knowledge representation language, and tools would be needed to assist developers in building and maintaining the knowledge base and user interface in parallel.

One of the key issues with the interaction is the degree to which we succeeded in providing the user with sufficient flexibility to match their own skills and support needs. We were continually concerned about responding to the accusation that LOD would be useful for inexperienced AOs or in a training mode but would be too slow for experienced AOs. Unfortunately, the requirement never to slow down the experienced AO is actually incompatible with a desire for better quality in the decision making. AOs would only be able to make decisions more quickly without using LOD if they were not adequately documenting and recording their work, i.e. they were doing it more quickly because they were carrying out the whole process in their heads and not documenting their thoughts.

The time-consuming parts of LOD are not related to the system's response times or the time taken to find the right form to fill in or assertion to make. If it were either of these then we believe it could be improved on. Rather it is with the filling in of the information. This is surely then the point — not should they have a different system from LOD, because all of our work indicated that LOD would be quicker than other support designs, but rather should they be made to use a system at all when it would undoubtedly slow them down by virtue of having to record information.

In retrospect, we feel that the most significant aspect of LOD3 was the way in which it combined ease of control and transparency to the user with logical inference capabilities and the ability to retrieve relevant legislation and guidance. Most work on knowledge based decision support in legal applications is based either on information retrieval or on logical encoding of legislation or on procedural support based on *expert* knowledge. Each of these, taken on its own, has shortcomings, as described in the following sections.

7.11.1. Information retrieval

Systems based simply on information retrieval tend to be too passive — the user has to know that they have a problem, what type of problem it is and where to start looking for an answer before the system is any use. Such a system would not necessarily be useful in improving the quality of decision-making.

It could be useful when people were dealing with a type of case which they had not handled before. It would not help, however, with the cases where people thought they knew how to handle a case but were wrong (e.g. because the conditions had changed recently). In fact the process of central, electronic, updating of manuals, etc. would mean that the possibility of the decision makers noticing that a set of conditions had changed while they were updating their manual would be lost. There have been examples in other organizations where having access to supporting guidance led the decision maker to think that they knew how to handle the case when in fact they did not — they were looking at inappropriate guidance.

This type of system would arguably help skills to develop if it meant that more people read the guidance, but would not have the major benefits which we were looking for. It would do nothing in terms of explanations to claimants, supporting appeals (except in that appeals officers would be another, perhaps more frequent, class of user), or monitoring. It could help with flexibility in terms of distributing the guidance and conditions to the decision makers more quickly — but it would not make them read it.

7.11.2. Logical encoding of legislation

Systems based purely on logical encoding of the legislation reflect a misunderstanding of what adjudication is all about - it is not just about the correct application of legal rules. The model of support in such systems is based on guiding the decision maker through a pre-defined network of rules. The emphasis which DSS staff all put on it is much more concerned with the specific facts of a case, the weighing of evidence and the role of interpretation.

The model of support which follows has two main features. Firstly, it requires that the users should predominantly be able to interact with 'real world' descriptions, objects and attributes rather than 'legal' terms and categories. Secondly, the role of the encoded legislation should be based on constraining the decision maker to justify their decision by reference to the facts of the case and the applicability of particular rules to those facts — the relevant network of rules is selected by the decision maker to justify their conclusions.

7.11.3. Expert procedural support

This type of support would attempt to identify some general procedures, strategies or task knowledge which could be used to construct a system which identified the 'best' way of handling a particular case or topic within a case and guided the user through these procedures as though they were being led by an expert. The problems with this suggestion are firstly, whether it is possible to build and maintain a useful system of this type for supporting adjudication, and secondly, whether it would be appropriate to do so.

Constructing a system of this type presumes that there is, in fact, a generalizable approach to handling cases which, if applied, would be better than that used by AOs. While it might be possible to sit down with an AO and explain the best way of dealing with a particular case, it is doubtful whether it would be possible to define a general procedure for tackling all cases. This attitude is actually reflected in the Adjudication Officer's Guide (AOG). If it had been possible to identify some general solutions would OCAO not have incorporated them into the AOG? In fact, the style of the AOG is explicitly and intentionally counter to such an approach. Similarly, the emphasis during training of adjudication officers is away from procedural solutions and towards the development of an understanding of the legislation.

The argument for this is that legal rules, and decision making associated with their application, are designed to apply to the general case rather than specific cases, and therefore the key role of the interpreter/applier of the rules is to know which ones should be used for the particular and peculiar combination of facts and evidence in a specific case. There is no logical 'general solution' which should always be followed — the solution is determined by the specific facts of the case, not the general 'type' of case. If this were not the case then we could expect that the legislation itself would specify the greater detail necessary to avoid ambiguity and 'misinterpretation'. Now it can be argued that although there is no *a priori* logical process applicable to all cases, there can still be frequently occurring 'groups' of problem which have a generally applicable 'practical' strategy associated with them. This is dangerous ground. Even if there are practical strategies which apply in 80% of cases, (and this is doubtful) it is necessary to ensure that the 20% of exceptions are clearly identified and handled appropriately — and there is no evidence that this is possible. This, in fact, is one of the important ways in which 'KBS in law' are crucially different from those for other decision making environments. In other areas, an 'optimum applicability'/'majority of cases' approach may be perfectly acceptable — the exceptions are not significant enough to make a difference. In law, exceptions are crucial and individual cases are extremely important.

Even if we had dismissed these considerations as 'idealistic' in their approach to the law and its application, we would still have had to consider the complexity and scope of the required knowledge base. This expertise would have to be elicited, as it is not currently available. Would OCAO be able to justify this extra effort on their part — involving far more effort than is required to produce the AOG? Had we any evidence that they would be able to agree about what knowledge went in? Would they be prepared to have this knowledge published — which by law they are required to do? People at OCAO have been characterized as having an excessively purist attitude to deciding cases. Would their approach be acceptable to 'real' AOs? Even if it were, the number of rules required would substantial. Updating the knowledge base according to changes in regulations and case law would be extremely complex and time consuming. The implications would be that less, rather than more, flexibility would be introduced. Were such a system to be built, it would be unlikely to go down very well with the potential users. They were always extremely, and probably justifiably, worried about the system 'taking over' and removing their freedom of choice. The introduction of an 'expert's' view of how the case should be handled would not be well received. It is also not clear that it would actually improve the skills of the AO. The skills which are required are those of being able to apply the general rules to the particular case. Being given 'standard answers' is acknowledged as being a very poor way of learning general principles. The best model of learning in these cases is acknowledged to be that of letting the individual try to apply the general principles and then commenting constructively on their approach.

7.12. CONCLUSION

After a long, and at times painful, evolution, during which the system concept became excessively complex before being simplified again, we arrived at a design which had a 'clear' user interface, appropriate use of logical rules and inference, and context-sensitive guidance relating to the interpretation of legal conditions. The incorporation of expertise in the system had been examined, but had been found to be inappropriate.

The resulting system made no assumptions about the amount of data (other than a bare minimum) which needs to be input from the claim form before beginning work on the case. Earlier versions of the system involved the prior inputting of all the claim data, but this was seen to raise problems. Some of the problems were practical — such as how would the information be input, by whom, was it inefficient if all the data were not needed to process the case, how would our system interface to existing computer systems? LOD3 allows any subsequent implementation option to be pursued, including access of some data from existing computer systems, or input of certain information by less qualified staff prior to decisions being made by AOs. A separate set of problems concerned the question of the status of the data — a degree of interpretation of the form completed by the claimant may be involved when filling in computer fields. It might therefore be necessary, as LOD3 allows, to require particular decision makers to interpret and enter some of the data.

The system provides a clear structure, within which users may move through the case in whatever order they wish, possibly suspending work on one case while further evidence is gathered, or revising some of the earlier decisions and re-examining the associated issues. Summaries are provided at appropriate levels of each topic so that the user can see precisely which issues they are currently working on. While the user is free to follow his or her own path through the case, the system will not allow the completion of a topic until the minimum necessary information has been dealt with, and will continue to highlight the outstanding issues requiring decision. We believe that this type of interaction supports the independence of the AO and also accommodates the different skill levels which AOs may bring to their use of the system. An experienced AO who knows their way around the conditions and the system should be able to go directly to the critical conditions and deal with them in a minimal amount of time. Less experienced AOs, on the other hand, may take a less efficient path, but will, in the process, develop a better understanding of the legal conditions they are applying.

On-line guidance plays a major part throughout the interaction. The system makes the whole right-hand side of the screen available for guidance and source texts to aid the AO. The sources include the Act, Regulations and Adjudication Officer's Guide, each of which are indexed for rapid access and are presented in a form which most closely matches the original source material as possible. The user of the system may access any part of the source text during the interaction with the system. More importantly, when they are involved in a specific part of the interaction — either filling in a form or working through a particular set of conditions — they may call up guidance specifically relating to the relevant condition or field on the form. In some circumstances the guidance might need to appear automatically — for example as a means of warning the AO that the conditions relating to this type of case have recently been changed by a commissioners decision and that they should therefore consider the newly available guidance with which they may not be familiar.

7.13. ACKNOWLEDGEMENT

The project gave us a rare opportunity to address a wide variety of issues relating to legal decision support, with the help of people from a wide variety of backgrounds. We thank the Alvey Directorate and the collaborators for their support, and all the project members for the parts they played in the development of LOD3 and its precursors.

CHAPTER 8

THE POLICY SYSTEM

Graham Storrs

8.1. INTRODUCTION

8.1.1. The structure of this chapter

This chapter describes the work of the policy application team in developing a series of policy support system prototypes and a series of public demonstrations based on these prototypes. The policy application was intended to demonstrate the feasibility of knowledge based support for policy-makers in the Department of Health and Social Security (the DHSS, later to become the DSS). This chapter contains no general material about the Alvey DHSS Large Demonstrator project: it is concerned only with the policy application. An brief introduction to the application area will be presented in order to provide an orientation to the problems and issues involved, although a fuller discussion can be found in Chapters 4 and 14. We present a brief history of the application in terms of the objectives of the policy application, the structure of the policy application Team and a chronology of significant events. This material is to provide both an orientation to the rest of the chapter and a framework of goals and objectives within which to understand the motivations for the various outputs generated by the policy application team. This is followed by a description of the four prototypes built during the project. The substance of the chapter is in the sections which describe the methods used to produce and evaluate the various prototype demonstrators and their associated knowledge bases and the evaluation

KNOWLEDGE-BASED SYSTEMS AND
LEGAL APPLICATIONS. ISBN 0-12-086441-X

studies that were performed. Lastly, there is a section describing additional experimental work, most of which was conducted in the last few months of the project and which serves to indicate some of the possible directions in which the work could be developed.

8.1.2. The nature of the policy application

The nature of policy-making within the DSS has been described in detail in Chapter 4. An important point to note here is that the policy workers at no time make a decision about policy, they simply make recommendations to the minister. It is the minister who must make decisions. The art of policy-making lies in the ability to understand the problems and the issues, to discover all of the options for action, to evaluate them on a wide range of criteria including political, ethical and practical, and then to present cogent arguments for and against each option. It is these tasks which a policy system must support.

In the early prototypes, P0 and P1, a six-stage model of the policy process was used. Although it proved to be an over-simplification, and required extension along the lines described elsewhere, it provided greater motivation for the knowledge based aspects of the policy prototypes, and helped to clarify the technical requirements to underpin a system to support certain aspects of the policy process. Briefly, in this model we identified the following six stages in the activity:

1. Verify that a problem exists.
2. Arrive at a precise characterization of the problem.
3. [Optionally] modify theories.
4. Generate candidate solutions.
5. Explore the consequences of the solutions.
6. Specify solution for legal draftsman.

All of these stages gave clear guidelines as to the kind of KBS support that could be provided for them. A full discussion can be found in [Bench-Capon 1987]. It proved, however, to be an over-constraining view of the process as a whole, imposing too much structure and not taking sufficient account of features such as the construction of arguments, which is the vehicle by which a policy issue is progressed. The two later prototypes therefore took on board this more exploratory conception of policy, as described in Chapters 4 and 14, while attempting integration with the more specific operations supported by the early prototypes.

8.2. THE HISTORY OF THE POLICY APPLICATION

8.2.1. The phases of the project

The Alvey-DHSS Large Demonstrator project can be thought of as having two major phases of approximately equal length. The first, from the project's inception in 1984 until about October 1986, is a period of exploration and analysis, marked by the existence of many small teams developing many, small prototypes. Much of what these teams were doing was developing an understanding of the application areas and testing the feasibility of techniques and approaches. There was also a certain amount of work on infrastructure and general-purpose software. At a social level, there was energy spent on team-building and learning to work in a large and widespread collaboration. For very many individuals there was a great deal of learning to be done, not only about the application areas but also about the tools and techniques that would be used on the project. At this time, the application teams, including policy, were each relatively self-contained and did all of the analysis, design and implementation within their areas.

In October 1986, a mid-term revie" of the project was completed and its results published. In brief, they were:

1. To reorganise the project into three 'applications' (previously there had been five).
2. To create a more formal split between analysis, design and implementation.
3. To use the Local Office application as the vehicle for demonstrating both the 'engineered and measured approach' and the construction of a 'large' knowledge base.

8.2.2. The policy application up to July 1987

The objectives of the application

As well as the overall project objectives, which are listed elsewhere (Chapter 2), the Policy Application was initially intended to produce (in the words of the proposal):

1. Policy database covering the principles, intent, explanation, justification and amendment of policy.
2. Advanced quantitative model to examine the financial and organisational implications of policy changes.

The sequence of events

A project workshop in summer 1984 was the real beginning for the policy team. At that meeting, the planning was done for the first six months of the project which included the initial analysis of the policy function. There followed a series of interviews which led to the production of a data flow diagram of the policy process and the six-stage model of policy decision making outlined above. A further useful outcome of this analysis was a hierarchy of policy concepts, intended to show the relationship between the terms used in the legislation, with those used in the formulation of policy goals, and the those used in making the legislative terms operational. The first six months of the policy application should be thought of as a probationary period as it was in this time that the feasibility of policy as an application area was assessed and the decision taken to pursue it further. The technical explorations of inference mechanisms appropriate to the support of policy making proceeded in parallel with this activity, as did the exploration of particular policy problems to do with poverty traps for widows and invalids. After the winter project workshop of 1984/85 there was a simulation of the widows' and invalidity traps and a constraint model for consistency checking/evaluation of effects of changes. The feasibility prototype (P0), based on this simulation, was demonstrated at the project workshop in summer 1985 and the feasibility study for the planning component was also completed by then. The addition of planning facilities to P0 was completed by October 1985. There followed a period of concentration on the interface to the functionality of P0 and a new prototype, P1, emerged in late 1986 followed by a much improved version (P1v2) ready for demonstration in summer, 1987.

8.2.3. The effects of the mid-term review

The policy application was, in the long-run, not so much affected by the mid-term review as other applications. It had been, until that time, a coherent and technically successful group and was widely considered to be one of the most interesting and challenging areas in the project. It had also been fortunate in having within it several of the project's most experienced and technically competent members. What is more, the difficulties of the period up to the production of P1 all came after the mid-term review. It survived the review, therefore, very little changed in terms of its scope and objectives. However, the constitution of the policy application Team did change considerably between October 1986 and July 1987. This period also found the team without any effective management and represents a period in which very little progress was made. The later (July 1987) reorganization of the project teams rectified this but the mid-term review can be though of as causing a long and wasteful hiatus in the progress of the policy application.

8.2.4. The policy application after July 1987

The objectives of the application

After the mid-term review, the objectives of the policy application remained unchanged. As the local office application was to be given the highest priority of the three and was to become the focus for work on large knowledge bases, the requirement for the policy application to produce a large knowledge base or even a complete demonstrator was removed. Instead, it was felt that the policy application could take more risks and be more experimental in its approach to providing support. Nevertheless, the policy application team were still required to produce a convincing demonstration of the feasibility of knowledge-based support for DSS policy makers. The new policy application team was headed by Graham Storrs, who had joined the team in October, 1985. However, Andrew Taylor who had run the team since the beginning of the project left after the reorganisation as did Justin Forder who had been a prominent member of the team until that point. Trevor Bench-Capon, another of the team's most prominent members, had a reduced involvement from about this time onwards after he took a lecturing appointment at Liverpool University. He did, however, continue to make a significant and important contribution.

The sequence of events

From its inception, the post-July 1987 policy application team had three main strands of activity: specifying and overseeing the production of the P1 (version 2) demonstrator, developing the requirements and designing P2, and developing the requirements and the design for P3. The P1v2 specification was produced in September 1987 and was built and was demonstrable by the end of the year. It was available for demonstration at the project workshop in February 1988. The P2 functional specification was produced in January 1988 and had its first public demonstration in October 1988. The system had been ready for public demonstration in July 1988 when it was reviewed by a DHSS policy maker. The P3 functional specification was produced in July 1988. P3 had its first public demonstration at the end-of-project demonstrations in April 1989. However, an earlier version had been previewed by the DSS in March 1989.

8.3. DESCRIPTION OF THE PROTOTYPES

In all, four demonstrators were produced:

P0 (Also known as the feasibility prototype.) This demonstrated the feasibility of using a logical model of the legislation to answer queries in order to identify policy problems. It allowed the specification of a class of people in whom the policy maker was interested and the use of the model to explore the effects of proposed changes to the legislation. In a later version, a knowledge-based planning component was added to guide the policy maker in deciding on possible corrective changes to the legislation in order to meet specified policy goals. P0 worked effectively but had a user interface that proved difficult for policy makers to understand.

P1 This had essentially the same functionality as P0 (without the planner) but had a considerably more sophisticated user interface. The interface was based on a model of the policy task and included notions such as policy folders and specialized stationery. It also introduced the notion of public world and private world versions of the legislation, corresponding to the actual legislation and a policy worker's private workings. Any number of private worlds could exist so that several policy options could be explored within the same policy problem. Queries were put to the system through forms and expression editors. These and the rule and attribute editors were used by selecting appropriate components from menus. The results of queries were in a formalized English. This prototype was improved in a further version, P1v2.

P2 This was a radical departure from the earlier prototypes and demonstrated support for the 'structuring' of policy problems (in a style similar to that used in 'outliners' or 'ideas processors') and the editing of detailed policy argumentation in a specially developed graphical representation. P2 attempted to show how the policy maker could be supported throughout the whole process of policy formulation and was strongly oriented to the Department's working procedures. Problem structuring gave rise to a set of subproblems. Each of these provided the context for detailed argumentation about policy options. This argumentation could be commented on and developed by other policy workers and then reviewed and evaluated by the originating policy maker. A set of selected policy options could then be grouped and reorganized into a coherent set of recommendations in a process we called rationalisation. P2 was widely demonstrated and was evaluated by the Department. In all cases it was well received.

P3 This system attempted to combine the knowledge based P1 functionality and the P2 functionality into a complete demonstration of the kind of support system that was possible for policy-makers. From all stages in the policy formulation process (problem structuring, detailed argumentation, etc.) the policy worker had access to the logical model of the legislation for the posing of queries or the 'what if?' exploration of potential changes. The policy maker could also retrieve stored arguments, examine legislation and other text and word-process his or her comments and recommendations. The argumentation formalism had been enhanced to allow meta-argumentation and the inference mechanism had been improved so that investigations involving several types of individual could, in theory, be undertaken at the same time. A number of improvements to the user interface were also made in response to the P2 evaluation. Unfortunately, a major feature of P3 — the direct use of the argument form as an interface to the logical model for query input and output — was not implemented in time for the end of the project. Several other P3 features also remain specified but unimplemented.

8.4. METHODS

8.4.1. Producing advanced decision support software

The project was begun at a time when the development of knowledge based systems was still very much a black art. That is, there were no widely accepted techniques for producing such systems in an engineered and measured way. This was, of course, doubly true of large knowledge based systems. Similarly, during the early part of the project, there were no methodologies for the analysis and production of highly interactive systems. At the time of writing, we can see such methods beginning to emerge but they are still at very early stages and none can be considered mature. As a result, we were forced to use what we considered best practice and to adopt and modify existing software engineering techniques. We opted very early for a prototyping approach and, in the first half of the project, aimed for producing a new prototype every six months after the initial analysis. In broad terms, P0 and P1 prototyped the knowledge representation and inference mechanisms, P2 prototyped argumentation support and P3 prototyped the integration of logic and argumentation. The project developed some guidelines on managing a prototyping development. These, essentially, treated each prototype as a small-scale software development in its own right with requirements and various levels of design documentation followed by implementation, testing and evaluation. In fact, this is exactly how the policy application has proceeded.

8.4.2. Analysis methods and the specification of requirements

The early analysis of the policy function was done in a manner derived from soft systems methodology. There was also considerable effort expended in producing a data flow diagram. This work was nearly all prior to the production of P0. After the mid-term review, analysis and the production of requirements specifications became the responsibility of the customer requirements team (also called the analysis team) and requirements specifications were to be delivered to the policy application team which would then produce a design specification for delivery to the implementation team. There was, after P0, a series of interviews with fairly senior policy makers and some detailed analysis of the contents of some policy files. The requirements specifications which emerged from these analyses used no formal or semi-formal notations and relied heavily on examples to illustrate the requirements. After the P2 requirements specification, no further requirements were produced for policy.

8.4.3. Design methods and the specification of designs

The policy application team did not use any proprietary design methods. The object-oriented nature of the programming environment and the toolkit leant itself naturally to a model-view-controller style of expressing the design and we found that entity-relationship diagrams were a useful notation for the model. Interface and interaction styles were specified by using the Apple Macintosh interface as a style guide but the constraints of the screen management tools in our development environment led us somewhat away from this in the actual implementation. Screen layouts were drawn in the specification as guidance only. For the most part, the design was done without following a method and was written in English rather than a formal or semi-formal notation.

8.4.4. Software development methods

The software for the policy prototypes was written in Loops and Lisp in the Xerox, InterLisp-D programming environment. Coding has always been from designs which were deliberately vague with the intention of leaving many of the low-level design decisions to the programmer. We called this technique Exploratory Programming. In practice, the programmers and members of the policy application team communicated frequently during the implementation period to review the emerging system, to clarify design concepts and, occasionally, to make design changes in the light of implementation considerations. Any major design changes were documented as amendments to the design specification.

8.4.5. Evaluation methods

The evaluation of the policy prototypes has been rather limited. There have always been two members of the policy application team who came from a policy background. Their input to the design and to the knowledge base building and their on-going critiques of the prototypes has provided continuous formative evaluation which has been very healthy for the application. On the other hand, there had been no evaluation of any of the prototypes (except for P2) before the end of the project. In a nine-month extension to the project, the P3 prototype was evaluated by the DSS and Lancaster University. The other prototypes have been publicly and internally demonstrated and such feedback as has arisen from this has been gleaned but its value has been rather small. For P2, a system was installed in a policy maker's office for several weeks. The policy maker, with the assistance of a team member, shadowed his own policy formulation work using P2 to get a feel for how the system might work in practice. The results of this were published within the DSS and were extremely positive in terms of the system's support for the policy maker's task and even for its usability. However, the results are still only one policy worker's opinions, one who was specially selected for his computer literacy and his favourable attitude to the project and its aims. The evaluation of P3 followed a similar pattern but problems with finding willing volunteers and live policy problems led to the end-result being rather vague and uncertain.

8.4.6. Knowledge base building

The knowledge bases for the policy application were never intended to be complete or necessarily a correct representation of the current legislation. The requirement was always to produce a knowledge base that would demonstrate the capabilities of the prototype. A variety of sources have been used throughout the duration of the project which have required a variety of methods. The content of the knowledge bases has not been sufficiently important to justify developing an underlying methodology which might have ensured accuracy.

Acquisition, analysis and encoding

The process of building a knowledge base can be thought of as having three stages. The first, acquisition, is where the raw data are is gathered by the knowledge engineer from whatever are the appropriate sources. The next step, analysis, is where the knowledge engineer takes the material that has been gathered and derives from it the structure and content of the knowledge base. This is expressed in the form of some kind of intermediate knowledge representation formalism. Lastly, in encoding, the knowledge engineer must enter the analysed knowledge into the target system in an appropriate formal notation.

Acquisition and analysis

The primary sources for policy knowledge bases have been the relevant Acts and Regulations although for P0 the Child Poverty Action Group handbook was also used. Normally, a distinction may usefully be drawn between domain and task knowledge. In the case of the policy system, the task knowledge is expressed as the policy system software and the explicit knowledge is purely domain knowledge. A major part of the analysis effort for the policy application team was in discovering just what was the task knowledge needed for policy making. The knowledge-base builders had a much simpler time in that the policy domain knowledge represented the legislation and did so in terms which are domain terms rather than real-world terms. Some small amount of real-world knowledge, assumed but not explicit in the legislation, needed to be included: (for example that male persons could not become pregnant), but this did not require a great deal of analysis. In general, the policy knowledge bases were so small that they could be verified and validated by inspection by the knowledge base builders and DSS experts. Further testing was performed by executing the logical model to see that the desired inferences were drawn.

Encoding

The rule or constraint languages devised for representing legislation in the policy systems were designed to be used by DSS policy makers and were supported by point-and-pick style editors to provide error-free and well-cued input. Consequently, the easiest way to enter a knowledge base into the policy systems was through the policy systems themselves. Unfortunately, none of the systems was sufficiently well-developed in time to make this possible and we had to use other tools (TEdit and KBB) to build the knowledge bases.

Comments on our knowledge base building experiences

There are two striking facts about the knowledge bases used in the policy demonstrations. One is that none of them was very large: in fact, all of them were small. The other is that they were built from scratch for each demonstration, there was no re-use, either of earlier knowledge bases or of knowledge bases produced elsewhere on the project. The two are, of course related. One reason why there was no re-use of earlier policy knowledge bases was the wholesale change in legislation consequent on the change from supplementary benefit to income support which took place during the life of the project. The P0 demonstration was oriented around a supplementary benefit problem while P2 and P3 were concerned with income support. An attempt was made to rewrite the P0 knowledge base as an income support one for re-use in P3 but this proved too difficult to manage and the attempt was eventually abandoned. Re-using knowledge bases from elsewhere in the project was also not possible. In claimant information, of course, there was no knowledge base built until the end of the project. In LOD and its precursors there was, again, the problem of the change to income support. There was also the much more serious problem that the LOD requirement for the structure and content of a knowledge base was very different from that of policy. The domains chosen for demonstrations differed. There were also differences in the uses that rules were put to in the two systems which meant that they were written differently, with different requirements for readability and function. Lastly, and related to this last point, the policy rules were written to be used as constraints while the local office rules were to be used as productions rather than as constraints.

The smallness of the policy knowledge bases is partly due to the fact that we did not manage to re-use and build on earlier knowledge bases in constructing later ones. It is also partly due to performance problems with the policy prototypes. The speed with which inferences are made in all of the prototypes means that large and complex knowledge bases would give unacceptably slow performance for the purposes of demonstrating them. Thus, for P1, we built a toy knowledge base of only a dozen or so rules. P0 with its purpose-built inference mechanism performed adequately with a knowledge-base of about 120 rules and P3, using the project's toolkit, was demonstrated with about 70 rules (each policy rule is roughly equivalent to five or six Horn clauses). It was also necessary, again so as to make the demonstrations comprehensible, to keep knowledge bases small in order to reduce the amount of material that is returned as a result of using the queries. In P1 and P3 we tried to ensure that no response contained more than 10 or 15 propositions. The pressures to keep knowledge bases small and the lack of a requirement to build a large knowledge base meant that the policy application did not feel it needed to use the knowledge base building methods employed by the local office team. Knowledge base building for policy tended to be by one or two people working intensely over a fairly short period (two to four weeks). This proved satisfactory for P0 and P1 but for P3 caused some problems. The knowledge base builders for P0 and P1 were experienced people with an understanding of the logical formalisms, the legislation and of conceptual modelling, The builders of the P3 knowledge base were relatively new to the project and had no previous experience in knowledge base building, legislation or logic. It may have been beneficial to have supported such inexperienced people with methods and tools similar to those used by the local office team even for building such a small knowledge base. However, it is more likely that training in conceptual modelling, logic and knowledge encoding would have been more advantageous.

8.5. ADDITIONAL EXPERIMENTAL DEVELOPMENTS

8.5.1. The reason for experimental work

It is clear that P3 is still a long way from providing the range and level of support for policy making that we can envisage. Throughout the project we deliberately kept the range of support at which we looked as narrow as we reasonably could. In particular, we excluded work on networking, access to external databases, statistical processing, numerical modelling and knowledge-base capture and maintenance. Instead, we concentrated on understanding the process of policy-making and on making the support that we do offer as deep as we can. Nevertheless, we still did not achieve all that we had hoped for even in this narrower range. To supplement the work on analysing, designing and building the prototypes, therefore, we undertook a small amount of speculative or experimental work where we thought there might be a chance of illustrating how we might enhance the capabilities of the final demonstrator.

8.5.2. The English expression of the knowledge base

In the P3 specification a desire was expressed to achieve anglicized output from the logical model. This desire was motivated by a need for readability, as the outputs as they stood were in the form of symbolic logic, and thus were relatively indigestible. Thus in July 1988 research began at Liverpool University to achieve anglicized output from the knowledge base. The program had three distinct phases, two of which have been completed. Phase one had the aim of taking a single triple and expressing that triple in an anglicized form, i.e. a sentence of English text. Thus in phase one there was to be a simple, one proposition to one sentence correspondence. Phase two took that work and expanded it, treating more than one proposition at a time but maintaining the one sentence to one triple correspondence so as to introduce cohesive ties in the output of related triples. The hope was to achieve more natural-looking text by the use of cohesive items such as pronouns. Phase three was to break up the one sentence to one triple correspondence, and express more than one triple in any one sentence, using logical connectives and argument forms to produce coherent and readable output text. The first phase studied the knowledge base and specified the subgrammar of English used to compose the knowledge base. In doing this, the output grammar for the system was also specified. Thus the problem of adequate coverage by the system was overcome by making the system address what it was required to cover in terms of grammar and cover that alone. The system has been rendered portable across applications, however, by the use of knowledge based tools to support the output grammar. These tools, such as a morphological analyser and production unit for verbs, are knowledge based and non-application specific. Hence, while the grammar is a limiting factor, the system as a whole is relatively portable between applications, as only the grammar, about 1% of the system as a whole, is application specific. While the results of this phase are perhaps no different from what could be achieved by associating pieces of canned text with triples, such a method would not have allowed extension into phases two and three. Phase two achieved a knowledge based categorization of English pronouns. This analysis looks for the semantic features of any given noun in context and then pattern matches the nouns semantic attributes against those of any given pronoun until a match is found. The system covers all standard English pronouns, looking at structural items such as case as well as semantic features such as sex marking and plural referents. Phase three used the Toulmin argument formalism to structure arguments into coherent paragraphs of text, as described in [Bench-Capon 1990].

8.5.3. Constraints and policy goals

This work is an application and to some extent an extension of the work of Sadri and Kowalski on integrity constraints in deductive databases. The benefit system has been designed to achieve many aims. These aims are liable to change over time and with successive governments. To give an example, a policy goal might be: if claimant earns more than a certain amount of money then he/she should not receive any non- contributory benefits. Provided that these aims or goals can be expressed in a logical formalism they can be treated as integrity constraints on the system as a whole. Updates to the knowledge base can be checked to ensure that they are not inconsistent with these policy goals. This provides a machine assessment of the acceptability of an amendment to the knowledge base. For further information on the work see [Kowalski *et al.* 1987].

8.5.4. Support for knowledge base revision

This work arose out of the work on the policy planner done for the feasibility prototype. An important task done by policy officers is to develop alternative solutions to problems that have been identified. Prototype 3 provides no support for this task. Work was started on a tool to aid the policy officers in the task of finding edits that would achieve the stated goal. This used the structure within the rules to generate a tree of possible solutions. No attempt is made to assess the suitability of these solutions since this is the function of the existing parts of the prototypes. The scenario for the use of this system is that once the problem has been clearly identified and can be expressed as a logical goal the system would in association with the user generate a set of possible solutions. The user would then create an environment with each of the more reasonable solutions. The effects of these changes could then be experimented with to ensure that other policy goals were not invalidated.

8.5.5. Extensions to the argumentation formalism

Work was planned for the final six months of the project to look into extensions of the argumentation form so as to better support the construction of macro-arguments and meta-arguments. It was also expected that some progress could be made on turning arguments in the form into readable English text. The prolonged illness of the researcher who was to have done this meant that the work could not be pursued. However, a subsequent research project led by Logica and partially supported by the UK Department of Trade and Industry, is looking at the use of argumentation in the design of safety critical software and will be looking at extensions to the argumentation form developed in the Alvey-DHSS Demonstrator.

8.6. THE FUTURE FOR DSS POLICY FORMULATION SUPPORT

The prototypes developed in the course of this project have, we believe, quite convincingly demonstrated the feasibility of providing this kind of advanced decision support for DSS policy makers. Nevertheless, there are many more aspects to the support that could be offered that are not apparent in P3 but which we have given some, and sometimes considerable, thought to. In this final section we consider some of these before presenting our view of what an installed DSS policy formulation support system might look like.

8.6.1. What to do with P3

Firstly, there are several sections of the functionality of P3 which were specified but which were not implemented due to lack of programming resource. It would be possible to do further development to P3 to add the facility to use arguments in our argument format as queries to the logical model of the legislation. This would leave it still incomplete. To finish P3, the missing two stages of the policy process, evaluation and rationalization, would need to be added. There are also several more query types that should be implemented (such as compare, and statistics). The rule base revision tool specified for P3 could then be added to complete the specified functionality.

8.6.2. P4

Beyond the additions mentioned above, which would be necessary to finish P3, there are several extra facilities that could be included that go considerably beyond the P3 specification. We might think of a system with these additional features as P4. We can think of the extra features of P4 as being either developments to the P3 functionality or additions to P3. In the "developments" category we might have:

1. *Improvements to the argument form.* At present this allows the construction of networks (chains) of micro-arguments. Chains as well as micro-arguments are labelled and can be used in other arguments thus permitting a degree of meta-argumentation. There is no support for the construction of higher-level (macro) arguments, there is no use of qualifiers in micro-arguments and there is no typing of micro-arguments. All of these things are possible and it is possible to conceive of a support system making good use of such features.
2. *More support for evaluation.* In the present design, the evaluation stage is by far the most poorly supported. It is possible to add a higher degree of automation if we have a more developed argument form. Arguments of certain types (arguments from authority, say) could be ranked as of inherently lower validity than others (logical arguments, for instance). Argument qualifiers could form the basis of a ranking. The attaching of cost and benefit weightings could also

support automatic evaluation, and so on.

3. *Support for solution generation.* The planner in P0 and the rule base revision tool specified for P3 are both attempts to provide support for the policy-maker to select optimal changes to the legislation so as to effect a policy option. Neither is an ideal solution: the planner because it relies heavily on heuristic knowledge that is inherently hard to maintain and the rule base revision tool, despite its generality, because its functionality is limited and probably quite difficult for a policy maker to use. A more generalized approach along the lines of the planner supported by guidance from the user might give a sufficiently powerful form of support.
4. *Interaction with the logical model in English.* The project has done some work on the expression of the knowledge base and of results from queries in a restricted English. For this side of the system to be more acceptable and useful to policy makers, more effort is required to enable English input and output when querying and editing the legislation model. To do this properly is beyond the state of the art but it is likely that a great deal can be achieved to make interacting with the system's logic formalism more painless for the user.
5. *Improved support for problem structuring.* P2 and P3 allow only strictly hierarchical decomposition of problems. This may be a useful discipline for the production of a final problem structure (in fact, this is one of the intuitions which motivated the design of KANT) but there are probably earlier stages in problem structure development where a looser format and more freedom to experiment with structures can be useful. There are also organizational and administrative functions which might usefully be included at this stage (e.g. circulation lists, access privileges to subproblems, etc.).

As well as these developments from the P3 'baseline' there are also a number of areas in which P3 offers no support whatsoever but where we know that support would be required in an operational system. In particular, we might single out:

1. *The storage and retrieval of arguments.* Policy-makers would find this facility extremely valuable and it could lead to a considerable cost advantage. A putative P4 would need to address the issues involved in the management of large volumes of stored argumentation some of which will contain text, some logic and some a mixture. There will be some of this material which will need to be maintained with its links to the current legislation, past legislation and the past and present versions of the knowledge base. Links to a variety of other textual material (such as reports, commissioners' decisions, etc.) will also need to be maintained.
2. *The process of commitment and maintenance of the knowledge base.*

In the present scenario, after the development of the policy argumentation, a recommendation would go to the minister and a decision would be made. The policy arguments and the associated knowledge base changes would be passed to solicitors for drafting as new legislation and would eventually become law. There is a set of procedures associated with this which need to be explicated and incorporated in the support offered. The issue is that once the workings of the policy branch becomes law, the public-world knowledge base must be updated to reflect the changes and any associated argumentation must be updated too. The new legislation text would also need to be added to the system and all three elements linked together appropriately (with any text and knowledge associated with the newly stored argumentation also being preserved for retrieval).

3. *Access to statistical and other databases.* A major resource for the policy maker is the data kept and maintained by government statisticians. However, policy makers often find this material difficult to access because of the problems associated with formulating a sensible query. A translation must be achieved between the needs of the policy maker for information on particular groups he or she is interested in and the actual data that are held in the databases. Often it is the case that surveys like the family income survey and the censuses simply do not have the right information in them to satisfy a particular query. However, it is not always straightforward to determine this as it relies on an understanding of the definitions of terms used by the policy maker and in the survey data, an understanding of the nature of the data (e.g. the sampling characteristics, the nature of any analyses done) and an appreciation of how the data are to be used. A subsystem of a policy support system which not only gave access to statistical databases or to statisticians but also helped the policy maker to formulate a query that matched his or her requirements to the type and quality of information available could be of enormous benefit.

4. *Facilities to support numerical modelling.* Problems concerning the costs of policy options can be incredibly complex and may involve dozens of interacting parameters. There is a great deal of work in academia and in government on large numerical models of the social security system. Direct, electronic access to such models for the purposes of evaluating options could be beneficial. Perhaps more useful would be the more rough and ready type of modelling that could be achieved by building crude numerical modelling capabilities into P4 and adding the appropriate information (perhaps gleaned from the statistical database interface) into the knowledge base. A little work on such a facility was done during the life of the project but was left incomplete when the researcher responsible

for it left because of sickness. It is an area that needs to be picked up again.

5. *Facilities for networking and group working.* The present scenario involves a whole group of policy workers working on any particular policy problem and the P2 demonstration, sketches the kind of support that we have imagined for this. However, we have not built facilities to support networked policy makers nor have we considered in detail the group dynamics of policy making in such an environment. We have not even explored the configuration management and access issues that such group working would raise.
6. *The proper integration of a policy support system with a largely paper-based organisation and legal system.* A thorough analysis would need to be undertaken to establish the exact boundaries of the P4 system and its interfaces with the rest of the organization and the rest of the world. It is on such seemingly trivial problems as the interface between a paper-based system and an electronic one that such schemes founder.
7. *There are the office automation aspects of an installable policy system.* What we mean here is the ability of the system to cope with the parts of a policy maker's job which are not on the main path of the policy function we wish to support. Tools such as word-processors, spreadsheets, databases, electronic mail, diagram editors and project management tools should all fit seamlessly with P4. Ideally they should all integrate with it, at least at the level of sharing data.

8.6.3. A vision of the future

One could envisage, in, say, five to ten years, after a period of further development to achieve the functionality outlined above, a situation where the whole of the DSS policy function is computerized and that a support system like P4 is in routine use. Each policy branch would be using powerful networked desktop computers. The system would support fully integrated office automation software which, in its turn, would be integrated with the policy support software. OCAO (perhaps) would be the repository of the legislation, argumentation and knowledge databases but each policy worker (and branch) would have his or her own local store of private workings and problems in hand. There would be facilities on the network for putting text materials into the databases and memoranda and reports would normally pass around in and out of the branches by electronic mail. Also on the network would be facilities for turning policy workings into printed form for the production of questionnaires, submissions, letters and so on. The system would have an integrated administrative support function to help schedule work, to manage the distribution and collection of policy work among the group and to filter and prioritize electronic mail. Each policy worker would have direct access to statistics and policy argument databases and could browse, on-screen, any of the acts and regulations, commissioners' decisions, case law and reports that he or she chose to. The system would have links out to statistics branch, treasury, regional directorate, office of the chief adjudication officer, solicitors branch, operations research branch, and perhaps elsewhere: pressure groups, other departments or agencies, perhaps even to the minister.

ACKNOWLEDGEMENTS

An earlier version of this paper was prepared for the DHSS Demonstrator Final Report. The author would like to thank Trevor Bench-Capon and Tony McEnery for their contributions to that version, some parts of which have survived into this one.

CHAPTER 9

THE CLAIMANT ADVICE SYSTEMS

Nigel Gilbert

There are two claimant information systems: the Advice System and the Forms Helper. Both systems aim to show how current IKBS and HCI technology could be used by large legislation-based organizations to assist in their interaction with the general public [Crossfield and Gilbert 1986]. The purpose of the Forms Helper is to help people fill in complex application forms. It has been designed to minimize the problems which many applicants experience in filling in conventional paper forms, thus reducing the likelihood of errors in the completed form. This benefits the organization in terms of increased customer satisfaction and reduced resources devoted to locating and correcting errors, as well as having obvious benefits for the form-filler. The Advice System aims to provide information to claimants and potential claimants about their eligibility for welfare benefits, the procedures they should use to make claims, and the social security system itself. It thus functions as an expert system, although unlike most conventional expert systems it is designed for untrained users. The Advice System demonstrates how IKBS can be used to provide a flexible and helpful information service to the general public on issues that are intrinsically complex, such as social security [Gilbert 1985a, 1985b].

KNOWLEDGE-BASED SYSTEMS AND
LEGAL APPLICATIONS. ISBN 0-12-086441-X

9.1. COMMON THEMES

9.1.1. Development methods

Rapid prototyping

The proposal for the project envisaged that development of demonstrators would proceed by means of 'rapid prototyping'. However, in 1984 this idea was ill-defined and there was little other than anecdote to indicate what constituted development by rapid prototyping. We therefore spent some time at the beginning of the project trying small-scale experiments and debating the merits of what we were doing. For the purpose of experimentation, we took rapid prototyping to be a development method which dispensed with formal design methods, designing by building and trying out alternative solutions, specifying by means of a 'prototype' rather than by written documentation, and using highly interactive programming tools.

It quickly became clear that 'rapid' is an imprecise and relative term. Some thought a cycle of design, implemention and evaluation over the course of a year was 'rapid'; others expected a cycle to be completed in a week. Our experience showed that there were major disadvantages associated with rapid prototyping:

1. One motive for rapid prototyping was that it allegedly allowed the designer to explore the design space quickly and thus select the best from a range of possible designs. In fact, although we were using probably the best prototyping software environment then available (InterLisp-D), construction of a single prototype to the point where it could be evaluated took months of work. This meant that major design decisions were made by default — the first design to be prototyped became the only one to be examined and therefore the one to be adopted.
2. It is impossible to design and build prototypes of very large and complex systems rapidly, because they are so large. The only practical method is to decompose the large system into much smaller modules and build prototypes of these. However, if a large number of modules are undergoing rapid evolution, the tasks of defining and maintaining common interfaces, of integration, and of promoting a common design 'philosophy' throughout becomes very difficult.

While we became sceptical about the value of 'rapid prototyping' itself, the alternative against which it has often been counterposed — design through the use of formal methods -- was also not seen as ideal. We were building systems whose precise functionality could not easily be predicted in advance. In addition, current methods for the formal specification of interfaces and, in particular, for human-computer interaction, were rudimentary and largely untried.

Combining rapid prototyping and specification

Over the course of the project we evolved a development method which seemed to avoid the worst disadvantages of both rapid prototyping and formal specification. Briefly, the development cycle consisted of the following stages:

1. Preparation of a requirements specification. The specification is based on exploratory research with potential users.
2. Construction of an initial prototype. The prototype embodies the designers' first ideas about how the requirements might be satisfied. It may be accompanied by experimental subsystems which present alternative solutions to some aspects of the requirement. No attempt is made at this stage to make the prototype robust or efficient.
3. Evaluation of the prototype in the light of the requirements specification. This may result in the requirements being revised or made more precise. In addition, some limited evaluation of the prototype may be carried out with users (although the opportunities for evaluation at this stage are restricted because the prototype is not sufficiently robust for user trials).
4. Experimentation with other approaches to improve the prototype in areas where it seems to be lacking.
5. Preparation of a functional specification. This specification abstracts a functional description of the final system from the prototype and the subsequent experiments.
6. Implementation of the system from the functional specification. This implementation is built paying attention to issues such as robustness, conformance to the functional specification and efficiency.
7. Evaluation of the implementation with users.

This cycle was followed for the development of both the Forms Helper and the Advice System.

9.1.2. Human-computer interaction

Because users of the Advice System and the Forms Helper needed to be able to perform tasks successfully with these systems without an opportunity for prior training and, for some users, without any prior exposure to computers, the HCI aspects of the design were recognized to be very important. Our recognition of the importance of the interface and interaction design for the success of the systems had several consequences:

1. Most of the early design work for the systems focused on the interface between user and computer. This contrasted with the focus of attention in, for example, the Local Office Demonstrator, which centred on problems of representing regulations.
2. It quickly became clear that much of the conventional HCI

literature, which dealt with issues like the design of character-based screens, the improvement of command languages and the construction of user-interface management systems, was almost entirely irrelevant to our interest in providing an easy to use system on large, high resolution screens to untrained users.

3. Instead, we came to believe that the design of the *interaction* (i.e. the flow of 'dialogue', however represented) was at least as important as the design of the *interface* (i.e. what the screen looked like), provided that some obvious guidelines about size of font and so forth were respected.
4. As a result of designing the systems 'from the user inwards', rather than from the desired functionality 'outwards', we developed views about how the systems' inferences were to be related to the users' interests. In particular, we came to be concerned about current understanding on 'user models' [Gilbert 1986, 1987a], 'discourse' [Gilbert 1987b] [Luff and Frohlich 1988] and 'explanation' [Gilbert 1988a] [Frohlich 1989].

9.2. THE CLAIMANT INFORMATION SYSTEMS TEAM

Unlike the other teams in the project, the claimant information systems (CIS) team was always clearly located in one place — the University of Surrey. Only three members of the CIS team have been from organizations other than the University of Surrey and they only stayed with the team for relatively short periods. This had some advantages and some disadvantages in comparison with drawing the team members from a wide spread of partners. The major advantage was the much greater productivity which could be achieved with everyone being on the same site. A second advantage was that the team was able to trade on its location in a university to develop good links with the academic community. The major disadvantage was that the CIS team was largely left to its own devices by the industrial partners who made few attempts to ensure that they were picking up exploitable items stemming from the team's work and did relatively little to influence that work to make it more relevant to their needs.

9.3. THE FORMS HELPER

9.3.1. The history of the Forms Helper application

Work on the Forms Helper started in October 1984. By June 1985 an initial 'proof-of-concept' prototype had been built. This prototype included most of the central ideas which were to be developed further in later versions: the 'electronic form' metaphor, the idea that the system should recommend to the user the next question to answer and the overall notion that neither the system nor the user should have enduring control over the interaction; instead there was to be 'mixed initiative'. This first prototype was, however, too slow to be usable and so a video demonstration of its main features was produced.

A second prototype was built in January 1986 which was significantly faster and more robust and this was used for conducting experiments with a small number of subjects, comparing their performance with the results of previous experiments using paper forms. The results of these activities led in the autumn of 1986 to the writing of a detailed specification for a second version of the Forms Helper [Frohlich and Luff 1986]. A team at ICL built this version during 1987. It was demonstrated at the 1987 Alvey conference and subsequently used in an evaluation carried out at ICL's Human Factors Laboratory under the supervision of the DHSS. The evaluation suggested further, relatively minor improvements which were incorporated in the final version demonstrated at the end of the project.

9.3.2. The objectives of the Forms Helper

The Forms Helper was designed to show how computers could help the general public fill in complex forms, in particular those required to claim welfare benefits such as income support. Many of the intended user population have little or no experience of using computers and know little about the legislation and regulations which determine eligibility for benefits. A primary design objective was therefore to construct a system which could be used easily without prior training. It would guide the form-filler in completing the form 'correctly' by drawing upon knowledge about the questions on the form, effective strategies for completing the form and the expectations of the organization which would process them, the DSS. The design had to support users filling in a variety of forms and therefore had to provide a 'shell' into which knowledge about each form could be inserted. Another objective was to demonstrate the utility of an architecture which would handle 'mixed initiative' interaction and investigate the value of this approach to human–computer interaction. Lastly, the design aimed to illustrate some general principles of effective human–computer interaction which could be applied to other systems [Frohlich *et al.* 1985].

9.3.3. The development of the Forms Helper

Defining requirements

Because the main objective of the Forms Helper was to make it easier for applicants to fill in complex forms, it was necessary to start with an investigation of what difficulties people have in completing conventional paper forms. Despite the considerable attention that had previously been devoted to the design of forms and, in particular, to the supplementary benefit and income support B1 application forms, relatively little was known about the way in which people fill them in. A study of form-filling behaviour was therefore mounted with four unemployed and four employed subjects who were asked to complete a copy of the B1, imagining themselves to be out of work and claiming benefit. Subjects were asked to read and think aloud and the verbal protocols were recorded and transcribed. Additional data came from the completed forms themselves and from observations made by the experimenter. It was found that subjects ignored large sections of the text on the forms — only about one-third of relevant question explanations and routing instructions were being read. It was also found that form-fillers made a significant number of 'disorientated progressions', that is, deviations from the expected route through the form. The great majority of these consisted of visits to questions which should have been avoided because they were irrelevant to the form-filler's circumstances. The effect of these visits to irrelevant questions appeared to be to disrupt the sense of the 'dialogue' between the form-filler and the form [Frohlich 1986].

Following the development of an initial prototype of the Forms Helper, a comparative evaluation of form-filling on paper and on the Forms Helper's 'electronic form' was carried out. Eight subjects were asked to fill out the supplementary benefit claim form as it was represented on the computer screen, while 'thinking aloud' about what they were doing. At the same time, the system logged the movement of the mouse cursor and key depressions against the system clock. The results showed that while the idea of computer support for form-filling had potential, the first prototype had serious inadequacies. The prototype Forms Helper did overcome the major problem found with paper forms, in that the system's routing recommendations guided users successfully through the set of questions relevant to their personal circumstances while avoiding irrelevant questions. Nevertheless, users did not find the system's help and guidance on how to answer questions useful, and the system was too slow and rather clumsy in several respects. The study thus identified a number of areas where design changes were required before the construction of the second version of the system [Frohlich 1987].

The specification of a complex human–computer interaction

The result of the evaluation of the Forms Helper prototype was that we had a much clearer idea of what the second demonstrator should look like and how it should function. This demonstrator was built in Manchester by the team at ICL, while the design and evaluation activities had been carried out in Guildford. It was necessary for the designers to convey precisely to the implementors what was required and we therefore began to investigate methods of formal and semi-formal specification for complex human–computer interfaces.

A number of methods of specification have been proposed, but the one which seemed to be most promising was based on ideas developed by Foley and van Dam [1982]. They suggest that human computer dialogues can be described at the conceptual, semantic, syntactic and lexical levels. A detailed specification of the second version of the Forms Helper was produced using this scheme [Frohlich and Luff 1989]. The exercise was successful in that the implementation team at ICL was able to build the system from the specification without frequent reference back to the designers.

9.3.4. Evaluation

The Forms Helper was evaluated by the ICL HCI Laboratory, Bracknell, under the supervision of the DSS. Twenty subjects, recruited from a local employment agency, were asked to complete both a paper income support claim form and the electronic version, using a split-half design in which some subjects used the Forms Helper first and then filled in the paper form, while others completed the paper form first and then tried the Forms Helper. The task was explained to the subjects, but no training was given. Their use of the Forms Helper was video taped and the tapes were analysed to identify any problems they encountered. A short attitude questionnaire was also administered to the subjects.

The results of the study showed a high level of acceptance for the idea of computer-based forms [Ottley *et al.* 1988]. Most users became confident of their ability to manage the technology, finding the system easy to use once they had got over their initial anxiety. They felt that the electronic form was easier to complete than the paper form. A number of small changes were suggested by the evaluation and the majority of these were incorporated into the final version. The study concluded that this type of system may well be acceptable to the general public in the right kind of environment.

The DSS also conducted an internal study of the costs and benefits which might accrue if the Forms Helper were to be installed in DSS local offices, providing clients with income support forms (but not forms for claiming other benefits) during office hours only. Making reasonable assumptions about hardware and maintenance costs, it was estimated that even this limited use of the system could save the DSS a very substantial sum, as well as providing a facility which would be welcomed by many social security applicants.

9.4. THE ADVICE SYSTEM

9.4.1. The history of the Advice System application

The proposal suggested that the Advice System would be the second of the claimant information systems to be built and design work on it did not begin until 1986. However, in early 1985, in anticipation of the need for a clear user requirement for the system, we started a study of potential users which continued into 1987. The results of this study were important in formulating the requirements specification [Buckland *et al.* 1987].

This requirements specification was used as the basis for the construction of an initial prototype which was demonstrated to the rest of the project in July 1987. A period of further research and design followed, culminating in a functional specification published in July 1988 [Robinson *et al.* 1988]. The demonstrator was built from this specification by the implementation team at ICL and was completed in time for the end of project demonstration in April 1989. However, the system ran very slowly, making it difficult to evaluate with users. The team therefore embarked on an almost complete reimplementation during the six months to September 1989. It was this third version which was eveluated in the period September to December 1989 and which is described in [Gilbert *et al.* 1990].

9.4.2. The objectives of the Advice System

Most expert systems have been designed for use by professionals who are able to bring both an understanding of the domain and some knowledge of computers to their interaction with the system. In particular, they can be assumed to know what the system is designed to do and what its limitations are likely to be. These assumptions about the user have to be relaxed as far as possible in a system designed for public use. The implications of designing for the public include: the concepts in terms of which the knowledge is structured must be either those comprehensible to the intended users or translatable to such concepts; the system should be capable of answering the types of questions which the users will wish to pose, not just those which are easy to answer using conventional techniques; and the structure of the interaction with the user ought to be one which is felt to be comfortable and natural. In addition, special methods have to be used to obtain a clear understanding of the requirements of a system designed for public use, since there is no well-defined and small set of users to approach, as would be the case in more conventional systems.

The primary purpose of the Advice System is to provide a wide range of types of information and advice of the kind that a trained welfare rights advice worker might offer. However it does not aim to duplicate many of the other roles which advice workers take on, such as letter-writing and form-filling, advocacy and representation, giving emotional support to clients and campaigning to change the benefit system. Its scope is restricted to financial benefits administered by the DSS (with some additions such as housing benefit, which is administered by local authorities). It is designed for English-speaking, literate users with the ability to use a keyboard and mouse and to read a computer screen. They could be interested in using the system on their own behalf or for someone without these skills and abilities. While a proportion of the intended user population will not fit this description, the technical problems of translation into other languages and providing alternative input and output technologies (such as touch screens) were not thought to be especially challenging in the context of the overall problem and were not considered in detail.

Because the system was intended as a demonstration, it was decided to include only part of the full range of social security benefits, those that are likely to be relevant to lone parents. This target group was selected because of the relatively high proportion of lone parents who claim social security benefits. One in seven families with dependent children is headed by a lone parent. In 1986, 55% of one parent families compared with only 7% of two parent families were dependent on social security. Apart from pensioners, one parent families have for many years been the largest group of people claiming benefits. Aiming the demonstration system at lone parents meant that knowledge about some classes of benefit, such as pensions and invalidity benefits, could be omitted, yet the system would still be capable of supporting a large number of users.

9.4.3. The development of the Advice System

Defining requirements

The intended users of the Advice System are drawn from the public at large and so it seemed appropriate to mount a research study to establish a set of user requirements. The study, which came to be known as the potential user study, focused on low income families because it was these who were most likely to need social security advice. Fifty low income households from inner city, urban and rural areas in south east England were randomly sampled using a complex stratified sampling design. A wider geographical spread might have been desirable, but this was not possible with the resources available. The design ensured that the sample was representative of the country as a whole along important dimensions. Respondents met one or more of three criteria: they had claimed a benefit in the past five months or had looked into doing so; they thought themselves eligible for a benefit; or they thought of themselves as living on a low income and were 'having difficulty in making ends meet'. The families were each interviewed twice, with an approximately nine month interval between visits. The interviews were tape recorded and transcribed before analysis. Topics covered in the interviews included: recent experience of claiming benefits and difficulties with form-filling; knowledge of the social security system; advice about social security from local support networks (friends and relatives, advice centres, medical and paramedical professionals and so on); factors affecting the propensity of households to claim; and experience with the use of computers and attitudes to new technology.

The results of the study were invaluable in defining the range of questions which potential users of the Advice System might want to ask about social security and claiming [Gilbert 1987b]. In addition, the study suggested the development of the concept of the 'claiming process' as a way of understanding individuals' and households' propensity to claim benefits. Previous work on this issue had largely confined itself to psychological theories about the attitudinal prerequisites for deciding to make a claim; the 'claiming process' examined in addition the effects of the household context and of previous and subsequent claims, suggesting a more complex and plausible model to explain why people apply for benefits and why some eligible people fail to claim [Buckland and Dawson 1989]. Another conclusion of the study was the reassuring one, for us, that most respondents in the sample would welcome having a computer to help them with information on social security. Nearly half the fifty-nine respondents felt that they did not at present know enough about the benefit system and that current sources of information were inadequate. Thirty eight of the fifty-nine said that they would use a computer to obtain benefit advice were one to be made available [Dawson *et al.* 1990].

Because it was decided that, to limit the scale of the demonstrator system, it would offer advice only for lone parents, a further study which concentrated on the situation of lone parents was conducted in 1988 and 1989. In this study, about fifty lone mothers and fathers were interviewed about their social and economic circumstances over the life course. This material has contributed to an understanding of the relationship between the level and form of social security income received by lone parents and their coping strategies. The domestic situation of one parent families has also been explored in the context of coping and household income strategies [Hardey 1989a, 1989b]. Throughout the development of the Advice System, the understanding of the experiences of claimants which was gained from these studies has made an important contribution to the design.

As well as approaching potential users, we thought it desirable to review existing arrangements for providing social security advice. Some twenty advice agencies were visited at the beginning of the project and advice workers interviewed about their work. With some difficulty, because of the requirement for confidentiality, interviews between advice workers and their clients at two advice agencies were tape recorded and transcribed. In addition, we recorded and transcribed a set of six Radio London phone-in programmes in which an advice worker responded to callers seeking information on welfare benefits. These sources provided a very useful foundation for specifying the requirements for the system as well as providing an inspiration for the design of the user-system interaction [Crossfield 1986].

Knowledge analysis and representation

Knowledge about benefits used in building the Advice System came primarily from public documents about the regulations and procedures governing the social security system, and information elicited directly from the DSS, the latter mainly for details about procedures which could not be found in official sources. The documents were of three kinds: 'official' regulations and manuals (for example, the DSS Adjudication Officers' Guide), published guides on welfare benefits (e.g. the Child Poverty Action Group's *National Welfare Benefits Handbook* and Rathfelder's *How to Claim State Benefits*) and DSS leaflets and forms. Little 'knowledge elicitation' of the conventional kind (involving intensive interviews with 'experts') was required for the analysis of eligibility and assessment, because most of the knowledge the system required was available in written form [Cordingley 1987, 1989]. However, procedural information was less well documented and therefore interviews with DSS staff and professional advice workers were also necessary.

The analysis of the procedural information included identifying procedures common to more than one benefit at each stage of the claiming process to see if a pattern could be isolated which would allow some generality across benefits. The procedures for one means-tested benefit were represented in a hierarchical procedural network. This network was then customized to each of the other benefits to allow for variations. The decision on how fine-grained to take the analysis of procedures was determined by considering the types of procedural questions claimants might wish to ask and the types of problem claimants most commonly experience.

Knowledge concerning the regulations governing eligibility for benefits was dealt with separately. Soon after beginning to study the task of analysing social security regulations, it became clear that attempting to encode regulations directly into some formal rule language was a very difficult task. Moreover, direct encoding meant that explicit links between the source material and the rules were difficult to construct. That in turn meant that the analysis was not available for scrutiny and maintenance. The first alternative to direct representation that we tried was a 'diagrammatic intermediate representation', a semi-formal graphical representation which could be linked back to the source and forwards to the rules which were derived from it [Cordingley 1988]. This approach proved the value of intermediate representations, but its graphical nature was found to be difficult to work with using the software then available — the graphs were large and awkward to navigate one's way round and there was no clear way to represent portions of the regulations which were referenced from several places, for example, to define 'presence in Great Britain'.

The graphical representation was therefore abandoned in favour of a hierarchical representation (like a word processor's 'outliner') with hypertext links between nodes created using KANT (see Chapter 11). Each node contained a semi-formal English version of a small portion of the regulations and (in the leaf nodes) a rule encoded in the Advice System's rule language. There were further links from the rules in the knowledge base back into these nodes and from the nodes into an index to the knowledge which had been encoded. This scheme is a great improvement over the graphical representation, being much more compact, easier to prepare and allowing links to be created between related items, although it suffered from the usual hypertext problem that users not intimately familiar with the complete structure can easily get lost.

There were two further difficulties in codifying knowledge about social security regulations. The first problem was finding some overall conceptual structure for the material. Social security regulations are enormously detailed and have been formulated incrementally over a long period of time. After some experiments with alternative structures, a modified version of the general arrangements employed by the Child Poverty Action Group in their handbooks was adopted. The second problem was that it was not easy to determine the appropriate level of detail at which to represent knowledge. The difficulty arises from the structure of the legislation and regulations, which tend to set out the general principle very briefly, but then overlay this with a great mass of exceptions and refinements for particular cases. Thus, to cite one from many curious examples, the regulations specify the position with respect to the receipt of child benefit of children born in an aeroplane over international waters; it is not worth encumbering a general public information system with such details. After a number of experiments with prototype knowledge bases, two methodological principles were adopted: firstly, the knowledge base was constructed 'bottom up' based on the questions which users would be able to answer; and, secondly, it was accepted that knowledge bases, like other software engineering projects, need to go through a process of successive refinement, possibly involving a series of prototypes, in order to achieve an adequate end-product.

Interaction design

Early attempts to design the interaction between the Advice System and its users used two methods: one method was to simulate various system components and the other was to derive models of interaction from an analysis of the advice worker and radio phone-in interviews. The simulations were carried out by members of the team playing the roles of system components and exchanging data and control instructions. There were problems with both methods. The former gave little guidance to the overall style of the interaction. Instead, the simulations tended to concentrate on the interactions between system components. The latter constrained the design of the interaction too much since advice workers often had quite different goals to those of the intended system. An overall model of the interaction that would inform specific design choices was needed. The Forms Helper had established the value of considering the interaction between the user and the system as a mixed initiative dialogue. We continued this line of research for the Advice System by reviewing two fields concerned with extended dialogues: the work on computational models of discourse in the field of computational linguistics and the studies of naturally occurring dialogues in the conversation analysis field of sociology.

The evaluation of existing computational techniques showed the difficulty of applying those that viewed discourse as planned or globally managed and the review of conversation analysis showed the advantages of viewing discourses as locally managed. It proved to be surprisingly easy to use the findings of conversation analysis to write interaction rules that solved the interaction design problem and, being based on conversation, these rules could easily be expressed independently of the domain of the system.

Interface design

Investigation into possible interfaces showed the difficulty of designing graphical representations of the concepts that the user and system would have to express. The choice of modelling the interaction on a conversation also implied that the user and system would have to communicate by utterances in natural language. Allowing the user to type utterances which the system would then try to understand was beyond the scope of the project. It also would not necessarily have provided the best means for users to express themselves. Instead we needed a way of allowing users to type only those utterances that the system could understand. We devised two schemes that would satisfy this requirement and tested them on a set of subjects. Using the first mechanism the user selected a topic from a menu that resulted in a further menu of more specific concepts being created. This process continued until the topics were expressible as sentences. The sentence the user selected would be their contribution to the dialogue. The second mechanism allowed the user to construct a sentence beginning from the initial word or phrase and proceeding to the punctuation at the end. Once the users had selected a phrase, a menu would appear that contained the next set of phrases which could continue their sentence. This process continued until the user selected a full stop or a question mark.

The results of these experiments pointed to a hybrid design in which the user selects topics down to a certain level and then selects phrases to construct one of a set of sentences about the last topic chosen. This design required two mechanisms: one to traverse the topics and one to generate phrases. Each of these mechanisms had a corresponding declarative representation; a 'topic tree' to describe the relationships between topics and a set of grammars to express the content of all utterances made by the user and the system. Both of these declarative representations had to relate to the referents mentioned in the knowledge base. The text generator that generates possible phrases is also used to generate complete system utterances.

9.4.4. Evaluation

At the time of writing, a number of lone parents are using the Advice System under laboratory conditions to evaluate the usability of the system as a whole. They are given the opportunity to explore what benefits might be available to them in their own situations. They are encouraged to comment verbally on what they are doing while they use the system and their interactions with it are logged for later analysis. Their comments and an interview held immediately after the trial are tape-recorded. In addition, a larger number of students are being given a 'scenario' containing a brief story about a hypothetical family and are being asked to use the system to find out what benefits the family is eligible for. Further details can be found [Gilbert *et al.* 1990] and in [Gilbert and Jirotka 1990].

The detailed results of these trials are not yet available, but a preliminary analysis of the data suggest that on the whole the design meets its objectives. The system's answers were considered to be clear and direct, and users appreciated their ability to ask as many questions as they liked. One user said the best thing about the system was that 'you can keep going round without it getting fed up.... you can go through different areas and different angles on the same thing'. The negative side of this was that the sessions were often quite long, frequently lasting an hour or more.

In general, users tended to seek out case level rather than domain or theory level answer types. In this way users were able to capitalize on the major capability of the system over information leaflets: that of giving personalised information. This attitude was captured by one user who said the system was 'better than ploughing through leaflets. It lets you into the heart of what you want to find out'. The trend was particularly evident for the lone parents, who had been given the freedom to explore the system for any kinds of answer they wanted. Out of a total of twenty-nine questions asked, twenty-one were for the case level answers, seven were for domain level answers, and one was for a theory level answer. These users asked primarily for quite specific answers with questions like 'Can I get housing benefit?' or 'How much income support can

I get?'. Most domain level answers were definitions of terms which users found useful in the process of answering system questions relating to their primary case level question. Theory level answer types were generally not requested except in cases where the system gave negative advice. Users reported trusting the system's answers and only became interested in the reasons underlying advice if it meant that they could not get a benefit they had expected to get.

The fact that users trusted the advice given did not mean that they were always satisfied with it. In fact a single system answer rarely gave enough information of the desired kind. Users often had trouble phrasing exactly the right kind of question at the interface, and almost always went on to ask a follow-up question on the same or a similar topic. This led to a highly interactive dialogue in which users explored an issue from a number of different angles. In the post-session interview, users confessed to being surprised at this, having expected a much more system-led dialogue in which they would answer a long string of questions before being given a single monologue on the benefits they could get. Several users spontaneously commented on the 'human qualities' of the talk, but reacted against the suggestion that it was 'like a conversation'. One user reflected a general feeling that the interaction was more formal or business-like than a conversation, by saying that 'It was more like a question and answer interview'. Another commented that 'It's better than a conversation because you can tell it to shut up and butt in'.

9.5. OTHER EXPERIMENTAL DEVELOPMENTS

9.5.1. Tools for qualitative analysis

As part of the potential user study, we tape-recorded two interviews with each of fifty families. These interviews were transcribed and common themes picked out from the transcripts. We had not gone far with the analysis before it became obvious that the technology we were using for the Forms Helper and the Advice System also had potential for assisting with the tedious and time-consuming task of sifting through many hundreds of pages of transcript. Thus was born the 'qualitative analysis tool' or QAT, a specification and prototype for a program to help with the analysis of any large body of textual materials. A description of user requirements and a requirement specification was produced in early 1986 and the rest of the project was persuaded that some resources should be assigned to building a prototype. This prototype, constructed over the period April to December 1986, was the project's first attempt to build a system with a significantly complex user interface. It was not a success, mainly because the difficulties of building such systems were not at that time properly appreciated and so the facilities which could be provided were very limited. However, the failure of the prototype was of considerable significance for the project as a whole: from its ashes was born the project's screen management tools and, because the project realised that the QAT would have potential not only for analysing interview transcripts but also for analysing documents such as legislation and regulations, QAT metamorphosed into KANT (Chapter 11).

9.5.2. Word incorporation parser

There are points in the dialogues between the user and both the Advice System and the Forms Helper where the user is asked for a date or a sum of money. We decided that we should allow users to input dates and amounts of money in any reasonable format, rather than forcing them to abide by some predefined style. This meant that these systems had to incorporate a parser capable of taking user inputs in many different formats and converting them into a standard one. Our first attempt used a chart parser, but this was found to be much too slow, taking of the order of three to five seconds to parse a single input. A second parser was built, based on a technique known as 'word incorporation' [Philips 1986]. This took between half and one second to parse a date, an acceptable response time. The parser used a grammar and dictionary which was developed to recognize inputs such as the following: 25th dec '86, 25/12, the 25th of December 1967, thirty five pounds, 35.00, three hundred and sixty five, 365, three hundred and 65, and don't know.

CHAPTER 10

MANAGING A LARGE COLLABORATIVE PROJECT

Charlie Portman

The Alvey-DHSS Large Demonstrator was a large project in several senses. It consumed over 35 person-years (115 different people were associated with the project during its lifetime). It consequently spent a lot of money each quarter. It lasted five years and took a significant slice out of the lives of its members. It was set up to tackle a large problem with several facets and ended up writing some large pieces of software and constructing quite large knowledge bases. Lastly, the project was large in a physical sense; it was spread from Lancaster to Guildford and from Liverpool to Cambridge across nine different sites.

10.1. ORGANIZATION

The project was preceded by a study phase which did the work needed to write the formal proposal — a document of 256 closely printed pages. The proposal outlined the project's structure and method of working so when the project started the organizational framework had already been defined. This framework was proposed in the absence of real experience of such a large, cross-culture collaborative project but seems, in hindsight, to have been well-chosen apart from the design control function which was probably inappropriate in the first few years of the project since it seemed to suggest that commonality would exist from the outset. This turned out to be an unreasonable view in the light of the scope of exploration needing to be done in the early years.

The project was initially organized with a top-level steering team,

KNOWLEDGE-BASED SYSTEMS AND
LEGAL APPLICATIONS. ISBN 0-12-086441-X

composed of senior representatives of the collaborating organizations, to which the whole project reported through the project manager. This team was intended to act as 'board of directors' to the project providing strategic guidance. It met quarterly throughout the life of the project, reviewing progress and plans and providing direction where needed. The project itself originally had an single applications team which was to investigate six different application areas, an integration and support team and a Design Control team each with a manager who reported to the project manager. To this structure was added an operations committee consisting of the team managers, the site representatives (where these were different) and the project co-ordinator.

During the life of the project this committee remained the main controlling group and was one of the main instruments for coordination and information passing between the groups. The terms of reference read (in part):

> 1. Purpose
>
> The Project's Operations Committee (OpsCom) is the executive body controlling the activities of the staff of the Project so as to meet the Project's objectives through the plans approved by the Steering Team.
>
> 3. Responsibilities
>
> OpsCom will:
>
> Approve team plans to meet the Project's objectives including exploitation.
>
> Approve overall plans for submission to the Steering Team.
>
> Allocate resources against approved plans.
>
> Formally review progress against plans agreeing tactics proposed by teams to react to changing circumstances.
>
> Co-ordinate cross-project administration and overall technical management.
>
> Represent individual collaborator's interests.
>
> Monitor the Project's external appearance.

In assigning staff to teams, personal interests and skills were given more weight than geography. This was a deliberate choice intended to test the problems in and solutions to distributed team-working. In many parts of the project's work this was found to be workable providing that extensive use was made of the various communication methods available. In other areas, particularly during integration of the final demonstration systems, the delays and lack of clarity of remote communication were overwhelming and the whole team was brought together for two or three weeks to complete the task. This seems to be a problem which improved communication technology alone cannot solve. The immediate presence of the participants is vital. One team was almost entirely on one site. This gave them much better intra-team communication but appreciably worse inter-team communication. This difference was reflected in their ability to meet their promises more closely than the other teams but also in the lack of common use of ideas and methods. This variance was not entirely bad as several good ideas, later of considerable use to the project, emerged but on the other hand there was undoubtedly some duplication of work. In the final analysis it seems that the way staff are assigned must take account of the state of knowledge, clarity of the definition of the work to be done and the nature of inter-site communications available. For exploration and development of a pluralist approach to a little-understood problem, the demonstrator's method of assignment was appropriate but for getting a well-specified job done in minimum time a site by site assignment of work and responsibility would have been easier to manage.

The role of project co-ordinator was particularly important. The coordinator handled the thousand and one administrative details needed to keep the project moving smoothly; these included collection of progress reports, updating and publishing name and address lists, making financial claims from Alvey and organizing the twice yearly project workshops.

A demonstrations and deliverables manager was appointed later with responsibility for planning and organizing public demonstrations and ensuring that all the other deliverables were produced.

The presence of dedicated 'central' management in the project was crucial to maintaining its coherence and giving 'outsiders' a common view of what was being done. Other demonstrators without this feature were much less coherent.

It seems that any project involving more than two sites or more than about eight people would benefit from this approach which would be needed to maintain a common direction and to resolve conflicting opinions.

10.2. CULTURE

A major difference between managing an Alvey collaborative project and an industrial project is in the prime motivations of the organizations and staff involved. In industrial projects staff are usually drawn from one organization (and its subcontractors) and all identify with the company's objectives. Secondary (divergent) objectives exist as well of course. In a project like the DHSS Large Demonstrator there is not this degree of focus; the collaborators have primary objectives which are quite different from one another and the staff tend to follow their parent organization's direction. To be effective, the project needs to align (some) of these objectives sufficiently closely with its own as to make progress possible.

In an industrial or a civil service context staff tend to operate in groups with leaders or managers who guide the activities of the unit and are able to commit the resources that they command within the constraints of their delegated authority. This model did not apply to the academic partners whose staff were more nearly equal colleagues with considerable personal control over their own activities, the 'principal investigator' did not have the ability to direct their work. Failure to recognize this at the outset was the cause of considerable puzzlement to both sets of parties.

Staff experience in any organization varies from person to person but experienced, senior staff can be expected to be well versed in their organization's culture, its motivations and *modus operandi* even though their personal views might well differ. However in an Alvey collaboration this experience was not common to all sites and this provided a rich source for misunderstandings as well as some unusual insights into the value and effectiveness of revered procedures, standards and attitudes. Interestingly neither the industrial group nor the academic group was homogeneous in itself either.

Alvey Large Demonstrators were not allowed to do 'research' nor to do 'product development'. This constraint required the project to walk a tight rope between the inclinations and experience of the academic parties on the one hand and that of the industrials on the other.

10.3. DESIGN CONTROL

The demonstrator was set up as a single project, rather than six separate ones, because it was believed by the proposers that there was an opportunity for considerable synergy between the methods, source material and resultant system components and that, therefore, more could be done with the money and people if they were to work together. One of the most difficult ideas to establish was that of 'design control'. It was intended that standards for analysis methods, software design, interfaces and reusable modules would be developed and adopted to improve the productivity of our experimental programming right from the project start. This concept was difficult to sell to nearly all parties, particularly in the early stages, the experimenters claiming that insufficient was known to set or adopt standards or that the imposition of standards was inappropriate and would slow down or completely inhibit their work. This situation made the design committee (DesCom) virtually useless in the early stages of the project. Changes were made in organisation were made to eliminate the separate design control team replacing it with a design committee. Later an implementation team was created responsible for all the project's demonstration software absorbing this responsibility for software design. These changes were largely as a result of the failure of the original intention that each team would produce the application for which they were responsible using common project software modules. The idea of a common analysis team was discussed but rejected; this may have been an error as some commonality of method and material did emerge in the last few weeks of activity. More could be done to reap the synergistic benefits earlier than was the case in this project, now that the experience has been won.

10.4. COMMUNICATION

Geographical separation reduces cohesion in any project and this lack must be overcome by corresponding increases in other means of communication such as telephone, mail, electronic mail, meetings, workshops and personal visits. These increased costs and are not a complete substitute for lunches together, meetings at the photocopier or coffee pot or a quiet pint in the pub.

All the methods mentioned above were used in the project. Telephone contact was useful but on many ocassions could not be used because of the absence from their usual location of the called party. The very flexible working hours of some project members made this situation even worse. The public mails were used to carry routine reports and bulk documents but were found, often, to be slow and unreliable.

A great deal of effort was put in to trying to get a working, reliable and easy to use electronic mail system as it was thought that this would overcome the time differences and delays just mentioned. Unfortunately it was found that, for some project members, the requirement to log on at frequent intervals — say daily — was too onerous and that, others found the technology too unfriendly and still others were unable to live with the reliability problems which we met. Despite these problems the project did make extensive and successful use of e-mail to co-ordinate its work and to distribute information rapidly. There were probably about ten regular users out of the thirty-five who had mailboxes and access to terminal equipment.

In addition to e-mail project members had access to a dedicated series 39 level 30 machine from their 1108/1186 machines and Macintoshes. The 3930 provided the project documentation system and drove a printer on each site.

Meetings of the steering team, operations committee (OpsCom) and of individual teams were held fairly regularly, often in London as the least difficult place for all to reach. Logica were very generous in providing the location on many occasions. In addition various special interest groups were set up and met a number of times covering matters such as software engineering, HCI, knowledge analysis and knowledge representation and inference. OpsCom held a number of 'extraordinary' or special meetings to discuss major issues such as the purpose and nature of demonstrations, reorganization, after Alvey and replanning.

One series, the special OpsCom meetings on demonstrations, was held using BT's Confravision service as an experiment. This enabled the northern and southern locations to meet in Manchester and London respectively and the two groupings to confer over closed circuit television. This method was held to be just cost effective and certainly saved some time at each end. However, it was not thought to be sufficiently good that face to face meetings could be reduced and hence did not become a regular channel of communication.

Project workshops were fairly popular with nearly all the project staff. They provided the opportunity for staff to meet one another in informal circumstances as well as the formal business which included project reports to bring everyone up to speed on the activities of other groups and to discuss problem areas. Demonstrations were also given of systems that had been developed since the last workshop. Sessions were also held to brain-storm solutions to problems being experienced and to agree the plans for the following period.

These events were meant to encourage social as well as work contact and also to provide an opportunity for steering team members, collaborators' management and the monitoring officer to meet the project staff en masse, hear the presentations and see the demonstrations that had been prepared. This was probably the single most effective mechanism to weld the project together and to generate and maintain *esprit de corps*. It was found that they should be held well away from any collaborator's site to ensure that the 'local' members did not disappear to deal with other matters at work or at home when they should have been socialising with their normally distant colleagues.

Traditions, like the 'project dinner' and the social afternoon developed as the series continued. Members will long treasure memories of one colleague falling in the Isis while punting, of recitations of Albert and the Lion in Exeter and tramping over various moors.

Nor were workshops without incident in the formal sessions: on at least one occasion technical disagreement erupted into strong argument and on another a scheduled talk was replaced by an improptu *cri de coeur* from the staff of one collaborator about their feeling of isolation from the rest of the group.

Personal visits between sites were encouraged for project members to discuss matters of mutual interest. However, it seemed that many members did not find this a very attractive option and such visits were the exception rather than the rule.

10.5. THE PROJECT DOCUMENTATION (PD) SYSTEM

Documentation proved a contentious issue. Management pressed for standards and the recording of documents in a common computer based system meant to be accessible to all project members. Investigators pleaded that their work was not yet fit to be published or so local that no-one else could possibly be interested, or they claimed that the system provided was too difficult to use or did not support their favourite document preparation system.

Over four hundred AlvINs and seven hundred PDs were deposited in the two systems over the five years of the project but it is certainly true that the system was of more use to the management of the project than to most of its members. This was partly due to 'technical' problems and partly to personal attitudes. Earlier provision of improved facilities and training would have helped but would not have eliminated the attitudinal problems, and so the onus was constantly on management to press for its use and to ensure that obstacles were removed quickly.

10.6. PLANNING

Naturally, the steering team required the project to provide a fairly detailed plan showing how the project expected to spend the considerable sums of money that the collaboration were investing and to show as each quarter passed how well the plan had been followed. Preparing the plans and reporting against them was one of the major activities of the management team.

Planning the work of the project was particularly difficult in the early years when effort was concentrated on investigating the user organization and its problems and exploring the IKBS state of the art and discovering what it could — and could not — do. These difficulties applied not only to the need to make plans at this stage but also to the need to adhere to them. The academic partners particularly felt restricted by the demand that they deliver predefined results by a pre-agreed date.

Most of the staff found difficulty in defining their 'milestones' in the early stages. Similarly, the concept of 'dependencies' was alien and restricting to the investigators, thus undermining the basic principles of network based planning.

Considerable difficulty was encountered in gaining mutual understanding both of the nature and strength of the commitments undertaken and the need to determine in advance the work required to create those demonstrations. Attempts to get team leaders to produce plans for central recording and publishing met problems in the lack of common nomenclature and notation. The tools initially used also proved a further hindrance as they ran on hardware only available to the group in Manchester.

Progress reporting remained a problem throughout the project because of the changes in direction at the detailed level as the investigations continued; however, a compromise in level of detail which enabled a reasonably coherent story to be maintained was found. It would seem that there should have been less detail in the proposal and that provision of suitable tools and training at the outset would have reduced, but not eliminated, these difficulties.

Resource levels specified in the project proposal were never completely reached partly because of the time lag in recruiting at the outset and when people moved on but also because some collaborators had difficulty in continuing to convince their superiors that the original statements were still valid. The industrial partners particularly had to be resold the value of the project to their changing ambitions and commitments. This lowering of available effort reduced the number of alternatives that could be explored but had only a minor effect on the scope and quality of the final systems.

It is likely that this problem would occur in any long term project because of the annual financial cycle common to most industrial companies.

10.7. TRAINING

It became clear that more effort should have been spent on training the group as a whole, and its leaders in particular, at a very early stage in a number of management techniques and in communication and presentation skills.

The abilities and inclinations of the staff varied tremendously across the project and many would have benefited greatly from some early exposure to existing techniques rather than having to use trial and error. Teams were asked to make presentations of their work at the half-yearly workshops and often fielded all their staff in an effort to make everyone feel involved. Many of the presenters, however, found this an ordeal and this lack of confidence together with their lack of preparation reduced the value of the presentation considerably. Formal technical training in programming in InterLisp-D was purchased from the supplier for at least one staff member from each site but little was available in the other technical areas in which the project became interested.

10.8. DEMONSTRATIONS

In the event most of the demonstrations occurring in the first three years were internal to the project although some initial prototypes were shown in 1985 and 1986 at the Alvey conferences at Edinburgh and Brighton.. Public demonstrations of substantial systems first took place at the 1987 Alvey conference held in Manchester and at the CCTA 'Computing in Government conferences' in 1987 and 1988 and the ITEX exhibition in 1988. The final set of public demos were held at the DTI, Kingsgate

House, in Victoria, London in April 1989.

Demonstrations were a very expensive exercise in resources and time. The work needed to prepare demonstrations was often underestimated leading, sometimes, to embarrassment at the event or regret subsequently.

Any future project should budget explicitly for this type of activity as 'squeezing it in' is very bad for progress on other activities. Some members enjoyed presenting the project's work at conferences and exhibitions but others found demonstrations very boring and felt that they were being taken away from 'real' work.

10.9. EXTERNAL

Alvey appointed a monitoring officer at the start of the project. The project was fortunate to establish excellent relations with him and to retain him throughtout the full length of the project. there was also representation from the CCTA on the steering team and on OpsCom. These two 'outsiders' provided a useful steadying influence providing guidance and criticism when needed of the work. They and senior members of the collaborating organizations (particularly the DHSS) were valuable in getting information and contacts with people doing related work. It certainly seemed that this was an effective but not too onerous or costly way for the funding organization to audit the spending of its funds.

As might be expected, the academic members were much more willing and able to give presentations and to publish papers in the learned journals: 114 documents were approved for external publication, 13 of which had non-academic authors.

Relations with the media were good and the project received much 'good press' including a brief piece in a television documentary.

While the project's public statements were usually received with interest and accepted as being an advance of the 'state of the art', a series of attacks from one researcher declaiming that our intentions were impossible caused a certain amount of unease. It was our conclusion that the problem lay in a misunderstanding of our intentions rather than a direct disagreement as to what was and was not feasible.

Two criticisms of the project were particularly pleasing. One, from the project monitoring officer was that: 'wherever I go in your Project they tell me the same story'. The other from one of the universities was that: 'our staff on your project seem more interested in doing project work than publishing papers'.

10.10. LESSONS

Managing a project like the Alvey-DHSS Large Demonstrator depends on developing and maintaining a common purpose and a common view of what the freedoms of and restrictions on the project members are.

Communication in all senses is the vital key to reaching and keeping this common view. Strong co-ordination is required to resolve differing views of equal partners, this should be as independent as possible. A great deal of travelling is inevitable, although use of e-mail and, perhaps, video conferencing, together with planning of meetings can keep this within bounds.

Requirements for procedures, planning, documentation, etc. should be well developed at the outset, although in a long project they will certainly need changes as time passes.

All activities should be 'budgeted', particularly the time and cost of demonstrations, conferences and workshops which are otherwise seen as an extra load by the team members. Creation of the final reports is also something that can 'fall off the end' if not planned and controlled.

It is, perhaps, interesting to speculate on the possible outcomes of such a project if the culture mix had been different. In an 'industrial only' project, for instance, it is likely that more tangible results in terms of software systems might have been produced but at the expense of a reduction in the scope and depth of exploration of many issues, particularly those relating to the claimants and their needs and to the policy branches. In an 'academic only' project, I imagine, the opposite balance would have been struck with a greater coverage but less complete demonstrator systems. It would be interesting to know whether the Alvey monitoring projects will support this view. In either case the project and its sponsors would have lost the beneficial effects of the intercultural interaction and the participants would have found the time they spent less stimulating and less fun.

PART IV

ISSUES

Building a knowledge based system in any domain raises certain issues. The idea of such a system is that it will perform by manipulating a knowledge base, and this requires that knowledge relevant to the domain be acquired, analysed and represented in a formalism suitable for execution. Further, the system must be used, which means that an interface to the user must be provided, and the system must be introduced into the organization and meet the business requirements of that organization. In this section issues related to these activities are discussed.

The legal domain has certain distinctive characteristics related to the fact that so much of the knowledge that seems appropriate for inclusion in a KBS exists in written form. Firstly there is the law itself, both statutes and the various statutory instruments made pursuant to those statutes. Then there are decisions made on individual cases which can serve as precedents for future cases. There are commentaries on the law, and, in the case of welfare benefits, books aimed at the lay public which set out to explain the law to those whom it affects. Also in welfare benefits law there exists voluminous guidance which instruct adjudicators in how they are to apply the law. If we go back to the formulation of law we find yet more documents which set out the intention behind the law and explain why certain solutions were adopted. Also in policy branches letters are written and parliamentary questions answered which further explain and justify the law. There is therefore a huge amount of disparate written material which could contain knowledge of relevance.

This material needs to be selected from and organized so that it can form part of the knowledge base. Elizabeth Cordingley was centrally involved in the knowledge analysis work done for the claimant information systems, and her chapter describes the approach taken there, and also draws on the experiences of her colleagues doing similar work with regard to the local office system. The chapter should serve to dispel any impression that because knowledge exists in written sources, the process of analysis in a realistically sized domain is a simple matter.

Once the knowledge to be represented has been decided upon, it needs to be represented. Systems have been built in the legal domain using the whole gamut of knowledge representation paradigms. The question therefore arises as to whether there is anything distinctive about the formalism required for the legal domain. In the early period of the Demonstrator a variety of knowledge representation techniques were used in experimental fashion in an effort to determine just what was required. After this period of experimentation a decision was taken to use a common formalism for all the prototypes, and this was to include features to meet the perceived requirements. Justin Forder and Trevor Bench-Capon were centrally involved in the design of this formalism, which became known as the project toolkit, and their chapter sets out the principles which it attempted to embody, and justifies them with reference to the particular demands that are made by the domain of law.

When thinking about the interface, it should be remembered that KBS in the legal domain are usually thought of as support systems. This means that the users of the systems will have been selected for qualities quite unrelated to their skills in using computers. Although regular users may be able to receive some training, this means that the systems need to be designed to be used by people with minimal computer skills. The problems are at their sharpest when they are designed to give advice to the general public, since this class of users cannot be expected to invest any time in learning to use the system. Paul Luff and David Frolich worked on the two Demonstrator systems aimed at the general public, and their chapter describes the style of interaction used in these systems, which they call mixed initiative interaction, together with the results of the extensive evaluation work carried out to examine the benefits of this style.

The typical picture of a person using a KBS is of an individual alone at a terminal. This picture suggests that the tasks supported should be tasks performed by an individual. This model fits both the adjudication support system and the claimant information systems, but will not do for the system targeted at the policy makers. There the field is too large, and the interested parties too diverse, for the task to be done by an individual working in isolation. Policy making is essentially a group activity. In his chapter Graham Storrs, who led the team working on the policy application, describes the issues involved in producing a KBS to support a group of people working in a co-operative fashion. These issues are not confined to policy making related to law, however: the co-operative working style is to be found at the strategic level of any large organisation.

The final chapter in this section discusses the organizational impact of introducing KBS. Introducing any form of computer technology will affect the working of the organisation into which it is introduced, and the working practices of the people working within it. Throughout the process of designing such a system, therefore, one needs to be aware of the implications of using it. Andrew Taylor, who was chiefly responsible for liaison with DHSS and determining the organizational requirements, discusses these issues, with particular reference to the kinds of KBS envisaged by the Demonstrator project.

All of these issues arise in building any knowledge based system, but they arise in a different way depending on the domain of application and the intended user. It is hoped that the discussions in these chapters will be of particular use to those building legal KBS, but also of value to those exploring KBS in other domains.

CHAPTER 11

ANALYSING TEXTS FOR KNOWLEDGE BASED SYSTEMS

Elizabeth S. Cordingley

Knowledge work — the selection of knowledge sources; knowledge elicitation, analysis, characterization and representation; KB design; and KB development — was a major focus of teams developing the Advice System (AS) and the Local Office Demonstrator (LOD). For them, knowledge work was regarded as an area in which there was potential for advancing the state of the art. It had value in its own right in the context of developing demonstrators. For the team developing the policy system, however, especially after the mid-term review when the LOD became the focus for developing an engineered approach to building large knowledge bases, there was no requirement to develop an increasingly comprehensive large knowledge base. The purpose of each policy KB was minimally to provide support for the particular aspect of the prototype being demonstrated. In fact, given the supporting role of the KB, the speed of inferences achieved before the end-of-project demonstrations in early April 1989, and the need to keep responses to queries small, large complex knowledge bases would have been counterproductive for the policy system. This chapter, therefore, focuses primarily on the approach to knowledge work adopted for AS and LOD, but includes comments on that of policy where appropriate.

The first three sections outline the impact on knowledge work of decisions about target users and the support they would need (section 11.1); the nature of the domain and how much of it to cover (section 11.2); and technical considerations relating to representation and inference

KNOWLEDGE-BASED SYSTEMS AND
LEGAL APPLICATIONS. ISBN 0-12-086441-X

(section 11.3). Section 11.4 discusses analysis undertaken by the application teams and its effect on knowledge-base design. Section 11.5 describes the strategies adopted by the teams for building their knowledge bases and how the structure of the teams influenced these decisions. approaches to analysis KB design and building.

11.1. TARGETING

The three objectives of the project which particularly affected knowledge work were:

1. To produce knowledge based decision-support solutions which enhance organizational effectiveness and quality of service.
2. To produce systems in which the multiple needs and varying skills of all the users are handled in a coherent manner, intelligently and sympathetically.
3. To produce systems embodying mechanisms for safeguarding the rights of individuals and the integrity of the system.

The concern with 'multiple needs and varying skills' led to the selection of three different sets of target users for the systems: D(H)SS headquarters staff for the policy system, D(H)SS local office staff for the Local Office Demonstrator, and D(H)SS 'customers' for the Advice System and the Forms Helper. Each target user group provided a special challenge for system design and knowledge work. They affected the selection of knowledge sources as well as the use, structuring and representation of knowledge gleaned from those sources. Consideration was given to creating a single knowledge base for all three systems with three different user interfaces, but there were several reasons for deciding against this. A particularly compelling one was that an Advice System might not be credible as an independent source of advice if it were developed and maintained by the organization administering the benefits rather than being developed independently and kept separate from D(H)SS knowledge bases. In the end each system which had a knowledge base had a separate one.

11.1.1. D(H)SS headquarters staff

The target users for the policy system were to be staff of the D(H)SS Policy Unit, exemplars of D(H)SS headquarters staff. The main application requirement for the policy team was to design a system to support policy workers in the way they undertook their task. It was to provide, among other things, facilities for problem structuring, detailed argumentation, evaluating and rationalising arguments which supported alternative policy options. 'Task' knowledge was expressed in the system software rather than explicitly in the knowledge base. 'Domain' knowledge, knowledge about the benefits (such as benefit rates, time limits, and conditions which must be met by claimants), was explicitly expressed in knowledge bases which were tailored to demonstrate other aspects of the prototype system for which they were designed rather than as a feature to be demonstrated in its own right. Whereas 'task' knowledge was driven by the target user group's working practices, 'domain' knowledge, the knowledge-base content, was driven by the need to 'demonstrate the capabilities of the prototype'. As the policy team relate in section 8.4.5 of the final report 'The knowledge-bases for the Policy application were never intended to be a complete or necessarily accurate representation of the current legislation.'

The P1 demonstration was able to meet its objective of illustrating technical aspects of the inference mechanism with only about a dozen rules. Other knowledge bases were rather 'larger': the feasibility prototype (P0), to demonstrate how the system would identify people caught in the invalidity trap, had a knowledge base which 'knew' of 15 benefits and contained 120 rules which referenced 112 attributes; P1 income support knowledge-base, a version of the P0 updated to reflect the change from supplementary benefit to income support had about 150 rules; P2 had no knowledge base as such but contained a collection of arguments set in a problem structure; and P3, the end of project demonstration, had a knowledge-base relating to national insurance credits with about 70 rules and 6 objects.

It was possible that these users would contribute to the expansion updating/correction of the knowledge base supporting their decision making and that the system would need to cover a range of benefits and claimant types.

11.1.2. D(H)SS local office staff

Target users for the LOD were to be D(H)SS local office staff. The DHSS operational strategy, from which this project was quite separate, already included plans for computer support for staff assessing supplementary benefit (later income support) claims, work typically undertaken by LOI grade staff.

The LOD was not intended to duplicate this support but to provide decision support for those dealing with difficult decisions and undertaking adjudication tasks, typically LOII grade staff.

One of the major concerns was that these users were, and would continue to be, personally accountable for decisions they took including those taken with the support of a decision support system. This meant they would need to be able to inspect work done on a case and the case information on which decisions had been based. For the purposes of a demonstration supporting existing procedures, it was important to present this information for inspection and processing in the form with which users were familiar. For this 'knowledge' of internal D(H)SS procedures and forms would be needed. Users would also need to be able to 'evaluate' suggestions offered by the system. Traditional support material, such as D(H)SS guidance and the reported decisions of tribunals and commissioners, made available for on-line browsing would need to be in a familiar format. Early analysis had shown that the format of support documents was rich in contextual clues whose loss in on-line representations would diminish the knowledge conveyed. The provision of browsing facilities would also mean that much support material need not be analysed for representation in the LOD knowledge base. Interpretation of the more ambiguous aspects of the benefit domain was thereby left with the user rather than the knowledge analyst; it was one way of making explicit that the system was to support rather than make decisions.

As the legal basis of decisions made by D(H)SS local office staff were the statutory instruments relevant to the benefit, these sources formed the basis for the explicitly represented knowledge in the LOD knowledge base.

Although preliminary work was undertaken in a number of areas, the main focus of local office application was supplementary benefits and then income support. It was thus scoped as an in depth single benefit system providing decision support for assessment of difficult cases and for adjudication.

Unlike the use envisaged for the Policy System, it was not envisaged that these users would maintain or enhance the knowledge-base although they might enter case information. Unlike for the Advice System, it was assumed that all relevant case information would be available before inferencing was undertaken so there would be no problem of providing suggestions to users on the basis of partial information.

11.1.3. D(H)SS 'customers'

For the Advice System (AS), target users were the D(H)SS 'customers' i.e. the members of the public who wanted information and advice about benefits and/or might want to claim one or more benefits. A wide range of computer-specific and general skills found among the public had to be recognized and catered for giving rise to the possible need for several levels of interaction with the Advice System and several levels of help and explanation. Analysis of how members of the public conceptualized their needs and the welfare provision of which they were aware required, as was an understanding of their common misconceptions and the kinds of explanation they found useful.

Much of this 'knowledge' was not, in the end, explicitly represented in the knowledge base of the Advice System, but the analysis did have a major impact on the way knowledge was structured and on the choice of object and attribute names.

Early studies of AS potential users confirmed sociological work on bureaucratic solutions to the problems of individuals. It had suggested that solutions, in this case details of claiming and welfare provision, would be expressed in the language and logic of the bureaucracy, 'legalese' and 'D(H)SS-speak, whereas problems would be expressed in personal everyday concepts and reasoning.

There could be no assumption that organizational concepts, terminology or the 'logic' used by the D(H)SS and parliamentarians would be known by, or be understandable to, members of the public. The difference in expression and reasoning had the further implication that sources, such as statutory instruments including Acts of Parliament, Regulations and their associated Schedules, originally thought suitable as a basis for building the knowledge-base of the AS would not be suitable as they stood. 'Translation' would be needed, and this would have to go further than the substitution of simple words for more complex, arcane terminology.

Bound up with the issue of adopting appropriate conceptualisation of domain knowledge was the issue of knowledge-base scrutiny. The AS analysts took the project objective of 'ensuring that mechanisms for safeguarding the rights of the individual' seriously, interpreting it to mean, among other things, that the building and the current state of the knowledge base should be such that members of the public, or their representatives, could inspect it (outside the normal sessional use) and make an informed judgement about its quality. This aim was consistent with the effort to develop a single 'intermediate representation' which would be meaningful to all parties interested in the quality of the knowledge base including domain experts, users or their representatives, systems programmers involved with coding and debugging the system, and those not involved with the development who might at some later time be involved with maintaining or extending the knowledge base (see the discussion below of how KANT was used for details of how this was undertaken).

The question was where in the development of the system was the translation to be undertaken. Partial translation into a world structure and concepts used by members of the public had already been undertaken by authors of popular texts such as the CPAG handbooks and Martin Rathfelder's *How to Claim State Benefits*. Unlike any that might be undertaken by the AS team, these 'translations' were already widely available in the public domain and had, through various editions, been so for some time. Their extensive use by advice givers and claimants could be expected to have brought errors, inconsistencies, deficiencies and misconceptions to light. There had already been public scrutiny of these 'translations' through use. This made these sources more suitable for the purposes of AS knowledge base building than official D(H)SS documents and statutory instruments used for the LOD system.

The Advice System was conceived of as providing advice on a

coherent set of benefits which demonstrated significant coverage of welfare provision relevant to its users. Its design challenge could be described as providing breadth of coverage (as opposed to depth which was a challenge for the LOD), demonstrating the ability to represent, and inference across, relations between benefits; and the ability to answer questions of many kinds including procedural questions such as what should a person do to claim a particular benefit, as well as non-procedural questions such as whether the person was likely to be eligible for a benefit, and if so how much the person could expect to get.

It is not surprising that members of the public do not define their lives in terms of distinctions important to the funding or administration of benefits.

A tribunal decision reported in *Welfare Rights Bulletin* 75 (p.3) concerned whether a shower for a disabled man constituted a 'medical need' or a 'domestic need', a distinction which is administratively important as it divides social security from NHS provision, but difficult to determine in the everyday world.

The 'cash' versus 'care' distinction which has defined the boundary between the social security and the personal social services is not always meaningful to claimants/clients. The 'health' versus 'medical' distinction which distinguishes the care provided by local authorities and that provided by the NHS is another distinction which is difficult to maintain in terms of life as it is lived.

It was decided that boundaries of the Advice System knowledge base should be set by reference to target cases associated with a group of people rather than a collection of benefits as a reflection of the teams concern to let the system be user-driven rather than organization-driven. It was decided to focus on lone parents as the target group because they were likely to be easily specified and eligible for a wide range of benefits.

It happened that benefits for the disabled and students were under review during the lifetime of the project as well as those covered by the social security review. It was uncertain whether regulations regarding them would be available for end-of-project demonstrations or whether they would already have come into effect by that time. So a decision was taken to narrow the scope of the target cases about which the AS would be able to advise to cases where the claimant would be a lone parent who was neither disabled nor a student nor, by the definition of lone parent used, retired. This allowed retirement pensions to be largely excluded from the knowledge base and was consistent with the decision not to devise an interface specifically appropriate to the disabled. It also allowed knowledge about disability including medical assessments, undertaken by medical rather than D(H)SS staff, to be excluded.

11.2. THE DOMAIN

The domain of application for the project as a whole was UK social security welfare benefits. Analysis of welfare provision, D(H)SS organisation, training for adjudicators and for local office staff who administered benefits, and the practices and problems of advice givers in non-D(H)SS advice agencies, and was carried out by social researchers in the claimant information team during the early months of the project. At this time it was anticipated that organizational and domain analysis for both the supplementary benefit application (as it was then) and the claimant information applications would be undertaken by social researchers on the CIS team at Surrey. This work and subsequent analysis of how members of the public experienced welfare needs and welfare provision showed how difficult it was to scope systems using this definition of the domain. It highlighted the difficulties in setting domain boundaries and in making decisions about what organizing principle should be used to structure domain knowledge.

11.2.1. Scope

It was particularly difficult to know what to include as UK welfare benefits for the purposes of the project. One view expressed early on in the project was that welfare benefits should be taken to be social security benefits administered by D(H)SS local office staff before the Fowler Review as this was the system with which evaluators would be familiar. This view would have been severely limiting, though, as it would have excluded all non social security provision of the kind delivered through the local education authority and local authority social services departments. It would exclude social security benefits which are administered for the D(H)SS by other central government departments, such as unemployment benefit which is administered by the Department of Employment. It would have excluded benefits such as housing benefit which are administered by local authorities. Benefits such as child benefit which are administered by the D(H)SS but are administered centrally rather than locally would also have been excluded.

The time boundary needed to be moved beyond the Fowler Review for the demonstrators to be timely at the end of the project. The analysts for LOD and policy were able to use early versions of Income Support Regulations for early work, however detailed analysis of the post-Fowler benefits by the CIS team which had decided to use sources in the public domain had to wait until the regulations were published. All of the systems developed during the project adapted to the change from pre-Fowler to post-Fowler benefits. In particular supplementary benefit was replaced by income support and FIS by family credit. It happened that the end of the project came at a time when it was not unreasonable to exclude transition arrangements and, as claimant histories were not held, reference to the superceded benefits could be avoided.

Organizational and administrative boundaries also needed to be breached for coherent packages of benefits to be covered by the Advice System. 'Experienced need' and advice seeking are widely known to cut across boundaries of administrative responsibility and funding sources. Though these boundaries are relevant to administering organisations and therefore to the process of claiming welfare provision, they do not usually constrain advice seeking. The advice sought is usually in terms of life experiences of the advice seeker, for example 'What happens when I reach retirement age?' or 'What's the effect of getting a divorce?'.

Organizational boundaries are also blurred during the process of gathering information needed to support a claim. A child benefit claim, for example, must be supported by a birth certificate. Hence advice about claiming child benefit may well need to include details about how to register a birth or get a copy of a birth certificate, even though these matters are not the administrative responsibility of the D(H)SS.

Organizations delivering welfare provision, including some D(H)SS local offices, recognise the boundary difficulties and have, as far as they are organizationally able, adopted a 'whole person' approach to claimants. Advice givers, not bound to an administrating organization are able to go even further in this direction as must a convincing Advice System. These objects had to be included in the knowledge base although little detail supported these non social security objects in the demonstrator, especially as it was being designed to be used by a member of the public without the attendance of any other advice giver.

11.2.2. Organizing principle for structuring knowledge

Several useful ways to structure the the knowledge emerged from domain analysis. The first was based on perceived rationale and emergent principles implicit in the structure and delivery of welfare benefits. Concepts like benefits 'as of right' as opposed to those which formed the 'safety net' of welfare provision went some way toward explaining why it was relatively easy to claim some benefits and was difficult to claim others. The insurance principle which underpins contributory benefits like unemployment benefit and statutory sick pay goes some way towards explaining why there are conditions relating to a claimant's contributions record for these benefits and not for others. This structuring of benefits was useful for constructing explanations and to provide warrants for system outcomes. It was used in the construction of rules to provide answers to these 'theory level' questions in the Advice System demonstrator.

Another structure was based on the concepts of welfare context and focal events/situations which occur in the life of potential claimants. Figure 3 (discussed in section 11.4.1 below) represents an attempt to combine disparate perspectives which it was thought might be useful in designing the interaction. It might have been the basis of a graphical user interface had that option been pursued.

Yet another knowledge structure for the domain could be based on organizationally relevant distinctions such as 'cash' versus 'care' which helps to define the boundary for social security (the 'cash' provision); contributory versus non-contributory, means-tested versus non means-tested which give a good indication of the kind of eligibility conditions a claimant must satisfy to get each category of benefit; income versus capital, a distinction used to structure knowledge for the LOD, which partitioned the information needed for two of the main aspects of means-tested benefits calculations.

As mentioned before, attempts were being made to construct the Advice System knowledge base in terms of concepts which were relevant to its users. This was to facilitate meaningful scrutiny and allow for the possibility that names for object and attributes might be directly useful for system–user dialogue. Using organizational and administrative distinctions as organizing principles to structure knowledge gave rise to difficulties with the user-driven approach.

The distinction between contributory and non-contributory benefits has both an organizational and a common-sense meaning. The two are not entirely consistent. D(H)SS staff use the term non-contributory to mean benefits paid out of the national insurance fund and dealt with by the 'contributory benefits side of the house' [Cordingley *et al.* 1985] but not based on a claimant's contributions record. Non-contributory benefits, in the common sense meaning of the term, are benefits you do not have to pay contributions to get. This would include all those mentioned so far (i.e. what D(H)SS staff refer to as non-contributory benefits) plus all those benefits paid for by parliament. The implication for the Advice System was that whereas it was be necessary to employ the technical distinction internally, for example in advising users about which local office to go to or, for D(H)SS offices which handled all the benefits and for the people using them, which part of the office to go to, it was inadvisable to use the term non-contributory in the dialogue with users. That made certain knowledge base distinctions and names unavailable to users during an AS session and would make scrutiny of the knowledge base more difficult for evaluators representing members of the public.

The distinction between means-tested and non means-tested benefits seems clearer to the public than the previous distinction, even though they might not express the distinction in these terms themselves. They are aware that for some benefits, especially income support, they must provide detailed information about their finances. The prospect of doing so prevents many of them from making any claim at all. The older version, family income supplement (FIS) and supplementary benefit (Supp Ben), of means-tested benefits family credit and income support were notorious for having the lowest take-up rates.

But there seemed to be confusion in the minds of some members of the public between information relating to means-testing and information relating to contribution records for contributory benefits. Both are financial and detailed.

11.3. REPRESENTATION AND INFERENCING

The choice of an object-oriented approach using entity-attribute-value (EAV) triples, the use of frames for classes and instances, and the use of constraints and rules for inferencing, described in detail and justified in Chapter 12 of this book, need not be rehearsed here. However, these choices had implications for what knowledge could be expressed and how that knowledge would be used by the demonstration systems. These implications are crucial to an understanding of the knowledge work of the project.

11.3.1. Time

The representation selected did not lend itself to dealing with time. Dates, for example the 'date of claim', could be represented. Durations of time could be calculated from these dates, but there was no temporal reasoning available. Expressing future eligibility was not straightforward enough to determine, for example, whether a person who was not eligible for a benefit 'today' would become eligible for that benefit in the future — given the passage of time and the only changes in material circumstance being those of the kind that could be predicted on the basis of the information available.

Hence the Advice System was developed only to be able to determine whether, for example, a claimant would be eligible for the benefit for the notional 'today'. If 'today' was the last day of eligibility there was no comment to that effect in the advice given. The restriction to advice about 'today' was implicit not explicit in the rules which were compiled into the systems source code.

Similarly, it was not easy to introduce time triggers, for example to alert the system user that a claim would have to be submitted by a certain date or the benefit time-limit would have been missed. Time-relevant advice could, however, be given by creating properties on frames to hold precomposed text which could be displayed to the user. But this use of properties to hold hard-coded messages is far short of what would be possible if there had been temporal reasoning available for knowledge base designers.

11.3.2. Migration of instances

Another limitation which was to cause considerable difficulty was the inability to create an instance when little of its detail was known and then have that instance 'migrate' through the class hierarchy, i.e. become the instance of a subclass of the original class and acquire a frame with slots for storing information about the additional attributes associated with the subclass, as more detailed information about its nature came to light. For very good reasons (see Chapter 12 below), classes described instances, i.e. expressed values which instances of that class could take, but did not represent instances, i.e. did not express which values instances did take. As soon as there was information pertaining to a particular instance of class, an instance entity had to be created. The information could then be stored in one of the slots of the frame for the instance. The difficulty is that information would typically be volunteered about, for example, a particular person (call this instance of PERSON *Terry) before it was known in detail what kind of person, in relation to the benefit system, *Terry was. If *Terry was an adult female, a whole collection of slots for attributes appropriate to adult females would have been needed such as whether the person was pregnant, whereas if *Terry were a male they would not.

11.3.3. Rich class structure

Initially it had seemed sensible to structure a knowledge base with a class for PERSON and a subclasses to represent kinds of person, e.g. CHILD and CHILDDEPENDANT and CHILDCLAIMANT and ADULT and ADULTCLAIMANT and ADULTDEPENDANT and WIDOW to name a few. The difficulty was that *Terry could not be created as an instance of the class PERSON and then subsequently become and instance of, say, the class CHILD and subsequently CHILDDEPENDANT as more details became known. One way to deal with the problem might have been to wait until it was known exactly what kind of person was being referred to before an instance to represent that person was created in the system. But that would require the user of the system to know how to categorize accurately in welfare benefit terms every person being referred to. It would also require that people being referred to had only one way of being properly categorized. Neither was the case.

One of the tasks of the Advice System was to help the user determine whether a person should be categorized in one way or another, for example as a dependant or not a dependant. And it was often the case that more than one category would apply. WIDOWS might also be EXPECTANTMOTHERS and/or LONEPARENTS and/or CLAIMANTS and/or DISABLED. So a rich class structure for classes like PERSON was not possible.

11.3.4. Perspectives

Another way to get around the problem was to use perspectives.

In one version of the AS knowledge base the class PERSON had an attribute called 'perspectives'. The 'perspectives' slot on the frame representing an instance of PERSON contained the set of 'perspectives' that could be applied to the person. This meant, for instance, that a person could be identified as a female, a lone parent, and a child benefit claimant. One implication of using perspectives was that inappropriate questions could be avoided. Males would not be asked questions about themselves being pregnant.

There needed to be attributes on the class PERSON which allowed perspectives to be associated with its instances. These were referred to as trigger slots. As soon as there was enough information to fill a trigger slot, such as that giving the gender to the person, the appropriate perspective, say 'female', would be associated with the instance of person and an instance of the perspective was created for that person, for example 'TerryAsAFemale'. Information which was female-specific and which could apply to all females would be stored in the slots of instances of the 'Female' perspective. The AS knowledge base was built using perspectives before technical difficulties with the Advice Manager module's use of perspectives were discovered and a third way of dealing with the problem was employed.

11.3.5. Huge frames

The third way of dealing with the problem was the one employed in the Advice System which was delivered at the end of the project. This solution, was both inelegant and inefficient, but it did work. The class PERSON was given all the slots which were needed by any of the subclasses of person. This meant that there was no need to 'migrate' an instance down a class hierarchy as there was no hierarchy down which to 'migrate'. The class PERSON ended up having more than 150 attributes. Every instance of the class PERSON had all 150+ slots whether they were a nonsense or not. Instances of newborn babies carried an overhead of slots relating to their marital status, their children, their school leaving age, and employment history. Although storage might not have been a problem, search was. Checking the values of all the slots of all the instances for possible deductions, as the inference engine did every time new information was made available, reduced performance.

11.4. KNOWLEDGE ANALYSIS AND KB DESIGN

Knowledge analysis was not a clearly defined activity in the project, especially in the early stages. In the final report, however, there is a characterization of knowledge analysis and knowledge encoding.

> We refer to the process of determining the essential structure of the [knowledge] source contents, and representing it in a semi-formal form, as 'knowledge analysis', and to the process of of taking such a semi-formal product and representing it in the chosen knowledge-representation scheme [e.g. the toolkit language] as 'knowledge encoding'.
>
> [Alvey DHSS Large Demonstrator 1984—1989 Final Report, p.23]

Most analysts were involved in a range of activities and naming them or apportioning our work between categories of activities was not usually necessary. The conception of 'knowledge analysis' used here, therefore, may differ in three ways from the way I understand large software development teams use the term: it was formative rather than summative; it often included synthesis as well as analysis; and the scope of knowledge examined was broader than typically used for knowledge base development.

11.4.1. Analysis as formative

The first difference is worth noting because of the potential confusion with the term analysis as used by software developers with a background in, say, mathematics or logic. Analysis, in their use of the term, is what happens to an artifact such as a knowledge base or a requirements specification after it has been developed. Analysis in this sense may, for example, include checks for internal consistency, incompleteness, or ambiguity. There are similarities to this understanding of analysis and the summative approach to evaluation in that it takes place after the artefact is created. Analysis in the sense I am using it here happens before that. It helps to formulate the product in the same way that formative evaluation feeds back into the process of creating whatever is being evaluated. The analyst will look for patterns and gaps in the undigested material and will try to clarify it. These activities are not unlike those undertaken by analysts who are checking for completeness and inconsistencies, so the distinction may seem unnecessary. Analysis of the kind undertaken on this project and by knowledge engineers working to capture requirements for a system, however, is typically performed on material relatively less digested for its purpose than that used by those taking a summative approach, and the analytical techniques are less mature. Analysis of the kind that I am referring to is still more of an art than a science.

11.4.2. Analysis including synthesis

Our 'analysis' involved the activities associated with the dictionary definition of the term — taking apart complex phenomenon distinguishing its elements by, for example, decomposition, critical examination, tracing things to their sources, and/or discovering general underlying principles and the expression, synopsis, of the results of these activities. It also included knowledge synthesis — a putting back together which could involve selection, integration, (more or less radical) restructuring, reconciliation of perceived conflicts, and reformulating of the analysed material as it was recombined. A simple synopsis of the elements distinguished during analysis was usually an intermediate product rather than the final outcome of our analysis.

11.4.3. Knowledge analysis as broad in scope

Our analytical activities involved more than studying material and extracting elements such as objects with their attributes and rules needed for building the knowledge base from our source texts — be they statutory instruments, books on the subject, or transcripts from specially conducted interviews. It also involved:

1. Studying the organization in which a system would be used or about which it needed to provide advice.
2. Considering the users to discover what they could be expected to know and how they could be expected to hold or refer to that knowledge.
3. Considering who would be the interested parties in scrutinising knowledge upon which the systems would depend and what representations of that knowledge would be both useful to them and to knowledge base builders and maintainers.
4. Analysing the tasks users would be undertaking and for which they required support.
5. Understanding the benefit system in the large, e.g. how groups of benefits related to one another, and in the small, e.g. detailed dissection of eligibility rules, contribution conditions, and assessment.
6. Understanding what was straightforward to staff or the public and what involved, sometimes hidden, complexity or misconceptions.
7. Understanding the status, e.g. the authoritativeness, currency, reliability of knowledge found in different sources, and the extent to which it is formalized within the organization.
8. Understanding how knowledge was used, including for which activities, its source, its flows, and the mechanisms for monitoring validating and maintaining it.
9. Understanding where concept substitution or paraphrasing was appropriate in transferring between legal and everyday language.
10. Understanding the demands and limits of the language and inference facilities being used to build the systems — not an easy task as these had not been finalized in the early stages of the project and were being developed in parallel to the analysis in the latter stages

of the project.

11. Understanding how knowledge of different kinds would be used by the system, distinguishing for example in the case of the Advice System between 'static' knowledge 'dynamic' knowledge and 'procedural' knowledge.

Each of the teams undertook a number of preliminary analysis exercises, all of which were knowledge analysis if the term is used broadly. Some analysis centred around particular benefits including single payments for supplementary benefits claimants, mobility allowance, widows benefits, and child benefit.

Organization and task analysis was also undertaken by the LOD team. There was a study of advice giving in independent (non-D(H)SS) advice centres. There was a study of potential users of both claimant information systems, i.e. the Forms Helper which did not have a knowledge base and the Advice System which did.

11.4.4. Advice System

The work on the Advice System (AS) gained momentum as the Forms Helper system was in its later stages of development: a sequential development pattern not adopted in as obvious a way by the other teams, each of which was producing successive version of a single system throughout the project. Knowledge analysis was undertaken by almost everyone on the team.

Members of the team working on designing the user–system interaction analysed naturally-occurring dialogues about benefits as part of their preparation for writing a set of interaction rules which were independent of the domain knowledge. The Oxford Concordance package (OCP) was used to examine the vocabulary and word use of fifty members of the public interviewed in the potential user study. The OCP software can, among other things, create a word list and word count or provide all examples of a word or phrase with as much context as required (e.g. the fifteen words preceding it and the twenty words following it). This analysis fed into the development of the lexicon of the advice system used in the dialogue with the user.

Colleagues developing the planner analysed D(H)SS procedures, developed appropriate planning operators and prepared semi-formal versions of procedural rules which we wrote in the toolkit language and added to the rules created for the non-procedural knowledge base. Classes and attributes needed for these rules were also added to the knowledge base through KANT structures as described in section 5 below. There were also rules developed for the planner which were not written in the toolkit language, but remained separate and made up the procedural knowledge base.

The analysis, design and development of the non-procedural (domain) knowledge base is the subject of the rest of this section and the AS portion of section 11.5. The analysis was centered at Surrey. I worked on it alone in the early stages. Two colleagues were seconded from the D(H)SS for a period to work with me at Surrey on the detailed analysis and representation of Child Benefit knowledge. Later a colleague from Logica moving between Cambridge and Surrey worked with me to complete the analysis and develop the AS knowledge base. We were always a small team and for most of the time working together in the same place.

The knowledge analysis for the Advice System went thorough several phases. During the first phase the benefit system as a whole was examined and represented in a number of different ways. By July 1986 the process of claiming a benefit had been modelled to show the kinds of knowledge an advice system in this domain might require; by September 1986 widow's benefits had been examined and a modification of systemic network grammar (e.g. [Bliss *et al.* 1983] used to represent some of its features; and by January 1987 an in depth analysis of child benefit had progressed far enough for various intermediate representations of its eligibility conditions to be designed and experimented with [Cordingley 1987]. The later stages involved completing a modified 'AND/OR' tree representing child benefit eligibility conditions in such detail that the 'leaves' of the tree related to information the claimant could be asked for, or would be information stored in the knowledge base. Lastly, once it had been decided that the system would give advice on cases where the (possible) claimant would be a lone parent and a range of appropriate benefits identified, analysis at a somewhat less detailed level was undertaken and they were represented in various forms including a class hierarchy and rules in the toolkit language. During this final stage static, dynamic and procedural knowledge were all subject of analysis and representation.

A brief discussion of four of the early exercises will give a flavour of the exploratory stage. Later development is treated in the section on KB building below.

It had become clear from studies undertaken by the Surrey team — the potential user study, the study of advice worker consultations, and radio phone-in programs — that members of the public did not conceptualize their problems or benefit provision in terms of administrative structures (Social Security, National Health Service, Manpower Services Commission, Local Authority and so on). Nor were distinctions related to funding (allocated by parliament and paid 'as of right', paid out of 'public funds' the national insurance scheme, industrial injuries scheme and so on) particularly pertinent to their view. Several conceptual maps of U.K. benefit provisions were developed putting Social Security Benefits in the wider context of benefit provision.

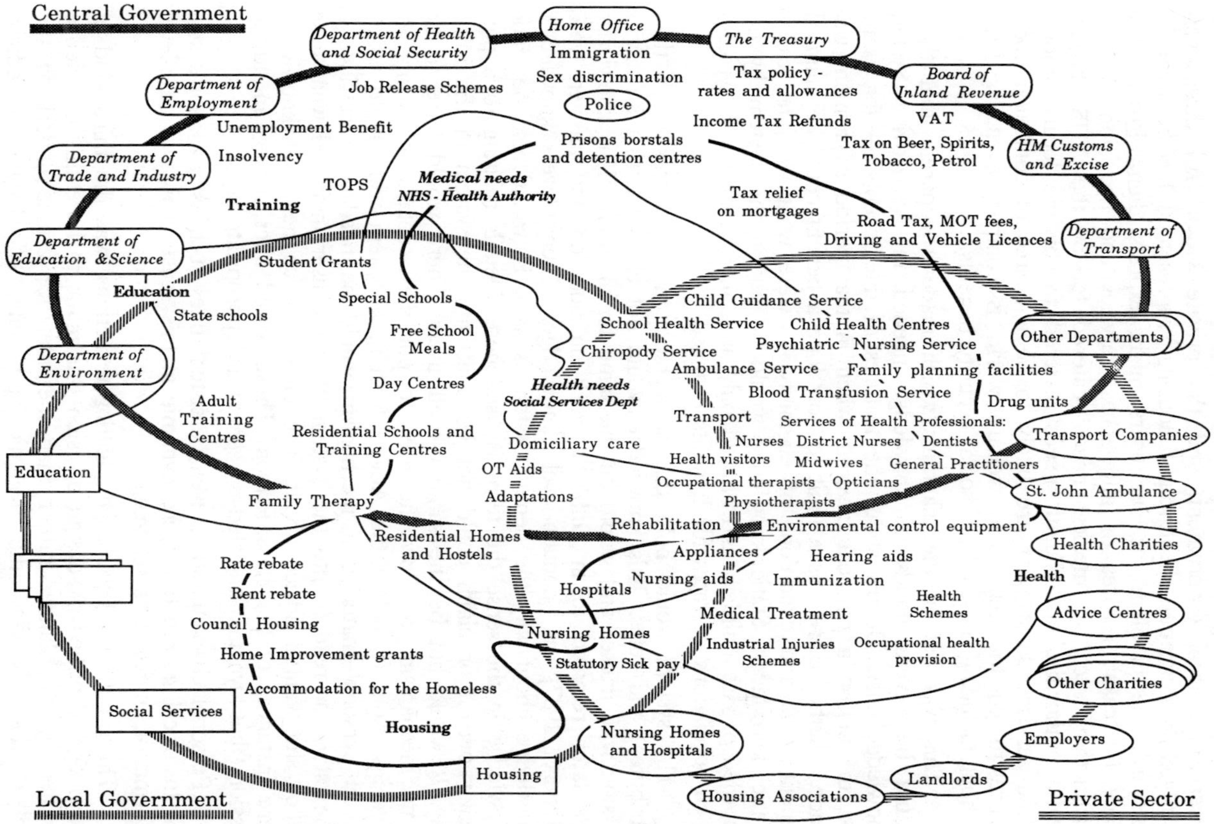

Figure 11.1 *Complexity of welfare provision*

The one in Figure 11.1 showed the complexity of welfare provision. Three sectors (represented by bold ovals) provided welfare — central government, local government, and the private sector. All three were involved in education, health and housing (represented by the irregular outlines), the problems as our users might express them. Provision is made by 'cash', rebates or allowances, services and provision in kind. Distinctions such as 'medical needs' catered for by the NHS through health authorities and 'health needs' catered for by the local authority social services department are likely to be a source of confusion about where to go for help. The welfare world is complex even, as here, without including most of the social security benefits.

This was one of the diagrams which made it apparent that there would be several kinds of knowledge needed in the Advice System knowledge base. Details about the features of the benefits — for example, the period a payment covered, when in that period a payment was made, whether there was a limit to how long a benefit could be claimed, benefit rates and conditions of eligibility — were what we later called 'static' knowledge. Static knowledge would be put in the system by the knowledge base builders and altered only as a maintenance task typically when regulations or rates for benefits changed.

The system would hold this as a hierarchy of classes (with their attributes) and rules. This knowledge would not change during an advice session with a user and would be the same for all users. This knowledge was later referred to in Gilbert's work on question and answer types [Gilbert 1987] as domain-level knowledge. Theory-level knowledge, knowledge about why the benefit system is as it is, would also be static knowledge in the sense the term is used here. Details relating to a particular person or claim could not be built into the system in the same way. It would not be the same for all users. There would have to be some mechanism to allow the user to put these details in during an advice session. If, unlike the Advice System, a system were build which stored personal material, a mechanism would be needed to retrieve it from store or read it into the system once the user indicated what case he or she wanted advice about. The objects which held this knowledge were instances of the class Person. These would alter during an advice session, thus dynamic knowledge seemed an appropriate label.

Personal characteristics, even persistent ones such as a person's sex, and historical information were dynamic in this sense. This was case-level information in Gilbert's scheme.

The procedural knowledge, relating to actions, was the third kind of knowledge identified. A design decision was made to have this knowledge handled by the planner rather than the inference engine underlying the toolkit which handled the dynamic and static knowledge. Procedural knowledge was, therefore, analysed separately. In the end, however, much

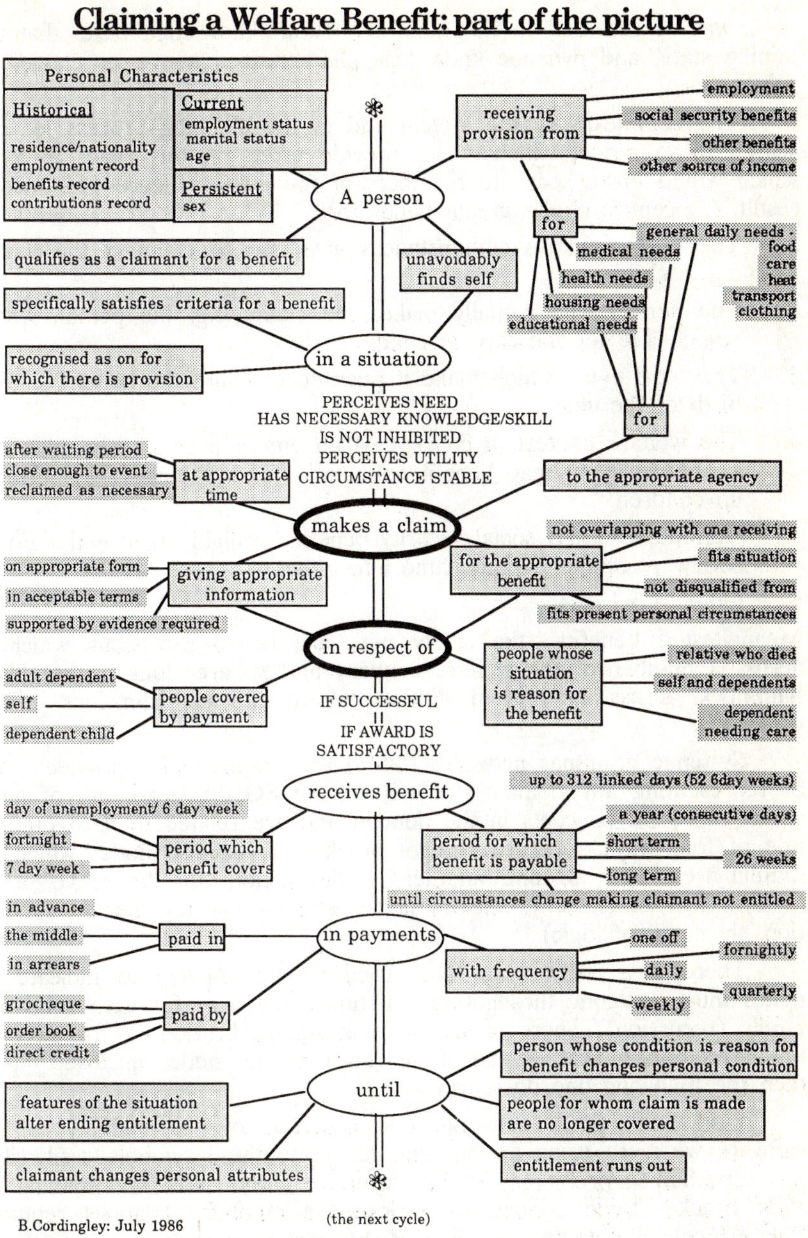
Claiming a Welfare Benefit: part of the picture
Personal Characteristics
Historical
residence/nationality
employment record
benefits record
contributions record
Current
employment status
marital status
age
Persistent
sex
A person
receiving provision from
employment
social security benefits
other benefits
other source of income
for
general daily needs - food care heat transport clothing
medical needs
health needs
housing needs
educational needs
qualifies as a claimant for a benefit
unavoidably finds self
specifically satisfies criteria for a benefit
recognised as on for which there is provision
in a situation
PERCEIVES NEED
HAS NECESSARY KNOWLEDGE/SKILL
IS NOT INHIBITED
PERCEIVES UTILITY
CIRCUMSTANCE STABLE
for
to the appropriate agency
after waiting period
close enough to event
reclaimed as necessary
at appropriate time
makes a claim
not overlapping with one receiving
for the appropriate benefit
fits situation
not disqualified from
fits present personal circumstances
on appropriate form
in acceptable terms
supported by evidence required
giving appropriate information
in respect of
people whose situation is reason for the benefit
relative who died
self and dependents
dependent needing care
adult dependent
self
dependent child
people covered by payment
IF SUCCESSFUL
IF AWARD IS SATISFACTORY
receives benefit
up to 312 'linked' days (52 6day weeks)
a year (consecutive days)
period for which benefit is payable
short term
26 weeks
long term
until circumstances change making claimant not entitled
day of unemployment/ 6 day week
fortnight
7 day week
period which benefit covers
in advance
the middle
in arrears
paid in
in payments
one off
fornightly
with frequency
daily
quarterly
weekly
girocheque
order book
direct credit
paid by
person whose condition is reason for benefit changes personal condition
features of the situation alter ending entitlement
until
people for whom claim is made are no longer covered
claimant changes personal attributes
entitlement runs out
(the next cycle)
B.Cordingley: July 1986

Figure 11.2 *Model of claiming a benefit*

of it was represented in the 'non-procedural' knowledge base, that containing static and dynamic knowledge characterized above, as classes and rules.

The complexity in the system and in the claiming process led to a search for a model which would provide order on this chaos in a way which would make sense to members of the public. Figure 11.3 was the result. Concentric circles create bands for:

1. The person whose circumstances give rise to claiming the benefit, e.g. a child.
2. The person who actually makes the claim, e.g. the person who is responsible for the care of child.
3. The focal event which make it possible to claim the benefit, e.g. the birth of the child.
4. The welfare context, a concept which emerged from this analysis as a useful way to map benefit onto real life experiences;, e.g. bringing up children.
5. Non-means-tested social security benefits available before the Fowler review recommendations came into effect.
6. Other provisions.

Means-tested benefits, 'the safety net', are broad provisions which go across a number of the welfare contexts and so are slung, rather like a hammock, across the bottom with arrows to indicate extensions in both directions.

Systemic grammar networks (SGN) are graphs which provide a way of representing any domain one wishes. An SGN is made up of nodes which represent concepts in the domain and are related to each other in one of four ways. Forward straight brackets, [, enclose nodes which are mutually exclusive of one another (a disjunction, the 'exclusive or' of logic). Curly brackets, {, enclose nodes which occur together (a conjunction, the 'and' of logic).

There is a curly arrow (not used on this figure) to indicate the nodes must be 'gone through' several times, say once for each child of a family (recursion). There is also a back square bracket,], for a conditional relation indicating that if all (and) of the nodes enclosed 'apply' then the following one does also.

Work with these networks was hindered by the inability on the software we were using at the time to create these symbols easily. This was especially a problem with the recursive curly arrow and making the curly bracket large enough to enclose the number of nodes required. This difficulty led to the labelling of the enclosing symbol with EOR for the 'exclusive or', AND (or 'and') for the conjunction and the conditional relations. These logical operators are sometimes (I think incorrectly)

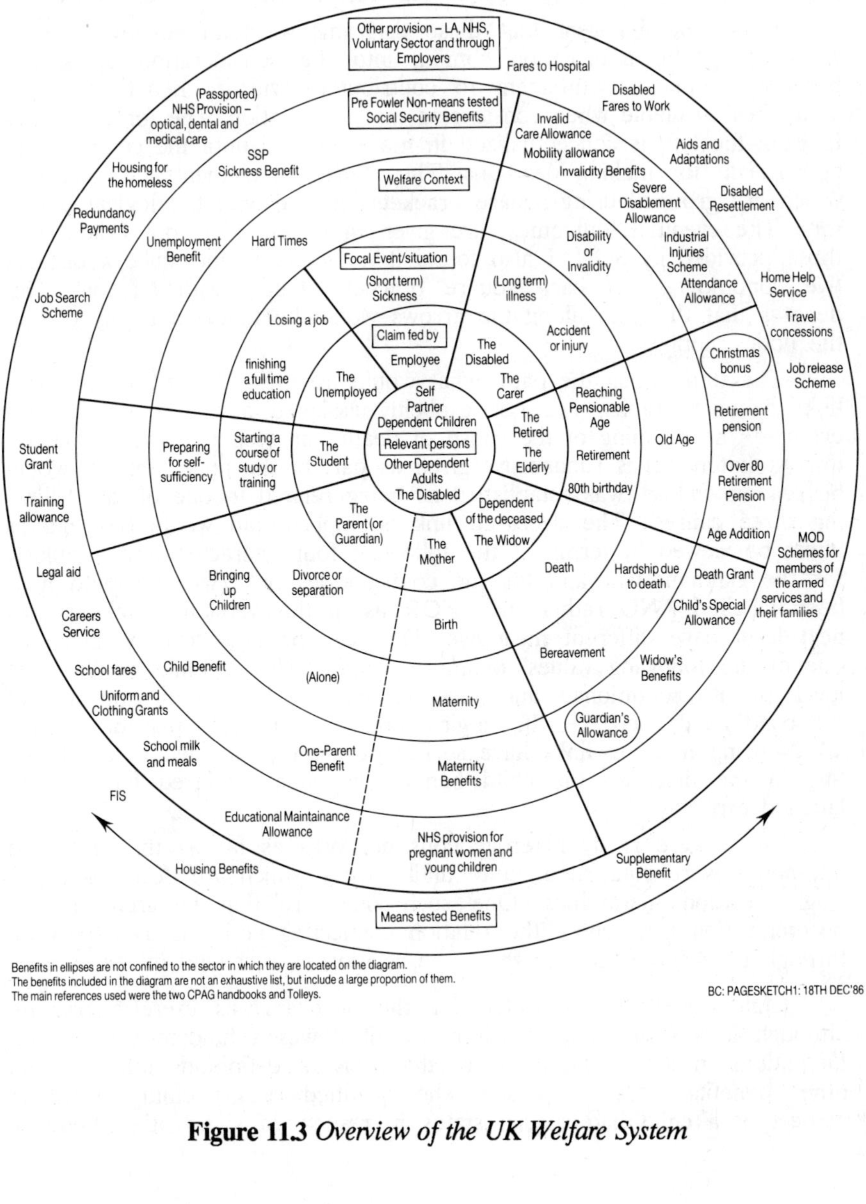

Figure 11.3 *Overview of the UK Welfare System*

called links, but I shall avoid using link in that sense here, reserving it instead for the concept of arc (denoted in the diagrams by horizontal lines or arrows). Labelling the brackets with their logical operators did not eliminate the need to 'teach' people to read the diagrams, but once the principles had been introduced, the label was there as a constant reminder about the easily forgotten feature, the meaning of the brackets.

It became apparent that these diagrams were an effective way of representing the information coming into the consideration of, say, a bereaved woman's entitlement to contributory widow's benefit and the 'outcomes' available when considering that information. The former comes in from the left, is conceptualized in more detailed until the concepts are appropriate for making decisions. They then are elements of conditions which are grouped using square brackets labelled with the logical operators. The eventual 'outcomes' are given in boxes, a symbol I added to those provided by SGN. I also found it necessary to introduce a disjunctive conditional, the back square bracket labelled with an 'or'. This denotes that the path along the arrows would be followed if any one of the nodes 'applies'.

The steps along the path, what would usually be called an arc or a link in most graphs, are not explicitly assigned any meaning. In this example, the meaning of the cause of death link (top left, the arrow following that node) is (unusually) given as part of the node label. It would be read in full as 'was established as being related to one of the following three causes'. The deceased link is implicit and would be read as 'must be viewed in terms of the following four characteristics'. Similarly for the claimant link and for the contributions link (which should have been labelled AND rather than EOR as in this version). Links at the next level have different meanings. They can be read 'can be given by one of the following values' or more simply 'is/was'. Links at the next level go into conditionals and have no meaning beyond the meaning of the conditional itself, i.e. 'if... logical operator... logical operator ... then ...'. Noticing that the links have such different meaning led to the labelling of the links on the child benefit diagrams produced later to be labelled explicitly.

These were richly heterogeneous networks as far as the links and the nodes were concerned: quite unlike trees, which are designed to be single relation hierarchies. One such single relation hierarchy is the decomposition tree where the relation connecting nodes is 'is a part of' throughout. Another is one where the relation is 'is a kind of' or 'is a'.

Child benefit was selected for the next analysis exercise because although it was a simple to claim benefit it was a fundamental benefit. Definitions in its regulations were the basis of definitions for terms in other benefits. Also a person who qualified to get child benefit in respect of a child had special status in respect of some other benefits.

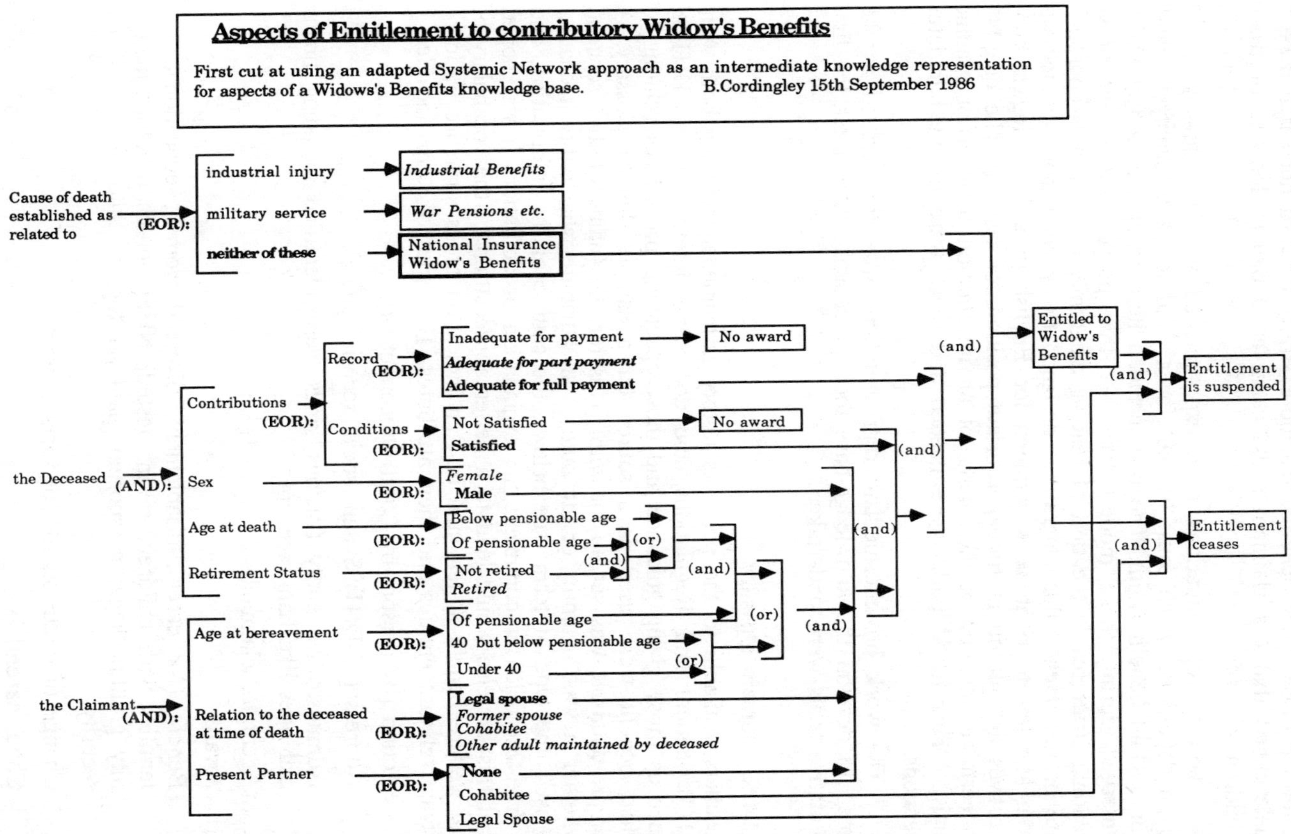

Figure 11.4 *Adapted systemic network for widows benefit*

Claiming those other benefits was more straightforward once it had been determined that the claimant could claim child benefit for one or more children.

Several representations were experimented with in showing the 3 main conditions which must be met for a child to be a 'qualifying child' for a child benefit claim. The one included here recognizes a fact which emerged during these modest trials — that people bring their prose reading strategies to the task of reading diagrams, whether it is appropriate or not. Hence this diagram is designed to be read from top to bottom and left to right as is common for English prose. The logical connectives are placed in the appropriate position for reading. The diagram is certainly in need of the talents of an information designer or graphic artist. 'Fast track' paths were needed and these were included in later versions.

The work on intermediate representations was not pursued as the need to develop the knowledge-base took precedence soon after the first tentative trials were undertaken.

11.4.5. Domain glossary

Leaflets available to the public, statutory instruments including both Acts of Parliament and Regulations, and documents internal to the D(H)SS such as those giving guidance and those specifying procedures relating to child benefit were used as a source for a sample domain glossary. A simple database was set up for with fields for the (name of the) concept, whether it was an entity or attribute, if an attribute what entity it characterised, the type of term (see below), the source of the information, and a free-text field for comments, an explanation or definition. It was hoped that this exercise would lead to a better appreciation of the vocabulary of the welfare benefit system and that an indication of its structure by identifying relevant entities and their attributes. The types of terms included:

1. Action (by person; by Local Office; set of).
2. Address (of D(H)SS unit; social security office).
3. Administrative entity (various kinds were identified including financial ones like bank account).
4. Agent for claimant.
5. Award.
6. Benefit (for carers; disablement; divorced women; educational; for families with children; means tested; NHS; non-contributory maternity grant;package; passported; paid on top of child benefit; social security).
7. Change of circumstance (of various kinds).
8. Child, parentless.

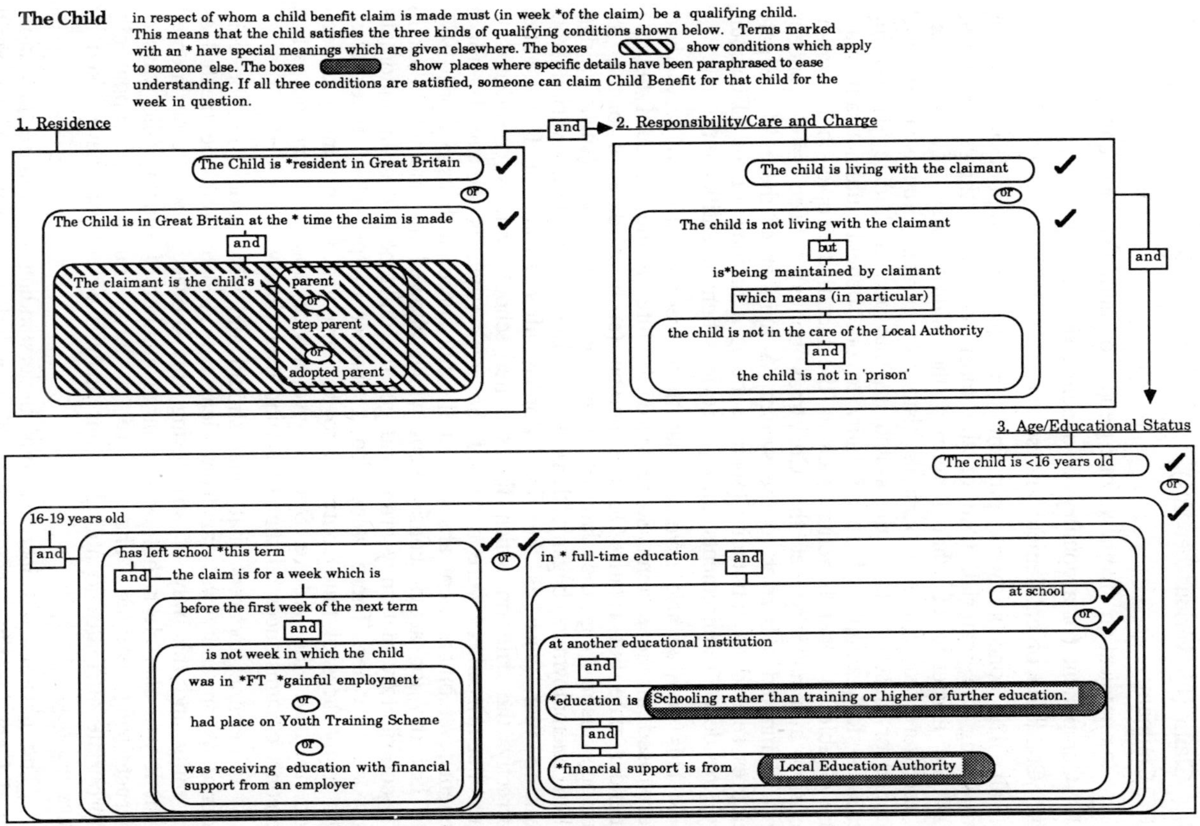
The Child
in respect of whom a child benefit claim is made must (in week *of the claim) be a qualifying child.
This means that the child satisfies the three kinds of qualifying conditions shown below. Terms marked with an * have special meanings which are given elsewhere. The boxes show conditions which apply to someone else. The boxes show places where specific details have been paraphrased to ease understanding. If all three conditions are satisfied, someone can claim Child Benefit for that child for the week in question.
1. Residence
The Child is *resident in Great Britain
or
The Child is in Great Britain at the * time the claim is made
and
The claimant is the child's
parent
or
step parent
or
adopted parent
and
2. Responsibility/Care and Charge
The child is living with the claimant
or
The child is not living with the claimant
but
is*being maintained by claimant
which means (in particular)
the child is not in the care of the Local Authority
and
the child is not in 'prison'
and
3. Age/Educational Status
The child is <16 years old
or
16-19 years old
and
has left school *this term
and
the claim is for a week which is
before the first week of the next term
and
is not week in which the child
was in *FT *gainful employment
or
had place on Youth Training Scheme
or
was receiving education with financial support from an employer
or
in * full-time education
and
at school
or
at another educational institution
and
*education is
Schooling rather than training or higher or further education.
and
*financial support is from
Local Education Authority

Figure 11.5 *Intermediate representations of child benefit conditions*

9. Circular.
10. Claim (for various benefits).
11. Claimant.
12. Communication (from various people or administrative units).
13. Component (of a country; of a name; of a form).
14. Condition of entitlement and so on.

In all, 429 concepts were put into the glossary without in any way exhausting the material. One of the most interesting things to emerge was the existence of what I termed the 'sluice gates' of the system. These were features of a person's history or current circumstances which opened or closed parts of the system to that person. Unlike 'passporting' features, for example where eligibility to one benefit automatically made one eligible to other benefits (such as the fact that people on retirement pension automatically get the Christmas bonus), 'sluice gate' concepts only eliminated a barrier to the system. A number of these 'sluice gate' features related to nationality (such as being a national of an EEC country), residence requirements and/or previous benefit entitlement.

This exercise also revealed that there were a variety of ways dates were used in the system. Some were absolute in the sense of being a calendar date but relative to the person (such as date of birth), the person's claim (e.g. the date of claim) or circumstance (such as date when unemployment began); there were 'fixed dates' which varied from year to year (such as the first Monday after Easter, if I remember correctly, the date on which the summer school term is considered to have begun); others were a day of the week (such as the pay-day for a benefit); yet others were absolute in the full sense, such as 5 April 1987, the last day for actual confinement which allowed the mother to claim non-contributory maternity grant and get the child benefit claim automatically sent to her. There were also a number of 'period of time rules'. The many faces of time continued to be intriguing, but we made a decision to have the Advice System give advice about a snapshot of a person's circumstances so that reasoning over time was avoided.

It became apparent that what should and what should not be considered as an entity was far from clear cut. A date could be treated as an entity and this way of structuring the knowledge was experimented with. It was also clear that were a large number of equally valid ways of characterizing entities. There were a large number of apparently appropriate attributes identified in our analysis which were never used by rules we began to write.

The glossary did increase our understanding of welfare provision, but did not identify a single compelling underlying structure which could be cited as the imperative for building the Advice System knowledge-base. Far more compelling, as it turned out, were the features and capabilities of the toolkit, discussed in the section on representation and inferencing above, and the content of the rules that emerged from careful study of the handbooks we used as sources for the final knowledge-base.

11.4.6. Local Office Demonstrator

In addition to the examination of specific benefits such as mobility allowance in the early days of the project, the Local Office Demonstrator team undertook organizational analysis and task analysis related to the adjudication of supplementary benefits claims and later analysed the task of making decisions related to income support claims.

Organizational analysis

The approach to organizational analysis used was based on the soft systems methodology of Peter Checkland. This approach accounts for the emphasis placed on the variety of organizational perspectives on the activities involved and in the knowledge associated with those activities. It also led them to view knowledge as part of organisational communication rather than a neutral objective commodity.

Task analysis

The task analysis involved a number of different elements. The explicit task of the local office decision maker was analysed, as was the knowledge used during the task. They produced an underlying model of how decision are made. Particular regard was paid to the type of knowledge used and its role in the decision making. They used:

1. Structured interviews, recording of task diaries, monitoring of problems and analysis of the results of individuals responsible for monitoring performance. The people interviewed have been determined by the previous organisational analysis.
2. Development of rational reconstructions of 'worked examples', including an analysis of the decision sequences, the results of decisions, the justifications of decisions and the authorising knowledge appealed to. Analysis of 'mistakes' in decision making and attempts to explain the origin of the mistake. This has required reference to texts on the nature of legal decision making as well as detailed discussion with trainers and monitoring officers.

[Alvey–DHSS Large Demonstrator 1984–1989 Final Report, p. 18]

Knowledge analysis

Context was seen as important for the LOD knowledge base. The team felt strongly that the source of knowledge should be clearly represented along with the knowledge and even be encoded with it in the system so users could examine it to see if the the perspective in the knowledge base accorded with their own. This feature was particularly apt in an environment where the status of the knowledge (e.g. guidance versus instructions) was a factor in the weight given to it and where users personally were legally accountable for the decisions they took, even those based on support from a computer system.

The team undertook both 'broad' and 'narrow' analysis. The former was the term given to the initial, domain-wide, stage of analysis, the identification and work on interconnected 'topics' such as membership of the family and amount with its related topics capital, income, and applicable amount.

The LOD 'domain knowledge base' was structured around the topics identified in this broad analysis which was carried out by a small number of analysts sharing material. 'Narrow analysis' described in some detail in the section on knowledge-base development and building below was the term given to work within the topic. It involved a larger number of analysts working at different sites and periodically checking with one another, until near the end of the project when they were able to gather at one site and share structures.

11.5. STRATEGIES ADOPTED IN DEVELOPING AND BUILDING KNOWLEDGE BASES

11.5.1. Local Office Demonstrator

The size of the LOD analysis team and their geographical spread encouraged them to devise strategies for independent but co-ordinated working. The fact that they were focusing on a single benefit, income support, and considering it in great detail meant that the same classes and attribute names would need to be used by a number of people. Their approach was to divide the work 'horizontally' with some of the same analysts working on more than one layer. The first layer was the 'broad analysis' in which the topics were identified and the portions of the source material linked to appropriate topics. During this analysis entities and their attributes were identified and named. This created 'data structures' and 'topic structures' which were used as source material for the next layer, the 'narrow analysis'.

> Narrow analysis focused on the rules within each topic, formalised their logical structure (representing the body of each rule as an AND/OR tree), and made a step towards formalizing the constituent propositions (i.e. the part which said what was being asked or concluded about the entity), the wording of which [was] copied directly from the source material (and then edited where necessary in order to give a more concise or less context-dependent representation while preserving meaning). The tool being used to support

> this work (KANT) allowed the representations of rules and their constituent parts to be linked to the relevant places in the source material; a different type of link was also used to link propositions for which guidance on interpretation was available...to the place in the source document where that guidance was provided. Topics could be handled substantially independently of one another once the links between them had been identified. The choice and naming of entities/classes was periodically co-ordinated between topics.
>
> As each set of semi-formal rules was produced, 'narrow analysis' continued by creating another set of structures indexed by the class of entity referred to and informal categories of proposition within each class (e.g. person/things to do with health) and accumulating copies of all the semi-formal propositions therein. The copies of propositions in these categories were linked back to the corresponding propositions in the semi-formal rules. The structures used at this stage were shared between the analysts; anyone was free to add content to the existing structure, but changes or extensions to the
>
> [Alvey–DHSS Large Demonstrator 1984–1989 Final Report, p. 25]
>
> structure itself had to be agreed between the analysts.

KANT might be described as a hypertext-like outliner with a number of additional facilities such as the recording of provenance (i.e. which analyst created or changed the nodes in the structure and when it was done) and in later versions the propagation of jeopardy (i.e. alerting the analyst that something a node depends on had been altered and should be inspected to see if the node as it stands is still valid). KANT had been designed to suit analysts who in the main had little or no experience with programming or using structured editors of the kind available on the Xerox machines we were using.

The encoding of the rules and creation in the knowledge base of classes (with their attributes) for the rules to operate on was carried out as a third layer of effort and was largely undertaken by people other than the analysts. The tool used for most of this work was either the structured editor available in the Xerox environment or the Knowledge-Base Builder (KBB).

Advice System

After recognizing the difficulties involved with handing over from an analyst to an encoder, one of the lessons learned in the work on the detailed child benefit knowledge, being few people to co-ordinate and both of us being interested in the full range of source to code transformations, the Surrey team adopted a vertical division of labour, rather than the horizontal one used by the LOD team. The range of benefits we were covering was divided into means-tested and non means-tested.

One of us took one, the other took the other. There were a number of classes and attributes in common, but many were different.

We made our growing lists of class and attribute names available to one another. We were able to resolve most conflicts and identify use of the same name to mean different things as we went along. We did our analysis and developed out KANT structures independently, then integrated our work into a single knowledge base which was 'owned' by and located at Surrey. With only one integrated knowledge base version control was simplified and necessary consistency easier to achieve.

Earlier exercises had indicated that starting to analyse a domain by looking for entities and their attributes had led to the creation of unnecessary (in the sense that they were never referred to in the rules we wrote) classes and/or attributes. So we decided to generate the knowledge base from rules to keep the knowledge base as lean as possible. The greatest boon to this style of development was the 'rule patch', a bit of computer program written at Surrey to provide new facilities for KANT. This patch enabled us to compile rules from KANT if the rules were written in the toolkit language and had been put in specially identified rule nodes of our KANT structures.

When the compiler noticed that a class or an attribute did not exist in the knowledge base we were able to create the classes and add the necessary attributes direct from KANT. We could also access the growing knowledge base via KBB which was a useful way of viewing and editing the class hierarchy and the attributes and was the simplest way to add a large number of classes and/or attributes at once, but it also caused problems of control. Using KBB rules, classes and attributes could be added to the knowledge base without having a corresponding KANT node available for inspection. It was tempting to use KBB especially when it was quicker than going through KANT, so the knowledge base got out of step with some of the KANT structures.

In later work, KBB and KANT were combined and the KANT structures were the knowledge base, nothing apart from what was in a KANT structure could be said to exist in the knowledge base.

Inspection of the knowledge base was of concern to the Advice System as it was for the LOD team, but in a different way. We did not anticipate that members of the public would inspect the knowledge-base as they used the system. Whereas the LOD team envisaged that their users would. Our concern was to make the transformations through which the knowledge went as it passed from source to encoded knowledge base available to scrutiny to all interested parties — including those representing the interests of members of the public, advice workers, D(H)SS, future developers of the system and those who would maintain it — separately from the use of the system. To this end our KANT structures contained several versions of each portion of the domain we represented.

Whereas LOD analysts made KANT nodes for each proposition and logical connector, so that a rule would be represented by a number of nodes, the AS knowledge base had whole rules represented in a single node. All nodes had a title field.

In nodes that contained rules, our analysis and formalisation of knowledge typically generated three other fields. The field containing the least formalized entry might contain text from the source, citation of the reference (title and page number), comments explaining any peculiarities of the knowledge, and reminders to the analysts about changes which had been made or needed to be made to the node. There was usually a field containing an English-like, semi-formal rule which was written to represent the knowledge in the original field faithfully. The third field contained the rule in the toolkit language.

The point of having the three fields juxtaposed and in the same node was to facilitate the inspection of the transformations through the three stages.

Towards the end of the project, when the facilities of KANT and KBB had been combined, an ICL colleague wrote a special 'patch' to make it also possible for our structures to have a fourth field in these nodes, one containing the compiled version of the rule. This meant we were able to inspect the rule the system actually contained and compare it to the one we had sent to the compiler. This enabled us to identify rules where, for example, through mistakes in placing parentheses propositions had been disregarded by the compiler. It was far easier to detect these truncated rules through inspection than through the creation and running of test examples.

A complex system of KANT structures was developed. It was able to serve as a 'progress chasing'/version control tool. It was able to show increasingly fine granularity of rules, i.e. where propositions in one rule were elaborated by other rules. In some structures links were made between KANT nodes representing the original rule and all those which further refined its proposition. Other structures were designed so that refining rules were 'children' of the top-level rule. Links were made between nodes where terms with crucial technical/legal meanings were used and nodes containing definitions for those terms. An effective glossary was thus created. It served not only to explain the meaning of terms but also as a check that the same meaning pertained throughout.

In some cases it was possible to make links between the original source material and nodes which made use of that material. We had not been given permission to make an on-line version of the CPAG handbooks, so a reference to the books was given when material from that source was first introduced.

It's fair to say that KANT and KBB provided extremely useful flexible tools which allowed analysts with different working styles and personal preferences to co-operate effectively in the analysis and construction of our knowledge base.as given when material from that source was first introduced. We did have an on-line 'KANTified' version of *How to Claim State Benefits* and so were able to make links between material in that source and versions of it used for the system.

11.6. CONCLUSIONS

A variety of analyses were undertaken. A variety of strategies for developing knowledge bases were adopted. The domain knowledge-bases which came into being each had its own character although the language for their formal expression was the same. This breadth of experience has been a strength of the project, allowing a number of lessons to be learned.

CHAPTER 12

KNOWLEDGE REPRESENTATION FOR LEGAL APPLICATIONS

Trevor Bench-Capon and Justin Forder

12.1. INTRODUCTION

The choice of knowledge representation is a crucial decision that must be taken when designing knowledge based systems, including those in the legal area. Over the years a number of paradigms for knowledge representation have become well established, and have been used to good effect across a range of different application domains. In fact, all these major paradigms have been used for legal applications: an examination of the literature will disclose KBS based on production rules, various kinds of structured objects such as frames and semantic networks, and first-order predicate calculus, as well as various mixtures. In all such systems, techniques developed for general use were straightforwardly applied to the legal domain, and many of these applications can be seen as successful to a degree. Experience has shown, however, that the paradigms do have practical differences that make them particularly suited to some areas and styles of applications. In this chapter we shall consider the demands placed upon knowledge representation by legal applications, and discuss how this should affect the way in which the knowledge representation task is tackled. First we shall consider how the application area impinges on a KBS through the life cycle of the KBS. Next we shall consider whether there are particular features of the domain which render the existing paradigms inadequate, and whether the claims made by such as [Greenleaf *et al.* 1987] and McCarty [1989] to the effect that special purpose knowledge representation techniques are required for the

KNOWLEDGE-BASED SYSTEMS AND
LEGAL APPLICATIONS. ISBN 0-12-086441-X

legal domain are justified. We shall then present the knowledge representation formalism developed for use within the three of the applications of the DHSS Demonstrator project, so as to illustrate our earlier conclusions, and indicate some of the problems encountered and areas where we consider further work necessary.

12.2. PHASES IN A LEGAL KBS AND CONSEQUENCES FOR KNOWLEDGE REPRESENTATION

Like any software application a KBS has a life cycle which includes the construction of the system, the testing of the system and a period of use, maintenance and enhancement. In each of these phases the fact that an application is in the domain of law will have considerable influence. It is that influence that will be considered in this section.

When constructing a KBS, it is necessary to consider the sources of knowledge available about the domain, and the nature of the knowledge to be represented. In the legal area a distinctive feature is the amount of knowledge that exists in written form. Not only may there be legislation itself, setting out the letter of the law, but there may also be reports of decisions made by adjudicators, perhaps transcripts giving the arguments presented by counsel, and commentaries and textbooks designed to instruct people in the law for a particular area. In many other fields, we cannot find texts corresponding to all of these categories. In the area of medical diagnosis systems, for example, we will find textbooks describing the symptoms and treatment of various diseases, and perhaps case histories as well, but there will be nothing corresponding to the legislation. For while the medical diagnosis system is ultimately about a real physical system, the human body, the legal KBS is ultimately about a conceptual system enshrined in legislation. The result of this is that the texts themselves need to be taken seriously in a legal application in a way in which they do not in a medical diagnosis application. It actually matters whether a legal case is real or hypothetical, and which case acts as a basis for a particular view of what the law is. Similarly it matters what the legislation says because the relationships and concepts under consideration owe their existence to this legislation. Any formalism for legal knowledge representation needs to be well adapted to the representation of these texts.

Of course, there exist examples of legal KBS which do not represent legislation at all, or only to a rudimentary extent: McCarty's TAXMAN, described in [McCarty 1977], and Rissland and Ashley's HYPO, described in [Rissland and Ashley 1987], would provide notable examples. The explanation for this is that this kind of system is motivated by a consideration rather different from that present in the majority of legal KBS. These systems set out to model the reasoning of lawyers, focusing on the way in which a single point of law might be resolved. There is therefore just one relevant phrase in the legislation. If we take the function of a legal KBS to provide support for the resolution of a whole case rather than a single point of law, we believe it is uncontentious to say that such a system must contain, as part at least, some representation of the underlying legislation. For example, Rissland and Skalak's CABERET system, described in [Rissland and Skalak 1989], combines rule-based reasoning, which directs attention to the points of law to be considered, with HYPO-like case-based reasoning to support the consideration of these points.

If we move from the construction of the knowledge base to its testing, we find again that the legal domain again has some special characteristics. It is a significant difference in legal applications that the answer produced by a system is of less importance than the means used to arrive at the answer. Almost all workers in the area have noted this feature with respect to the role played by explanation. Most domains can aim at providing the right answer, and the explanation is given mainly to allow the user to invest some confidence in the answer, or to aid the system builder in debugging the knowledge base when a wrong answer is given. In a legal expert system in contrast, the method of arriving at an answer is of more importance than the answer itself, since it needs to correspond to a potentially successful legal argument, and to be available to the user so that he can strengthen or counter the points made depending on the side he wishes to argue. The user of a legal KBS wants to know how to win his case, not just that he ought to win it. This force of this point is not, however, confined to explanation, but affects also the knowledge representation: since the conclusion must be demonstrably based on acceptable legal reasoning the knowledge used in the system must also be demonstrably sound. How is such a demonstration to be achieved? Unfortunately it cannot be done by running sets of test cases through the system, but only by an actual scrutiny of the knowledge base itself. Which means that the knowledge base has to be in a form which is accessible to the expert who can assess its correctness, and has to be structured in a way which corresponds to the sources from which it derives. Of course, the representation will be a paraphrase, and it is well known that paraphrases are legally unacceptable in general: nonetheless the closer the represented knowledge to the source, the more acceptable and capable of validation it will be.

Two chief consequences arise from the need for the knowledge base closely to follow the source, and to be available to the expert for audit. Firstly, there needs to be sufficient flexibility of syntax to accommodate the different ways of expressing equivalent statements that might be used in the legislation. Use of a canonical form inhibits intelligibility by forcing rearrangement of the source form. Secondly, the statements in the representation must be truly declarative. While almost all knowledge representation paradigms have declarativeness as an aspiration, in practice the use of, for example, conflict resolution strategies in production rule systems, means that it is not possible to detach a piece of a knowledge base from its context and consider its correctness in isolation. In many application areas, where we are interested in the effect of the representation, this matters only in so far as it makes the validation of the knowledge base a harder task. But in the legal domain, where the correct decision is only part of what is required, it presents a more serious problem.

The same point is reinforced when we consider the maintenance of a legal KBS. Maintenance is a more pressing problem for a legal KBS than in many other areas. For while, if we are building a medical expert system we can expect the functioning of the human body to remain fairly constant (although knowledge of it may improve, and fashions in diagnosis and treatment change), legislation can be, and is, amended with disturbing frequency, and at any time a new decision on a given point may alter what the law on that particular matter is. Thus a legal knowledge base must be constructed with the certainty that those parts of it concerning legislation and case law will alter. Such alterations in legislation are typically localized: words are added to or deleted from a particular paragraph or section. It is desirable that the corresponding changes to the knowledge base be similarly localized, and this can only be so if the structure of the knowledge base reflects that of the legislation.

Lastly we need to mention the use of the system. Because the person who is using the system is concerned with a legal decision, for which the responsibility is his, the process of using the system must make sense to him. The role of explanation was noted above, but we should also consider the questions that are put the user and the terms in which they are asked. Such transparency in use must also be supported by the underlying knowledge representation, and again the closer the representation approaches to the form and structure of the sources, the more comprehensible the process will be.

From the early days of KBS it seemed that law was a very natural area of application, because it was just the features of declarativeness and flexibility, mentioned above as crucial for legal applications, which were claimed to distinguish KBS from conventional systems. In practice, however, these qualities were often overstated for existing paradigms, and might be further compromised in order to achieve other system goals. A certain degree of disillusion has resulted. The lesson is that these features, especially declarativeness, while present to some degree in any knowledge representation paradigm, need to be taken especially seriously when building a legal application.

12.3. ISOMORPHISM TO LEGISLATION

In the previous section we stressed the need to make the represented knowledge correspond to the structure of the represented source. In this section some of the implications of this for a knowledge representation formalism is examined.

There should be identifiable items within the knowledge base which correspond to the items found in the legislation. If working within a rule based paradigm, this would mean ideally something like a single rule to express the content of each regulation, definition, etc. The need for isomorphism thus requires the syntax of rules to be sufficiently expressive to allow this one to one correspondence. Furthermore, the internal structure of a rule should map clearly onto its representation in the legislation — clauses should follow in the same order, linked by the same connectives. Neither of these conditions is fulfilled by PROLOG-style formalisations — for example, a definition of the form:

S1 A person shall be P if, and only if, he is Q or R and S

would be represented by the two Horn clauses:

HC1 p(X):- q(X).
HC2 p(X):- r(X), s(X).

Leaving aside the problem that one part of the biconditional in S1 is represented by the treatment of negation as failure within this paradigm (defended in Kowalski (1989)), this has done some small violence to the form of the original statement. HC1 and HC2 in fact translate

S2a A person shall be P if he is Q
S2b A person shall be P if he is R
S2c No person shall be P unless he satisfies the conditions in S2a and S2b

Whilst S1 and S2 are logically equivalent, there may well have been a motive in choosing to express the conditions for P-ness in the form of S1 rather than S2. Moreover, neither HC1 nor HC2 can properly be considered in isolation. Thus several of the motives for isomorphism, particularly considerations deriving from ease of representation and scrutability for validation are lost by the need to translate into a normal form. This may of course, be seen as no more than syntactic sugar, but the practical considerations suggest strongly that this sweetening should be provided.

The issue of grain size of predicates within rules is also important. Consider the following example from [Bench-Capon *et al.* 1987], which discusses the appropriate representation of Regulation 6 of the Conditions of Entitlement Regulations (relating to a now defunct benefit, supplementary benefit). The regulation states:

> [a claimant is not required to be available for employment if] he is regularly and substantially engaged in caring for a severely disabled person

Now this could be formalised in a variety of ways. Simplest would be the purely propositional

```
F1 a-claimant-is-not-required-to-be-available-for-employment
  <- he-is-regularly-and-substantially-engaged-in-caring-for-a-
     severely-disabled-person
```

This may be adequate for some purposes, but fails to reflect any of the internal structure of the constituent propositions, most notably in this case, that the same person is the subject of both. So we could move to a predicate calculus representation with unary predicates:

```
F2 is-not-required-to-be-available-for-employment(X)
     <- regularly-and-substantially-engaged-in-caring-for-a-
        severely-disabled-person(X)
```

But these unary predicates could be decomposed further:

```
F3 is-not-required-to-be-available-for-employment(X)
  <- regularly-and-substantially-engaged-in-caring-for(Y,X)
     & is-a-severely-disabled-person(Y)
```

Or even

```
F4 is-not-required-to-be-available-for-employment(X)
  <- engaged-in-caring-for(Y,X,regularly)
     & engaged-in-caring-for(Y,X,substantially)
     & is-disabled(Y,severely)
```

What determines which of these representations is best is the utility of making the decompositions. In particular we need to know whether the components into which we decompose are used elsewhere: if they are not it is unlikely that much will be lost by not making the decomposition. These considerations of grain size of predicate have consequent implications for the expressive power of the knowledge representation formalism. Here, F2 requires that we have more than propositional logic, F3 that we allow reference to more than a single individual, and F4 that we do not restrict ourselves to binary relations. (Of course we could rewrite F4 using only binary relations, but this would again represent a departure from isomorphism.) Although systems have been built using propositional logic, and a quasi-propositional logic allowing no more than F2, we cannot say at the outset that F4 would not be appropriate and so should make provision for this in our knowledge representation formalism.

So far, the demands made on the representation have stayed within the bounds of well-known formalisms. A specific problem, however, derives from the fact that legislation typically contains explicit references to other pieces of legislation, either within the same statute or elsewhere.

This point is well discussed in [Routen 1989] and [Routen and Bench-Capon 1990]. Subsection 2 of section 79 of the United Kingdom Housing Act 1985 provides a representative example:

> 79 (2) Subsection (1) has effect subject to:-
> (a) the exceptions in schedule 1 ...
> (b) sections 89(3) and (4) and 90(3) ... and
> (c) sections 91(2) and 93(2).

This can be catered for in existing formalisms by substituting an explicit representation of the material contained in each of the sections referred to in the representation of section 79(2), producing a flat formalisation, that is one without any cross-reference. An approach taken in [Sergot *et al.* 1986b], and [Bench-Capon *et al.* 1987]. This lessens the correspondence to the source form, and introduces inescapable redundancy. The pitfalls of this with regard to construction, validation, maintenance and use of the system are discussed at length in [Routen and Bench-Capon 1990].

An alternative approach, again compatible with existing formalisms, is to introduce new predicates corresponding to the truth values of the cross-referenced sections. While introducing less redundancy, this again causes deviation from the structure of the source form, and has the undesirable effect of creating this deviation at the "far end" of the reference — so amendments introducing new cross-references will cause non-local changes. What is needed is a mechanism within the knowledge representation formalism to allow such cross-references to be made explicitly.

12.4. ADEQUACY OF EXISTING PARADIGMS

So far we have considered ways in which existing paradigms might be used to build a legal KBS. There are, however, those who would argue that there are features of the legal domain which require a representation that is specific to the legal domain: for example [Greenleaf *et al.* 1987], and [McCarty 1989]. Greenleaf *et al.* base their argument on the need for the representation to be well adapted to use by lawyers, who they see as the natural builders of such applications, and this means that 'the form of representation must be such that expression in that form comes naturally to lawyers'. McCarty's motive is different: his belief is that if legal knowledge based systems are to progress beyond the limited success produced by current systems, a deep conceptual model is required. Because there are many common sense categories, such as time, action, belief and permission, underlying the representation of a legal problem domain, a knowledge representation language that faithfully mirrors the structure of these categories is required. In [McCarty 1989] he proposes the basic features of such a language, which he calls a Language for Legal Discourse.

These arguments are of a quite different sort. The first is an appeal to the convenience of the notation used in representation: if one accepts that it is lawyers who should build these systems, and one believes that lawyers would find a particular style of representation congenial, then the argument holds. It does not, however, claim that existing paradigms are inadequate, but rather that there are pragmatic advantages in a specialized representation. McCarty's argument is deeper, in that it does claim that existing paradigms are inadequate. McCarty's argument is a more general form of the widely held view that because much of law is concerned with the creation of rights and duties, the representation of norms must be central, and hence some form of deontic logic is a *sine qua non*. For a helpful discussion of this see [Jones 1989]. The issues arising from the claims about the adequacy of existing paradigms to represent these fundamental structures is as yet unresolved. Attempts have been made to represent some of the categories put forward by McCarty in first order predicate calculus. For an example of the treatment of deontics see [Moore 1980]; for an example of the treatment of temporal matters see [Kowalski and Sergot 1986] and the brief discussion of the issue towards the end of this chapter. Others would claim that the need for all of these categories is not proven for all legal KBS; for specific discussions of this with regard to deontics see [Sergot 1985] and [Bench-Capon 1989]. More work is needed on these issues before useful conclusions can be drawn.

One further feature of legal knowledge, not much discussed in the literature, which seems of prime importance is the role of definitions in legal knowledge.

12.5. DEFINITIONS

It has been noted in [Sergot 1985] that:

> substantial amounts of legislation are, or can be taken to be, essentially definitional in nature. Much legislation can be viewed as a high-level specification of some legal relationship or property.

This is certainly true for a good deal of the social security legislation which formed the basis of the DHSS Demonstrator systems, and has been observed elsewhere in such diverse areas of the law as the law relating to nuisance, discussed in [Schildt 1989], and Netherlands Dismissal law, treated in [Koers *et al.* 1989]. That the definitions found in legislation are an essential part of a legal KBS is now almost universally accepted. These definitions may not be the only knowledge required for a system, although systems (e.g. [Sergot *et al.* 1986b]) have been built which contained only this knowledge. Because much of the knowledge to be represented consists of definitions, however, we need to be aware of the differences between analytic statements, which express a definition, such as:

D1. a bachelor is an unmarried man

and synthetic statements, which record true universal generalisations, such as

D2. Catholic priests are unmarried men

Both of these statements would be formalised in first order predicate calculus as:

D3. $(\forall x)(Fx \rightarrow Gx \& Hx)$

but this formalization loses the different information conveyed in the original statements. Part of the difference lies in the fact that the definition gives necessary and sufficient conditions, whereas the universal generalization gives only a sufficient condition; but this is not all: for while finding that a person was not an unmarried man would lead us inevitably to conclude that he was not a bachelor, whereas whilst this finding would lead us to suppose that he was not a Catholic priest, further evidence might lead us to reject instead the universal generalisation. It must be recognized that Catholic priests could marry, and might one day be women.

In [Brachman 1985], which offers an admirable critique of some of the shortcomings of frame representations as widely used, Brachman discusses definitions. Having established that frame systems which permit the cancellation of default values cannot be used to express necessary conditions he suggests that they are entirely inadequate when dealing with sufficient conditions, and so cannot begin to express the difference between a definition and a universal generalization. He then cites two arguments designed to suggest that this is unimportant: that no lexical items have complete definitions (e.g. [Bobrow and Winograd 1979]), or that criterial definition is impossible for the majority of terms in which AI systems are interested (e.g. [Reiter 1978]). These arguments are clearly not good enough to rebut Brachman's criticisms in general, and this is even clearer if our domain is law. For the law is a field in which definitions, in the quasi-mathematical sense, are available, and where the need to give different treatment to definitions is evident. This latter point is clearly shown in [Schildt 1989] where, because of the nature of the domain, definitions give rise to conjunctions, which are closed, and the empirical observations of case law give rise to disjunctions, which are open-ended. In his JURIS system $(P \& Q)$ is not equivalent to $\neg(\neg P \vee \neg Q)$, since with P and Q false the first would be false and the second would be unknown (to allow for the possibility of further clarification of the concept under consideration). This makes a sharp distinction between definitions and generalizations, but it restricts the use of conjunctions to definitions and of disjunctions to generalizations whereas we believe that such a distinction needs to be pervasive in an area such as law where definitions are of such prime importance. The consequence for knowledge representation is that it must provide an appropriate means of distinguishing between a definition and a universal generalization. The suspicion is that the unsatisfactory treatment of definitions in frame systems as commonly used underlies the statement in [Koers *et al.* 1989] that 'frames will be of little use for legal knowledge representation' (p. 53).

In any definition the distinction between the term being defined and the terms being used to define it is important. In a first order predicate calculus formalization such as D3 this information is lost. While this does not affect the deductive inferences that can be made on the basis of a definition, it is important for the way in which definitions are used. Thus, for example, we can sensibly say that a person becomes a widow when their husband dies, but not that their husband dies when they become a widow. These considerations are likely to be of importance when explaining arguments turning on definitions, and generally when reasoning about them. Thus, given the central role of definitions in law, it is highly desirable for this reason also that the knowledge representation formalism supports definitions in a comfortable and explicit manner.

12.6. USEFULNESS OF FRAMES

In the above discussion we said that frame representations as currently used did not fit well with legal representation because of their unsatisfactory treatment of definitions. None the less frames do have wide appeal, and this appeal is explicable in terms of what Ringland calls in [Ringland 1988] their 'bundling' aspect. When people conceptualise the world they find it natural to think in terms of objects with attributes, and of different classes of objects with characteristic and different attributes. This notion lies very deep in our conceptual framework, as is indicated by Somers, e.g. [1963] and Kiel, e.g. [1979]. Given that this is a natural way of thinking about the world, and that one use of frame-like representations is to effect this kind of division, it seems unwise to reject such systems because of the failings above. What is needed rather is a different approach to frames which will avoid the above objections, whilst retaining the notion of distinct types of object with characteristic attributes. Turning again to definitions, including those to be found in legislation, we find a very common form to be that which says 'an X is a Y which is P', such as a 'a bachelor is a man who is unmarried'. This kind of definition does, of course, fit very well with a frame hierarchy, with the defined term being a subclass of the term used in the definition with the indicated restriction on some of its attribute values. Notice, in contrast, that when we represent such definitions in ordinary predicate calculus we get

$$(\forall x)(\text{bachelor}(X) <\!-\!> \text{man}(X)\ \&\ \text{unmarried}(X)).$$

Here the difference in role of the two terms in the definition are lost. We believe this distinction to be important and worth reflecting in the representation, and this is sometimes very conveniently done by means of an inheritance hierarchy.

12.7. INCOMPLETE INFORMATION AND VAGUENESS

Another feature of the legal domain, is that ultimately a decision is made. When a case is brought before a competent adjudicator, he cannot plead ignorance. This means that he must decide on the basis of the facts available to him, although it is rare that his information will be complete and certain. Also, law notoriously exhibits 'open texture', that is some of the terms used will be vague and their application capable of resolution only by application of the proper decision making mechanism. These features, which are often confused, have led some to argue that a knowledge representation facility for the domain must include facilities for explicitly representing this. The converse has been argued in [Bench-Capon and Sergot 1988] and [Schildt 1989], which suggest that these topics can be handled through the use made of a classical bivalent representation, rather than by adapting the representation. None the less any representation must be capable of supporting reasoning with incomplete and open-textured information.

12.8. THE ALVEY–DHSS DEMONSTRATOR TOOLKIT

The Alvey–DHSS large Demonstrator project gave an opportunity to explore and develop many of the ideas discussed above. After investigating a range of existing paradigms the project developed its own knowledge representation and inference Toolkit for use in the three legislation-based applications that were its concern:

1. Supporting the assessment of welfare benefit claims.
2. Advising potential benefit claimants.
3. Supporting the development of new benefit policy.

The project gave a unique opportunity to explore representation and use of legal knowledge in these contrasting and important applications. Each of the three applications had to use a large, maintainable knowledge base, and was subject to the kinds of constraint discussed in the preceding sections. Welfare benefits legislation is subject to particularly frequent amendment and any useful system would have to be able to respond quickly to such changes. This led us to emphasize three of the features discussed above, namely that its structure should reflect the structure of the sources from which it derived, that it should be modular, and that the meaning of components should be clear from inspection (independent of other components).

The Toolkit's knowledge representation language is purely declarative, being soundly based on classical predicate logic, and provides sufficient flexibility of syntax for the representation to reflect the structure of the clauses in the source form of the knowledge being represented. The first aspect ensures that the meaning of any statement in the representation is unambiguous and can be determined without reference to other statements in the system. The second aspect allows a clear correspondence between statements in the source and statements in the formalism. Both aspects work together to support validation by inspection and to facilitate maintenance.

The considerations advanced towards the end of the last section led to a mixed paradigm which would allow the representation and use of classes, instances, rules and constraints. Attributes of an instance hold numeric or symbolic values, or other instances. Values can represent sets/ranges of possibilities, allowing reasoning with incomplete or imprecise information.

The Toolkit is supported by an assumption-based truth maintenance system (ATMS), based on [deKleer 1986], which allowed applications to use assumptions to achieve results which would require non-monotonic reasoning in other systems.

12.8.1. Design

The knowledge representation and inference facility was restricted to those features which were well understood and capable of being implemented in a sound, logical manner. This ruled out some perceived application requirements, such as the need to support reasoning about time. The reasons for this were both pragmatic, in that we saw no advantage in implementing facilities of dubious provenance, and motivated by the belief that a better understanding of the need for such facilities, and some insight on how they might be implemented, could be gained from building upon a sound and well understood foundation.

12.8.2. Classes, instances, slots and values

All the applications needed to be able to represent and reason about multiple individuals, their attributes and their relationships. To support this, the Toolkit provided a frame-based system.

As the discussion of Brachman's views suggested 'frames' are commonly used for knowledge representation without precise definition of or distinction between the class/subclass and class/instance relationships. The loose definition of inheritance permits liberal use of default values to achieve a variety of imprecisely specified aims, in ways which are inconsistent with classical logic. Following the principles outlined above, we represented the definitions of types of individual referred to in the source material by classes, defining them in terms of their attributes and the types of those attributes. Individuals were represented by instances of these classes. For economy of expression, the classes were organized into a class/subclass lattice supporting a strict logical interpretation of inheritance, as outlined below. Giving definitions of the different sorts of individual in this way helps support the distinction between analytic and synthetic statements discussed earlier and sets limits on what can meaningfully be said in rules or constraints. A class hierarchy of this sort thus achieves the aim of sensibly decomposing the objects into the domain into types with characteristic bundles of attributes, and provides a well-founded language in which additional information about the domain can be expressed. Classes in such a system correspond to logical types rather than to the 'typical members' of the conventional frame systems. Readers familiar with the KRYPTON system of Brachman *et al.* [1983] may notice some similarities with that system: in fact the Toolkit was designed independently of reference to that system, and the similarities arise out of a common motivation for the two formalisms.

Such class defines its instances by specifying the names and types of the slots which its instances contain. Some of this information may be contained directly within the class definition, and some may be found by inheritance from one or more superclasses. A class always embodies a more specific definition than any of its superclasses — slots may be added but not deleted, and inherited slots must have the same, or a more restrictive (but compatible), type as that given in the superclass. If a slot is inherited from more than one superclass, its type must result from the intersection of the types of the inherited versions of the slot (or a further restriction on this). The strictness of this inheritance mechanism means that it does represent genuine necessity, rather than the more nebulous notion associated with cancelable inheritance.

The available slot types were:

1. Numeric, with type giving permitted range.
2. Literal, with type enumerating a set of mutually exclusive literal values (Boolean attributes were represented using literal slots with values True, False).
3. Instance-valued, with type giving the permitted class of instances (instances of subclasses of the named class were also, logically, instances of the named class, and so might be held in the slot).

The claim assessment and advice applications needed to be able to reason in the face of incomplete information about individuals. The policy application needed to reason about groups of people rather than individuals. Both these requirements were met by allowing attributes to hold ranges of possible values, and reasoning on the basis of these.

Values in literal and numeric slots represented the current possible set of values for the attribute represented by the slot. This interpretation of slot values enabled negation to be handled by taking the complement of the denied value with respect to the slot type. Values in instance-valued slots were divided into the names of instances known to be in the slot, and the names of instances known not to be in the slot (allowing an appropriate, though incomplete, treatment of negation).

The representation of attribute types and values was such that some reasoning could proceed in the absence of complete information, without invalidating the classical interpretation of negation.

All the applications needed limited second-order facilities (e.g. to allowing summation of money owned by the members of a family). To make this possible without requiring a closed-world assumption, instance-valued slots could also contain cardinality information (represented as a numeric range), and a limited set of second-order functions was provided, e.g. for summing some slot value over the set of individuals held in a given instance-valued slot. The provision of cardinality information also allowed an improved treatment of negation.

12.8.3. Rules and constraints

While all the applications needed some kind of rule language to relate slot values within or between instances, the nature of support required appeared to vary between applications.

The declarative reading of a logical statement licenses deductive conclusions about any of its propositions. Sometimes, however, the intention of such a statement is to allow a particular conclusion to be drawn. The claim assessment and advice applications had 'input' and 'output' data which could be distinguished at the time of building the knowledge base, whereas in the policy application the distinction between 'input' and 'output' data varied according to the problem being considered. This distinction, mentioned earlier in Chapter 4, was recognized by providing 'rules', which had one 'head' proposition distinguished as the conclusion, and 'constraints', which gave equal status to all their propositions. Constraints were thus more general than rules, but where the 'output' slot was known in advance the use of a rule was more efficient.

Rule bodies and constraints could be of arbitrary complexity, allowing the decomposition of the knowledge base into individual rules and constraints to reflect the decomposition used in the source material.

Variables in rules and constraints were typed with the classes of individuals over which they were quantified. In classical predicate logic such typing information has to appear in the form of additional conditions in the body of the statement, thereby losing a valuable distinction between the roles of such conditions. Typing a variable with a non-leaf class allowed the effect of the rule to be inherited by its subclasses, so giving economy of expression. Rules and constraints could also refer to particular instances by name. A constraint was a well-formed logical statement built from propositions, negated propositions, and the connectives 'and', 'or' '=>' and '<=>'.

A rule had a single head proposition (possibly negated), 'if' or 'iff' as its neck, and a well-formed logical statement built from propositions, negated propositions, and the connectives 'and', 'or' '=>' and '<=>' as its body. The use of this variety of logical operators obviated the need to translate into a normal form, and so allowed the constraints and rules to mirror the structure of the source material.

Each of the above-mentioned slot types had a corresponding proposition type for testing/asserting particular values. Additional proposition types allowed the values of numeric slots to be related by equations or inequations containing arithmetic expressions and second-order functions.

Inference was data-driven (i.e. forward-chaining). New data drove a matching process, with successful matches resulting in the generation of activations. These were added to an agenda; when the application requested it, activations were scheduled in most-general-first order (possibly causing more activations to be generated), until no further activations remained.

12.8.4. Hypothetical reasoning

Applications also required the ability to make assumptions about input data without commitment so that users could change their minds, and so that 'what if?' investigations could be performed. In the policy application, such hypothetical reasoning could extend to the investigation of variations on constraints corresponding to possible changes in legislation.

Others have used 'non-monotonic logics' to support such things as default reasoning, retraction of assertions and 'what if?' investigations. We chose instead to underpin our monotonic logical language with an explicit assumption-based framework for hypothetical reasoning (based on the work of deKleer). While being invisible to the logical formalism, this framework allowed the application system to explore the consequences of alternative beliefs and to keep track of the dependencies between conclusions and assumptions. This meant that while all inference was sound in classical terms the application could use the results within the context of explicit sets of assumptions to provide the facilities mentioned above.

The ATMS was used to allow slot values, and the existence of instances and rules/constraints, to depend on externally-defined assumptions. The ATMS automatically maintained the status of all derived information with respect to the available assumptions, and allowed retrieval of information to be done under any (consistent) set of assumptions (a set of assumptions is called an 'environment'). All the information in a slot could be retrieved, so that the dependence of the slot value on different assumptions could be examined. The dependency information maintained by the ATMS could be accessed by the application, allowing explanations to be constructed externally to the Toolkit.

Any inconsistent assignment of values to a slot caused the environment(s) under which the incompatible values would jointly hold to be marked as inconsistent. No useful inference or retrieval could proceed under an inconsistent environment.

12.9. POSSIBLE FUTURE WORK

The Toolkit developed in the DHSS Demonstrator project supported many of the features that we identified as being desirable for a legal application. It was not a radical departure from existing knowledge representation paradigms, but rather represented the imposition of a discipline of the use of existing paradigms so as to enforce the declarative reading and avoid some of the problems that would occur were declarativeness to be violated.

It was not, however, a complete solution. The initial decision to implement only facilities we were clear about inevitably meant that limits of expressiveness were encountered. This section describes additional lines of work that could be pursued to remedy some of the shortcomings.

12.9.1. Backward chaining

Despite an intention to provide both forward and backward chaining, difficulties in combining backward-chaining and hypothetical reasoning resulted in only the former being implemented, since an ATMS sits far more naturally with this style of inference, Backward chaining is useful for restricting the input data to those required to determine a given conclusion, but if hypothetical input data may be entered, and if inference is restricted to paths leading to the goal (as is usual in backward chaining systems), inconsistencies in the input data (which are by definition impossible if the data are not hypothetical) may go unnoticed. One remedy, which takes particular account of the focusing nature of backward reasoning, would be to use a backward search from the goal to select the relevant input data, and to allow forward inference to occur when the data is input. The advice application implemented this strategy outside the Toolkit, and it would seem a useful extension for a variety of applications.

12.9.2. Rules, constraints and definitions

The limitations on the syntax of rules, though reasonable at first sight, led to unanticipated problems in their interpretation and use. While constraints did not suffer from these problems, when used for definitions they could not show the distinction between the term being defined and the terms being used in the definition. This distinction is not important to the inference mechanism, but it could be important to the user interface, and is important to the builders, validators and maintainers of the knowledge base. The ability to annotate clauses to show these distinctions would be valuable.

12.9.3. Multiple use of rule/constraint components

Legislation commonly contains cross-references to small substructures in remote pieces of legislation, e.g. 'A person who satisfies paragraph 3 of Regulation 11...'. While the Toolkit generally allowed the representation of rules or constraints with the same grain size as the original legislation, in cases such as this we have either to duplicate the cross-referenced material, or to decompose into multiple rules the structure containing the cross-referenced item. The first approach introduces undesirable redundancy, while the second is clumsy and requires an awareness of what cross-references exist (or may come into existence). More work is needed not only on the representation aspects but also on the tools to support maintenance of heavily cross-referenced structures.

12.9.4. Existence, identity and migration within the class lattice

Frame-based systems are generally not good at handling existential statements (e.g. 'Some of Mary's children are under 6'), having multiple representations which turn out to represent the same individual (e.g. 'the person claiming child benefit for Jimmy' and 'Mary'), or at allowing an individual to be represented and reasoned about before its type is fully known (e.g. 'the animal that bit Henry'). These problems are all related, and are compounded when hypothetical reasoning is allowed. The Toolkit was limited to using instance names as unique 'rigid designators' of individuals of fixed classes. These are important problems, but they are so closely coupled that all of them need to be solved before the full benefit of solving any of them can be felt.

12.9.5. Temporal reasoning

All applications would have benefited from temporal reasoning facilities, but we were no such facilities were provided by the Toolkit. Some work was done on a variant of the event calculus of [Kowalski and Sergot 1986] using explicit assumptions of persistence rather than negation as failure, but there was not time either to assess its appropriateness for the applications or to attempt to mechanize it efficiently. There is as yet no consensus in the AI community with regard to the appropriate handling of time; promising representations exist, but control of inference remains a serious problem.

12.9.6. Modal reasoning

The policy application would have found it valuable to be able to perform some limited amount of modal reasoning, so that the desirability of states could be reasoned about as well as their truth, and so that conclusions as to what should be the case could be drawn, as well as conclusions as to what is the case. The need was not felt in the other two applications, because in those applications the user has no control over what the law is, but is charged only to apply it. The rights and wrongs of the matter are therefore no concern of his, and he must treat what the law says ought to be true as if it really were true, and he does not engage in any specifically normative reasoning. See [Bench-Capon 1989] for a fuller discussion of this point. No such facilities have been provided, but investigation of how they might be incorporated would be valuable.

12.10. CONCLUSION

In this chapter we have described some of the features that we feel need to be taken into account when choosing how to do the knowledge representation for a legal KBS, and we have described a formalism produced for that purpose. The example formalism is to some extent a justification for some of the points made in the early stages of the chapter, and to some extent their source. In conclusion we would like to make a distinction between two aspects: expressiveness and what could be termed engineering principles, the first concerning what can be built, and the second how it should be built. The first determines what can be represented in a formalism: the formalism of the Toolkit is for example inadequate in its treatment of time and modal knowledge. Given this inadequacy, applications can still be built, but their functionality will be limited: thus in the policy application all the distinctively modal reasoning must be performed by the user, although he is supported in this by the non-modal reasoning of the system. Thus the system will tell him that Q follows from P, but he must himself conclude the undesirability of P from the undesirability of Q. The legal domain does make certain demands on the expressiveness of a representation, and the nature of the application to be built will depend on how well these demands are met. This explains why a technically unambitious system such as the Retirement Pension Forecast Advisor described in [Spirgel-Sinclair 1988] can be built using the very restricted representation provided by ADS expert system shell, whereas the highly ambitious TAXMAN III of McCarty requires his extensively elaborated language for legal discourse. In these terms the facilities offered by the Toolkit fall between the two, as does the ambition of the applications supported.

In terms of engineering considerations, which concern how the application is built rather than what is built, the legal domain also makes demands. We suggested above that these suggest that the representation must be truly declarative and support an isomorphic representation of source material. Our belief is that the Toolkit scores well with regard to these points. But is should be noted that these considerations do not determine the range or styles of applications that can be built, but rather the utility that they will have in practice.

Legal applications will doubtless continue to be built using a variety of knowledge representation paradigms: what we have done here is to offer issues for consideration, and some pointers to how we feel they should be resolved.

CHAPTER 13

MIXED INITIATIVE INTERACTION

Paul Luff and David Frohlich

13.1. INTRODUCTION

There are a number of important ingredients to the success of any knowledge based system. Many of these have been discussed in other chapters of this book. For example, the function of the system should be fitted to the requirements of some target user group (Chapter 3). Its knowledge representation and inference capabilities should allow it to fulfill this function accurately and efficiently (Chapter 12). Its knowledge-base should be coherent and scrutable (Chapter 11). Communication at the human–computer interface should be based around some clear metaphor for interaction (Chapter 5), and the cost of developing and maintaining the system should be outweighed by the benefits of operating it (Chapter 10).

However, there is another ingredient which is rather more difficult to characterize but is equally important in making the system useful and usable. This is the dynamic property of the interaction which the system supports. In many ways the interactional dynamics of a knowledge based system is the ingredient which binds all other ingredients together. Ultimately, users interact with a 'virtual system' whose behaviour is more than the sum of its constituent parts; behaviour which is unfolded to them, bit by bit, in an on-going interactional sequence. If the system fulfils some function for users, it must do so through the particular pieces of information it provides to them spontaneously or in response to

KNOWLEDGE-BASED SYSTEMS AND
LEGAL APPLICATIONS. ISBN 0-12-086441-X

activities they perform. If it is to make inferences specific to this function, it must obtain facts from users in the right order and form, and report important results to them at the right place in the interaction. If the system is to project some clear metaphor at the interface, it must do so in the actual details of its individual responses to user inputs, and at a pace which is not overly costly to users or the organizations in which they work.

This chapter describes a series of explorations in the design of new forms of interactional dynamics for knowledge based systems. More specifically, it reports a number of discoveries in the design of what might be called *mixed initiative interaction*, in which the control of the dialogue is shared between user and system. These discoveries were made in the process of designing and evaluating the claimant information Demonstrators introduced in Chapter 9. In contrast to that chapter, we focus here on the evolution of interaction design ideas for the Forms Helper and the Advice System, and describe their consequences for usability. We argue that there are numerous forms of mixed initiative interaction which have mixed consequences for interaction itself, but that an appropriate mixing of initiative can considerably improve the usefulness and accessibility of knowledge based systems.

This chapter begins with an examination of the dimensions of mixed initiative interaction, and goes on to use these dimensions to describe the particular mix of initiative embodied in two versions of the Forms Helper and the final version of the Advice System. The chapter ends with a discussion of implications for the design of knowledge based systems.

13.2. DIMENSIONS OF MIXED INITIATIVE INTERACTION

Mixed initiative interaction is said to be a characteristic of human conversation involving 'the change of initiative or control from one participant to another' [Nickerson 1981, p. 55]. In this respect it is unlike an interrogation which is controlled exclusively by an interrogator. It is related to a number of other properties of conversation such as *bidirectionality, apparentness of who is in control* and *shared rules for the transfer of control and structure* (cf. [Nickerson 1981].

Bidirectionality refers to the two-way exchange of information which distinguishes a dialogue from a monologue. It necessitates a switching of speaker and listener roles at least once in the conversation. At one level, initiative can be said to reside with the party currently occupying the speaker role, and mixed initiative to a shared ability to switch roles. However, at another level, initiative might reside with the party governing the switching of speaker and listener roles. Mixed initiative in this sense has to do with the negotiation of who is 'in control' at any moment irrespective of who is currently speaking. The apparentness of who is in control is an important aspect in such negotiation, and in any conversational situation there will usually be some kind of structure to the way control is negotiated and exchanged. Observations of human conversations structure have led to the proposition of certain rules for the transfer of control (e.g. [Sacks *et al. 1974]*.

There is growing appreciation of the need for mixed initiative dialogue, especially in interactions with knowledge-based or expert systems. A common criticism is that existing dialogues are too tightly controlled by the system, and do not allow the user an active enough role in the process of obtaining advice and information (e.g. [Coombs and Alty 1980]. This has led to the development of more cooperative problem solving systems in which the responsibility for arriving at the correct solution is shared between user and system [Kidd 1987]. Similar trends are evident in the design of dialogues with intelligent tutoring systems. Attempts are being made to make the kind and level of information given out by such systems more responsive and reactive to student interventions in its presentation (e.g. [Cawsey 1989], [Moore and Swartout 1988]. Moran [1987] has described this trend as a move towards greater *interactivity* in interactive systems.

Despite this endorsement of mixed initiative styles of interaction, there is currently no recognised set of dimensions along which initiative can be described as 'mixed'. This makes it very difficult even to discuss the mixed initiative properties of any existing system, much less to compare the effectiveness of various mixtures across systems.

For this purpose we propose a simple terminology to do with the possible ways in which the initiative or control of a human computer conversation can be allocated and switched between parties. These are as follows:

Starting	Who has the initiative to start the interaction?
Overall mixture of initiative	Who has control of the interaction ?
Local mixture of initiative	
Taking from	How can the user take the initiative from the system?
Taken from	How can the initiative be taken from the user?
Giving to	How can the user give the initiative to the system?
Given to	How can the initiative be given to the user?
Stopping	Who has the initiative to stop the interaction?

We distinguish between who is in overall control from who is occupying the speaker role. When discussing the local mixture of initiative we define activities from the user's viewpoint that help to distinguish mixed from non mixed initiative systems. Any system whose interaction cannot be described in these terms is not a mixed initiative system. This is because the terms are expressed as possible *transitions* of initiative and cannot be applied to completely system or user-led systems in which the initiative remains with the same party throughout.

They also help to make clear the extent to which the initiative in any interaction can be mixed. This will show up in the combination of descriptions under each heading. For example, an interaction which is started and stopped by the system but susceptible to temporary user interruptions, might be described as one in which the initiative can be taken but not given by each party.

Lastly, the same terms are useful for describing the way in which initiative is mixed in practice. Such descriptions are essential in any discussion of the advantages of mixed initiative interaction, since it is perfectly possible to design a system which supports a switching of initiative which is never used by either party.

In the rest of this chapter we use this terminology to describe the design and evaluation of three styles of interaction, varying in the extent to which initiative was shared within them. The aim of this exercise is to identify common problems in the design and use of mixed initiative systems and to indicate the success or otherwise of various solutions we have explored.

13.3. MIXED INITIATIVE INTERACTION WITH THE FORMS HELPER I

13.3.1. Design

Interface

The Forms Helper is an electronic form-filling system. Users are presented with a representation of the form on the screen. They answer the questions displayed on it by either typing into free-text areas on the form or by selecting options with the mouse. An example screen display of the first version of the Forms Helper is shown in Figure 13.. The pages of the form appear on the right of the screen. On each page are a number of questions. As all questions on a particular topic cannot fit on to a page, pages are grouped into sections. At the bottom right-hand corner of the page is a page-turning device. By selecting this, the user can either turn to the next page or return to the previous one. On the left of the screen are a number of additional devices. At the top left is an area for displaying system messages to the user. Below this area is a device for selecting sections of the form. To match the paper form, the electronic version was also divided into sections. This panel allowed the user to go to the first page of any section. It also indicated the section

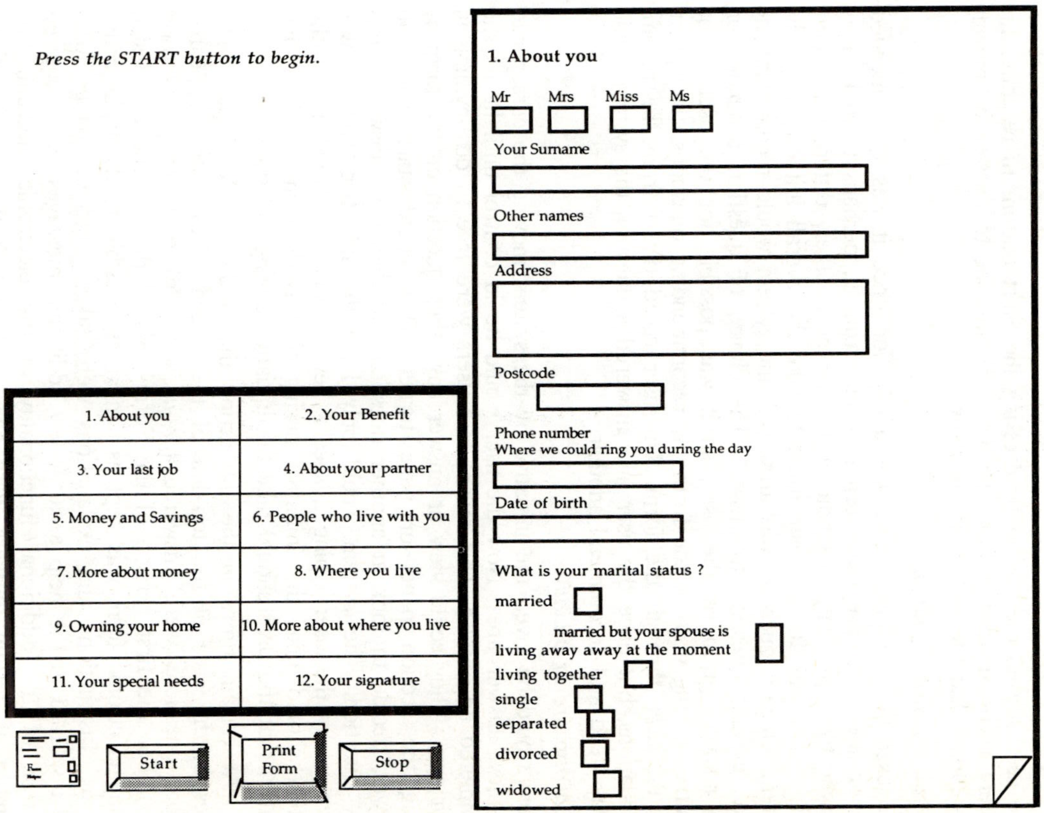
Press the START button to begin.
1. About you
2. Your Benefit
3. Your last job
4. About your partner
5. Money and Savings
6. People who live with you
7. More about money
8. Where you live
9. Owning your home
10. More about where you live
11. Your special needs
12. Your signature
Start
Print Form
Stop
1. About you
Mr
Mrs
Miss
Ms
Your Surname
Other names
Address
Postcode
Phone number
Where we could ring you during the day
Date of birth
What is your marital status ?
married
married but your spouse is living away away at the moment
living together
single
separated
divorced
widowed

Figure 13.1

the user was on, if the section had been visited and whether the section had been completed. At the bottom left of the screen are three buttons, one to start the system, one to stop it and one to print out a paper version of the form.

Starting

The user started the system by pressing the Start button. In response the system recommended a first question for the user to answer by moving the cursor into the region of the answer.

Overall mixture of initiative

The user did not have to answer a question once it was recommended. He or she could use their turn to divert from it, perhaps to look at an answer to a previous question or to answer another, different question. This was a way for allowing users to take the overall initiative from the system. Once a question was answered, the system would recommend the next relevant question to answer. The choice of question depended on the answers given by the user, so it was possible for the user to be 'routed' a long way on the form. By recommending questions, the system led the user through the form. The user could divert from the recommendations, but once the user had answered a question the system would always lead and recommend another.

Local mixture of initiative

Users would be given the initiative by the system moving the cursor into the next answer area. Now the user would be in control until he or she completed an answer. This meant that users were free to do anything in their turn. They could view or answer any other question on the form by using the section panel or page turner. They could start typing an answer, decide to look at another question and then start answering this new question. The system would only have the initiative when it was given it, by the user typing a special key. It was not intended that the system should take the initiative during the user's turn nor, for that matter, that the user should take the initiative during the system's.

At certain times in the interaction the system would display messages in the area at the top left of the screen. These either appeared before questions were answered (*pre-answer help*) or after (*post-answer help*). For the first version of the Forms Helper the content and design of the electronic form was kept as similar as possible to its paper counterpart. Instructions and explanations were taken from the paper form and displayed in the help area. A few additional messages were required because of the additional functionality of the electronic medium. For example, if certain answers were given, the system using a few rules could infer certain things. As the form was for a welfare benefit, these facts were mainly about the eligibility for that benefit. These inferences were displayed in the help area. The system could understand numbers, dates and amounts of money entered in a wide variety of ways. When the user entered text of these types which the system could not understand, it would display a message.

Stopping

At any point in the interaction the user could stop the system (by pressing the Stop button) otherwise the system would continue recommending questions to answer until all relevant questions had been answered. This included any questions that had been skipped by the user. These were returned to after all other relevant questions had been attempted. Only when the user had answered all the relevant questions did the system stop cycling through the form. A message appeared in the help area to signal that no more answers were needed.

13.3.2. Evaluation

Methods

Following a study of paper form-filling [Frohlich 1986], a similar study of electronic form-filling was carried out using Forms Helper I. A mixture of employed and unemployed people tried to fill in a representation of the claim form for supplementary benefit (the 'B1') using the system. This was the form used in the previous study. Users were asked to read and 'think aloud' as they interacted with the system, tape recordings and observational notes being made of their comments. It was also possible to produce a paper version of the completed form at the end of the interaction and a log, kept by the system, recorded both user and system actions as they took place. All these materials could be combined to study what had taken place. More details of the methods and results of this study are given in [Frohlich 1987]. In the following sections we concentrate on those findings that relate to the mixed-initiative nature of the interaction.

Starting

For the evaluation of the first version of the Forms Helper we gave the users some training beforehand and as users only had to select the Start Button there is little to say about how users initiated the start of the interaction.

Overall mixture of initiative

Although the system led the interaction and recommended questions to the user, we found that the users selected a large proportion of questions to answer. The mean proportion of user-selected question visits initiated by the user was 37.4% [Frohlich 1987], some subjects initiating over half the visits. Even though it was possible to be led through all the questions by the system, the lowest proportion of visits initiated by a user was 15%.

One of the reasons users selected so many questions was not to answer them, but to look at them. When paper form-fillers have a problem with a particular question, they try to understand that question by reading the questions that follow and depend on it [Frohlich 1986]. Though this context is useful, it leads people to 'capture' questions that are not relevant to them. Often by ignoring routing instructions, they see questions that they think they should answer and try to answer them. The design of the first version of the Forms Helper intended that, by displaying all the questions on the form and skipping the irrelevant ones, the user would be given the context but discouraged from giving unnecessary answers. Unfortunately, the system skipping questions disrupted the interaction, especially as this often meant going onto a new page. Users tended to use their turn to see what had just happened in the system's. Luckily, as the system would only recommend relevant questions it was hard to answer a series of irrelevant ones. The system kept taking the user away. This is illustrated in the following example. This shows questions recommended by the system and those answered by the user. The captured questions are indicated by arrows (≫ ≪).

(1)

System	**Are you living with your parents, relatives or friend as part of their family?**	
User	Yes	
System	**What is the name of the head of the household ?**	
User	George	
System	**We can help you with things like clothes for a new baby, money to replace worn out furniture or bed clothes or expenses if you move home Do you want a leaflet ?**	
≫	**Does the money you pay for where you live cover all your heating costs**	≪
User	Yes	
System	**We can help you with things like clothes for a new baby, money to replace worn out furniture or bed clothes or expenses if you move home Do you want a leaflet ?**	
≫	**Do you have any joint tenants who share the rent and bills with you?**	≪
User	No	
System	**We can help you with things like clothes for a new baby, money to replace worn out furniture or bed clothes or expenses if you move home Do you want a leaflet ?**	
≫	**Do you pay board or lodging ?**	≪
User	Yes	
System	**We can help you with things like clothes for a new baby, money to replace worn out furniture or bed clothes or expenses if you move home**	

	Do you want a leaflet ?
User	Yes
System	**Are you, or any of the people you are claiming for, pregnant ?**

DH

In this case, after answering the second question, the user is recommended another one some six pages further on in the form. The user returns to try and answer questions he has seen near the first two. After each answer the system takes him back to the same question: the next relevant one. This is the worst case of capturing questions in any of the trials. The inconvenience of finding the way back to an irrelevant question is too great to continue like this for long. On paper forms there is no such penalty so form-fillers can go on answering irrelevant questions indefinitely.

Local mixture of initiative

There were three other, more local, reasons why the proportion of user-initiated question visits was relatively large: the first one is a problem of giving turns and the second and third are problems of taking turns.

Giving to and Given to. The first problem occurred when the users were given the turn and could not give it back to the system. This happened when the system recommended a question and the user decided not to answer immediately. If they selected a new section on the form to view some questions or look at previous answers they could get lost. The only way the system could take the turn and recommend a question would be for the user to give it the turn. The user gave turns by completing answers. This meant it was the user's responsibility to go back and find the recommended question. The section panel offered some assistance indicating which sections had been visited, but it did not help in finding the page within the section on which to find the question. Some users found ingenious methods of combining the page-turning device with the section menu to return from a visit to a distant page.

Taking from and Taken from. As already mentioned, the system was not designed to take the turn from the user. It could only be given a turn. This proved to be a problem when the system had to provide information to the user during the course of the interaction. In an attempt to keep the form from looking cluttered we designed the system so that all help would appear in the top left-hand corner of the screen; a prominent position that would remove instructions and explanations from the question and answer area. Even so, users tended to focus on the right hand side of the screen where they were reading and answering questions and miss statements volunteered by the system on the left. Furthermore, when help both followed an answer and preceded the next question, users were confused to which question the help applied. Figure 13.2 shows an example of this happening: where help both follows the user's second answer and precedes the system's next question.

	Help and Explanation Area	*Form*
System		**Is your home very difficult to heat because of things like damp and very large rooms ?**
User		Yes
System		**Why is it difficult to heat ?**
User		very large rooms and high ceilings
System	**You can find out more about this in leaflet SB17 'Help with heating costs'.**	
	Do not count people who live as part of your family.	**Does anyone pay you for rooms or property that you let?**
User		No.
		ST

Figure 13.2: Pre- and post-answer help in Forms Helper I.

The design of the transfer of turns between Forms Helper I and the user meant there was no way for the system to interrupt and take a turn to give help. We had a location on the screen for it, but no place in the interaction.

Although we had intended the Forms Helper not to take turns from the user the design of the interface meant that this could happen. Most computer systems that use a mouse have two interface objects that indicate where a particular action will occur in relation to the screen. A 'cursor' marks the place the mouse is 'pointing to', that is where presses of the mouse button would apply to, and a 'caret' indicates where typed characters will appear. This means there are two places the user could be focused on. We wanted to have just one. The Forms Helper's 'cursor' would follow movements of the mouse and characters as they were typed. The one cursor would always be showing where the users' actions were taking place. We also reserved the action of pressing the mouse button, 'clicking the mouse', to ticking multiple choice answers and pressing buttons. Selecting a question was done by moving the cursor over a free text area for a small amount of time. This design implied a different level of mixture of initiative, that of who had control over the cursor. When the user moved the cursor with the mouse he or she had control of it. When the user either entered an answer area, typed a character or completed an answer the system had control of it. If the user moved the cursor slowly over a text area the system would act as if the user had selected that question and move the cursor to the first typing position in the box. This may not have been what the user intended. He or she could have been heading for another question, the page-turner or the section panel. To the users the cursor appeared to be dragged from them, the system had interrupted the user's turn. To regain control, the user had to move the mouse again and so a battle over the cursor would commence. The user either could concede defeat and complete the answer or, by moving the mouse quickly away from the answer area, escape. This problem was exacerbated by a small bug at the interface. Sometimes if the user typed when the cursor was not over any answer area rather than ignoring the input, the system would output it into the next box the cursor moved over. The battle now involved the user removing unwanted input as well as trying to get control of the cursor. Note also, that by moving over another answer area, pre-answer help to a different question would appear in the help area.

Stopping

At the end of the interaction the system returned to questions skipped by the user. As these questions were likely to be spread over a number of different pages, the system would make large movements through the form resulting in some users becoming disoriented. In fact, no user initiated finishing the interaction. As most could not answer particular questions they never got the message to say they had finished. Instead, the system kept going back to those questions and the user kept skipping them until, eventually, they were either encouraged to press the Stop Button or told that they could go.

13.4. MIXED INITIATIVE INTERACTION WITH FORMS HELPER II

13.4.1. Design

Interface

The second version of the Forms Helper was designed to overcome some of the problems users had had with the first version while retaining features that were found to work. Figure 13.3 shows the screen layout. The form appears towards the middle of the screen and now there is only a page selection device on the left. The distinction between sections and pages is lost and all movement between pages, initiated by the user, is performed using this device. There is no page turning device on the form. Again, answers are of two kinds: multiple choice and free text, but now help is divided into three kinds, each displayed at a different location on the screen. General help about using the system appears in a large area at the bottom of the screen. When any question is selected, pre-answer help appears in a box to the right of the form and level with the question. In this box there is an option for the user to request help for that particular question, either for a rewording of a question or for an example answer. The third kind of help, post-answer help, appears in a box in the middle of the screen after a question is answered. A progress indicator shows what proportion of questions, of those known to be relevant, have been answered by the user. This appears below the form and above the general help box.

Starting

By analysing user difficulties with learning to use the first version of the Forms Helper it was possible identify the training required to introduce them to the second version before using the second version. So, the interaction with the second version commences with a training sequence. On the whole, this sequence is led by the system and imitates the style of the main body of the interaction. Users learn to use the mouse, ask for help and answer questions, by the system taking them through a training form. When the user is asked to select a particular form to fill in, he or she chooses an option in response to a question that appears on a page of the training form. Users are also encouraged to select questions and move around the training information. Answering the final question on the training form will result in the first page of the real form being displayed and the first question being recommended. There is no need for any special Start button as the system takes the first turn by introducing the user to the mouse.

Overall mixture of initiative

The overall style of the interaction remains the same in the second version; the user completes an answer to give the turn to the system, the system recommends the next relevant question to give the turn back to the user.

Local mixture of initiative

The details of the turn transition have changed. Rather than the system moving onto a new question when the user selects an option (for multiple choice options) or types a special 'continue' key (for free-text options), users press the Continue key to complete both types of answer. This aims to clarify to the user when they are giving the turn to the system. There is now only one way of doing this.

We have also tried to avoid the problem of 'question capture' by not displaying irrelevant questions on the form. In the second design only questions that are known to be relevant are displayed. When users have the turn they can only use their turn to answer relevant questions. This is a large departure from a paper form on which the Forms Helper was originally based. No longer is the form of a static size with a fixed number of questions, some of which the user is routed past. Now the form 'grows' as the user fills it in. 'Question capture' was a problem of both paper forms and Forms Helper I. This new design aims to avoid it. The design has also has implications on the interaction. Giving the turn to the system not only results in a next question being recommended but can also result in a new set of questions being displayed. Certain questions, called filter questions, become very important to the

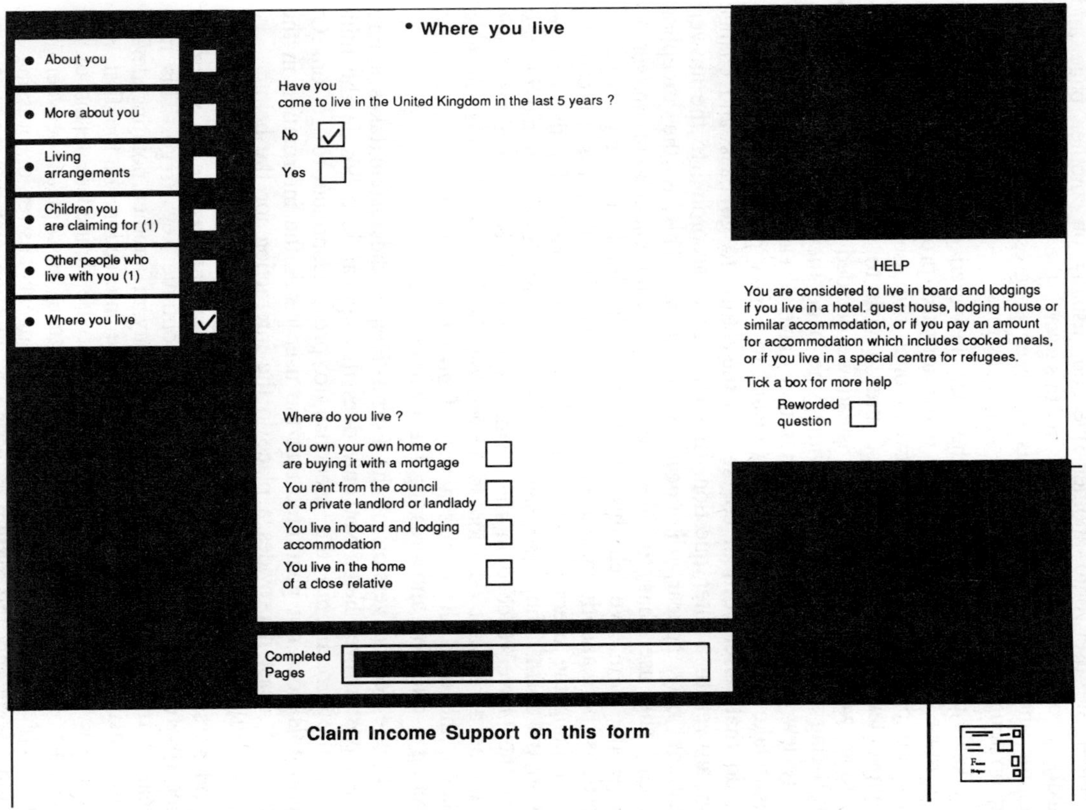
About you
More about you
Living arrangements
Children you are claiming for (1)
Other people who live with you (1)
Where you live
• Where you live
Have you come to live in the United Kingdom in the last 5 years ?
No
Yes
Where do you live ?
You own your own home or are buying it with a mortgage
You rent from the council or a private landlord or landlady
You live in board and lodging accommodation
You live in the home of a close relative
HELP
You are considered to live in board and lodgings if you live in a hotel. guest house, lodging house or similar accommodation, or if you pay an amount for accommodation which includes cooked meals, or if you live in a special centre for refugees.
Tick a box for more help
Reworded question
Completed Pages
Claim Income Support on this form

Figure 13.3

unfolding interaction. Answering one of these questions can cause the system either to display some new questions and recommend the first or to move the user onto another question, usually on another page and usually another filter question. In this way the interaction is more dynamic and smoother, growing as the user progresses through the form and no longer skipping over irrelevant questions.

With the form growing as the user answered questions it would be even more difficult for users to make forward progressions. New questions and pages could appear between ones the user had already visited. The problem of users getting lost after a visit to a page further on in the form would be even worse. Instead we decided to constrain users to only being able to go forward within the page they were on. They can still review questions on pages that they have already been to, but they cannot take the initiative and go forward to a new page. Only the system can do that. Users can of course use their turn to go back and change their answer to a filter question. In such a case, according to the answer, questions may appear, disappear or reappear. This is the exception though. The user has to take the initiative and change an answer to change the form. We felt this was more desirable than having irrelevant questions permanently displayed and available for all users to capture. Constraining the users in this way makes it much harder for them to get lost in the form. They also have a guide, the page index, to the furthest point they have reached in the form. As the form is growing there will always be a relevant question to answer on the last page of the form. In addition, the user always has a way of giving the turn to the system; by selecting a question and pressing the Continue key.

In the second version of the Forms Helper the system takes a turn to give post-answer help. Not only does this appear in a box in the middle of the screen, but the user has to press Continue to go on. Of course, this does not guarantee that the user reads the information in the box, but at least it provides a place in the interaction for the help.

The battle for control over the cursor no longer occurs in the second version. Once the user starts typing an answer he or she must either delete all their input or press the continue key to go. This may appear restrictive but it alleviates the necessity of another pointing device. It also clarifies the meaning of a turn in the interaction. In the first version of the Forms Helper the turns were to be defined in terms of the boundaries of each activity. The system's turn took place between the user completing an answer (either by selecting an answer or pressing the continue key) and the system selecting a question (by moving a cursor into the next answer area) and the user's turn took place between this selection and the user completing the answer. The battle over the cursor shows how the boundaries were not well enough defined. While the user had the turn the system could still interrupt and select a question. The new design marks the transition of turns clearly. Users always give the turn by pressing the continue key. When they have the turn they are in control, the system cannot take it away from them.

Stopping

Forms Helper II no longer cycled around questions indefinitely. Users were given two chances to answer a question. After skipping a question a second time the system no longer recommended it. Also, as users no longer could make forward progressions in the form after going through the final page, the system was bound to recommend a question that had been recommended before. Unlike the first version, there were no hidden pages the user could have skipped.

The change of the Forms Helper to a more dynamic system meant that more care had to go into redesigning the electronic version of the form for the new system. Consideration of the dynamics of the interaction with the form had to be taken into account when choosing the ordering of questions and pages. Filter questions tended to be placed at the top of a page where questions could unfold beneath them. Also, it was possible to make the the order of pages more coherent then the comparable paper form now that certain questions need not be displayed.

13.4.2. Evaluation

An evaluation was carried out to discover if the second version of the Forms Helper system was acceptable to users (Ottley 1988). This was carried out on a larger sample of users and the results of this were generally positive. Users found the system easy to use and follow, felt confident in using it and they felt they knew what they were doing when they were filling in the computerized form. Unfortunately the results of this study were not sufficiently detailed to give information about users' interactions with Forms Helper II so little can be said of the mixed-initiative aspects of the revised system.

13.5. MIXED INITIATIVE INTERACTION WITH THE ADVICE SYSTEM

13.5.1. Design

Interface

The Advice System is a question-answering knowledge based system. Its interaction is based on the organisation on natural conversation (see [Frohlich and Luff 1989]. A typical screen display of the Advice System is shown in Figure 13.4. The screen is divided into two parts. On the left is a transcript of part of the interaction as it progresses. Completed utterances appear here. The system's and users' contributions are distinguished by a different typeface. This transcript only records the past utterances that can fit onto the visible area of the screen. The oldest ones scroll off the top. On the right is the area in which users construct their utterances. There are two phases to constructing an utterance. Firstly, the user selects a topic to talk about and then the user constructs an utterance on that topic. Topics are selected from a series of menus that contain topics in which the choices are each more specific than the last and utterances are constructed, phrase by phrase, until there is a possibility to complete the sentence, with one of a variety of terminators. This phrase selection mechanism is similar to that described by Tennant *et al.* [1983]. Although most utterances can be constructed from selecting phrases from menus, numbers, amounts and names have to be typed into text boxes. For this reason text boxes may also appear as options in the phrase being constructed. In addition to topic and phrase options, buttons can be selected on the right-hand side of the screen (these appear at the bottom of the area). They are intended to give the user a quick way to say one of four things. These are: asking for a rephrasing of something the system said, asking for a reason behind something the system said, asking to leave the system and interrupting the system. When the user presses one of these or completes a sentence with a terminator the corresponding utterance is added to the left-hand side of the screen as a record of what has been said.

Starting

The start of the interaction is based on openings of telephone conversations with the user cast in the role of the caller. In contrast to Forms Helper II, the user has the first turn in the interaction. The user summons the system, the system replies and identifies itself. The user then has to identify himself or herself. Then follows a special sequence that is led by the system. As in the second version of the Forms Helper the start of the interaction is the place where training takes place. For the Advice System this involves helping the user to learn how to use the topic and phrase menus. The user is first encouraged to make a few statements about himself or herself and then to raise the first topic of the conversation by asking a question. Once the user has asked this question the main body of the interaction begins.

Overall mixture of initiative

In comparison to the Forms Helper, the Advice System is based on the idea that the user asks the questions and the system answers them. In fact, the Advice System depends on the user asking questions. It cannot give advice otherwise. This is why it is necessary to complete the starting sequence with a user's question. Once the user has asked this question, the system may be able to answer the question immediately or, before answering, it may have to ask a series of questions in return. While the system is trying to answer a user's question it effectively leads the interaction. When the system is asking a question it is possible for the user to ask another one in reply, perhaps, to discover what the question means. The user now leads the interaction. It is possible to view the

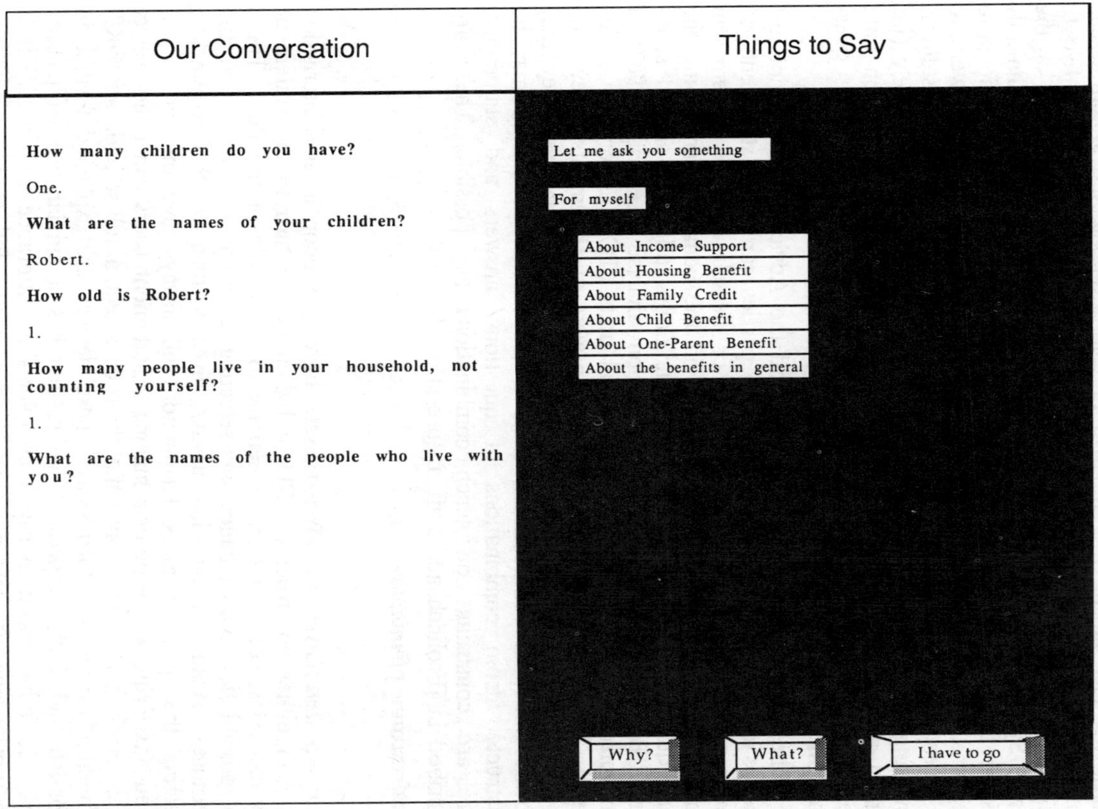
Our Conversation
How many children do you have?
One.
What are the names of your children?
Robert.
How old is Robert?
1.
How many people live in your household, not counting yourself?
1.
What are the names of the people who live with you?
Things to Say
Let me ask you something
For myself
About Income Support
About Housing Benefit
About Family Credit
About Child Benefit
About One-Parent Benefit
About the benefits in general
Why?
What?
I have to go

Figure 13.4

mixture of initiative in the interaction of the Advice System on various levels, the user having the initiative to ask questions, the system taking control in order to find an answer and the user taking the initiative to ask another question. In fact, we have designed the interaction of the Advice System to restrict the number of levels to three. It is technically feasible for the system to handle an arbitrary number of questions to questions, but we felt users may not then be able to relate answers to the questions. If the user asks a second question while the system is answering another one, and the system cannot answer it immediately (i.e. without asking further questions) it holds over the second question until later. The user is then given the opportunity to ask the 'held-over' question again.

The interaction between the user and the Advice System is not just a series of questions and answers. Both parties can make statements. A user can volunteer facts about himself or herself and the system can inform the user of facts it has deduced in the course of answering the user's question. It is possible to hold the floor and make several statements. Borrowing terms from conversation analysis [Levinson, 1983]; a turn consists of several turn constructional units (TCUs). For the Advice System, TCUs can either be questions, answers or statements. They need not be just about the topic of the conversation (substantive) they may also be about the conversation itself (meta). Although a turn may be constructed from combinations of questions, answers and statements, there are constraints on which combinations are possible. These are described in [Frohlich and Luff, in press].

Local mixture of initiative

Giving to and Given to. When users have the floor in the interaction they can either construct a TCU and then give a turn to the system or they can construct a TCU and then try to keep hold of the floor. These two possibilities are signalled by selecting different terminators to the utterances. Asking a question always gives a turn to the system. So selecting the question mark terminator will always give the turn away. When answering a question or making a statement users can either select a '...' terminator to hold onto the floor or select a full-stop or an 'OK?' terminator to give the turn away. These devices are explained further in [Frohlich and Luff, In press]. The system has a similar way of passing turns. If it has more to say it completes an utterance with a '...'. If it does not it ends its statement or answer with a full stop. As with the user, the system asking a question automatically gives the turn away. So the user is given a turn when the system ends its utterance with a full stop or a question mark.

Taking from and Taken from The user can also take the turn from the system. After the system has made a TCU followed by '...', a button appears for a period of time. Selecting this button gives an opportunity for the user to interrupt the system and then construct a turn. Similarly, the system can take the turn from the user. Despite ending a TCU with a '...' it is possible for the system to interrupt a user's turn. This occurs when there is something wrong with the user's utterance, for example if the user fills out a text box incorrectly or if the user makes a contradiction. In these cases the system initiates a repair sequence to deal with the trouble [Frohlich and Luff 1989].

Stopping

As mentioned earlier, the Advice System relies on the user asking questions to continue with the interaction. We devised a way of encouraging further questions by designing a series of 'preclosings' that suggested topics for further questions [Frohlich and Luff 1989]. In the first preclosing, using information from the topic menus, the system asks whether the user wants to ask another question on the same topic as the last. If this is declined then users are asked, in a second preclosing, whether they want to ask a question on a related topic. This topic is either related to the last question in terms of the menus or derived from a simple heuristic. If this second opportunity is declined then the users are asked whether they want to ask another question on any topic whatsoever. If this third chance is turned down then the system enters a closing sequence, where the system and use say goodbye to each other.

The preclosing sequences are also the places where the user is given the opportunity to ask again questions that have been held over. Like the start of the interaction, these sequences for negotiating new topics and the end of the interaction are controlled by the system. They should also be completed by the user asking a question. The Advice System does supply another device for ending the interaction. At most times a button, labelled 'I have to go', is available on the bottom of the right-hand side the screen. By selecting this the user can initiate the end of the interaction.

13.5.2. Evaluation

Methods

A small-scale evaluation of the Advice System was carried out to assess its usability. Further details can be found in [Gilbert and Jirotka 1989]. The behaviour and comments of five lone parents and twenty undergraduate students were recorded as they each interacted with the system for approximately one hour. Lone parents were simply asked to explore the system for any information which might be useful or interesting to them. Students were asked to discover specific kinds of benefit information on behalf of a hypothetical lone parent called Maggie. One-half of the students were given the job of finding out eligibility and assessment information about the name of and amount of the benefit Maggie might be able to get, while the other half were asked to obtain procedural information to help her in the process of claiming a benefit. A procedure known as *co-operative evaluation* was used in which subjects were encouraged to describe their experience of interacting with the system to an evaluator who was present throughout the session [Wright and Monk 1989].

Users were also interviewed after the session. All dialogue between the user and the evaluator was tape recorded and all user and system actions were automatically logged by the system.

Starting

There was a major problem with the way initiative was shared at the start of the interaction. It had to do with closing the opening sequence. After the initial summons-answer and identification sequence, users were given the initiative by the system to 'tell me something about yourself and your situation'. Most users did not quite know what to do with it. They began by volunteering statements but never knew when to stop. Several users had to be restrained from working systematically through over two hundred available user statement options before going on to ask their first question.

Indeed, the fact that users had to ask questions of the system to get advice was not clear in this initial period. Users appeared to arrive at the machine with a general expectation that they would have to feed in extensive details about themselves before being given a description of their eligibility for a range of benefits. One user expressed this by saying; 'I thought I would have to put a lot of information in and it would give a summary answer at the end', ASLOGANN2. By giving users initiative to feed in such details at the start of the interaction, the system unwittingly confirmed this expectation. As users could not predict the moment when initiative would be taken from them by the system to deliver useful advice, the best strategy seemed to be to hold on to the initiative to continue inputting further statements. This was despite the fact that there was a simple method of giving the initiative back to the system; by saying 'No' to the system's repeated question 'Do you want to tell me anything else?'.

Overall mixture of initiative

Once past the opening sequence, the overall mixture of initiative appeared to become a lot clearer to users. They realized quickly that the system required a question to supply an answer, and had no choice but to formulate a first and then further questions to control the rest of the conversation.

However, some student users who had been asked to explore the range of benefits available to lone parents in general, expressed unease at being in control of the conversation for so long. This seemed to be related to the fact that answers to domain level queries of this type are provided by the system in the next turn. Thus, users asking a series of domain level questions would be encouraged by the system to ask further questions about every fifth turn as shown below. Interestingly, the system takes the local initiative for speaking away from the user with preclosing questions like: 'Do you want to ask another question about what benefits are available?', but leaves the overall initiative for controlling what is said in the hands of the user. Users themselves appear to tire of this after four or five cycles.

(2)

User	What benefits are available to lone parents on a low income? (3.4)
System	**Income Support...** (10.5) **Housing Benefit...** (10.5) **And Family Credit...** (10.8) **Do you want to ask another question about** **what benefits are available?** (92.4)
User	Yes (0.3)
System	**Go ahead. You may have to wait a** **few seconds for the lists** **to appear on the right hand side of the screen.** (109.3)
User	What are the conditions for getting Income Support? (3.0)
System	**To get Income Support you must** **be working part-time or not at all,** **have less than £6000 in capital, and** **an income below a certain level...**

ASLOGCTELIG

Relief from control usually arrives after the asking of a case level question like 'Can I get Income Support?'. Users may find the initiative taken from them at this point, as the system begins to question them for facts about the person concerned. Within these cycles of system-led dialogue, users are happy to respond to system questions until they encounter a problematic question. As with the interaction on the Forms Helper, such an encounter becomes an occasion for digressing away from the current system question. The following kinds of insertion sequence were common forms of digression on the Advice System, and illustrate the value of giving users opportunities for taking initiative from the system. Typically, such initiative is exercised locally to resolve difficulties in the comprehension of system utterances.

(3)

System	**Do you have a 'commercial arrangement' for paying your rent?**
	(37.1)
User	What?
	(0.6)
System	**A commercial arrangement is a formal arrangement set up by the landlord or landlady to make a profit.**
	(35.5)
User	No

ASLOGLUCY1

Local mixture of initiative

Taking from. We have just seen how users sometimes took the initiative away from the system in order to resolve some local breakdown in communication. This was done by selecting the 'next turn repair initiator' 'What?', or more rarely 'Why?'.

Other occasions on which users took initiative from the system involved the use of different devices. For example, several users selected the Let Me Speak button to *self-select* between the parts of a complex system answer. This was used in two ways. In the first, users self-selected to ask a different question as soon as they recognized that the answer to the last question was not the kind they wanted. In the second, users self-selected to volunteer information made relevant by the beginning of the answer. This is shown in the sequence below, in which a student user volunteers the fact that Maggie is not receiving any one-parent benefit, after becoming convinced by the first part of the system answer that this is a benefit Maggie should be getting. Her expectation in volunteering this information was that 'now it should tell me I should be getting some'.

(4)

User	Who can get One-Parent benefit?
	(3.0)
System	**One-Parent Benefit is for people who are lone parents...**
	(10.3)
User	Let me speak...
	(130.6)

The amount of One-Parent Benefit I am getting
is £0 a year.

ASLOGSGELIG

Users also used the '...' punctuation to hold the floor after providing an answer to a previous system question. This was most commonly done to volunteer further information in order to clarify what has just been said. This is shown in the excerpt below, where the user tries to indicate that although she is working, her work is only part-time because of her responsibilities in looking after her child.

(5)

System **Are you working in a paid job at present?**
(5.7)
User Yes...
(8.1)
I am not available to take a full-time job.

ASLOGCLELIG

Taking the initiative from the system did not always work so smoothly. A variety of problems in the switching of initiative had to do with confusion over the ownership of utterances appearing on the right-hand side of the screen. Although users were told clearly at the beginning of the interaction that all utterances on the right represented their talk to the system, there was a tendency for them to hear some of these as system talk to them.

Part of the problem was the ambiguous nature of the language used. Both user and system talk was expressed in the first person, so that each party referred to themselves as 'I' and to each other as 'you'. Thus any utterance such as 'Let me tell you something', could be read in two ways. Utterances on the right of the screen were particularly prone to misinterpretation because although they could only be *selected* by the user, they were *generated* (as options) by the system. This led to a dangerous combination of ambiguous user utterances being presented to users by the system itself. One user expressed the general confusion in saying 'I didn't expect there to be two me's, ASLOGNFELIG'.

The effect of hearing user talk as system talk was to obscure the apparentness of who was currently speaking. This in turn affected the way users might or might not try to take the initiative from the system. For example, users who saw the 'Let me speak' button incorrectly as a system utterance, reported being deterred from interrupting. In this case, the fact that this button was displayed between the separate parts of a complex system answer, appeared to encourage the perception of 'Let me speak' as a filled pause serving to inhibit self-selection.

An alternative interpretation of 'Let me speak' led users to select it as a method of returning the initiative to the system; specifically to encourage continuation of an answer already begun. In practice, selecting 'Let me speak' has the opposite effect. The reasons for this behaviour are harder to understand, but may be related to a correct belief that utterances on the right-hand side of the screen are not actually spoken until selected. By selecting what they thought was a system utterance requesting continued use of the floor, some users may have been trying to activate and acknowledge the request.

Lastly, a tendency of the system to perform a low-level operation called *garbage collection* led to a general problem in micro-initiative. Garbage collection is a function carried out by the underlying software to 'clean up' the internal state of the system. It is carried out at irregular intervals and can last for irregular periods of up to a second. Its effect on the user is to de-activate the mouse and display the cursor in inverse video. This means that any mouse click made to select some screen option within the garbage collection period is not registered by the system and consequently fails to effect the corresponding function.

This can have quite devastating consequences for the switching of initiative by user operations. If users are attempting to take the initiative by clicking on the 'Let me speak' button during a system pause, and happen to depress the mouse button during a garbage collection period, they may fail to secure the floor before the system resumes speaking. The effect is less severe in cases where screen options are displayed continuously, but undesirable consequences may still ensue. For example, several users attempting to select punctuation at the ends of their utterances were slow to realize the selection had failed, and waited several seconds for the system to respond. In general, garbage collection acts as a form of system inattention which users must learn to recognize and avoid from the colour of the cursor.

Taken from. There appears to be only one case in twenty-five dialogues in which the initiative was actually taken from the user by the system. This was because the system is designed to take the initiative only when an invalid or contradictory statement is input as part of a list. Such utterances were themselves relatively rare and tended to occur in isolation, usually in answer to prior system question. This, then, is an example of an available facility for switching initiative which is rarely used in practice.

The one occasion of its use is interesting as it demonstrates a problem with a particularly ambiguous statement about the number of children the user currently gets child benefit for. It is phrased in such a way as to encourage the typing of a name or relationship within a text box which really requires a number. Note the way in which the initiative for repairing the initial utterance is persistently and unhelpfully passed to the user by the system. Ironically, when the user tries to *retain* the initiative after her second attempted repair, the system takes it from her (last turn below):

(6)

User	I am getting child benefit for My son child/children OK? (1.5)
System	**No...** (0.4) **I don't understand that. Please try again.** (21.4)
User	I am getting child benefit for Jon child/children. (0.7)
System	**I still don't understand that. Please try again.** (28.7)
User	Why? (0.5)
System	**Sorry I can't answer that.** (5.4)
User	What? (0.3)
System	**Sorry I can't answer that.** (25.66)
User	I am getting child benefit for My child child/children... (0.8)
System	**I still don't understand that. Please try again.**

ASLOGSGELIG

Giving to. An initial period of learning was required for users to learn how to give initiative to the system. The principal methods involved selecting appropriate kinds of punctuation mark from the screen at the ends of input utterances. This was not immediately obvious to several users who exhibited a tendency to attempt to terminate utterances with the return key or a generalized mouse click.

The two simplest methods for users to give initiative to the system worked extremely well. Stop ('.') punctuation was selected after most user answers or statements, while query ('?') punctuation was the only possible option for terminating user questions.

Rather surprisingly, two less orthodox methods were also used to good effect. 'OK?' punctuation was selected to terminate utterances when the user was not completely happy with them, as shown at the beginning of sequence (6) above. This happened with 'Don't Know' answers, potentially invalid textual inputs and utterances which users felt to be semantically incomplete in some way. An example of the latter case is shown below, and relates to the user's reticence to state that she is in a paid job when she is actually working part-time. It is interesting to note that whatever response the system gives to the user's 'OK?' acts to reassure users. If the system, answers 'No' before initiating repair, the user is relieved to find the system recognises their concern over the previous utterance. If the system answers 'Yes', as in the following case, the user is reassured that the concern has been dismissed:

(7)

User I am working in a paid job at present OK?
(1.3)
System **Yes...**
(0.2)
Do you want to tell me anything else?

ASLOGKBPROC

A 'Your turn' user statement was provided as a method for users to give back the initiative to the system without actually saying anything. Several users manouvred themselves into a position in the conversation from which they gratefully escaped with this option. This usually involved holding or taking the initiative from the system to make an utterance which subsequently could not be found among the question or statement options. An example of this is shown below:

(8)

System **Income Support is for people on low incomes who are not working full time...**
(7.9)
User Let me speak
(29.4)
[Select Let me ask you something]
(4.0)
[Retract Let me ask you something]
(5.4)
[Select Your Turn]
(0.5)
System **Because people on low incomes who are not working full time are entitled to financial support...**

ASLOGCTELIG

In one sense the meta-questions 'What?' and 'Why?' can also be seen as a way of giving the local initiative to the system, usually to repair some breakdown in communication. However, these have already been discussed as ways of taking initiative at a higher level away from the system, as in the midst of a series of system questions and user answers. This paradox illustrates the complex nature of initiative and its movement in conversational interactions, and the multiple functions served by a single method of switching.

Two general problems with 'What?' and 'Why?' are illustrated in sequence (6). First, users never really knew which of the two were most likely to produce the most satisfactory system answer. In fact sometimes neither was chosen and a 'Don't Know' user answer was chosen as a generalised way of initiating system repair. Second, these utterances only apply to the immediately prior utterance. This means that they could not be used in situations where users wanted to query the whole of a previous segment of dialogue or to apply both questions sequentially to a previous system utterance. Thus in the example (6), the system applies the user's 'What?' to the system's previous 'Sorry I can't answer that' utterance, rather than to its original 'I still don't understand that. Please try again'.

Lastly, the problem of interpreting some utterances on the right hand side of the screen as system utterances also affected the giving of initiative to the system. Users sometimes selected a 'Let me tell you something' topic option at the top of the screen in order to get the system to tell them something. One user even reported expecting yes/no options to follow this operation; as if the statement had been activated as a system question equivalent to 'Do you want me to tell you something?' In addition, the user continuation marks '...' were sometimes selected for the same purpose.

Given to. It was not always clear to users when they had the initiative to speak. Again, misinterpretation of the 'Let me tell you something' option as a system utterance, led some users to wait for the something it seemed to want to tell. Further unnecessary waiting resulted when users failed to recognize that the system had finished generating the next list of topic or phrase options for them to choose from in constructing the next part of their current utterance. This reflects a micro-level at which users can be given the initiative to speak in the interaction. Once they receive the floor to construct an utterance, they must be given progressive lists of utterance options in a series of micro-exchanges within their own turn. The problem mentioned above, has to do with knowing when a micro-exchange has been completed.

An unusual case in which the initiative was given to users was in a conversational juncture. These were designed to allow users to retract their current question, and involved the system periodically asking 'Do you want me to carry on trying to answer your question?'. Users reacted to this in two main ways. When the system asked the question prior to the beginning of a system answer they always answered 'yes', to continue towards an answer. When it asked the question in the middle of a long system answer they usually answered 'no', believing that the system had come to an end of what it wanted to tell them. In both cases they were surprised to be given the initiative to stop the system trying to answer their question, and several users tried to account for the behaviour in terms of the system getting 'fed up' with them or trying to 'cop out' of answering their questions.

Stopping

Pre-closings worked extremely well as a method of encouraging users to supply further questions to the system or to decide to close the conversation. An example of this is given in sequence (1) above. In these sequences the initiative for directing the course of the conversation which began with the user at the beginning of the conversation is being returned to the user through meta-system questions suggesting possible next topics.

One minor problem resulted from some duplication in the naming of topics in the topic hierarchy used to classify the set of possible user questions. There were topics of the form 'About income support' for each major benefit under both the 'For myself' and 'For lone parents in general' divisions of the question topic tree. After asking a number of general questions under the 'For lone parents in general' topic, several subjects got stuck down this branch after deciding to ask a specific question about one of the named benefits. They were led quite naturally to keep answering 'yes' to the system's preclosing question 'Do you want to ask another question about (Income Support)' , when in fact they should have said 'no' to switch topic at a higher level than the one being recommended.

All users were reassured by the 'I have to go' button which appeared on the right hand side of the screen during most of their turns. However, this was seldom used in practice to close the conversation, as the natural place for users to want to leave the conversation was after a system answer. At such points users found themselves in a pre-closing sequence which did not allow them access to the 'I have to go' button. When asked if they knew how to get out of the interaction after expressing a wish to leave, several users set about searching for an opportunity to say 'I have to go' whilst being led out systematically through three preclosings. At other times in the interaction, some users were tempted to use the 'I have to go' option to escape from the current screen, but never did.

13.6. CONCLUSION

This chapter has aimed to show the importance of attending to the dynamics of the interaction when designing knowledge-based systems. Small changes in these dynamics can greatly alter the way people use systems. We have also presented the dynamics by describing activities the user and system performs at the start, in the body and at the end of the interaction. In particular, we have described the interaction at two levels, the overall level of control and the local, and examined the places where transfer can take place at the local level in terms of the giving and taking of turns. This may not be enough. In the Forms Helper interaction, the system had overall control guiding users from one question to the next. At a more local level, when users were given the turn they need not answer the suggested question. They could divert from it and answer one of their own choice. Similarly, when a user was answering a question posed by the Advice System, the user could hold onto the turn after answering and volunteer a statement. Though both activities occurred during what has been defined as a user's turn, they both appear to be taking the initiative from the usual 'flow of the interaction'; in some ways 'taking a turn' from the system. This may imply that the notion of 'mixed initiative' should be further refined, perhaps in terms of multiple levels of initiative.

We have largely been concerned in this chapter with the way control can be transferred between users and the two systems. It is possible to see other issues of initiative arising. When problems occur in the interaction, when either the user or system has trouble with what has gone in the other's turn, then it is the responsibility of one of the parties to indicate that a problem has occurred and either's responsibility to correct the problem. Forms Helper II initiated the correction of a user's 'error' by putting a message at the bottom of the screen. It was then the user's responsibility to correct it, though they did not have to. When users had problems, they could also initiate repair by asking the system for help. Both the Advice System and its users could initiate a special sequence when they had problems with the other's turn. We have also looked at the way either the system or the user can initiate the start, the end and, with the Advice System, new topics for the interaction. Rather than refining the definition of mixed initiative, it may be more useful to examine the way people use the resources given to them by a computer system to perform these activities. Conversation analysis already has such a terminology for looking at the way people interact with each other in conversations. The way turns are taken in conversations has been examined [Sacks *et al.* 1974]. So has the repair of trouble in conversations [Schegloff *et al.* 1977], the openings of conversations [Schegloff 1968], the closings of conversations and the negotiation of new topics [Schegloff and Sacks 1973].

These factors can only be examined when the initiative or control of an interactive system can be taken by both the user and the system. We have described two different types of system that have attempted to do this. It would be interesting to examine the nature of the mixed initiative interaction with other types of computer system, especially those that differ from ones presented here. It remains to be seen what factors can be identified to describe mixed initiative systems that are less 'conversational'; those where turns take place simultaneously, those where turns are spread around a computer screen and those where turns appear on different media.

CHAPTER 14

GROUP DECISION MAKING

Graham Storrs

14.1. POLICY MAKING WITHIN THE DSS — THE NATURE OF THE PROBLEM

It is with the policy system that we are particularly concerned in this chapter as it is only in this application that a significant amount of group working needs to be catered for.

The DSS is a very large organization with about 93,000 staff administering roughly five million claims each year from approximately 500 offices around the UK. There are a great many people involved in monitoring and formulating policy on behalf of the minister in central policy branches and the regional directorate. In the policy branch concerned with formulating the policy for income support, one of the main social security benefits, there were as many as 300 people involved.

Most of the day-to-day work of a policy worker involves the explanation of policy. Queries about the way the legislation is working or the justification for legislation arise as a result of questions being asked in Parliament, from pressure groups, from concerned individuals, or from reviews within the policy branches themselves. Typically, such queries

An earlier version of this paper was presented at the First European Conference on Computer Supported Cooperative Work, London, September 1989.

KNOWLEDGE-BASED SYSTEMS AND LEGAL APPLICATIONS. ISBN 0-12-086441-X concern perceived anomalies or injustices. However, the social security legislation is, on the whole, the way it is because of the policy of the department. Such queries, therefore tend to elicit explanations rather than to initiate the revisions of the law that the inquirer is often seeking.

Thus, on receiving a query, from whatever source, the policy worker's first task is to establish whether a genuine anomaly exists. If it does not, an explanation may be issued. If it does, then action must be taken to establish whether corrective action is necessary and, if it is, to take steps to correct the anomaly. Corrective action may involve a change in or a refinement of existing policy and/or a change to the existing legislation.

14.2. POLICY MAKING WITHIN THE DSS — THE NATURE OF THE TASK

Let us assume that a problem requiring corrective action has been identified. The problem will, typically, be 'owned' by a single policy maker. This person will commence the work of finding an acceptable solution to the problem by reviewing it. This normally involves the production of a 'policy review paper'. This outlines the current state of the legislation, of the Department's policy, of the effects of the legislation that are perceived as being problematic, gives any other relevant background information (such as statistical data, statements by ministers, the findings of other reviews of the area, etc.), and may suggest and partially evaluate some candidate solutions. It is also the role of the review to set the scope of the problem (by saying what is and is not included) and by providing criteria for evaluating candidate solutions.

In our analysis of the policy process, we refer to this phase as 'problem structuring'. Problem structuring may be a solitary task or it may involve others, depending on the size and scope of the review. However, when others are involved it is normally only in the role of information provider to the problem owner. Occasionally there will be meetings and less formal consultations during this phase to clarify the current policy or to seek ideas for solutions.

The original review paper will be circulated to several others. Some of these will be subordinates of the owner and others will be colleagues in other branches or directorates. It is the role of the owner's subordinates to elaborate the arguments in the review paper, to suggest other and more detailed solutions and to evaluate all the candidate solutions. They will, however, sometimes have something to say about the overall problem structure and may suggest new structures which imply different solutions and will affect evaluations of already suggested solutions.

The main purposes of circulating the review paper outside the originating branch are: to alert others who may be affected by the problem;

to make others aware of the kinds of solution being offered so that possible interactions with other areas of the social security legislation or its administration may be revealed; and to seek evaluations of the candidate solutions and the arguments behind them from the sometimes very different perspectives that other directorates bring to bear.

Everyone who receives the original policy review paper will comment on it. This may take the form of marginal notes on the original or a short memo but is more likely to be in the form of a complete, new policy review paper. On receiving back these comments, the owner must understand them, digest them, amalgamate them and otherwise use them to inform the writing of a new review paper. If the owner is happy with the statement of the problem, the efficacy of the chosen solutions, and the coherence of the case in favour of those solutions (and for rejection of the rejected solutions), then a document is produced recommending the chosen solutions to the minister. However, it is more likely that there will still need to be much more work done before a clear and supportable set of solutions is arrived at. This means sending out the second version of the review paper to either the same or a different set of subordinates and colleagues for further work and comment.

Even when a set of recommendations to the minister have been submitted, the Minister may reject them or ask for various modifications. In fact, this is quite normal for early submissions. When this happens, the owner must begin a new cycle of producing a review paper, sending it for comment and then preparing a new set of recommendations. On a particular policy problem we analysed, which was to do with a very small part of the income support legislation and was recommended to us as fairly typical for its type, yet small, complete and not too complicated, there were a total of twenty people who became involved, more than forty full review papers were written as well as a host of notes and memos and five sets of recommendations were made before the minister was happy with the solutions proposed. The whole process took two years from start to finish. Many policy problems take longer times to resolve and some are under continuous review.

14.3. ISSUES IN GROUP WORKING

There are many interesting aspects to the way policy is made in the DSS but we will concentrate here on the way that groups work together to solve a policy problem. Firstly, we look at some of the unusual features of the group itself, then of the problem and lastly of the dynamics of the task.

14.3.1. The group

One striking aspect of group work among policy makers is that they tend not to view their task as group work at all. Indeed, the number of meetings held about a particular policy problem is very small and typically involve only a very few of the people working on the problem, so face-to-face contact with other members of the group is rare. The individual's perception of his or her task is that they are given a problem to work on and then work on it. They are not unaware of the wider organizational setting for their task but tend to consider their input as being an individual effort.

The group that works on any particular problem is liable to be widely separated in space and time. That is, very few members of any particular group will be in the same office, or building or, increasingly, even the same town at the same time during the solving of the problem. This is not helped by the DSS policy of rotating staff, especially the more senior staff such as would typically work on a policy problem, around jobs and around regions on a regular basis (about one move every three years). This means that many of the individuals in a group and even the owner are likely to have changed during the life of a policy problem.

14.3.2. The problem

Another striking characteristic of policy problems is that there is no obvious process for solving them. It is also clear that deciding the criteria for the evaluation of candidate solutions is just as much a part of the problem as the finding of the candidate solutions in the first place. This latter is especially true where the solutions proposed are changes to policy rather than changes to legislation. Rittel and Webber [1984] have expressed the notion that for a certain class of problems (wicked problems) to understand what the problem is is, in itself, to identify acceptable solutions to the problem (see also [Simon 1984] for a discussion of this type of problem). The kinds of strategic planning problems they discuss seem very similar to the policy problems the DSS deal with. To quote Rittel and Webber:

> The formulation of a wicked problem is the problem! The process of formulating the problem and of conceiving a solution (or re-solution) are identical, since every specification of the problem is a specification of the direction in which a treatment is considered. (p. 137)

They also say:

> The information needed to understand the problem depends on one's idea for solving it. That is to say: in order to describe a wicked problem in sufficient detail, one has to develop an exhaustive inventory of all conceivable solutions ahead of time. (p. 136)

Clearly, this is just not possible as the space of potential solutions is infinitely large. When people solve such problems, Rittel and Webber argue, they identify feasible solutions on the basis of 'realistic judgement'. What this seems to amount to is a constraining of the solution space by excluding those types of solution which are thought to be 'unrealistic'. Judgements about what is and what is not a feasible solution must be based on criteria to do with the goals, the power, the resources and the beliefs of the planner. Essentially, these criteria are used to define constraints on the type of characterization that is acceptable for the problem and hence on the type of solution that may be proposed. Solutions which violate these constraints are not acceptable.

A further difficulty that these problems pose is brought about by the size of the groups working on them, by the mobility of the group members, and by the length of time problems take to solve. Both of these factors lead to difficulties with access to, amount of, and retention of information. The DSS has a significant problem with the capture, the organization, and the retrieval of information during the solution of a policy problem. In essence the only visible information is in the review papers and any external sources that are introduced. The related problems of forgetting, information overload, 'tunnel vision' and ignorance of the workings of other group members are all potential dangers in the policy making process.

14.3.3. Problem solving dynamics

The organizational structure of the DSS policy function works very well in overcoming most of the difficulties inherent in the policy problem. In particular, the distribution of problem solving over a large group of individuals with different organizational perspectives and expertise is effective at trapping most of the potentially harmful interactions between different policies and different parts of the legislation. Unfortunately, the cost of this is the extremely slow speed of the process. This in turn raises the problems of information capture, organization and access mentioned above which, in their turn, require further care and thus slow down the process even further.

One of the most important organizational devices for ensuring the coherence of the final solution is to give the problem to a single individual to own. The process is essentially one of this individual iterating towards a solution with the assistance of a large group of expert colleagues. The individual ownership of problems ensures that each solution is internally coherent while the distribution of the problem solving effort helps to ensure consistency across the whole of DSS policy and legislation.

The drawbacks of this type of organization are largely in the limits of the cognitive capacities of the individuals involved (no single person can foresee the ramifications of a change in legislation across the whole of the social security law — only a rather small part of it), and in the nature of the communications between group members.

Communications are particularly interesting as a source of difficulties. The flow of information during policy work is illustrated in Figure 14.1. The diagram is somewhat simplified because it is possible for an owner's subordinate to delegate the work to or ask for comment from his or her own subordinates, as, indeed, may the owner's colleagues in other branches or directorates. Apart from telephone calls and the rare face-to-face meeting, the major medium for information transfer is the policy review paper. These papers are typically documents of perhaps fifteen or twenty A4 pages of single-spaced text (including tables) and usually have one or more annex which may well be much larger than the main document.

The review papers and annexes are usually very well written, with good, clear English style and well-formed arguments. However, they are, inevitably, rather dense in their information and argument content. Furthermore, policy makers, in writing their policy documents, rely heavily on tacit knowledge of and shared assumptions about the political culture in which they operate — so there is often as much to be read between the lines as there is on them.

What this implies for the policy worker is that each paper is a very complex communication that must be unravelled and analysed and understood before it can be responded to. Naturally, this task is many times duplicated for the owner of the problem. Each paper that is produced is the end-product of a great deal of work. This work is kept, if it is kept at all, in the individual policy worker's personal files. These are eventually archived but are not easily available to the group during the problem solving period (nor afterwards, since the archives are very difficult to search). This means that many arguments that appear in review papers are incomplete in that assumptions, data and so on on which they were based do not make it into the paper but stay in the personal file. This places an additional burden on the reader of a review paper to judge the validity of his colleagues conclusions without the benefit of full visibility of their reasoning.

An even more extreme manifestation of this problem is that the repeated iteration involving new issues of the owner's review paper means that most of the group is working always with the digested and summarized comments of their colleagues rather than the original material so that duplication is always a danger, and the opportunity to spot another's mistakes is not available. Indeed, the problems of retrieval of past policy decisions and, especially, of the reasons behind them, very often means that the justification for the legislation and the policy behind it is reconstructed anew each time it is required by a

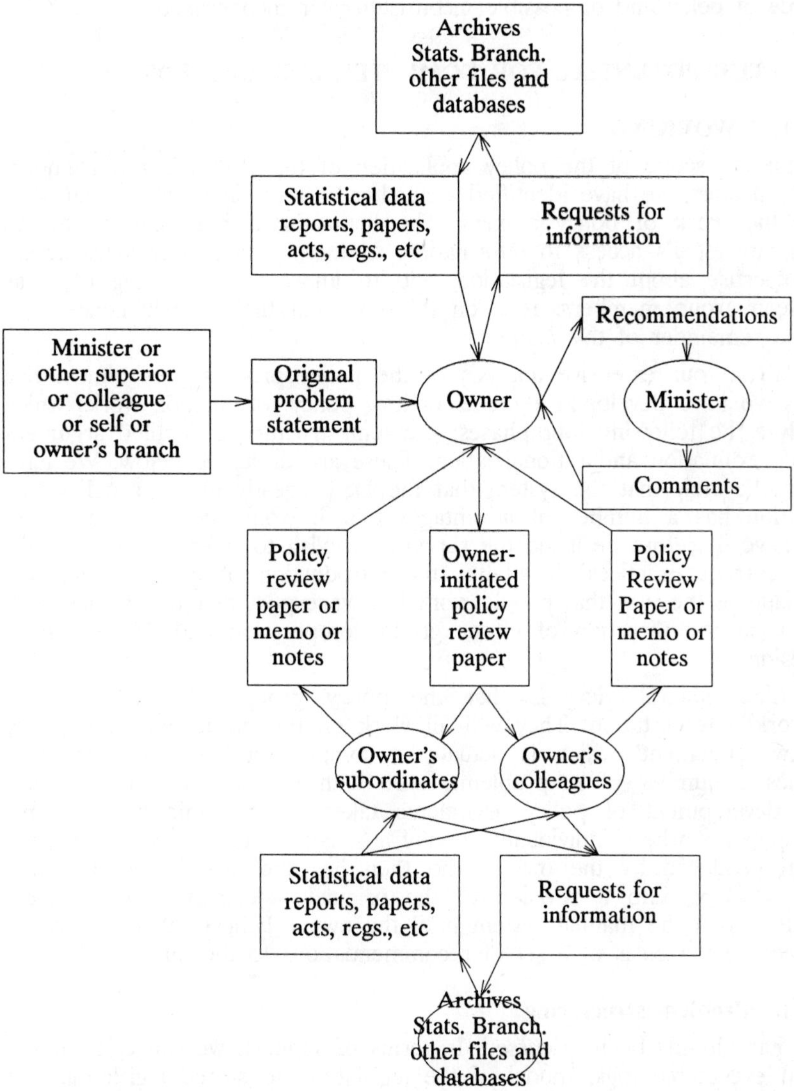

Figure 14.1: *The flow of information during policy problem solving.*

policy branch. This situation is clearly unsatisfactory as it is another source of delay and of possible inconsistency or incoherence.

14.4. THE POTENTIAL FOR COMPUTER SUPPORT FOR GROUP WORKING

Within the scope of the policy application of the DHSS Large Demonstrator project, we have identified a number of ways in which we can support the work of policy makers. The main thrust has been to extend each individual's access to information, to extend each individual's access to expertise about the legislation, and to improve the sharing of ideas between group members. It is on this last area that we will concentrate in the remainder of this chapter.

From our extensive analysis of the policy process over almost five years we have developed a model of how policy formulation works which involves the following four phases: problem structuring, detailed argumentation, evaluation and rationalization. These are discussed below. We have taken the view that the system that the DSS already uses for policy formulation has a number of advantages that it would be good to retain. We have therefore designed the support we wish to offer to mesh closely with current practices. Inevitably, the introduction of computer support will change the way that people work but we expect that the changes will all be in the direction of closer group co-operation and greater group cohesion.

The general view is that the policy group will each have a networked workstation. They will all work on the production of a policy review 'document' which is actually a complex problem structure that defines a number of subproblems, each with its own internal structure. The development of policy arguments takes place within subproblems. The policy workers individually modify a structure and detailed argumentation produced by the owner who then has the task of consolidating their working into a revision of the original 'document'. This process iterates as in the manual system until the owner believes that it is ready to become the basis of a set of recommendations to the minister.

14.4.1. Problem structuring

This has already been discussed. In terms of support, we can offer access to an executable logic model of the legislation, to stored legislation text and to stored policy arguments. However, problem structuring is an essentially individual activity under the present organization.

14.4.2. Detailed argumentation

In this activity, the owner or, more likely, another policy worker in the group, is developing a detailed policy argument within an element of the problem structure. It is in this area that the greatest amount of support can be given.

As well as access to an executable logic model of the legislation, to stored legislation text and to stored policy arguments, we provide a standard form for expressing arguments. The rationale behind the use of a standard argument form was that for the group to co-operate more effectively on the development of policy, they needed to have a common language and a common set of objects that they were manipulating.

The argument form we use is a modification of one developed by Steven Toulmin [1958]. This is based on the assumption that the forms of arguments can be expressed using a simple syntax. Toulmin distinguished macro-arguments (which are of some indeterminate size at least as big as a paragraph of text) from micro-arguments (which are at least as small as a paragraph of text). The form he devised is for describing micro-arguments and it is the micro-arguments developed by policy makers during the detailed argumentation phase of their work that we offer support in the creation, manipulation, storage and retrieval of. It will be useful to briefly review the reasons for the particular form that Toulmin devised.

If we make an assertion, Toulmin argued, we commit ourselves to the claim that it involves. If that claim is challenged, we will, normally, produce some facts to support it. The facts themselves may be challenged and, if so, will require their own support so that they may be agreed and the argument may progress. This gives us a basic and simple distinction between a claim and the data which support it. Of course, the claim may still be challenged, not now on the basis of its factual support but on the question of why we believe those data support that claim. What the challenge demands are the "rules, principles, inference licences or what you will" that justify the step from data to claim. Such justifications Toulmin calls warrants: 'general, hypothetical statements which can act as bridges and authorise the particular step to which our argument commits us'. The basic form of an argument is shown in Figure 14.2.

The nature of our warrant will affect the amount of force that the argument gives to the claim. That is, we will need to qualify the claim on the basis of the warrant we have used. There are also conditions of exception or rebuttal which indicate circumstances in which the general authority of the warrant would not hold. What is more, the authority of the Warrant itself may be challenged in which case we need to provide explicit support for it in the form of a backing. A backing is a statement of facts which, in the particular field of argument we are in, can safely be taken as certain or self evident. Toulmin's complete argument form is

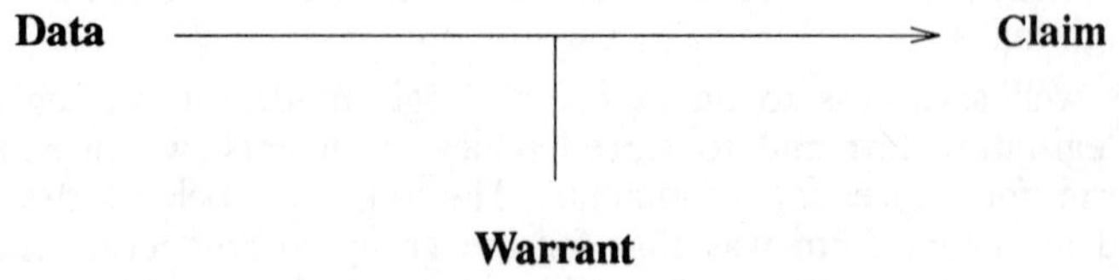

Figure 14.2: Toulmin's basic micro-argument form

now as shown in Figure 14.3.

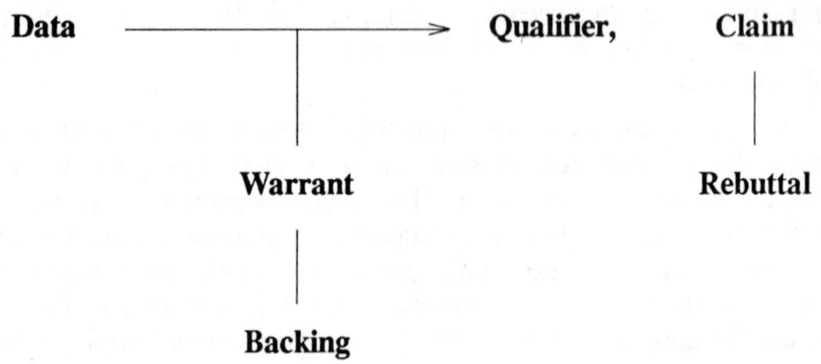

Figure 14.3: Toulmin's complete micro-argument form

There have been some slight modifications so as to produce a computer-manipulable form of micro-argument structure and, especially, to ensure that micro-arguments may, where possible, be integrated with the logic model of the legislation. However, what we are offering policy workers is essentially the same as Toulmin's form.

The main benefits that a standard form for micro-arguments give to policy workers are:

1. The components of an argument (e.g. assumed data, inference warrants) are either explicitly stated or are explicitly omitted. In the

jargon of rhetoric or argumentation - see [Dixon 1971]; Perelman and Olbrechts-Tytecha [1969] — this will affect the force of the argument. In particular it will make obvious how an argument may be challenged or rebutted.

2. Arguments become easily manipulated by policy workers who can use graphical editors to create and amend complex argument structures compounded from many micro-arguments. In particular, the particular policy arguments that one worker has created become the actual objects for manipulation of subsequent workers.
3. Arguments are easily manipulated by the computer. They can be stored, indexed, searched, retrieved, checked, linked to the legislation text and the logic model as appropriate, displayed and combined and recombined as necessary.
4. Just as there is a single body of legislation that all policy workers refer to and work on, so there is (in theory at least) a single, coherent body of arguments which developed the policy behind and derived the particular form of that legislation. A computer-manipulable argument form allows the possibility of making this set of arguments available to all policy workers as a baseline from which to develop new policy and legislation.

14.4.3. Evaluation and rationalization

These two phases involve the owner gathering in, at the end of each iteration, the detailed argumentation of the others, extracting the suggested options, the arguments for them and any evaluative arguments for or against them and applying a range of evaluation 'perspectives' (based on the department's policy goals and the arguments for them). This will yield a set of potential solutions for each of which a coherent argument should be available. By manipulating these and the overall problem structure, the owner will be seeking to develop a set of arguments for these options which are mutually consistent and satisfy the evaluation criteria. This we have called rationalization.

The rationalization of the chosen solutions then becomes either the new problem structure to be passed out to the rest of the group, or the basis for the preparation of a set of recommendations to the minister.

14.4.4. Knowledge based support

It is fundamental to a policy maker's job that he or she should understand the social security legislation. The quality and quantity of this knowledge varies according to the exact role of the policy maker however. Senior policy makers are aware of the general form of the legislation within their areas of specialization but not of the detail. They also require an acquaintance with the legislation in related areas. More junior members of the team have a more detailed knowledge of the legislation which is more narrow in its scope. In this way, the knowledge required for policy formulation is itself widely distributed within and between policy groups.

It is certainly the case that the most major concern of a policy maker is that all of the possible options for change are discovered and evaluated. However, close behind this is the concern that changes to the legislation which are proposed in one area should not have unforeseen and undesirable ramifications in other areas. Indeed, a great deal of the interaction between policy groups and with other interested parties (e.g. external pressure groups) is largely for the purpose of exposing proposals for legislative change to expert critiquing so as to avoid such problems.

As an aid to detecting such unwanted interactions between different parts of the legislation, the policy system provides a representation, in first-order logic, of the legislation. In our prototypes, we have modelled only small parts of the legislation but a fully operational system would be expected to model the whole of the social security legislation and parts of related legislation. There is also a need to add a little real-world knowledge (such as that men cannot become pregnant) where such knowledge is assumed and used but not made explicit in the acts, regulations or case law.

To use this logical model of the legislation, the policy system provides the users with the ability to describe classes of people in which they are interested and then to query the model about how these people interact with the benefit system. There is a range of queries constructed for this purpose. The policy maker may also use rule editors to modify the knowledge base — in effect modelling proposed changes to the legislation. The system supports a notion of public and private versions of the legislation. The public version is the model of the actual legislation. Any work that a policy maker does on possible changes to the legislation is done within a private version. These private versions exist as versions of a subproblem within the overall problem structure and can be associated closely with the detailed argumentation so that particular chains of argument and even particular micro-arguments can be associated with a particular set of knowledge base changes.

14.5. EVALUATING THE POLICY SYSTEM

It is extremely difficult to discover whether systems with the objectives of the policy demonstrators fulfilled their purposes. It is not only that the objectives for these systems were vague (which they inevitably were) but also that there are no adequate metrics of suitability for purpose that could be applied. We are left, ultimately with having to ask potential users of the system for their personal opinions (more or less well-informed by some degree of experience with the prototypes) on the matter. Within this framework, we can vary some of the parameters. We can ask users during development and use their responses to guide further development (formative evaluation) or we can ask them after we have finished and use their responses as a rating or judgement of the system (summative evaluation). We can also be more or less realistic in the kind of experiences they have with the system, varying their exposure between a short presentation and an extended trial in their normal working milieu. We can also ask about different aspects of the system to be evaluated. We could ask, for instance, about the validity of the task model it embodies, or about its usability, or its suitability as a support tool. We can vary the number of potential users we asked — asking more would increase our confidence in any responses. Lastly, we could vary the degree of structure, formality and detail of the experiences we provide, the questions we ask, and the answers we expect.

There have always been two members of the policy application team who came from a policy background. Their input to the design and to the knowledge base building and their on-going critiquing of the prototypes has provided continuous formative evaluation which has been very healthy for the application.

All the early policy prototypes were evaluated only by demonstrations. However, in the last three months of the project, a system was installed in a policy maker's office. The policy maker, with the assistance of policy application team members when necessary, 'shadowed' work he was doing on a current policy problem using the prototype in order to get a feel for the adequacy of the system. He was judging it against a set of criteria to do with the accuracy of the policy formulation model it embodied, the quality of its support for the policy formulation tasks, and its usability as a piece of software. The results are reported elsewhere (an internal, DSS report) but they were, generally, very positive on all three sets of criteria.

Nevertheless, despite this favourable evaluation, it must be borne in mind that the evaluator was chosen for his friendly attitude to the project and its aims and his computer literacy. The evaluation is simply the opinions of this one man whose exposure to the system was rather limited. However, coupled with the very positive responses that we have had to demonstrations of the system to many other policy workers, we are probably justified in thinking that the system would be well liked as a support tool.

We also sought some views on the cultural acceptability of such computerized support for DSS policy makers. This too has been encouraging. The evaluation we have done and the demonstrations we have given have been enough to convince the DSS of the potential of the policy system. The Department has now completed a longer (nine months) evaluation study which again involved placing systems in policy makers' offices and using them to shadow real policy formulation work.

This study, which was completed in December 1989, concluded that the approach showed considerable potential but its final recommendations are unknown at the time of writing. It is expected that further development work may be commissioned.

14.6. CONCLUDING REMARKS

In the DSS policy function we have encountered a rather unusual instance of group working. The particularly odd thing about it is that the 'group' is widely dispersed in space and time. Yet it is a problem which calls for the bringing together of a great many people with a wide range of expertise and with widely differing perspectives. The particular methods that the DSS have employed to use such groups is itself interesting and effective.

Our proposed computer support for this function has, as far as possible, preserved the advantages of the current practice. The main technical difficulties we have had to overcome were in the development of a suitable model of the policy process and in finding a computer-manipulable and yet usable, standard language for the core of the policy worker's task the creation and manipulation of arguments. We currently have a prototype system encompassing all of the types of support discussed above which was demonstrated at the end of the project in April 1989, which had been evaluated by the DSS in the three months prior to that and has now undergone a subsequent nine month evaluation in the DSS.

CHAPTER 15

ORGANIZATIONAL AND SOCIAL IMPLICATIONS

Andrew Taylor

Throughout the project a substantial amount of effort was expended considering and attempting to address some of the important organizational and social issues raised by the systems being developed. This work focused not only on the specific analysis of detailed aspects of the working practices of potential users but also on the more general questions of:

1. The applicability of methodologies for organizational analysis for KBS.
2. Issues concerning the cost benefit justification of such systems.
3. The possibility of predicting the future effects of the systems.
4. The roles of various groups and individuals within an organization introducing such systems.

This chapter outlines the range of organizational issues which arise with these systems, describes how they were addressed within the specific project work and assesses the possibility of methodologies or prescriptive recommendations which could improve the handling of these issues.

15.1. INTRODUCTION

The terms of reference, and subsequent organization and planning of the project, did not include any major objective to consider, directly, the social and organizational aspects of the systems. Whether this was a

KNOWLEDGE-BASED SYSTEMS AND
LEGAL APPLICATIONS. ISBN 0-12-086441-X

reasonable or desirable decision (and this question was itself the subject of disagreement within the project) it was nonetheless a given constraint to the work. Throughout the project, however, questions were often asked, typically by those responsible for exploiting the systems, concerning what benefits the systems could provide. Similarly, the potential end users, along with socially concerned observers of the work, frequently questioned us about the effects the systems could have on the working practices of the decision makers and the quality of service offered. It was also apparent that it would have made little sense to develop 'requirements statements' for the systems which did not match any real organizational need or take account of the context within which the systems would have to operate.

These various external expectations supported the specific interests and concerns of the analysts working on the project in considering the organizational features of the systems. During the last few years the importance of such issues has become more generally acknowledged — not least through the clearly apparent failure of systems which have not paid sufficient attention to such factors. As a result, the demand for methodologies which can help with the identification of suitable application areas, the identification of user requirements, the whole process of knowledge acquisition and the evaluation of systems and knowledge bases, has grown to be the major area of concern for those developing these knowledge based systems. More widely there has been a call for the adoption of a new conception of 'knowledge' and a corresponding change to the proposed role of the technology.

Not surprisingly, the experiences of our project have led us to conclude that there are no easy answers or recommendations appropriate for any of these organisational and social issues. Indeed there is nothing in the technology *per se* which encourages us to believe that it holds out particular dramatic benefits and opportunities, nor in contrast that it is bound to have undesirable and detrimental effects on working practices. Similarly there are no general and guaranteed recommendations on how to achieve successful solutions. So much depends on factors such as the size of the system and the scope of its impact, the degree of involvement of users and the extent of integration of the systems with their existing tasks and objectives. This makes it difficult to draw general conclusions from the work of our project. It is therefore necessary to explain the sense in which the project experiences have highlighted important issues.

The issues which we have concentrated on are likely to be more important to large scale, internally developed applications to support a specific defined task and designed with clear business objectives in mind. In this it contrasts with, say, the Latent Damage Adviser of Capper and Susskin [1989], which is smaller, more generic and less defined in terms of its expected usage. This contrast should not be underestimated — it is as considerable as the difference between say, a generic time recording system written on a spreadsheet for use on a PC within any organization and a fully sophisticated financial and administrative system built for a specific company. The distinction has much to do with the extent to which the system constrains its possible uses. We can, for instance, imagine a spectrum from a most general unconstrained system but where the user is required to provide a great deal of interpretation and judgement of relevance of the results of the system, and on the other extreme a specific, focused and targeted system incorporating constraints on which issues need to be addressed and how. Our concerns have been less with the generic capabilities for any interested individual and more with the specific needs of an organization and the particular roles of its decision makers.

This chapter characterizes the stages in the development of these KBS at which 'human' issues are of particular importance, the difficulties presented within the project and some of the techniques and methodologies which were used. It will also consider some of the issues and complexities which are still unresolved and draw some general conclusions about the future work required to address these issues.

15.2. STAGES

Organizational issues arise in five key areas of the development of a knowledge based decision support system. Without assuming that these can be characterized as distinct stages they fall into a general sequence of the following:

1. Opportunity identification and definition of objectives.
2. Requirements development and revision.
3. Knowledge analysis.
4. Introduction into the organization (incl. 'job design', internal marketing, training).
5. Evaluation, validation and acceptance, maintenance and future development.

This section will consider what is involved generally in each of these and also some of the particular issues present with legal applications which may not be so apparent in other domains but are still likely to be problematic.

15.2.1. Opportunity identification and definition of objectives;

The identification of a system which it is appropriate, and worthwhile, to develop is undoubtedly the most crucial stage — but is also, it seems, the least rigourously addressed. The dangers of a poor selection are considerable. On the one hand, the system may be supporting tasks which have little relevance or importance to the organization — or which the human decision makers have no difficulty with and carry out in the most cost effective manner already. On the other hand, it is quite easy to select a task and role for the system for which it is just not feasible to construct a support system. This may be to do with limitations of the technology, the 'damp squib syndrome' — that it cannot perform sufficient tasks to be of help, or the knowledge required for the knowledge base is unfeasible to elicit and encode. Alternatively it can be that systems have undesirable effects which cannot be controlled by the organization, the 'time bomb syndrome'.

The potential for such mistakes in legal domains appears to be considerable. Simple encodings of the legislation as logical rules are an example of systems which are mostly irrelevant and inappropriate to support decision makers in law, or which are too limited on their own to provide any significant support. Such mistakes are easily recognizable and can be addressed at an early stage — although it can be worrying to see developers blindly assuming that some good use must be possible for these logical encodings if only someone could design a suitable interface for them. More serious is the danger of underestimating the complexities of decision making in law and the ramifications of interfering with delicate organizational balances that have been established over many years. Similarly, the conceptual complexities of reasoning by analogy or of identifying strategies for addressing particular legal problems are such that, unless the knowledge required and procedures for applying it are already available and explicit, it must be at least extremely ambitious to believe that a knowledge engineer (even one with a training in law) could elicit them. It was for these reasons that we dismissed early on the idea that the encoding of 'expert knowledge on how to tackle assessments' was a feasible possibility. The danger of undesirable consequences from inappropriate systems is more worrying still. Problems of law, by their very nature, invoke issues of overlapping and competing interests. In many ways the law itself provides a ground for the negotiation of differences. In such an environment the occurrence of intricate complexities is unavoidable, and the adoption of any simplistic interpretation highly dangerous. Part of the answer must be to link any system closely with existing organization procedures for monitoring and controlling the decision processes.

The key questions which need to be addressed at this stage, therefore, include the following:

1. What are the key business priorities, particularly those associated with expertise and decision making?
2. Which tasks, linked to these business priorities, seem 'susceptible' to KBS solutions (based on analysis of the tasks, mistakes, constraints, nature of decision making and knowledge used, etc.)?
3. What are the potential business benefits of possible systems and so

what feasibility and evaluation criteria should be applied to an assessment of proposed systems?

4. What is the organizational feasibility of the system? (based on an analysis of the scope of activities supported, the context in which the system would be located, job design and 'monitoring and control' procedures).
5. What is the technical feasibility of producing a useful and workable system (based on estimates of the complexity of required functionality, scope and complexity of required knowledge, usability criteria and system adaptability)?

The project was presented with a number of challenging problems when trying to address these issues. Firstly, there were uncertainties pertaining to the objectives of the organization. It was clear that there was no single, definitive view on the objectives of the organization but rather a plurality of perspectives each with their own legitimacy. The degree of correspondence between the activities actually being carried out within the organization and the stated objectives was frequently minimal or at least uncertain. The long term plans of the organization included proposals for radical change in responsibilities and accountability which in effect questioned the possibility of any system remaining relevant. Secondly, there were problems in discerning the tasks to support and consequently the organizational feasibility of possible systems. It was particularly difficult to establish the precise uses of different knowledge items. There exists a plurality of sources and flows of the knowledge, along with mechanisms for monitoring, validating and maintaining the knowledge, which vary in their formality, impact and pervasiveness. Often the 'official' accounts did not match the actual practices of individuals and local groups.

Thirdly, we believe that an important feature of all legal domains when addressing these issues is the fact that decision making in law, and indeed policy development, takes place within a framework of time constraints and risk assessment. It is always conceivable that a particular issue could be researched and considered in exhaustive and painstaking detail only to confirm the initial assessment of the situation. The skill is to recognize where potential risks lie and to address issues to sufficient depth to remove as much risk as reasonable within the time constraints. One of the great potentials of knowledge based support systems must be that they could change the current balance in such assessments for the better.

15.2.2. Requirements development and revision

Requirements analysis for knowledge based support systems seems too often to be considered something which is not particularly difficult to perform — after all, systems analysts have been carrying out a very similar task for traditional systems for many years, and why should these systems be peculiarly difficult? The answer is that previous systems were typically built around explicit manual procedures, the form and content of which were not a particular matter of concern to decision makers. In contrast, the tasks which KBS are trying to support are typically the central areas of skill, experience and individuality of the decision makers. The key issue with requirements definition for KBS, therefore, is to decide whose requirements the system is intended to address and, usually more difficult, who has the authority to sanction a statement of requirements. The problem is that decision making is seldom 'one thing', rarely occurs in only 'one place', and is usually carried out by a whole variety of individuals with different skills, levels of experience, responsibilities and approaches. So how do we identify a 'single' requirement? Equally it is often dangerous to separate out components of an overall task and provide support for these while neglecting the important, and usually dynamic, links between the components supported and the wider set of tasks [Brown and Taylor 1990].

Legal applications present a particular set of issues for requirements analysis and specification — issues which we would argue are always present but which legal applications cannot ignore. This is based on the problem of following a so-called participative approach to systems development. Simply, the requirements for a system cannot be grounded on what people want, let alone what they say that they want, but has to take account of what they are obliged to do, and therefore what they need. Unfortunately, experienced decision makers can still be found who are contravening the conditions empowering them with their authority. What is even more likely is that they will not be able fully to understand the effects (either positive or negative) of any support systems.

The conclusion is that requirements analysis for these types of system need to consider the nature of the decision makers tasks, and the role of any support capabilities, in a far greater depth than that for traditional systems. In particular it needs to consider the following questions:

1. Which decision making tasks are going to be supported by the system and how do these relate to each other (based on an analysis of which tasks require most support and what type of support they require, how interdependent the tasks are)?
2. Which organisational groups and what different 'types' of user will be supported (based on an analysis of organisation groups and boundaries, different user 'profiles')?
3. What support will be provided and how will the user access this

support (based on evaluations of different support possibilities and definitions of allocation of task between system and user)?

4. What knowledge will be included in the system and how much of it (based on an analysis of the various sources, structures and uses of knowledge by the users)?
5. Which features of the requirement are critical for the success of the system and its usability?

The particular issues for the project were centred on the variety of competing but equally valid answers to these questions. This resulted from the variety and multiplicity of:

1. Types of user, levels of skill, organization groups and boundaries involved in the activities.
2. Tasks in the decision making and the relative proportion of time and effort spent on each; the environment of decision making (including constraints of time, interruptions, etc.) the situations in which 'problems' arise and the mechanisms for their resolution.
3. Sources of knowledge and information, degree of their formality, approaches to their application, perceived reliability and authority of the knowledge, its boundaries of relevance and significance for the decision making.

As a result, the proposal of any requirement had to acknowledge that any single model of the decision making process and role of the system would be inadequate. The requirement statements had to support the multiplicity of uses and users. In addition to these general problems the crucial feature of legal applications in terms of requirements development has, for us, been the need to acknowledge that a 'right decision' or 'successful policy' is, on its own, insufficient as an outcome of the decision process. Of equal, or indeed greater, importance is the need for the evidence, reasoning and judgement behind the decision or policy to be explicit and well argued. Indeed, it is clear that it does not make sense to talk of a right decision or a successful policy in the absence of such a reasoned justification.

15.2.3. Knowledge analysis

Knowledge analysis is frequently thought of as being the responsibility of the more technically-oriented knowledge engineer rather than the organizational analyst. While there are many aspects of knowledge analysis which are so oriented, it is naive and dangerous to believe that decisions about the scope of knowledge to be included in a system, the form of its presentation and its organization, and the procedures for maintaining and updating it, do not raise organizational issues of considerable importance.

Particular problems arise in legal applications because of the interconnectedness of the various conditions, and the variances in status or levels of authority of the different possible knowledge sources.

It has been said, [Harlow and Rawlings 1984] that the calculation of a claimant's income, notional income and capital resources, in accordance with the regulations, raises complex questions of property, tax and matrimonial law more suited to a Chancery judge than to a benefit officer or lay tribunals. There is an argument for encoding each overlap in rules, but even ignoring questions of knowledge base maintenance and coherence, the design of the interface would probably result in the user having to deal with what could appear as a multiplicity of apparently unconnected questions occurring unexpectedly within an area with which they thought themselves familiar. In particular, from our own experience, the three main areas where potential 'dangers' exist are:

1. The ambit of the law to be represented as rules, once a has been made on the style of representation of the law as rules.
2. How to give the user 'optimal' access to case-law.
3. The under or overestimation of the importance of published guidance on interpreting the relevant law.

It is obviously unacceptable to argue that the existing mechanisms of choosing what information should be made available should be extended to KBS support. The current decisions are inevitably constrained by, as well as taking advantage of, the mechanisms available. New mechanisms must require new decisions.

The questions which the organizational analyst needs to address, therefore, include the following:

1. What are the different sources of knowledge, how do they relate to each other in terms of authority and what are the differences in how they are used, how are they 'kept up to date' within the organisation?
2. What are the different types of knowledge and how do they relate to the decision making tasks? What is the difference in terms of their authority and status, and what implications does this have for the ways in which the knowledge can be presented to the user?
3. What is the structure of the knowledge to be incorporated in the system, what is the significance of this structure and how does it delimit the scope of knowledge which has to be included within the system?
4. How are we to plan and control the process of building the knowledge base, and how are we to maintain and amend the knowledge base (including sizing, distributed development, documentation)?

Legal domains hold special problems for knowledge analysis, and these problems were certainly manifest throughout our project. This is ironic in view of the fact that the application areas were originally preferred because of the apparent avoidance of issues of knowledge elicitation. The particular difficulties lay in establishing precisely what status and role the different knowledge sources had, the ways in which they were structured, and why, and the relations between the different knowledge sources along with their uses. The domain of law may appear encouraging in that large quantities of knowledge are seemingly explicit. We concluded that the assumptions implicit in this knowledge and its form of presentation, and the extent of the knowledge required to apply the explicit conditions, mean that an unusually complex set of issues surround the selection, representation and subsequent presentation of any legal knowledge.

15.2.4. Introduction into the organization

Throughout the five year project, and particularly during its last twelve to eighteen months, considerable time and effort was spent in promoting the work of the project within the Department of Social Security, explaining what we had done and why to a large number of people, attempting to make them aware of the issues they would be presented with if they chose to take the work further. However, the majority of issues concerning the introduction of the systems into the organization were still left unaddressed. Our estimation was that it would take at least another three years to address these outstanding issues satisfactorily. In the case of the policy system this was exacerbated by the fact that the integration of the systems would of necessity have to progress at a rate determined by the use made of the system by the policy makers themselves. Unfortunately, in the KBS community at large there appears to be a view that once the systems have been produced people will 'know what to do with them' and be able to integrate them into the working practices of the organization effectively. In fact this is made worse by the presumption that analysis of job design issues will take the main features of the system as 'given'. Instead of an approach which argues that 'now we have got a system how can we adapt roles responsibilities and organization to make best use of it' we need one which considers what features the system has to have in order for it to meet the requirements of the roles, responsibilities and organization.

The general model of issues requiring to be addressed identified three groups of consideration. Firstly, there is the technology itself — what it can do and what it is needed to do to support the specific class of users, what it demands from the organisation in terms of keeping it operable and valid. Secondly, there are questions of the roles and responsibilities of the users of the system; how they should be adapted; what additional tasks are required (again for both the users and the creators/maintainers of the knowledge base). Thirdly, there are issues of cultural acceptability including what is considered as 'good working practice', plus the management and policy decisions on how the service provided by the organization can be enhanced by the systems. In addition to these three, continuing, sets of issue, there are some issues which are purely concerned with the introduction of the system. These include the internal marketing of the system to the key owners and decision makers (i.e. the promotion and development of a commitment to the ideas and principles of the system and its design), training in the system (including in the construction and amendment of the knowledge base), and the issue of phased introduction of the capabilities.

The questions of job design are inevitably raised at and included in the requirements definition, but also in the opportunity identification stages.

At this stage the principal questions which need to be asked include:

1. Who needs to be involved as sponsors of the system, assessors of the acceptability of the system capabilities and arbiters on what features should be included?
2. What is an appropriate and acceptable allocation of tasks between user and system; what new tasks will be required to improve the decision making and to maintain the new system including requirements for monitoring and control for evolution of the system performance?
3. What evaluation criteria for usability, and for assessing the implications on the work environment, should be accepted and how should they be applied so as to evolve an acceptable system?

While the project was unable to address these issues in any comprehensive manner, it became apparent that the issues of introducing this technology into organizations are particularly critical in legal domains. The primary concern is that the risks of getting it wrong are considerable in organizational, legal and political terms. The role of the decision maker and the range of their empowered decisions is crucial to the whole organization but also outside its direct control in a way that few other organizations would face.

The number of interest groups and the adversarial nature of the relationship between these various interests implies that the knowledge and support required must both be adaptable to the needs of specific users and also sympathetic to the alternative views. Legal and policy domains also involve a whole range of issues relating to the confidentiality of, and accountability for, decisions. Who requires or is allowed access to certain information, which decisions need to be recorded and with what level of justification, what advice it is permissible and appropriate to offer, are all issues with which the system may interfere.

The differences between the adjudication support and policy systems are considerable in terms of the status and individual freedom of the users.

It can only be expected that in other legal domains equally extreme differences will arise. In particular the professional legal community is particularly conservative in its use of technology; it combines connotations of power and mystique with its expertise and knowledge; it is a domain where the personal style, individuality and skill of the lawyer is dominant.

15.2.5. Evaluation, validation and acceptance, maintenance and future development

Issues of evaluation and quality assurance arise not only with regard to a delivered system but also to the changes to that system which ensure that it maintains its validity and relevance. For this reason, evaluation cannot really be separated from questions of maintenance. Too often the term evaluation is limited to verification and validation of the system in terms of its meeting the requirements specification, containing valid knowledge and providing correct answers, inferences and advice. This provides assurance that the system 'does what we wanted it to do'; the other, and perhaps more important issue, however, is 'whether we were right in wanting it to do that in the first place'. In terms of legal applications there are four aspects of parameters that can be considered:

1. The legal correctness of the knowledge base.
2. The legal and political appropriateness of the functionality of the system.
3. The organizational suitability and usefulness of the knowledge base.
4. The quality contribution which the system will make to the decision making.

It may be felt that these issues of quality assessment really go beyond the province of what the KBS system designer can hope, or indeed be expected, to address. Surely, it may be argued, the system developer can only work to a clear specification with objective performance criteria and can therefore only be expected to establish that the delivered system actually meets these requirements. In our experience, this view has been shown to be excessively naive and essentially untenable in many areas of KBS developments. Firstly, the requirements specification needs to be negotiated with the system users who cannot be expected to understand the impact of consequences of many of the design decisions. Secondly, the performance criteria cannot be expected to be 'objective' when the decision making itself is subject to interpretation, discretion and alternative evaluation, and when the task cannot be segmented without destroying the underlying coherence and logic of the decision making.

Thirdly, both the scope and the detail of the requirements and the performance criteria are unavoidably subject to change — in time and sometimes across locations and users.

While it is possible to define a limited subset of functionality and knowledge for which objective criteria can be established, in the process of narrowing down the area of 'quality assurance' the value of the resulting system is appreciably, perhaps even dangerously, reduced. The overriding lesson for us has been that a conception of evaluation as a single discrete event or checkpoint which objectively assesses the acceptability of a system is really misplaced. Any system has to undergo evaluation and assessment of its reliability not dissimilar to that which would be placed on a human decision maker.

15.2.6. Techniques, methodology and outstanding issues

A wide variety of techniques were used during the project to address these wide range of issues. Soft Systems Methodology (SSM) [Checkland 1980] was used as a key part of the organizational analysis. Its particular advantages were seen to lie in its emphasis on the variety of organizational perspectives concerning both the activities of the organization and the knowledge used by them, and the explicit consideration of the monitoring and evaluation of decision making. In this way it was possible to establish where exactly support was required and how it could best be provided, along with the associated issues of validation and maintenance of the knowledge. Traditional social science techniques were applied for eliciting models of the decision processes and conceptions of the knowledge used. Primarily this involved (structured and unstructured) informant interviewing, but to a lesser degree included the use of construct theory and protocol analysis. Particular emphasis was placed on the training, monitoring and guidance-provision aspects of the tasks. Underlying all of these techniques it was essential to understand the role of knowledge as part of a dynamic, negotiated, organizational communication rather than some neutral objective commodity which could be stored in a machine. User committees were therefore established including representation from each of the major interest groups. Substantial effort was devoted to selecting and developing the interest and commitment of these representatives and their colleagues.

By far the most important single factor in the successful aspects of the design, however, was the element of creativity and conflict in the design team and the development of arguments to justify the selected designs. In essence the motivation behind the design needed to be 'sold' to the potential users. The importance of these human skills led us to question the eventual relevance of a search for methodology to address these issues.

The most effective design is one which integrates the user and system in an adaptive and novel manner — opening up the possibilities for new ways of working. To achieve this the designer must be able to understand both the user's task and the capabilities of the technology. But they also need to be creative in the development and 'selling' of solutions. This may include the use of some methods in a limited way; it is also likely to depend on simulation and prototyping, with evolutionary development of systems.

It depends centrally, however, on the skills of the designer in creating quality designs and in convincing the user of the value of the systems and the opportunities they present for change. This point can be best brought out by comparison with other design tasks. Unfortunately, the usual model for system design is a comparison with engineering (VLSI, control systems, etc) or computer program design. Yet the nature of the task which we are trying to support encourages different comparisons — with architects, interior designers, or even better with lawyers and policy makers themselves. For these people are actually concerned with creating solutions for their 'clients' which satisfy the tacit needs of the clients in ways in which these clients themselves would not have thought possible.

Such comparisons help to explain why the idea of methodology may be less than constructive. For with architects, lawyers and policy makers the idea of a methodology for their task would be so limiting that it would become ludicrous. They may readily use checklists, guidance, and collected know-how, but not an overall methodology *per se*. Methodology is useful once the requirements for support have been designed — they give the assurance that these requirements will be implemented as intended. So there is a necessity for a language to express requirements in a formal way and guarantee their accurate implementation.

Equally, some methodologies can be helpful in the initial exploration of the context of the requirements (for example SSM) but all our experience has shown that the prime importance is in the design process itself, and none of the methodologies can directly address this design stage. Instead of trying to extend existing methodologies so that they could support this 'creative task' we believe that we should be developing specialist design skills. The answer to the question 'how can we ensure good systems and organizational design?' is that we should use good designers.

15.2.7. Issues

There are certain critical organizational and human issues which remain outstanding from the project and which we were able to address only in ad hoc and opportunistic ways. The concluding section of this chapter considers some of the most important of these and assesses the implications in terms of future developments. Four issues are particularly problematic for kbs developments in legal applications. The first concerns the nature of justification of the system and ownership, particularly in the light of the multiple interest groups. The second concerns the extent to which the responses of users are reliable. The third involves bounding the application and the knowledge base and the associated assumptions on what knowledge the users will provide for themselves. Lastly, there is the underlying issue of the indeterminacy of the likely effects of the system and its implications for design.

1. Ownership and Justification

It has been emphasized throughout this paper that it is important to establish answers to the questions: Who owns the system? Who should use it and for what purposes? Who should be responsible for authorising the knowledge contained in the system? Who is targeted to benefit from the system? In particular, we should not expect, for a sophisticated system in a large organisation, for any of these to be the same individual or group. Equally, we need to identify which objectives should be selected for the system, what costs are acceptable and what level of return is expected.

The difficulty is that most organizations either proclaim or manifest confused, contradictory and 'irrational' objectives. The policies of any organization are typically developed on the basis of a delicate balance of organizational, political and individual interests, combined with an understanding and acknowledgement of the practical (both administrative and financial) constraints involved in implementing these policies. In practice, therefore, there is a multiplicity of competing objectives and a plurality of distinct, and frequently competing, interest groups. It is not sufficient just to acknowledge the existence of this multiplicity of objectives and interests, nor to believe that it is acceptable just to bring the various interests together in a discussion of the design of the system. It would be naive to believe that in such a circumstance the influence and responsibility of each group would be equally considered. How, then, do we reconcile these interests? It cannot be acceptable, however tempting, simply to follow the wishes of the commissioning group — not least because those commissioning the system often will not have the authority and power to make the system successful.

Applications in the domain of law are particularly susceptible to these issues. The law itself is designed to focus on these issues of overlapping interests and the negotiation of rights, agreements and compromises. In the same way, therefore, that the law cannot be seen as subject to the interests of one group, any system to support the legal decision making must consider the impact on the balance of relationships between those making the decisions and those impacted by those decisions.

2. Reliability of Users

The design and evaluation of any system is largely dependent upon the responses to the system of the users to whom it is presented. Our problem has been that what users may say is not always a reliable basis for establishing either what they are thinking, what they will do in specific circumstances, or their role in the organization and their contribution to organizational objectives. The conclusion has to be that users responses to systems cannot be taken at face value and we need to be careful in deciding precisely what their responses tell us about the design of the system. This may seem strange at first sight. Why on earth should users not 'tell the truth'?

There are a number of elements to this issue. The most extreme and perhaps least likely case is where users are being intentionally malicious and obstructive.

Obviously if we have reached such a position then something has gone fundamentally wrong in the setting up of the project or the evaluation. More probable are the possibilities that:

1. They are being misleading out of self-interest for protecting their current work practices and roles; for example, they may be worried about the potential effects of the system on their working practices, they may be frightened of the technology and the possibility of it showing up their own limitations — or even the apparent straightforwardness of their job.
2. They are answering different questions to the ones we are trying to ask; for example, they may be answering on someone else's behalf rather than in terms of what they personally think, they may be trying to help us by making assumptions as to what we would like to know.
3. They are unable to articulate precisely what it is that they know; for example, they may not think in terms of the plans, data, knowledge and logical inferences which are the constructs of the system designer and implicitly built into the operation of the system; their knowledge may be 'tacit' or based on craft skills which it is impossible or inappropriate to represent explicitly.
4. They themselves do not know what 'the truth' or 'the correct answer' is (even though they may think that they do) and in some cases perhaps no-one can know for sure; for example adjudication officers make mistakes and have misconceptions about their roles and responsibilities (this is an example where their is a presumption that there is a 'correct' answer). Alternatively different policy makers carry out their tasks in different ways (this makes no assumption that there is a single 'right' way).
5. There is no truth in the sense which we are looking for it — people do not work with conceptual, cognitive or mental models, but only with specific contextual based responses to separate situations; in the extreme truth may just be a construct of the observer.

The problem is that so much of the analysis behind the design of any system, but especially of KBS, depends upon some model of the users tasks and decision processes. In some cases, however, a valid model may not be identifiable, or may in the extreme only reflect the analysts and designers own conceptions.

Limiting or scoping the system and the knowledge base

It was noted earlier that decisions have to be made on what statutes, case law, guidance and human 'know-how' or arguments should be included in the system and in what manner. The problem with excluding certain statutes is that those cases where the omitted statutes would have effect may be incorrectly handled. With systems such as the Local Office Demonstrator, such a limiting of scope may be clearly identifiable to the user — the system does not handle 'trade dispute' or 'student' cases for example. With systems like the Policy Demonstrator, however, the implications are less easy to determine — we cannot know anything about the implications of the omitted legislation. In contrast, the problems associated with including inappropriate legislation are not only practical (that unnecessary and costly effort is expended in creating and maintaining the knowledge base, or that users are presented with an unwieldy and laborious interaction) but may be conceptual in terms of misleading or confusing the user about the potential significance of the rather obscure conditions.

Problems with case law are perhaps more complex. How do we avoid the 'overloading' of the user with an excessively large volume of apparently relevant cases?

If we are providing access to individual cases, how is it possible to communicate why the case is significant and what its relevance may be for the case under consideration by the user? Although it may be an oversimplification, a distinction can be made between cases that expound a general principle and therefore have a widespread impact and those which give detailed consideration to the facts of a case, and are distinguished from other similar cases.

A case may be significant in that it expands or explains the meaning of certain words — sometimes this explanation may take the form of a 'rule' which clarifies or illustrates a term, at other times it may be a more general discussion of a term or phrase. It therefore appears that some case law may contain 'knowledge' which could be encoded as rules while many cases do not. On what basis should we decide which knowledge is appropriate for what form of representation? How should the difference between rules derived from case law and those from statute be presented to the user?

Guidance and 'know-how' raises similar and potentially more varied problems. Some guidance is in the form of declarative rules, some procedural; some is illustrated and expounded with examples, others as general discussion of factors to consider. Not all guidance has the same status - having different grounding in the legislation. How important is the sequence, form and structure of the presentation of guidance? How much guidance is it appropriate to give, particularly if the frequency of it being needed is small? How important is the source of particular expertise or know-how — and to what extent is it necessary to make this source explicit?

The issues of scoping really centre on three general questions:

1. What can we safely assume the user to know and understand — in terms of the interpretation of rules, the significance of facts, cases and arguments, and the status of the different knowledge sources?
2. What 'degree of coverage' is required in terms of the number and variety of cases which should be supported by the system and how should we make clear what is not supported?
3. Who can decide on the contents of the knowledge base and how can they assess how successful they have been in their scoping of the system?

It is clear that the only way of answering these questions is to accumulate sufficient experience and to reflect on it in a critical manner. The problem is that, currently, we have no such experience as to how to limit the knowledge base in ways which will not jeopardise the success of the system. Equally, the need for critical reflection is often neglected. This brings us to the final general issue.

Indeterminacy of the effects of the system

It is increasingly apparent that with more advanced systems, the likely effects of their introduction are indeterminate at both the organizational level and at the level of individual working practices. Equally, however, the process of design tends to assume that the impact of a system is predictable and identifiable. The general approach, in effect, is to model the organization, model the users tasks and knowledge items, identify those tasks (or subtasks) which could be performed by a system and then design the system to replicate these processes and carefully link in to the existing network of manual procedures. The fundamental problem with this approach is that it assumes the activities of the user are both determinate and inflexible, and also assumes that a system can satisfactorily replicate the required performance within the subtasks. In fact users will typically adapt (or even subvert) the systems to serve new organizational and personal objectives. Similarly, in the domain of human decision making and interpretation, systems perform less well than human experts and often produce 'unnatural' results in the interaction.

The answer seems to be to design new tasks for the users which take advantage of the features of systems by integrating their particular assets with the human skills, rather than try unsuccessfully to replicate human processes.

Our concern is really with the extent to which the design should be closed and specific. Given that users will want to feel supported but unconstrained by the system, and given that the particular ways in which they may use the system will vary and adapt, it is better to design an environment where the specific interaction is determined by the user rather than by the system.

15.3. CONCLUSIONS

This chapter has tried to emphasize the range and variety of organizational issues arising with regard to the introduction of KBS in legal applications.

The general conclusion is that the majority of the issues are as yet unresolved and largely unaddressed. This should be worrying for any organization considering such a development — and in particular those who stand to be affected by the system. Unfortunately there is little evidence from past systems development that much will be done to address these issues until there is some failure which is ascribable to them. For those organizations that wish to pre-empt such failures, this author would recommend three general principles or considerations.

Firstly, the introduction of these systems cannot be seen simply as a process of analysis and development carried out by system designers and handed over to users. Greater emphasis needs to be placed on the processes of presentation, introduction of the system into the organization, continuing evaluation of the use of the system, and regular changes to the system based on the monitoring of its effects. In principle this may not seem different from traditional systems development. The concern is that with systems which come so close to the central decision processes of people in the organization, and have the potential for substantial effects, far more continuous effort is required to monitor the effects and respond to necessary changes.

Secondly, there is the general question of the relevance and appropriateness of methodology for addressing these issues. Earlier in this chapter it was argued that methodology had to be secondary to design skills and the creativity and sensitivity of individuals. These individuals, it follows, should ideally be skilled in organizational analysis, knowledgeable about the capabilities of the technology and able to explain these to non-technical users, and thoroughly conversant with the decision processes and practice of the domain. These are highly specialist skills which there is little evidence of in the systems design community. External consultants seldom have the time to build up the depth of understanding of a particular environment and organization. Equally, however, trained or practising lawyers cannot be expected to have sufficient expertise — not only because they lack the technical and organizational perspectives but also they have little general knowledge of the practices and procedures outside their own domain of experience.

The required role is really one of an 'internal consultant' who can be specifically developed to bridge the gap between users and technical designers. Few organizations are developing such people, however.

Lastly, in terms of their social impact, it is probably important to maintain a reasonable perspective on the dangers associated with these systems. The chances of systems failing due to insufficient consideration of the human issues are considerable. The likelihood of undesirable social consequences resulting from these systems is more questionable. Certainly, focusing on the technology *per se* is likely to serve little purpose when the organizational stereotypes and managerial expectations have by far the greater impact. The objective of organizational analysts should be to demonstrate the options available and the formative context in which decisions are made so that the political nature of the decisions is not hidden behind the inevitability of the technology.

CHAPTER 16

KBS APPLIED TO LAW: A FRAMEWORK FOR DISCUSSION

Trevor Bench-Capon

16.1. INTRODUCTION

In this final chapter I shall not attempt to catalogue the lessons of the Alvey–DHSS Demonstrator project, both because these are to be found in the foregoing chapters, and because every participant in that project will have brought away rather different expperiences from it. Instead I want to advance a framework which can be used to discuss various different applications of KBS to law: this will help to place the various applications of the Demonstrator in perspective, and can be used as a basis to compare them with other work in this field.

The framework proposed takes as its starting point the characteristics of the legal domain. These characteristics serve both to distinguish this domain from the other domains to which KBS may be applied, and to link the very different applications that are found in that domain. These characteristics derive from the nature of the source material that can be included in a KBS. The discussion will begin with a fairly detailed look at a particular social security benefit — sickness benefit — so as to tease out these characteristics. This benefit has been chosen because it is an important and representative contributory benefit, with a long history. A fuller discussion of it, and other social security benefits may be found in [Ogus and Barendt 1982]. Although focused on a particular benefit, the points will hold good for all social security benefits, and I believe are also applicable to other sorts of administrative law, and, indeed, to law in general.

KNOWLEDGE-BASED SYSTEMS AND
LEGAL APPLICATIONS. ISBN 0-12-086441-X

16.2. SICKNESS BENEFIT

Some laws, such as those which prohibit theft and murder, are so universal that it is tempting to think that there have always been such laws. Indeed, it is difficult to imagine a society which did not have laws forbidding these crimes. These laws do, however, serve to fulfil important social goals, and were created to help achieve those goals. This fact, that laws are made for a reason, and the consequent need to consider what this reason is and how it shapes the law, is important everywhere, but the process of legislation being used to translate social goals into action is seen particularly clearly in the case of laws instituting benefits.

If we consider our chosen example of sickness benefit, we find that since quite early times there has been some kind of recognition that the more fortunate members of society should help to sustain the existence of less fortunate members who are, through no fault of their own, unable to make provision for their own needs. Typically, a person in a developed society is able to provide for himself because he has a job and is paid (or, in popular parlance 'earns') the money he needs to do so, or is a dependant of someone with such means. There are, however, certain common contingencies which prevent a person from working to receive the money necessary to provide for himself and his dependants. Most notably, people become too old to work ('retirement'), they are unable to find a job ('unemployment'), or they fall ill, and so are incapable of doing work ('sickness'). Of course, different societies have at different times taken different views on how society should respond to such contingencies: one strand of thought, expressed in the fable of the Ant and the Grasshopper, would be that a person should save in good times so that he can see himself through the hard times. In the UK provision for these various contingencies was for many years through the Poor Law, but this was extremely basic, and most people wanted to avoid the squalid poverty of the workhouses. In the nineteenth century therefore, trade unions and friendly societies developed in part to enable the better-off workpeople and artisans to pay into a fund while in work to insure themselves against these contingencies, so that their income could be maintained through them and they would not be forced to rely on the Poor Law. Such coverage was, however, voluntary and less than universal, so that many were still forced on to the inadequate provision of the Poor Law. This led to the view that what was needed was a national and compulsory insurance scheme which would provide universally the benefits of membership of the voluntary schemes. Eventually this was to lead to the National Insurance scheme, which provided for these contingencies, including sickness.

Thus when sickness benefit was introduced there was a clear intention on the part of government to provide for the maintenance of the income of those normally in work whose earning capacity was diminished by sickness. This intention has remained and we find it currently given effect by section 14 of the Social Security Act 1975:

14(1) Subject to the provisions of this section, a person who satisfies any of the three conditions in subsection (2) below shall be entitled

(a) [provision for Unemployment Benefit]

(b) to sickness benefit in respect of any day of incapacity for work which forms part of a period of interruption of employment.

Further elaboration of the notion of a day of incapacity for work is given in section 17:

17(1) For the purpose of any provision of this Act relating to unemployment, sickness,or invalidity benefit

(a) subject to the provisions of this Act, a day shall not be treated in relation to any person —

(i) [provision relating to a day of unemployment]

(ii) as a day of incapacity for work unless on that day he is, or is deemed in accordance with regulations to be, incapable of work by reason of some specific disease, or bodily or mental disablement.

Section 14(1)(b) expresses the intention quite clearly; the person should be incapable of work, and this incapacity should be an interruption of his employment. The presumptions are therefore that he would normally have an income from employment, but should be temporarily incapable of realizing this income. Section 17(1)(ii) is a slight elaboration of this, attempting to exclude malingerers by a stricter definition of incapacity of work, and places the onus of proof on the claimant. It is therefore a faithful reflection of the intentions, but it is stated in very general terms and, as it stands, it is likely to be too vague to be applied by the lay adjudicators who administer the scheme. Thus the legislation stands in some need of clarification.

Clarification comes in two ways: by regulations and by decisions in particular cases. In section 17(1)(ii) reference is made to regulations which can state circumstances in which a person may be deemed to be incapable of work. Such regulations are made under section 17(2):

17(2) Regulations may —

(a) make provision (subject to subsection (1) above) as to the days which are or are not to be be treated for the purpose of unemployment, sickness or invalidity benefit and a maternity allowance as days of unemployment or incapacity for work.

Such *enabling legislation*, as it is called, allowing regulations to be made to give more precision to a concept introduced in the primary legislation, is a very common feature of benefit legislation. In part this division exists for the convenience of the legislators in that regulations are easier to make and amend than is the primary legislation, but there is also something to be said for the conceptual separation achieved by using the primary legislation to enunciate the broad concepts and using regulations to bring about any fine tuning that may be required. The following are examples of regulations made under this power. Regulations made to clarify the notion of a day of incapacity for work are found in the *Social Security (Unemployment, Sickness and Invalidity Benefit) Regulations 1983*. Regulation 3(1) provides an example of a specific circumstance in which someone is deemed to be incapable of work:

3(1) A person who is suffering from some specific disease or bodily or mental disablement but who, by reason only of the fact that he has done some work while so suffering, is found not to be incapable of work by reason thereof, may be deemed to be so incapable if that work is

(i) work which is undertaken under medical supervision as part of his treatment while he is a patient in or of a hospital or similar institution; or

(ii) work which is not so undertaken and which he has good cause for doing,

and from which, in either case, his earnings do not exceed £26.00 in the week in which that work is performed.

An example of a regulation prescribing circumstances disqualifying a person from sickness benefit is

17(1)A person shall be disqualified from receiving sickness or invalidity benefit for a period not exceeding 6 weeks as may be determined in accordance with sections 97-104 if —

(a) he has become incapable of work through his own misconduct, except that this disqualification shall not apply where the incapacity is due to venereal disease or, in the case of a woman who is not a wife, or being a wife, is separated from her husband, to pregnancy.

Thus we can see that the regulations go into quite specific detail, even naming particular ailments in some cases, and help to clarify what is found in the primary legislation. Regulation 3(1) is meant to make explicit that a person should not be prevented from doing, and being paid for, therapeutic work which may speed his recovery, and regulation 17(1) is meant to ensure that people do not profit by their own misconduct, whilst not allowing free rein to the moral censure of the adjudicator.

The other way in which the legislation may be clarified is by decisions in particular cases. When a decision is made, the party against whom the decision goes may appeal. In the social security system of the UK the first appeal is to an appeals tribunal, and there is a further right of appeal to a social security commissioner. A Commissioner's decision may be considered of sufficient significance for it to be reported, in which case it is held to set a precedent which should be followed in subsequent cases. What we have then in a reported decision is a definitive application of the law to the facts in a particular case, and the suggestion that the decision should be followed in subsequent cases. Of course, no two cases will be exactly alike and so there will be room for interpretation as to whether the facts are sufficiently similar for the precedent to apply. Nonetheless, reported decisions do afford useful clarification.

As an example of the kind of clarification that can be achieved through reported decisions, consider one relating to regulation 3(1)(i) quoted above. In R(S)3/52 (the numbering system indicates the benefit to which the decision relates, the number of the decision and the year of the decision, so that R(S)3/52 was the third decision reported on sickness in 1952) we find:

> C, suffering from tuberculosis, was engaged for two-and-a-half days a week in a factory specially operated for the rehabilitation of tuberculosis victims. He attended hospital as an out-patient once every two months. It was held that he was a patient 'of' (though not 'in') a hospital

The point at issue was whether the claimant could be regarded as a patient of a hospital given the infrequency of his visits. Given that the case has come to this level of appeal it is probable that the adjudicating officer had thought not, but the commissioner held otherwise. The artificiality of the rule, as interpreted, is further shown by R(S)5/52 where it was made clear that had the claimant been under the supervision of a specialist without attending a hospital his claim would have failed. Nonetheless, given the decision in R(S)3/52 it is clear that attendance need not be all that frequent. Another example of clarification through reported decision is the interpretation of 'good cause' in 3(1)(ii) it has been made clear that medical reasons will typically suffice, whereas the simple intention to earn some extra money will not (R(S)4/79 and CS 8/79).

Regulations and reported decisions do serve to clarify the broad concepts set out in primary legislation, but even at this level of detail it is often hard for the adjudicator to be sure how to proceed in every case. He is, for one thing, not a medical expert so that the question of how the adjudicator can ascertain that a person is suffering from a 'specific disease or bodily or mental disablement' which is sufficient to render him incapable of work, and what he is to accept as satisfactory evidence arises. The answer is partly to be found in regulation 2(1) of the *Medical Evidence Regulations* which requires that the claimant furnish evidence of incapacity either 'by means of a certificate in the form of a statement in writing given by a doctor' or by 'such other means as may be sufficient in the circumstances of any particular case.' Thus the first thing that an adjudicator will look for is a doctor's statement, and normally such a statement will be taken by the adjudicator sufficient to satisfy the conditions without need to consider the details of the legislation. Where this is absent the case is more difficult, although commissioners' decisions have shown that a statement of incapacity from an employer is insufficient (R(S)13/51), whereas hospitalisation — even for tests which subsequently prove negative — does raise a presumption of incapacity (R(S)1/58). The problem is that the facts that are actually available to the adjudicator, that a claimant is in hospital, or that he possesses a medical certificate, do not match exactly to the description of the facts required in the legislation. Similar considerations arise when considering the contributions record of the claimant, or his age, when the law requires that he be in a certain age range, but the ascertainable facts are in the form of birth certificates or other evidence. There is therefore a problem of interpretation, of applying the law to the discoverable facts.

In many areas of law, skill in interpretation, involving both a knowledge of the law and of relevant past decisions as well as an understanding of English and a certain degree of common sense knowledge of the world, will be a good part of what makes a person expert in that field of law. Essentially, each of these experts will be operationalizing his knowledge so as to map onto the facts available to him. Different experts may operationalize their knowledge in different ways, regarding different facts as relevant, and perhaps drawing different conclusions on the basis of the available facts. In the case of sickness benefit, as in the other areas of social security, however, this operationalisation has been to some extent codified. The office of the chief adjudicating officer produces a manual for the guidance of adjudicating officers which contains a written version of much of the expertise they need to deploy. Even this detailed guidance will require some interpretation, but it does mean that a great deal of the expertise required for interpretation is explicit. This is not, however, the only way the relevant knowledge can be operationalized, and there exist other manuals, such as the welfare rights handbooks published by the Child Poverty Action Group, which also attempt to present the law in an applicable fashion. Such guides are used both by claimants themselves and by those who advise claimants, such as Citizens Advice Bureaux workers. The ways in which these guides operationalize the law differ from that found in the adjudicators' manual both because the perspective of use differs, in that they are concerned to indicate potential title rather than to support an authoritative legal decision, and because the facts available to the two groups differ. As examples of this last point, consider the case of the age of the claimant, which is presumably known by the claimant, whose word will be simply accepted by his advisor, but which will require to be established by supporting evidence to satisfy the adjudicator; or the case of contributions record of the claimant which can be definitively established by the adjudicator by an inquiry to the Department's records, but which must be estimated by the claimant and his advisor on the basis of his remembered work history. The existence of formal and universally applied guides is perhaps unusual, but in many other areas of law there exist commentaries and textbooks which are used by the would-be expert in a very similar fashion.

The other component of an adjudicator's expertise is his knowledge of procedures. As well as knowing, for example, that he requires a birth certificate to establish the age of the claimant, he also knows how to go about obtaining this information: whether he should write to the claimant, whether he should request the original or a photocopy, or whatever. This is perhaps most clearly seen in the case of contributions records: there the adjudicator knows that he must send a request to the appropriate part of the Department on a specified form, and what boxes will be ticked if the claimant's record is satisfactory. In this case he need have no knowledge of what the contribution conditions are — he knows what he must *do* to discover if they are satisfied. He will also know a number of administrative procedures, so that he can take the correct action on accepting or rejecting a claim. Thus the expertise of the adjudicator will consist of a number of acquired relationships between facts which he can discover and the questions he must decide and a number of procedures which help him to discover facts, resolve questions and take appropriate actions.

When the claim is decided and payment made or withheld, this payment or withholding is itself a fact, and it is possible for interested parties to relate this to other facts about the people receiving and not receiving the benefit. This gives the opportunity to evaluate the working of the whole system: the policy maker who formulated the original legislation can compare the state of affairs that the legislation has brought about with the original goals that motivated the legislation, and decide whether they are achieved or not, and so whether the legislation should be amended. For example, it may have been unforeseen that a consequence of the legislation in regulation 3(1)(i) would be that an infrequent attender of a hospital would be able to avail himself of the therapeutic earnings provision. If this consequence was both unforeseen and in conflict with the goals which motivated the provision, then the relevant legislation will require amendment. Similarly, if the exclusion of someone who consulted a specialist without attending a hospital was unintended. So the state of affairs consequent of legislation will be evaluated by the policy makers, but it will also be evaluated by other interested parties. Pressure groups, for example, often detect what they consider to be conflicts between the consequences of legislation and what they believe to be the goals of the legislation, and mount campaigns for change. Evaluations from different groups will be performed from different perspectives, and may give rise to different conclusions.

16.2.1. A model of legal source knowledge

With this element of evaluation we have come full circle, and are back with the prospect of revising legislation to more closely align effects with intent, or perhaps even with modifying the original intent itself. The relationships described in the foregoing discussion can be summarised in diagrammatic form to give a model of the types of knowledge involved in the formulation and application of law (see Figure 16.1).

This model captures all the elements that we found when looking at sickness benefits. In other cases some of the levels will contain less knowledge than others: for example a new benefit will require time for a body of case law to be established. Also different fields of law may tend to place more or less importance on the different sorts of knowledge, but I would contend that these elements are to be found everywhere. Lastly, one should notice a key difference between the nodes, which broadly represent a body of knowledge, and the arcs which include procedural knowledge enabling this knowledge to be applied.

In the next section we consider how such a model can be used to focus a discussion of legal knowledge based systems.

16.2.2. Applying the model to legal KBS

Given the model we can firstly divide tasks into those which operate at a single level and those which effect a transformation across levels. Thus one task is to discover what a piece of legislation really means. In [Allen and Saxon 1987] there is a good discussion of the various ways in which a particular section of a statute may be interpreted, according to how we interpret words such as 'except', 'if' and 'unless' which give rise to differing logical structures for the statute. The tool they propose to assist in this interpretative process, which they call 'normalization', thus operates wholly within the legislation level. Similarly, tools designed to support the conceptual retrieval of case law are operating within that level. Other systems support the transformation from one level to another; many of the consultative style expert systems in the domain support the mapping of legal concepts into the facts available to the user. Moreover, given the possibility of alternative mappings appropriate to different classes of user, there may potentially be several systems at a given level.

Applying this to the systems described in this book, we can see that the policy system was intended to support the transformation from intentions to legislation, and that the advice and local office systems were both designed to support the transformation from legal concepts to ascertainable facts, but each appropriate to a different user group.

The model thus shows us that there are many possible types of task which are carried out in the legal domain, and we can characterize a KBS by reference to which task it supports. More importantly, given the correspondence between the levels at which the tasks are carried out and

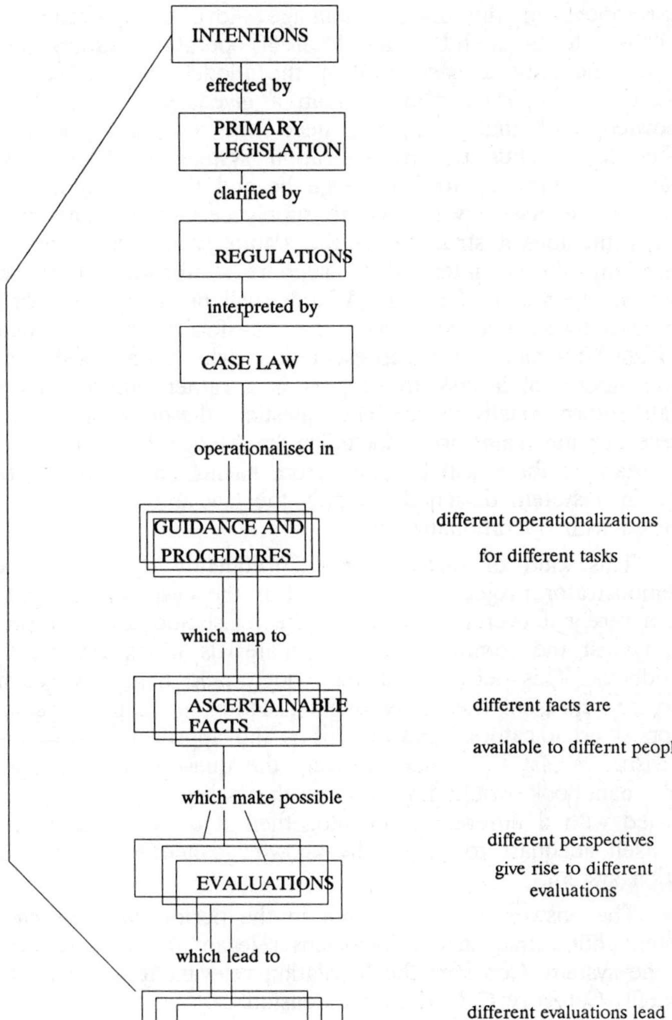

Figure 16.1

the knowledge used to carry them out, we can begin to see what sorts of knowledge should be incorporated within them. For typically different KBS will draw their knowledge from different levels; thus the knowledge represented in the British Nationality Act system of Sergot *et al.* [1986] is drawn almost exclusively from the level of legislation, whereas that represented in the Latent Damage Advisor of Capper and Susskind [1988] is to be found at the level of operationalisation, and of mapping to the facts of a case. From the model we can see that a system intended to operate wholly within a given level needs to represent the knowledge of that level, but need not represent knowledge from any other level. Thus the normalization system of Allen and Saxon need make no reference to knowledge beyond the statute itself, although the user of the system will need to supply certain elements of judgement to clarify the logical structure of the statute when using the system. In contrast any system intended to support a transformation between levels, such as the Latent Damage Advisor, will need to represent knowledge at the two levels between which the transformation is to take place. The British Nationality Act representation, which was designed without any clear notion of a task to support is a rather different case, to which I shall return briefly later. The question therefore arises as to whether there are any gains from including knowledge from other levels; whether for example there will be gains from having any representation of legislation in a system designed to apply the law and hence predominantly concerned with operationalization.

This kind of question arose frequently during the course of the Demonstrator project. In practice it is the case that the adjudicating officers rarely if ever consult either the legislation or the reported decisions as against the summary of these materials which can be found in their handbook. This being so, it was widely held that it would not be necessary to represent the underlying legislation at all in a system designed to support adjudicators. Indeed this is the approach of the Latent Damage Advisor. Whilst the model answers the question as to why the adjudicators' handbook would not support the policy application, since it is concerned with a different level altogether, it does not explain why it is not by itself adequate to supply the knowledge needed for building an adjudication system.

The answer to this lies not in the performance or capability of the system, but rather in considerations relevant to the on-going practical use of the system. Consider the legislation relevant to a relatively unimportant benefit, Category C Retirement Pension.

The UK Social Security Act states:

39(1) Subject to the provisions of this Act —

(a) a person who was over pensionable age on 5th July 1948 and satisfies such other conditions as may be prescribed shall be entitled to a Category C retirement pension at the appropriate weekly rate.

To interpret this we need also to bear in mind:

27(1) In this Act 'pensionable age' means —

(a) in the case of a man, the age of 65 years; and

(b) in the case of a woman, the age of 60 years.

Now if we consider the kind of knowledge that an expert adjudicator might apply to decide claims for this benefit, we might see him allowing claims of men aged 101 and women aged over 96. This would certainly pick out the correct group of people and would be the most convenient expression of the knowledge if the claim form gave the age of claimant. It does, however, 'compile in' both a certain amount of arithmetical expertise and knowledge of the current date, as well as the interaction between 27(1) and 39(1). If the claim form contained not the age of the claimant but the date of birth, however, this would not be the most convenient expression of the knowledge, since a calculation would be required to get the age from the date of birth, and the expert would be likely instead to operationalize the knowledge as 'men born before 5/7/1888 and women born before 5/7/1893'. This still conflates 27(1) and 39(1). The point here is that when experts operationalize their knowledge they will amalgamate knowledge from a variety of sources in the way which is of most use to them.

As far as performance and correctness goes either of these operationalizations, neither of which make any reference to the legislation, would be perfectly adequate. But consider now the question of maintenance of such a system. The initial expression, with its explicit reference to an age would become out of date within the year, and so the representation would need to be amended every 5 July. Or suppose that 27(1) was amended, perhaps to introduce a pension age common to both men and women: then the operationalization in terms of date of birth would no longer be acceptable. The point is not that changes need to be made: that is inevitable. The problem is that using the expertise alone we have no way of telling which parts of our representation need to be changed in order to respond to given changes either in legislation or in external circumstance. Similar problems arise with respect to validation of the knowledge base; expertise, by bringing together different knowledge elements tends to make the justification for particular items harder to establish. These points are discussed more fully in [Routen and Bench-Capon 1990]. Lastly, should it be necessary to explain and justify decisions in terms of the legislation, then this cannot be done from the operational knowledge alone.

The situation with expertise can thus be represented by Figure 16.2.

The expertise, as the diagram indicates, mixes together knowledge from a variety of levels in the model and often adds something else as well. Representing the expertise directly would mean that the separation of the knowledge into its component parts — essential for validation, maintenance and explanation — would be more difficult. Thus it might advantageous to represent the different levels separately. The model also

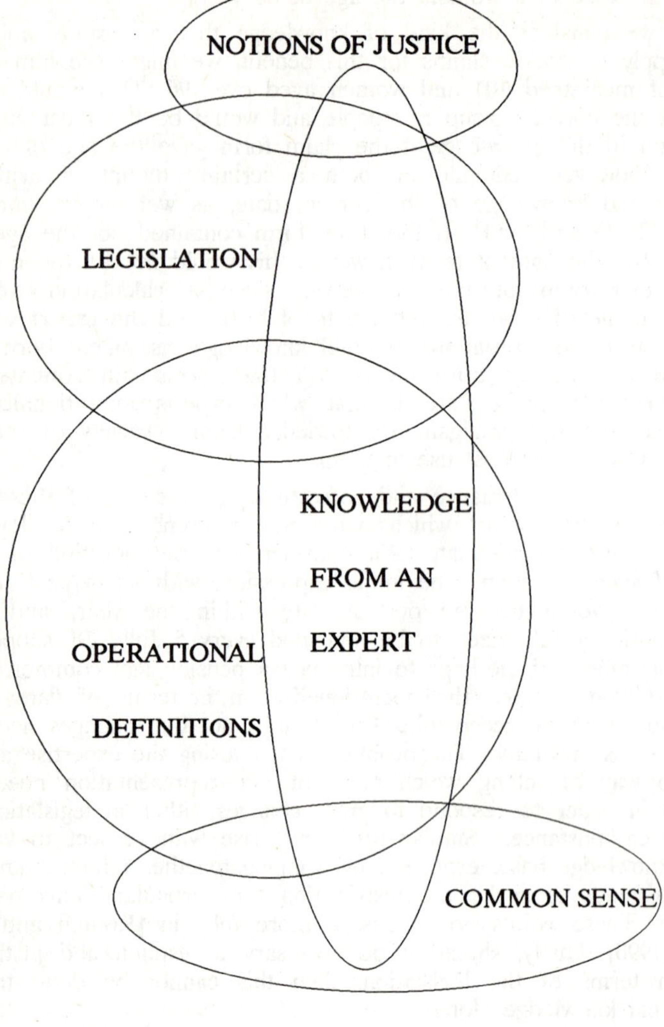

Figure 16.2

suggests why representing only legislation such as was done with the British Nationality Act cannot form the basis of a satisfactory system for adjudication. For, although this knowledge is incorporated into the expertise, explaining why such a system would not be wholly useless, there is so much else involved in the expertise that it cannot hope to be adequate unless augmented by this additional knowledge. Indeed it is precisely this extra knowledge which tends to make the system useful and usable.

The implications for building KBS in law are that we need to identify the task we want to support quite specifically, and this will establish what knowledge is essential to the system. Expanding the system to include higher and lower levels of knowledge will be of help in so far as it imposes structure and discipline on the representation, but will not necessarily give any extra capability.

Thinking in terms of expertise can also help to clarify the scale of ambition of the system. If we consider the TAXMAN system described in [McCarty 1977], we see an ambitious system that wants to solve the kind of very hard case that would become the concern of the Supreme Court, (or the House of Lords in the UK). For such a landmark case existing expertise cannot be of assistance, for the case is unlike any that has been encountered before. Here, then, it will be necessary to return at very least to the underlying legislation, if not to the goals which motivated the legislation. In extreme cases it may even be necessary to consider the validity of the goals themselves so as to apply concepts of fairness and justice, in which case we will need to represent an extra, higher, level of ethical principles as well. In such hard cases as these, existing operationalizations such as might be got from an expert are not enough: rather we need all the knowledge that such an expert could use so that we may develop an appropriate operationalization from first principles. This in turn explains McCarthy's desire for a 'deep conceptual model', as evinced in [McCarty 1989].

The implications for those who wish to build KBS in law are twofold. Firstly, that it is important to identify the task which the KBS is supposed to support. This may be no easy matter, given the many levels which can be worked within or moved amongst. Nonetheless it is vital to the success of a KBS that it should make distinctions: a KBS designed to support members of the public will simply not work if used by adjudicators. The second implication is that, having identified the task, it is necessary to decide which sources are to be used. The task will determine which must be included, but it may be desirable to extend the representation beyond what is necessary so as to add structure, or the capability to deal with questions of natural justice, or whatever. But this extension must be a conscious decision: representing knowledge at additional levels will inevitably complicate the task. Thus if one is building an application to support advisors of the public, it will be more difficult if one starts with the legislation than with the expertise of actual advisors, where much of the requisite knowledge will have been pre-digested and pre-structured. There could be compensating gains, in terms of maintainability or of correspondence with some other application, but one should be sure of the need before embarking on the extra effort that such a more ambitious approach will entail.

16.3. CONCLUSION

The area of KBS in law covers a multitude of very different applications, from those concerned to tease out the logical structure of a given piece of legislation, through those which are supposed to support a particular person in applying the law to specific cases, to those which help a person to complete a form necessary to claim a given benefit. This variety of applications should be unsurprising given the multitude of tasks which are connected with the law, the variety of ways in which such tasks can be supported, and the apparent multiplicity of competing material which could be used as the basis of a legal knowledge base. What I have attempted to do in this chapter is to delineate the various sources and to show how the knowledge used can serve to define the task, and vice versa. In turn this means that specifying the task which one wishes to support can help to identify the knowledge that one needs to incorporate in the KBS. Of course, with knowledge, there can never be too much of a good thing (*pace* Bacon) and so it is always open to the builder of a legal KBS to go wider than what he strictly needs to build an adequate application. There will be some advantages from this: perhaps an increase in structure and maintainability if the legislation is included, and perhaps an ability to cope with a wider range of legal reasoning if notions of justice can be somehow included. The important thing is to recognize what the application demands, and so to scope the ambition and knowledge to represent accordingly. My aim in putting forward the model described in this chapter was to enable a rationale to be given to such decisions.

BIBLIOGRAPHY

Allen, L.E.: (1957) Symbolic logic: A razor-edged tool for drafting and interpreting legal documents, *Yale Law Journal* 66, 833-879.

Allen, L.E.: (1980) Language, law and logic: Plain legal drafting for the electronic age. *Computer Science and Law* (Niblett, B., Ed.). Cambridge University Press, New York, 75-100.

Allen, L.E.: (1982) Towards a normalized language to clarify the structure of legal discourse. *Deontic Logic, Computational Linguistics and Legal Information Systems* (Martino, A.A., Ed.). North-Holland, Amsterdam, 349-407.

Allen, L.E., Saxon, C.S.: (1985) Exploring computer-aided generation of questions for normalizing legal rules. *Computing Power and Legal Language* (Walter, C., Ed.). Greenwood/Quorum Press, New York, 1988, 243-316.

Allen, L.E., Saxon, C.S.: (1986) Analysis of the logical structure of legal rules by a modernized and formalized version of Hohfeld fundamental legal conceptions. *Automated Analysis of Legal Texts* (Martino, A.A., Socci, F., Eds.). North-Holland, Amsterdam

Allen, L.E., Saxon, C.S.: (1987) Some problems in designing expert systems to aid legal reasoning. *Proc. First International Conference on Artificial Intelligence and Law, Boston,* ACM Press, 94-103.

Alvey (1989) *Alvey-DHSS Large Demonstrator 1984-1989 Final Report*

Andretta, M., Lugaresi, M., Zambon, F., Losano, M., Nannini, N.: (1988) I linuaggi formali applicati alla representazione di testi normativi: il progetto PROLEG. *Proc 4th International Congress on Computer Science and Law, Rome.*

ARCA (1988) *Annual Report of the Chief Adjudication Officer.* HMSO.

Ashley, K.D.: (1985) Reasoning by analogy: A survey of selected AI research with implications for legal expert systems. *Computing Power and Legal Reasoning* (Walter, C., Ed.). West Publishing Co., St. Paul, Minn.

Ashley, K.D.: (1987) Modelling legal argument: Reasoning with cases and hypotheticals. PhD thesis, Department of Computer and Information Science, University of Massachusetts. COINS Technical Report 88-01. To be published by MIT Press.

Ashley, K.D.: (1989) Toward a computational theory of arguing with precedents. *Proc. Second International Conference on Artificial Intelligence and Law, Vancouver,* ACM Press, 93-102.

Ashley, K.D., Rissland, E.L.: (1986) Toward modelling legal argument. *Automated Analysis of Legal Texts* (Martino, A.A., Socci, F., Eds.). North-Holland, Amsterdam, 19-30.

Ashley, K.D., Rissland, E.L.: (1987) But, See, Accord: Generating 'Blue Book' citations in HYPO. *Proc. First International Conference on Artificial Intelligence and Law, Boston,* ACM Press, 67-74.

Ashley, K.D., Rissland, E.L.: (1988) Waiting on weighting: A symbolic least commitment approach. *Proc. AAAI-88, Minneapolis,*

Bain, W.M.: (1984) Toward a model of subjective interpretation. Research Report 324, Dept. of Computer Science, Yale University.

Bajaj, K.K., Dubash, R.K., Kamble, A.S., Kowalski, R.A., Murthy, B.K.: (1989a) Indian Import Policy and Procedures as a Logic Program. *Proc. Third International Conference on Logica, Informatica, Diritto* (Martino, A.A., Ed.). Istituto per la Documentazione

Bajaj, K.K., Dubash, R.K., Kowalski, R.A.: (1989b) Central government pension rules as a logic program. *Knowledge Based Computer Systems* (Ramani, S., Chandrasekar, R., Anjaneyulu, K.S.R., Eds.). Narosa Publishing, New Delhi, 19-28.

Bellord, N.J.: (1980) Tax Planning by Computer. *Computer Science and Law* (Niblett, B., Ed.). Cambridge University Press, New York, 173-182.

Bellord, N.J.: (1983) *Computers for Lawyers.* Sinclair Browne, London.

Belzer, M.: (1986a) Reasoning with defeasible principles. *Synthese* 66, 1-24.

Belzer, M.: (1986b) A logic of deliberation. *Proc. Fifth National Conference on Artificial Intelligence* 38-43.

Belzer, M.: (1987) Legal reasoning in 3-D. *Proc. First International Conference on Artificial Intelligence and Law, Boston,* ACM Press, 155-163.

Bench-Capon, T.J.M.: (1987) Support for policy makers: Formulating legislation with the aid of logical models. *Proc. First International Conference on Artificial Intelligence and Law, Boston,* ACM Press, 181-189.

Bench-Capon, T.J.M.: (1988a) Logical Models of Legislation and Expert Systems. *Expert Systems in Law,* (Fiedler, Haft and Tranmuller, Eds.), Attempto Verlag, Tubingen, 27-41.

Bench-Capon, T.J.M.: (1988b) Applying Legal Expert Systems Techniques: Practical Considerations. *KBS in Government 88* (Duffin, P., Ed.), On Line Publications, 205-214.

Bench-Capon, T.J.M.: (1989a) Representing counterfactual conditionals. *Proc. Artificial Intelligence and the Simulation of Behaviour, Brighton,* (Cohn, A., Ed.). Pitman, 51-60

Bench-Capon, T.J.M.: (1989b) Deep models, normative reasoning and legal expert systems. *Proc. Second International Conference on Artificial Intelligence and Law, Vancouver,* ACM Press, 37-45.

Bench-Capon, T.J.M., Robinson, G.O., Routen, T.W., Sergot, M.J.: (1989) Logic programming for large scale applications in law: A formalisation of Supplementary Benefit legislation. *Proc. First International Conference on Artificial Intelligence and Law, Boston,* 190-198

Bench-Capon, T.J.M., Sergot, M.J.: (1988) Towards a rule-based representation of open texture in law. *Computing Power and Legal Language* (Walter, C., Ed.). Greenwood/Quorum Press, New York, 39-60.

Berthoud, R.: (1984) *The reform of Supplementary Benefit: Summary of findings,* Policy Studies Institute, London.

Biagioli, C., Fameli, E.: (1987) Expert systems in law: An international survey and a selected bibliography. CCAI *(Journal for the Integrated Study of Artificial Intelligence, Cognitive Science and Applied Epistemology)* 4, 4

Biagioli, C., Mariani, P., Tiscornia, D.: (1987) ESPLEX: A rule and conceptual based model for representing statutes. *Proc. First International Conference on Artificial Intelligence and Law, Boston,* ACM Press. 240-251.

Bing, J.: (1980) Legal norms, discretionary rules and computer programs. In *Computer Science and Law* (Niblett, B., Ed.). Cambridge University Press, New York. 119-136.

Bing, J.: (1984) *Handbook of Legal Information Retrieval* North-Holland, Amsterdam.

Bing, J.: (1986) The text retrieval system as a conversation partner. *Yearbook of Law, Computers and Technology:* Volume 2 (Arnold, C., Ed.). Butterworths, London. 25-39.

Bing, J.: (1987) Designing text retrieval systems for 'Conceptual Searching'. *Proc. First International Conference on Artificial Intelligence and Law, Boston,* ACM Press. 43-51.

Birnbaum, L.: (1982) Argument molecules: A functional representation of argument structure. *Proc. Third National Conference of the American Association for Artificial Intelligence*

Birnbaum, L., Flowers, M., McGuire, R.: (1980) Towards an AI model of argumentation. *Proc. First Annual National Conference on Artificial Intelligence* 313-315.

Bliss, J., Monk, M., Ogborn, J.M.: (1983) *Qualitative Data Analysis for Educational Research a guide to the use of Systemic Networks,* Croom Helm, London.

Bobrow, D.G., and Winograd, T.: (1979) KRL: Another Perspective, *Cognitive Science* 3 (1), 29-42.

Boguraev, B.: (1985) User modelling in cooperative natural language front-ends, in G. N. Gilbert and C. Heath, *Social action and artificial intelligence,* Gower, Aldershot.

Brachman, R.J.: (1985) 'I Lied About the Trees' or defaults and definitions in knowledge representation, *AI Magazine,* 80-93

Brachman, R.J., Fikes, R.E., and Levesque, H.J.: (1983) KRYPTON: integrating terminology and assertion, in *Proceedings of AAAI-83,* Morgan Kaufmann: Los Altos, California.

Branting, L.K.: (1989) Representing and reusing explanations of legal precedents. *Proc. Second International Conference on Artificial Intelligence and Law, Vancouver,* ACM Press, 103-110.

Brody, D.A.: (1980) The post-Macomber cases in a TAXMAN II Framework: A preliminary analysis. Technical Report LRP-TR-5, Laboratory for Computer Science Research, Rutgers University, New Brunswick, NJ, 1980.

Browne, J., Taylor, A.: (1990) Indivisibility, inseparability and indiscernibility: some problems with simulations for complex domains. *Simulation in the Development of User Interfaces.* (Hamilton, I. Ed.) Taylor and Francis

Buchanan, B.G., Headrick, T.E.: (1970) Some speculation about artificial intelligence and legal reasoning. *Stanford Law Review* 23.

Buckland, S., Dawson, P.: (1989) Household claiming behaviour, *Journal of Social Policy and Administration.*

Buckland, S., Hardey, M.: (1988) The extended household: low income families in affluent villages, Social and Computer Sciences Research Group, University of Surrey.

Buckland, S., Cordingley, E.S., Frohlich, D.M., Gilbert, G.N., Luff, P.: (1987) Initial Requirements Specification for the Advice System, Social and Computer Sciences Research Group, University of Surrey.

Capper, P.N., Susskind, R.E.: (1988) *Latent Damage Law - The Expert System.* Butterworths, London.

Castaneda, H-N.: (1975) *Thinking and Doing.* D.Reidel. Dordrecht.

Cawsey, A.: (1989) Explanatory dialogues. *Interacting with Computers* 1, 69-92.

Chan, D.: (1984) A logic based legal expert system. MSc thesis. Department of Computing, Imperial College, London.

Charniak, E., McDermott, D.: (1985) *An Introduction to Artificial Intelligence.* Addison-Wesley.

Checkland, P.B.: (1980) *Systems Thinking, Systems Practice.* Wiley

Ciampi, C.: (ed.) (1982) *Artificial Intelligence and Legal Information Systems* North-Holland, Amsterdam.

Cook, S., Hafner, C.D., McCarty, L.T., Meldman, J.A., Peterson, M.A., Sprowl, J.A., Sridharan, N.S., Waterman, D.A.: (1980) The applications of artificial intelligence to law: A survey of six current projects. *Proc. AFIPS National Computer Conference*

Coombs, M.J., Alty, J.L.: (1980) Face-to-face guidance of university computer users-II: characterising advisory interactions. *International Journal of Man-Machine Studies* 12, 407-427

Corden, A.: (1982) New light on claiming FIS: implications for take-up, *Poverty, 53.*

Cordingley, E.S.: (1986) Overviews of the UK Welfare Benefits System, in Buckland, S., Cordingley, E.S., Frohlich, D., Gilbert, N., Luff, P., (January, 1987) Initial Requirements Specification for the Advice System, Appendix C.

Cordingley, E.S.: (1987) Knowledge Acquisition for the Advice System, *Proceedings of the first European Workshop on Knowledge Acquisition for Knowledge-Based Systems, Reading University, England,*

Cordingley, E.S.: (1988) Intermediate representation for extended office systems, *Proceedings of the IFIP TC8/WG8.4 International workshop on Office Knowledge: Representation, Management and Utilization,* North-Holland

Cordingley, E.S.: (1989) Knowledge elicitation techniques for knowledge-based systems, *Knowledge elicitation principles, techniques and applications* (Diaper D., Ed.) Ellis Horwood, London.

Cordingley, E.S., Buckland, S., Dawson, P.: (1985) What's a DHSS Local Office: The DHSS 'HQ' Perspective, Alvin 131, DHSS Demonstrator Project at Surrey.

Cordingley, E.S., Gilbert, G.N.: (1987) Alvey DHSS Demonstrator: Advanced Information Technology for Legislation Based Organisations and the public they serve *BURISA Newsletter* 81.

Cranston, R.: (1985) *Legal Foundations of the Welfare State,* Weidenfeld & Nicolson,

Cross, G.R., deBessonet, C.G.: (1985a) The implementation of CCLIPS. (June 1985). *Computing Power and Legal Language* (Walter, C., Ed.). Greenwood/Quorum Press, New York, 1988, 89-98

Cross, G.R., deBessonet, C.G.: (1985b) Representation of legal knowledge for conceptual retrieval. *Information Processing and Management* 21, 1, 35-44.

Crossfield, L.P.: (1986) Explanation in regard to a Welfare Benefits Advice System, *Proceedings of the first Alvey Explanation Workshop, University of Surrey,*

Crossfield, L.P., Gilbert, G.N.: (1986) Introducing expert systems into a large legislation-based organisation, *Expert systems and knowledge engineering* (Berthold, T., Ed.) North-Holland, Amsterdam. 95-100.

Dawson, P., Buckland S., Gilbert, G.N.: (1990) Expert systems and the public provision of welfare benefit advice, *Policy and Politics.*

deBessonet, C.G.: (1980) A proposal for developing the structural science of codification. *Rutgers Computer & Technology Law Journal* 8, 1, 47-63.

deBessonet, C.G.: (1982) An automated approach to scientific codification. *Rutgers Computer & Technology Law Journal* 9, 1, 27-75.

deBessonet, C.G.: (1983) Legislative technique and automated systems. *Proc. Third Congress on L'Informatica Giuridica e le Comunita Nazionale ed Internazionale Rome*

deBessonet, C.G.: (1984) An automated intelligent system based on a model of a legal system. *Rutgers Computer & Technology Law Journal* 10.

deBessonet, C.G., Cross, G.R.: (1985) Representation of some aspects of legal causality. *Computing Power and Legal Reasoning* (Walter, C., Ed.). West Publishing Co., St. Paul, Minn., 205-214.

deBessonet, C.G., Cross, G.R.: (1986) Conceptual retrieval and legal decision-making. *Automated Analysis of Legal Texts* (Martino, A.A., Socci, F., Eds.). North-Holland. Amsterdam, 219-227.

deKleer, J.: (1986) An assumption-based TMS. *Artificial Intelligence* 28 127-162.

Denning: (1986) Introduction to *Neligan's Digest of Social Security Commissioners' Decisions,* HMSO.

Dick, J.P.: (1987) Conceptual retrieval and case law. *Proc. First International Conference on Artificial Intelligence and Law, Boston,* ACM Press. 106-115.

Dixon, P.: (1971) *Rhetoric.* Methuen.

DSS: (1989) Supplementary Benefit, Family Income Supplement and Housing Benefit Take Up, 1985-6, Technical Note, Analytical Services Division, Department of Social Security.

Dworkin, R.: (1967) The model of rules. *University of Chicago Law Review* 35, 14.

Dyer, M.G, Flowers, M.: (1985) Toward automating legal expertise. *Computing Power and Legal Reasoning* (Walter, C., Ed.). West Publishing Co., St. Paul, Minn., 49-68.

Foley, J.D and van Dam (1982) *Fundamentals of Interactive Computer Graphics,* Addison-Wesley

Frohlich, D.M.: (1986) The organisation of form-filling behaviour *Information Design Journal,* 5, 45-59.

Frohlich, D.M.: (1987) On the re-organisation of form-filling behaviour in an electronic medium, *Information Design Journal,* 5, 111-128.

Frohlich, D.M., Luff, P.: (1986) Interaction design specification for the Forms Helper, Social and Computer Sciences Research Group, University of Surrey.

Frohlich, D.M.: (1988) Conversational dynamics for emergent explanations, *Proceedings of the fourth Alvey Explanation Workshop, Manchester.*

Frohlich, D.M., Crossfield, L., Gilbert G.N.: (1985) Requirements for an intelligent form-filling interface, People and computers: designing the interface (Johnson, P. and Cook, S., Eds.) Cambridge University Press, 102-117.

Frohlich, D.M. Luff, P.: (1989) Some lessons from an exercise in specification using Foley and van Dam's interface documentation method, *Human Computer Interaction* 4, 121-147.

Frohlich, D.M., Luff, P.: (1989) Conversational Resources for Situated Action, *Proceedings of CHI '89.* ACM SIG-CHI.

Frohlich, D.M., Luff, P.: (In Press), Applying the technology of conversation to the technology for conversation. *Computers and Conversation* (Luff, P. Gilbert, G.N., and Frohlich, D.M., Eds.) Academic Press, London.

Gardner, A.v.d.L.: (1983) The design of a legal analysis program. *Proc. Fourth National Conference of the American Association for Artificial Intelligence*

Gardner, A.v.d.L.: (1984) An artificial intelligence approach to legal reasoning. Report STAN-CS-85-1045, Department of Computing Science, Stanford Univ. Also published by Bradford Books/MIT Press.

Gardner, A.v.d.L.: (1985) Overview of an artificial intelligence approach to legal reasoning. *Computing Power and Legal Reasoning* (Walter, C., Ed.). West Publishing Co., St. Paul, Minn., 1985., 247-274.

Genesereth, M.R., Greiner, R., Grinberg, M.R., Smith, D.E.: (1984) The MRS dictionary. Memo HPP-80-24, Stanford Heuristic Programming Project, Stanford Univ.

Gilbert, G.N.: (1985a) Computer help with welfare benefits, *Computer Bulletin*, 1, 2-4.

Gilbert, G.N.: (1985b) Decision support in large organisations, *Data Processing* 27, 28-30.

Gilbert, G.N.: (1986) User models: can they be good enough?, *Proceedings of the first Alvey Intelligent Interfaces Workshop, Abingdon*

Gilbert, G.N.: (1987) Questions and answer types, *Research and development in expert systems IV* (Moralee, D.S., Ed.) Cambridge University Press, 162-172.

Gilbert, G.N.: (1987a) Cognitive and social models of the user, *Human-computer interaction -- Interact '87,* (Bullinger, H-J. and Shackel, B., Eds.) North-Holland. Amsterdam. 165-172.

Gilbert, G.N.: (1987b) Questions and answer types, *Research and development in expert systems IV* (Moralee, D.S., Ed.) Cambridge University Press, 162-172.

Gilbert, G.N.: (1987b) Advice, discourse and explanations, *Proceedings of the third Alvey Explanation Workshop, University of Surrey,* 94-109.

Gilbert, G.N.: (1988a) Explanation as process, *Proceedings of the fourth Alvey Explanation Workshop, University of Manchester*

Gilbert, G.N.: (1988) The Alvey DHSS Demonstrator Project: Applying IKBS to social security, *Artificial Intelligence* (Buchberger, E., Goranzon B., and Nygaard K., Eds.) Oslo: Universitetsprlaget.

Gilbert, G.N., Buckland, S., Frohlich, D.M., Jirotka, M., Luff, P.: (1990) Providing advice through dialogue, *Proceedings of ECAI '90,* Stockholm.

Gilbert, G.N., Jirotka, M.: (1990) Planning procedural advice, forthcoming in *Interaction with Computers.*

Gilbert, G.N., Luff, P., Crossfield, L., Frohlich, D.M.: (in press) A mixed initiative interface for expert systems: the Forms Helper, *International Journal of Man-Machine Studies.*

Gold, D.I.: (1987) Specification and implementation of an expert system in law. DPhil thesis. Oxford Univ.

Gold, D.I., Susskind, R.E.: (1986) Expert systems in law: A jurisprudential and formal specification approach. *Automated Analysis of Legal Texts* (Martino, A.A., Socci, F., Eds.). North-Holland, Amsterdam, 625-642.

Gordon, T.F.: (1989) Issue spotting in a system for searching interpretation spaces. *Proc. Second International Conference on Artificial Intelligence and Law, Vancouver,* ACM Press. 157-164.

Gray, G.B.: (1985) Statutes enacted in normalized form: The legislative experience in Tennessee. *Computing Power and Legal Reasoning* (Walter, C., Ed.). West Publishing Co., St. Paul, Minn., 467-493.

Greenleaf, G., Mowbray, A., Tyree, A.L.: (1987) Expert systems in law: The DATALEX Project. *Proc. First International Conference on Artificial Intelligence and Law, Boston,* ACM Press. 9-17.

Gunthner, F., Lehmann, H.: (1984) Automatic construction of discourse representation structures. *Proc. Tenth International Conference on Computational Linguistics* 398-401.

Gunthner, F., Lehmann, H., Schunfeld, W.: (1986) A theory of representing knowledge. *IBM Journal of Research and Development* 30, 1, 39-56.

Hafner, C.D.: (1978) An information retrieval system based on a computer model of legal knowledge. PhD thesis. Univ. of Michigan, 1978. Also published by UMI Research Press, Ann Arbor, Michigan.

Hafner, C.D.: (1981) Representation of knowledge in a legal information retrieval system. *Information Retrieval Research* (Oddy, R., Robertson, S., van Rijsbergen, C., Williams, P., Eds.). Butterworths, London.

Hafner, C.D.: (1987) Conceptual organization of case law knowledge bases. *Proc. First International Conference on Artificial Intelligence and Law, Boston,* ACM Press. 35-42.

Haft, F., Jones, R.P., Wetter, T.: (1987) A natural language based legal expert system for consultation and tutoring: The LEX project. *Proc. First International Conference on Artificial Intelligence and Law, Boston,* ACM Press. 75-83.

Hammond, P.: (1983) Representation of DHSS regulations as a logic program. Report 82/26, Department of Computing, Imperial College, London, 1982. Also in *Expert Systems 83: Proc. Third Technical Conference of the British Computer Society Specialist Group*

Hammond, P., Sergot, M.J.: (1983) A PROLOG shell for logic based expert systems. *Expert Systems 83: Proc. Third Technical Conference of the British Computer Society Specialist Group*

Hammond, P., Sergot, M.J.: (1984) *APES Reference Manual.* Logic Based Systems Ltd, Richmond, Surrey, England.

Hardey, M.: (1989a) Lone parents and the "home", *Men, women and the home* (Allan, G. and Crow, G., Eds.) Macmillan. London.

Hardey, M.: (1989b) One parent families and their homes, The meaning of home and neighborhood Symposium, The National Swedish Institute for Building Research.

Harlow, C., Rawlings, R.: (1984) *Law and Administration* Weidenfeld & Nicolson,

Hart, H.L.A.: (1961) *The Concept of Law.* Clarendon Press, Oxford.

Hayes, P.J.: (1979) The logic of frames. In *Frame Conceptions and Text Understanding* (Metzing, D., Ed.). de Gruyter.

Hellawell, R.: (1980) A computer program for legal planning and analysis: Taxation of stock redemptions. *Columbia Law Review* 80, 7, 1363-1398.

Hellawell, R.: (1981) CHOOSE: A computer program for legal planning and analysis. *Columbia Journal of Transnational Law* 19, 339-357.

Hellawell, R.: (1982) SEARCH: A computer program for legal problem solving. *Akron Law Review* 15, 635-653.

Hilpinen, R.: (1971) *Deontic Logic: Introductory and systematic readings.* Reidel, Dordrecht.

Hohfeld, W.N.: (1913) Fundamental legal conceptions as applied in judicial reasoning: I. *Yale Law Journal* 23.

Hohfeld, W.N.: (1917) Fundamental legal conceptions as applied in judicial reasoning: II. *Yale Law Journal* 26.

Howe, L.E.A.: (1985) The 'deserving' and the 'undeserving': practice in an urban local social security office, *Journal of Social Policy,* 14, 49-72.

Humphreys, A.M.: (1988) Proposals for a statute law database. MSc thesis. Department of Computing, Imperial College, London.

Hustler, A.: (1982) Programming law in logic. Report CS-82-13, Department of Computer Science, Univ. of Waterloo, Canada.

Jones, A.J.I.: (1987) On the relationship between permission and obligation. *Proc. First International Conference on Artificial Intelligence and Law, Boston,* ACM Press. 164-169.

Jones, A.J.I.: (1989) Deontic logic and legal knowledge representation. *Proc. Expert Systems in Law, Bologna,* To appear in *Ratio Juris* (1990).

Jones, A.J.I., Purn, I.: (1985) Ideality, sub-ideality and deontic logic. *Synthese* 65.

Jones, A.J.I., Purn, I.: (1986) 'Ought' and 'Must'. *Synthese* 66.

Jones, R.P.: (1986) The LEX project, IBM Scientific Centre, Heidelberg and University of Tuebingen. In *Yearbook of Law, Computers and Technology:* Volume 2 (Arnold, C., Ed.). Butterworths. London.

Jones, S.: (1980) Control structures in legislation. In *Computer Science and Law* (Niblett, B., Ed.). Cambridge University Press. New York. 157-169.

Jones, S., Mason, P., Stamper, R.: (1979) LEGOL 2.0: A relational specification language for complex rules. *Information Systems* 4, 4, 293-305.

Kamp, H.: (1981) A theory of truth and semantic representation. *Formal Methods in the Study of Language* (Groenendijk et al., Eds.). Mathematical Centre Tract, Amsterdam. Reprinted in Truth, Representation and Information (Groenendijk et al., Eds.).

Kedar-Cabelli, S.: (1984) Analogy with purpose in legal reasoning from precedents. Technical Report LRP-TR-17, Laboratory for Computer Science Research, Rutgers University, New Brunswick, NJ.

Kerr, S.: (1982) Deciding about Supplementary Pensions: a provisional model, *Journal of Social Policy,* vol. 11, 505-517.

Kidd, A.: (1987) Cooperative problem solving systems, *Proceedings of the HCI '87 Conference, University of Exeter,* 7-11 September

Kiel, F.C.: (1979) *Semantics and Conceptual Development: an Ontological Perspective,* Harvard University Press.

King, J.J.: (1976) Analysis and KRL implementation of a current legal reasoning program design. Unpublished. MIT.

Kolodner, J., Simpson, R., Sycara-Cyranski, K.: (1985) A process model of case based reasoning in problem solving. *Proc. Ninth International Joint Conference on Artificial Intelligence* 284-290.

Koers, A.W., Kracht, D., Smith, M., Smits, J.M., Weusten, M.C.M.: (1989) *Knowledge Based Systems in Law* Kluwer Law and Taxation Publishers, Deventer, Netherlands.

Kowalski, R.A.: (1989) The treatment of negation in logic programs for representing legislation. *Proc. Second International Conference on Artificial Intelligence and Law, Vancouver,* ACM Press. 11-15.

Kowalski, R.A., Sadri, F., Soper, P.: (1987) Integrity Checking in Deductive database, *Proceedings of 13th Conference on Very Large Data Bases, Brighton.*

Kowalski, R.A., Sergot, M.J.: (1986) A logic based calculus of events. *New Generation Computing* 4, 1, 67-95. Also *Knowledge Base Management Systems* (Thanos, Schmidt, Eds.). Springer-Verlag, Heidelberg.

Kowalski, R.A., Sergot, M.J.: (1987) Directions for computer logic applied to law. *Journal of the Law and Computers Association of Japan* 5.

Kowalski, R.A., Sergot, M.J.: (1990) The use of logical models in legal problem solving. *Law, Computers and Artificial Intelligence* (Narayan, A., Bennun, M., Eds.). Ablex. Also to appear in Ratio Juris, 1990.

Lakhani, H.M.: (1988) Stock Exchange regulations in logic. MSc thesis. Department of Computing, Imperial College, London.

Leith, P.: (1982) ELI: An expert legislative consultant. *IEE Conference on Man/Machine Systems.*

Leith, P.: (1983) Hierarchically structured production rules. *The Computer Journal* 26.

Leith, P.: (1986a) Clear rules and legal expert systems. In *Automated Analysis of Legal Texts* (Martino, A.A., Socci, F., Eds.). North-Holland, Amsterdam, 661-680.

Leith, P.: (1986b) Fundamental errors in legal logic programming. *The Computer Journal* 29, 3.

Levinson, S.C.: (1983) *Pragmatics,* Cambridge University Press, Cambridge

Loevinger, L.: (1949) Jurimetrics: The next step forward. *Minnesota Law Review* 33.

Loewer, B., Belzer, M.: (1983) Dyadic deontic detachment. *Synthese* 54, 295-319.

Lowes, D.: (1984) Assistance to industry: A logical approach. MSc thesis. Department of Computing, Imperial College, London.

Luff, P., Frohlich, D.M.: (1988) Discourse dynamics and dialogue design, Social and Computer Sciences Research Group, University of Surrey.

Matthewman, J.: (1986) *Tolley's Social Security and State Benefits 1986,* Croydon: Tolley Publishing Company Ltd.

McCarty, L.T.: (1977) Reflections on TAXMAN: An experiment in artificial intelligence and legal reasoning. *Harvard Law Review* 90, 837-893.

McCarty, L.T.: (1980a) Some notes on the MAP formalism of TAXMAN II, with applications to Eisner v. Macomber. Technical Report LRP-TR-6, Laboratory for Computer Science Research, Rutgers University, New Brunswick, NJ.

McCarty, L.T.: (1980b) Some requirements for a computer-based legal consultant. Technical Report LRP-TR-8, Laboratory for Computer Science Research, Rutgers University, New Brunswick, NJ. Also in *Proc. First Annual National Conference on Artificial Intelligence*

McCarty, L.T.: (1980c) The TAXMAN project: Towards a cognitive theory of legal argument. *Computer Science and Law* (Niblett, B., Ed.). Cambridge University Press, New York. 23-43.

McCarty, L.T.: (1982) A computational theory of Eisner v. Macomber. *Artificial Intelligence and Legal Information Systems* (Ciampi, C., Ed.). North-Holland. Amsterdam.

McCarty, L.T.: (1983a) Intelligent legal information systems: Problems and prospects. *Rutgers Computers and Technology Law Journal* 9, 2, 265-294. Also in *Data Processing and the Law* (Campbell, C., Ed.). Sweet and Maxwell, London, 125-151

McCarty, L.T.: (1983b) Permissions and obligations. *Proc. Eighth International Joint Conference on Artificial Intelligence.* 287-294.

McCarty, L.T.: (1986) Permissions and obligations: An informal introduction. In *Automated Analysis of Legal Texts* (Martino, A.A., Socci, F., Eds.). North-Holland. Amsterdam. 307-337.

McCarty, L.T.: (1988a) Clausal intuitionistic logic. I. Fixed-point semantics. *J. Logic Programming* 5, 1, 1-31.

McCarty, L.T.: (1988b) Clausal intuitionistic logic. II. Tableau proof procedures. *J. Logic Programming* 5, 2, 93-132.

McCarty, L.T.: (1988c) Programming directly in a non-monotonic logic. Technical Report LRP-TR-21, Computer Science Department, Rutgers University, New Brunswick, NJ.

McCarty, L.T.: (1989a) A Language for Legal Discourse I. Basic features. *Proc. Second International Conference on Artificial Intelligence and Law, Vancouver,* ACM Press. 180-189.

McCarty, L.T.: (1989b) Computing with prototypes (Preliminary report). Technical Report LRP-TR-22, Computer Science Department, Rutgers University, New Brunswick, NJ.

McCarty, L.T., Sridharan, N.S.: (1980) The representation of conceptual structures in TAXMAN II. Part One: Logical templates. Technical Report LRP-TR-4, Laboratory for Computer Science Research, Rutgers University, New Brunswick, NJ.

McCarty, L.T., Sridharan, N.S.: (1981) The representation of an evolving system of legal concepts: II. Prototypes and deformations. Technical Report LRP-TR-11, Laboratory for Computer Science Research, Rutgers University, New Brunswick, NJ.

McCarty, L.T., Sridharan, N.S.: (1982) A computational theory of legal argument. Technical Report LRP-TR-13, Laboratory for Computer Science Research, Rutgers University, New Brunswick, NJ.

McCarty, L.T., Sridharan, N.S., Sangster, B.C.: (1979) The implementation of TAXMAN II: An experiment in artificial intelligence and legal reasoning. Technical Report LRP-TR-2, Laboratory for Computer Science Research, Rutgers University, New Brunswick, NJ

McGuire, R., Birnbaum, L., Flowers, M.: (1981) Opportunistic processing in arguments. *Proc. Seventh International Joint Conference on Artificial Intelligence* 58-60.

MacRae, C.D.: (1985a) User control knowledge in a tax consulting system. In *Computing Power and Legal Reasoning* (Walter, C., Ed.). West Publishing Co., St. Paul, Minn.

MacRae, C.D.: (1985b) Tax problem solving with an IF-THEN system. In *Computing Power and Legal Reasoning* (Walter, C., Ed.). West Publishing Co., St. Paul, Minn. 595-620.

MacRae, C.D., MacRae, E.C.: (1985) An expert system for tax research: Interacting with knowledgeable users. (June 1985). In *Computing Power and Legal Language* (Walter, C., Ed.). Greenwood/Quorum Press, New York, 351-376.

Marshall, C.C.: (1989) Representing the structure of a legal argument. *Proc. Second International Conference on Artificial Intelligence and Law, Vancouver,* ACM Press, 121-127.

Martino, A.A.: (ed.) (1982) *Deontic Logic, Computational Linguistics and Legal Information Systems* North-Holland, Amsterdam.

Martino, A.A., Socci, F.: (eds.) (1986) *Automated Analysis of Legal Texts* North-Holland, Amsterdam.

Mehl, L.: (1958) Automation in the legal world: From the machine processing of legal information to the 'Law Machine'. *Mechanisation of Thought Processes (Proceedings of a Symposium held at the National Physical Laboratory),*

Meldman, J.A.: (1975) A preliminary study in computer-aided analysis. MIT Report MAC TR-157, M.I.T., Cambridge, Mass.

Meldman, J.A.: (1977) A structural model for computer-aided legal analysis. *Rutgers Journal of Computers and the Law* 6, 27-71.

Mendelson, S.: (1989) An attempted dimensional analysis of the law governing Government appeals in criminal cases. *Proc. Second International Conference on Artificial Intelligence and Law, Vancouver,* ACM Press, 128-137.

Michaelsen, R.H.: (1982) A knowledge based system for individual income and transfer tax planning. PhD thesis. Univ. of Illinois.

Michaelsen, R.H.: (1984) An expert system for federal tax planning. *Expert Systems* 1, 2.

Michaelsen, R.H., Michie, D.: (1983) Expert systems in business. *Datamation*

Moore, R.C.: (1980) Reasoning About Knowledge and Action, Technical Report 191, SRI International.

Moore, J., Swartout W.R.: (1988) A reactive approach to explanation. *Proceedings of the Fourth International Workshop on Natural Language Generation.*

Moran, T.: (1987) Research issues for advancing HCI. *Proceedings of the HCI '87 Conference.*

Neligan: (1986) *Neligan's Digest of Social Security Commissioners' Decisions* HMSO

Niblett, B.: (ed.) (1980) *Computer Science and Law* Cambridge University Press, New York.

Nickerson, R.S.: (1981) Some characteristics of conversations. *Man computer interaction: human factors of computers and people.* (Shackel, B., Ed.) Sijthoff and Noordhoff, The Netherlands

Nitta, K.: (1985) KRIP: A knowledge representation system for laws relating to industrial property. Research Report, Information Processing Group, Electroctechnical Laboratory, Sakura-mura, Ibaraki, Japan.

Nitta, K., Nagao, J., Mizutori, T.: (1986) KRIP2: A knowledge representation and inference system for procedural law. Research Report, Information Processing Group, Electroctechnical Laboratory, Sakura-mura, Ibaraki, Japan.

Ogus, A.I., Barendt, E.M.: (1982) *The Law of Social Security,* Butterworths, London

Ottley, S.: (1988) HCI Lab DHSS Demonstrator Evaluation - Final Report. Unpublished Report.

Ottley, S., Charyszyn, S., Rosato, C.: (1988) *HCI Lab DHSS Demonstrator Evaluation -- Final Report,* ICL.

Pattaro, E., Casadei, G., Sartor, G.: (1989) An expert system project in environmental law (IRI-Project). *Proc. Expert Systems in Law*

Perelman, C.: (1963) *The Idea of Justice and the Problem of Argument.* Routledge and Kegan Paul, London.

Perelman, C., Olbrechts-Tyteca, L.: (1969) *The new rhetoric: A treatise on argumentation.* University of Notre Dame Press.

Peterson, M.A., Waterman, D.A.: (1985) Evaluating civil claims: An expert systems approach to evaluating product liability cases. *Computing Power and Legal Reasoning* (Walter, C., Ed.). West Publishing Co., St. Paul, Minn. 627-659.

Phillips, J.: (1986) A word incorporation parser, *AISB Quarterly,* 59, 14-18.

Popp, W.G., Schlink, B.: (1975) JUDITH, a computer program to advise lawyers in reasoning a case. *Jurimetrics Journal* 15, 4, 303-314.

Reichman, R.: (1981) Modeling informal debates. *Proc. Seventh International Joint Conference on Artificial Intelligence, Vancouver* 19-24.

Reiter, R.: (1978) On Reasoning By Default, *Proceedings of TINLAP-2,* Urbana Illinois, 210-18.

Rescher, N.: (1966) *The Logic of Commands.* Routledge and Kegan Paul, London.

Reynolds, J.C.: (1970) Transformational systems and the algebraic structure of atomic formulas. *Machine Intelligence* 5 (Michie, D., Ed.). Edinburgh University Press.

Ringland, G.: (1988) Structured Object Representation, *Approaches to Knowledge Representation,* (Ringland, G.A., and Duce, D.A., Eds.) Research Studies Press, Letchworth. 81-100

Rissland, E.L.: (1983) Examples in legal reasoning: Legal hypotheticals. *Proc. Eighth International Joint Conference on Artificial Intelligence, Karlsruhe.* 90-93.

Rissland, E.L.: (1984) Learning how to argue: Using hypotheticals. *Proc. First Annual Conference on Theoretical Issues in Conceptual Information Processing, Atlanta.*

Rissland, E.L.: (1985a) Argument moves and hypotheticals. *Computing Power and Legal Reasoning* (Walter, C., Ed.). West Publishing Co., St. Paul, Minn.

Rissland, E.L.: (1985b) The ubiquitous dialectic. *Proc. Sixth European Conference on Artificial Intelligence Pisa.*

Rissland, E.L.: (1989) Dimension-based analysis of hypotheticals from Supreme Court oral argument. *Proc. Second International Conference on Artificial Intelligence and Law, Vancouver,* ACM Press. 111-120.

Rissland, E.L., Ashley, K.D.: (1987) A case-based system for trade secrets law. *Proc. First International Conference on Artificial Intelligence and Law, Boston,* ACM Press. 60-66.

Rissland, E.L., Ashley, K.D.: (1989) HYPO: A precedent-based legal reasoner. In *Recent Advances in Computer Science and Law* (Vandenberghe, G., Ed.), Kluwer.

Rissland, E.L., Skalak D.B.: (1989) Interpreting Statutory Predicates, in *Proceedings of the Second International Conference on AI and Law, Vancouver.* ACM Press.

Rissland, E.L., Soloway, E.M.: (1980) Overview of an example generation system. *Proc. First Annual National Conference on Artificial Intelligence*

Rissland, E.L., Valcarce, E.M., Ashley, K.D.: (1984) Explaining and arguing with examples. *Proc. National Conference on Artificial Intelligence (AAAI-84)*

Rittel, H.N.J., Webber, M.M.: (1973) Dilemmas in a General Theory of Planning, *Policy Sciences* 4, Elsevier, Amsterdam, 155-169

Rittel, H.W.J., Webber, M.M.: Planning Problems are Wicked Problems. *Developments in Design Methodology,* (Cross, N., Ed.) Wiley. 135-144.

Roberts, H.: (1988) Knowledge representation for procedural law. MSc thesis. Department of Computing, Imperial College, London.

Robinson, P., Luff, P., Jirotka, M., Hardey, M., Gilbert, G.N., Frohlich, D.M., Cordingley, E.S., Buckland, S.: (1988) Functional specification for the Advice System, Social and Computer Sciences Research Group, University of Surrey.

Routen, T.: (1989) Hierarchically organised formalisations. *Proc. Second International Conference on Artificial Intelligence and Law, Vancouver.* ACM Press. 242-250.

Routen, T.W., Bench-Capon, T.J.M.: (1990) Hierarchical Formalisations, forthcoming in *International Journal of Man-Machine Studies.*

Roy-Burman, J.: (1988) Database modelling of the physical and conceptual structure of statute law. MSc thesis. Department of Computing, Imperial College, London.

Ruoff, T.: (1984) *The Solicitor and the Automated Office.* Sweet and Maxwell, London.

Sacks, H. Schegloff, E.A., Jefferson G.: (1974) A simplest systematics for the organisation of turn-taking in conversation, *Language,* 50, 696-735

Schank, R., Rieger, C.J.: (1974) Inference and the computer understanding of natural language. *Artificial Intelligence* 5, 4, 373-412.

Schild, U.J.: (1989) Open-textured law, expert systems and logic programming. PhD thesis. Department of Computing, Imperial College, London. To be published by Ellis Horwood.

Schegloff, E.A.: (1968) Sequencing in conversational openings, *American Anthropologist,* 70, 1075-1095

Schegloff, E.A., Jefferson G., Sacks, H.: (1977) The preferences for self-correction in the organization of repair in conversation. *Language,* 53, 361-382.

Schegloff, E.A., Sacks, H.: (1973) Opening up closings, *Semiotica,* 8, 289-327

Schlobohm, D.A.: (1985) A Prolog program which analyzes income tax issues under Section 318(a) of the Internal Revenue Code. *Computing Power and Legal Reasoning* (Walter, C., Ed.). West Publishing Co., St. Paul, Minn. 765-815.

Schlobohm, D.A., Waterman, D.A.: (1987) Explanation for an expert system that performs estate planning. *Proc. First International Conference on Artificial Intelligence and Law, Boston,* ACM Press. 18-27.

Schunfeld, W. (1985) Prolog extensions based on tableau calculus. *Proc. Ninth International Joint Conference on Artificial Intelligence* 730-732.

Sergot, M.J.: (1980) Programming law: LEGOL as a logic programming language. Department of Computing and Control, Imperial College, London.

Sergot, M.J.: (1982) Prospects for representing the law as logic programs. *Logic Programming* (Clark, K.L., Tarnlund, S-A., Eds.). Academic Press, London, 1982.

Sergot, M.J.: (1983) A query-the-user facility for logic programming. *Integrated Interactive Computer Systems* (Degano, P., Sandewall, E., Eds.). North-Holland, Amsterdam, 1983. Also in *New Horizons in Educational Computing* (Yazdani, M., Ed.). Ellis Horwood

Sergot, M.J.: (1985a) Representing legislation as logic programs. (August 1985) *Machine Intelligence* 11 (Hayes, J.E., Michie, D., Richards, J., Eds.). Oxford University Press, 1988, 209-260.

Sergot, M.J.: (1985b) Logic programming and its applications in law: A brief tutorial introduction. (June 1985). *Computing Power and Legal Language* (Walter, C., Ed.). Greenwood/Quorum Press, New York, 1988, 25-38.

Sergot, M.J., Sadri, F., Kowalski, R.A., Kriwaczek, F., Hammond, P., Cory, H.T.: (1986a) The British Nationality Act as a logic program. *Communications of the ACM* 29, 5, 370-386.

Sergot, M.J., Cory, H.T., Hammond, P., Kowalski, R.A., Kriwaczek, F., Sadri, F.: (1986b) Formalisation of the British Nationality Act. *Yearbook of Law, Computers and Technology:* Volume 2 (Arnold, C., Ed.). Butterworths, London.

Sharpe, W.P.: (1984) Logic programming for the law. M.Tech. thesis. Brunel University.

Sharpe, W.P.: (1985) Logic programming for the law. *Research and Development in Expert Systems: Proc. Fourth Technical Conference of the British Computer Society Specialist Group on Expert Systems.* (Bramer, M.A., Ed.). Cambridge University Press.

Sherman, D.M.: (1986) Blueprint for a computer-based model of the Income Tax Act of Canada. LL.M. thesis. York University, Toronto.

Sherman, D.M.: (1987) A Prolog model of the Income Tax Act of Canada. *Proc. First International Conference on Artificial Intelligence and Law, Boston,* ACM Press. 127-136.

Simon, H.A.: (1984) The Structure of Ill-Structured Problems. *Developments in Design Methodology* (Cross, N., Ed.) Wiley. 145-166.

Smith, J.C.: (1976) *Legal Obligation.* University of Toronto Press.

Smith, J.C., Deedman, C.: (1987) The application of expert systems technology to case-based law. *Proc. First International Conference on Artificial Intelligence and Law, Boston,* ACM Press. 84-93.

Sommers, F.: (1964) Types and Ontology, *Philosophical Review,* 73, 522-527.

Spirgel-Sinclair, S.: (1988) The DHSS Retirement Pension Forecast and Advice System, *KBS in Government 88,* (Duffin, P., Ed.) Blenheim On Line, Pinner. 89-106

Sprowl, J.A.: (1979) Automating the legal reasoning process: A computer that uses regulations and statutes to draft legal documents. *American Bar Foundation Research Journal,* 1, 1-81.

Sprowl, J.A.: (1980) Automated assembly of legal documents. *Computer Science and Law* (Niblett, B., Ed.). Cambridge University Press, New York. 195-205.

Sridharan, N.S.: (1978a) A flexible structure for knowledge: Examples of legal concepts. Technical Report LRP-TR-1, Laboratory for Computer Science Research, Rutgers University, New Brunswick, NJ.

Sridharan, N.S.: (1978b) AIMDS User Manual, Version 2. Technical Report CBM-TR-89, Department of Computer Science, Rutgers University, New Brunswick, NJ.

Sridharan, N.S.: (1980) Some relationships between BELIEVER and TAXMAN. Technical Report LRP-TR-7, Laboratory for Computer Science Research, Rutgers University, New Brunswick, NJ.

Stamper, R.: (1976) The automation of legal reasoning: Problems and prospects. LEGOL Project Report L6, LSE Systems Research Group, London School of Economics and Political Science, London.

Stamper, R.: (1977) The LEGOL-1 prototype system and language. *The Computer Journal* 20, 2, 102-108.

Stamper, R.: (1979) Towards a semantic normal form. In *Data Base Architecture* (Bracchi, G., Nijssen, G.M., Eds.). North-Holland, Amsterdam.

Stamper, R.: (1980) LEGOL: Modelling legal rules by computer. *Computer Science and Law* (Niblett, B., Ed.). Cambridge University Press, New York. 45-71.

Stamper, R.: (1986) A non-classical logic for law based on the structures of behaviour. *Automated Analysis of Legal Texts* (Martino, A.A., Socci, F., Eds.). North-Holland, Amsterdam.

Stamper, R.: (1989) The role of semantics in legal expert systems and legal reasoning. *Proc. Expert Systems in Law.*

Stamper, R., Tagg, C., Mason, P., Cook, S., Marks, J.: (1982) Developing the LEGOL semantic grammar. *Artificial Intelligence and Legal Information Systems* (Ciampi, C., Ed.). North-Holland, Amsterdam, 357-379.

Stathis, K.: (1987) A logic-based system for an application in law. MSc thesis. Department of Computing, Imperial College, London.

Studnicki, F., Polanowska, B., Stabra, E., Fall, M., Lachwa, A.: (1982a) The research project ANAPHORA in its present stage of development. *Coling '82 Abstracts* (Hajicova, E., Ed.). North-Holland, Amsterdam, 273-276.

Studnicki, F., Polanowska, B., Stabra, E., Fall, M., Lachwa, A.: (1982b) A semantic approach to automated resolving of interdocumental cross-references in legal texts. *Computing in the Humanities* (Bailey, R.W., Ed.). North-Holland, Amsterdam. 1

Suphamongkhon, K.: (1984) Towards an expert system on immigration legislation. MSc thesis. Department of Computing, Imperial College, London.

Susskind, R.E.: (1986a) Expert systems in law: A jurisprudential inquiry. DPhil thesis. Oxford Univ., 1986. Published by Oxford University Press.

Susskind, R.E.: (1986b) Expert systems in law: A jurisprudential approach to artificial intelligence and legal reasoning. *The Modern Law Review* 49, 168-194.

Susskind, R.E.: (1987) Expert systems in law: Out of the research laboratory and into the marketplace, *Proc. First International Conference on Artificial Intelligence and Law, Boston,* ACM Press. 1-8.

Susskind, R.E.: (1989) The Latent Damage System: A jurisprudential analysis. *Proc. Second International Conference on Artificial Intelligence and Law, Vancouver.* ACM Press. 23-32.

Sussman, G., Winograd, T., Charniak, E.: (1971) Micro-Planner Reference Manual (revised). A.I. Memo 203A, Artificial Intelligence Laboratory, M.I.T., Cambridge, Mass.

Szolovits, P., Hawkinson, L.B., Martin, W.A.: (1977) An overview of OWL, a language for knowledge representation. MIT/LCS/TM-86, Laboratory for Computer Science, M.I.T., Cambridge, Mass.

Taylor, A.: (1988) Adjudication, Policy and Organisation: The Example of Social Security Decision Making, *KBS in Government* (Duffin, P. Ed.) Blenheim, London. 215-226.

Tennant, H.R., Ross K.M., Thompson C.W.: (1983) Usable natural language interfaces through menu-based natural language understanding in *Proceedings of CHI '83*

Toulmin, S.: (1958) *The Uses of Argument.* Cambridge University Press.

Toulmin, S.: (1972) *Human understanding: The collective use and evolution of concepts.* Princeton University Press.

Toulmin, S., Rieke, R.D., Janik, A.: (1979) *An Introduction to Reasoning.* MacMillan Press, New York.

Twining, W.L., Miers, D.: (1982) *How To Do Things With Rules* (2nd Edition). Weidenfeld and Nicolson, London.

von Wright, G.H.: (1963) *Norm and Action.* Routledge and Kegan Paul, London.

Walter, C.: (ed.) (1985) *Computing Power and Legal Reasoning* West Publishing Co., St. Paul, Minn.

Walter, C.: (ed.) (1988) *Computing Power and Legal Language* Greenwood/Quorum Press, New York.

Waterman, D.A., Anderson, R.H., Hayes-Roth, F., Klahr, P., Martins, G., Rosenschein, S.J.: (1979) Design of a rule-oriented system for implementing expertise. Report N-1158-ARPA, The Rand Corporation, Santa Monica, Calif.

Waterman, D.A., Paul, J., Peterson, M.A.: (1986) Expert systems for legal decision making. *Expert Systems* 3, 4, 212-226.

Waterman, D.A., Peterson, M.A.: (1980) Rule-based models of legal expertise. *Proc. First Annual National Conference on Artificial Intelligence.* 272-275.

Waterman, D.A., Peterson, M.A.: (1981) Models of legal decisionmaking. Report R-2717-ICJ, Institute for Civil Justice, The Rand Corporation, Santa Monica, Calif.

Waterman, D.A., Peterson, M.A.: (1984) Evaluating civil claims: An expert systems approach. *Expert Systems* 1.

Welfare Rights Bulletin 75, London: Child Poverty Action Group.

Wright, P., Monk A.: (1989) Evaluation for Design in *Proceedings of the HCI '89 Conference, University of Nottingham,* 345-358.

Index

ABF 8, 29
acceptance issues 319–20
Adjudication Officer's Guide (ADG) 78–9, 85–6, 92, 160–1, 163
adjudication support system 77–94
  aims of 80–2
  capital conditions 90
  categorization problems 89
  domain complexity 88
  historical background to 78–80
  interrelationship between factual information and legal conditions 90
  outstanding problems 91–4
  problems of categorization 88
  problems of interpretation 89
  procedural complexity 87–8
  requirements of 82–91
  rules 87
  source material 83–7
  tasks 87–91
Advice System 124–7, 183, 189–97, 213, 266
  conceptual model for 125–6
  defining requirements 191–3
  development 185, 191–6
  evaluation 196–7
  history of application 190
  interaction design 194–5
  interaction rules 126
  interface design 195–6
  knowledge analysis 193–4
  knowledge base 241–4
  knowledge representation 193–4, 227–36
    regulations and procedures 123–4
  objectives of 190–91
  primary purpose of 190
  target users 214, 216–18
  user interface 126
algorithmic programs 20
algorithmic representations 20
Alvey-DHSS Demonstrator project vii, 1, 69–74, 199–208
  applications 71
  breadth of remit 72
  close relationship with customer organization 72
  communication methods 203–4
  culture 201–2
  demonstrations 206–7
  design control 202–3
  documentation 205
  external publication 207
  interdisciplinary nature of 70–71
  lessons 208
  monitoring officer 208
  opportunities of 69–74
  organization 199–201
  phases of 167
  planning 205–6
  project introduction into the organization 317–19
  prototypes 137–8
  size of applications 73
  size of project 69–70
  training 206
  see also Toolkit
Analytical Legal Databases 51
ANAPHORA 41
APES 36–9
argument form 303–5

artificial intelligence vii, 6, 7
Assumption-based Truth Maintenance Systems (ATMS) 59, 256, 259
Atomically Normalized Form (ANF) 51
axiomatic theory 35

BASIC 20, 23
bidirectionality in mixed initiative interaction 266–8
British Nationality Act 1981 vii, 37, 39, 72, 338, 340

C program 21
CABERET 247
case-based reasoning 64
case law 10–11, 53–60, 84, 324
CCLIPS 8, 49, 51, 52
Child Poverty Action Group 334
CHOOSE 20
Citizens Advice Bureaux 334
civil code systems 11
claimant information systems 183–98
  development methods 184–5
  experimental developments 197–8
  team organization 186
  tools for qualitative analysis 197–8
  see also Advice System; Forms Helper
classification 9–14
  by activity 9–10
  by computational formalism 10
  distinguishing between statutes and case law 10
  fixed interpretations of the law 12–14
  open texture 12
COBOL 23
common knowledge base 129–38
  example of 129–36
common law systems 10, 11
computational formalisms 10, 27, 32
computer-aided instruction (CAI) 19
computer programs, law in 3–67
conceptual models 49–53
constructive ownership of stock 30
CORPTAX 20, 23, 30, 46, 48, 49, 52
Corpus Juris Mechanicum (CJM) 54, 55
court decisions 11
CSK rules 58, 60
customers, knowledge based systems for 115–17

database retrieval 65
DataLex 21, 22, 32, 64, 65
data-processing applications 23, 36
decision making 17, 77–8
  see also adjudication support system; group decision making; policy makers
decision nets 21
deductive reasoning 13–14
definitional law 39, 40
DENDRAL 7
deontic concepts 62–3
deontic logic 62–3, 252
deontic modalities 63
Discourse Representation Theory 42
divorce law in Scotland 29
document drafting 9
document retrieval 5–6, 9, 49–53
domain glossary 236–9
drafting of legislation 43–5

electronic form-filling system 268
ELI 28
EMYCIN 18, 28
environmental law 37
ESPLEX 29, 52, 96
evaluation issues 319–20
expert systems 8, 18, 26–8

first-order generalization 56, 57
flowcharts 20–1, 28
Forms Helper 119–24, 127, 183, 186–9, 266
  design concept 121–3
  development 184, 187–9
  'electronic form' approach 121–3
  electronic help and support 123–4
  evaluation 189
  history of application 186–7
  interactive computer system 120–21
  objectives of 187
  target users 214
  training form 124
  user requirements 119–20
Forms Helper I, mixed initiative interaction 268–75
formulation of legislation 95–113

garbage collection 288
government grants 37
group decision making 295–308
group working 297–302
  computer support 302–6
  see also policy formulation
guidance issues 324–5

Hohfeldian concepts 44
human-computer interaction 185–6, 188
human issues, outstanding 321–6
HYPO vii, 8, 64, 66–7, 72, 246, 247

Immigration Act 1971 37
import and export regulations 38
Income Support (General Regulations) 1987 83
Income Tax Act of Canada 30, 31
information retrieval 159–60
information sources 6
Internal Revenue Code 30, 31, 49
IRI-Project 37
Istituto per la Documentazione Giuridica (IDG) 8, 50, 52

JUDITH 8
JURIS 253
justification 322

KANT 217, 227, 241–3
knowledge analysis 224–40, 315–17
  Local Office Demonstrator (LOD) 239–44
knowledge base 240–4
  Advice System 227–36, 241–4
  limiting or scoping 324
Knowledge Base Builder (KBB) 241–3
knowledge based systems (KBS) vii, 69–73, 77, 95
  framework for application to law 329
  model application to 336–42
  public use of 115–28
knowledge representation 245–63
  adequacy of existing paradigms 251–2
  and inferencing 222–4
  and phases of KBS 246–8
  backward chaining 260
  classes, instances, slots and values 256–8
  definitions 252–4
  design 256
  future work 260
  hypothetical reasoning 259
  implications for formalism 249–51
  incomplete information and vagueness 255
  rules, constraints and definitions 258, 260
  Toolkit 255–9
  usefulness of frames 254
knowledge structuring, organizing principle for 220–2
knowledge work 213
  domain of application 219–22
  scope of 219–20
  targeting 214–18
KRYPTON 257

landlord and tenant legislation 37
Language for Legal Discourse 7, 34, 41–2, 52, 64, 251
Latent Damage Act 1986 18, 19
Latent Damage Advisor 72, 310, 338
Latent Damage System 18–19, 37
law in computer programs 3–67
LDS (Legal Decision making System) 14–15
legal analysis 19, 20, 23, 29
legal disputes 9, 18
legal domain, characteristics of 329
legal rules 13
legal source knowledge, model of 336
LEGOL 5, 8, 23, 29, 32–6, 39, 52
LES 21
LEX 29, 42–3
LEXIS 50
LIRS 8, 52
Lisp 172
litigation 9
Local Office Demonstrator (LOD) 139, 174, 213, 324
  early objectives 140–1
  initial areas of investigation 141–3
  knowledge analysis 239–40
  knowledge base 239–44

local office application 143–4
prototypes 144–5
target users 215–16
Local Office Demonstrator 1 (LOD1) 145–8
Local Office Demonstrator 2 (LOD2) 148–51
Local Office Demonstrator 3 (LOD3) 151–63
design of 153–7
evaluation of 157–62
expert procedural support 160–2
information retrieval 159–60
logical encoding of legislation 160
requirements of 152–3
summary of system 162–3
logic programming 8, 26, 29, 30, 35–43
logic sentences 35
logical consequences 27
logical normalization of legislation 95
LOI users 143–4
LOII users 143–4
Loops 172

maintenance issues 319–20
Medical Evidence Regulations 333
micro-arguments 303–5
mixed initiative interaction 265–94
dimensions of 266–8
with Advice System 279–92
with Forms Helper I 268–75
with Forms Helper II 275–9
MRS 58

Neligan's Digest 85
NORMA 33–5, 39, 52
normalization 43–4, 51
Norwegian Research Centre for Computers and Law (NRCCL) 8, 65

objective definition 311–13
obligations 62–3
OCAO 143, 152
open texture 12
opportunity identification 311–13
organizational issues 309–27
outstanding 321–6
OWL 54
ownership 322
Oxford Concordance package (OCP) 227

parser 42–3
patent law 37
pension regulations 37, 38
permissions 62–3
policy argumentation process 100
Policy Demonstrator 324
policy development 97, 103
constraints on 104
policy environment 97–9
policy formulation 45, 97–106
conceptual components 99–101
correctness of 111
detailed argumentation 303–5
issue clarification 107
issue explanation 107–8
issue verification 106
knowledge based support 106–10, 112–13, 305–6
lack of specified goals 110–11
nature of problem 295–6
nature of support 110–11
nature of task 296–7
option evaluation 109
option generation 108–9
potential benefits of support system 104–6
problem solving dynamics 299–302
reasoning about classes not cases 110
requirements of support system 104
solution specification 109
solution verification 109
system evaluation 306–8
types of knowledge used in 101–4
see also group working; policy support system
policy justification 110
policy support system
analysis methods 171
anglicized output 176
application after July 1987 169
application up to July 1987 167–8
argumentation formalism 177
description of prototypes 169–71
design methods 172
design specification 172

evaluation methods 172–3
experimental developments 175–7
further work on 178–81
future of 181–2
history of application 167–9
knowledge base building 173–5
knowledge base revision 177
methods 171–5
nature of application 166
prototypes 165–82
requirements of 104, 171
software 171–2
policy system, integrating facilities of 111
Poor Law 330
problem structuring 296, 302
procedural law 41
product liability 15
project introduction into the organization 317–19
PROLEG 38
PROLOG 10, 28–32, 36, 38, 39, 43, 62, 249
prototype-plus-deformations structure 61–2
prototypes 137–8
public use of KBS 115–28

qualitative analysis tool (QAT) 197–8
quality assurance 319
Query-the-User 36

ratio decidendi 55–8
requirements analysis 314
requirements specification 314
Retirement Pension Forecast Advisor 263
R × F = D equation 24–6
risk assessment 313
ROSIE 15, 28
rule-based formalisms 28–30

SAL (System for Asbestor Litigation) 15
SARA 64, 65
scientific codification 51
SEARCH 20
sickness benefit 330–42
social issues 309–27
Social Security, information provision for claimants 116
Social Security Act 1975 331
Social Security Act 1986 83
Social Security benefit entitlement decisions 78
see also adjudication support system
Social Security benefits 37
Social Security claimants 117–19
rates of take-up 117
Social Security legislation 37
Social Security (Mariners Benefits) Act 1975 84
Social Security (Unemployment, Sickness and Invalidity Benefit) Regulations 1983 332
Soft Systems Methodology (SSM) 320
special-purpose formalisms 40
Statuatory Sick Pay legislation 37
statutes 10–11, 53–60
stock exchange regulations 37
syllogism 55
systemic grammar networks (SGN) 232

tableau calculus 43
tasks 75–6
TAXADVISOR 18, 24, 28
TAXMAN vii, 7, 34, 39, 40, 246, 341
TAXMAN I 7, 29, 45–9, 51, 52
TAXMAN II 7, 45–9, 52, 60–4
TAXMAN III 263
text animator 19
theorem-proving methods 45
3-D 62
time bomb syndrome 312
time constraints 313
Toolkit 263
in knowledge representation 255–9
Trustee Act 1925 84
turn constructional units (TCUs) 282–3

US Uniform Commercial Code 50
user reliability 322–4

validation issues 319–20

WESTLAW 50
word incorporation parser 198

The A.P.I.C. Series

General Editors: M.J.R. Shave and I.C. Wand

1. Some Commercial Autocodes. A Comparative Study*
   E.L. Willey, A. d'Agapeyeff, Marion Tribe, B.J. Gibbens and Michelle Clarke
2. A Primer of ALGOL 60 Programming*
   E.W. Dijkstra
3. Input Language for Automatic Programming*
   A.P. Yershov, G.I. Kozhukhin and U. Voloshin
4. Introduction to System Programming*
   Edited by Peter Wegner
5. ALGOL 60 Implementation. The Translation and Use of ALGOL 60 Programs on a Computer
   B. Randell and L.J. Russell
6. Dictionary for Computer Languages*
   Hans Breuer
7. The Alpha Automatic Programming System*
   Edited by A.P. Yershov
8. Structured Programming†
   O.-J. Dahl, E.W. Dijkstra and C.A.R. Hoare
9. Operating Systems Techniques
   Edited by C.A.R. Hoare and R. H. Perrott
10. ALGOL 60 Compilation and Assessment
    B.A. Wichmann
11. Definition of Programming Languages by Interpreting Automata*
    Alexander Ollongren
12. Principles of Program Design†
    M.A. Jackson

* Out of print.
† Now published in the Computer Science Classics Series.

13. Studies in Operating Systems
R.M. McKeag and R. Wilson

14. Software Engineering
R.J. Perrott

15. Computer Architecture: A Structured Approach
R.W. Doran

16. Logic Programming
Edited by K.L. Clark and S.-A. Tärnlund

17. Fortran Optimization*
Michael Metcalf

18. Multi-microprocessor Systems
Y. Paker

19. Introduction to the Graphical Kernel System (GKS)
F.R.A. Hopgood, D.A. Duce, J.R. Gallop and D.C. Sutcliffe

20. Distributed Computing
Edited by Fred B. Chambers, David A. Duce and Gillian P. Jones

21. Introduction to Logic Programming
Christopher John Hogger

22. Lucid, the Dataflow Programming Language
William W. Wadge and Edward A. Ashcroft

23. Foundations of Programming
Jacques Arsac

24. Prolog for Programmers
Feliks Kluźniak and Stanislaw Szpakowicz

25. Fortran Optimization, Revised Edition
Michael Metcalf

26. PULSE: An Ada-based Distributed Operating System
D. Keeffe, G.M. Tomlinson, I.C. Wand and A.J. Wellings

27. Program Evolution: Processes of Software Change
M. Lehman and L.A. Belady

28. Introduction to the Graphical Kernel System (GKS): Second Edition Revised for the International Standard
F.R.A. Hopgood, D.A. Duce, J.R. Gallop and D.C. Sutcliffe

29. The Complexity of Boolean Networks
P.E. Dunne

30. Advanced Programming Methodologies
Edited by Gianna Cioni and Andrzej Salwicki

31. Logic and Computer Science
Edited by P. Odifreddi

32. Knowledge Representation. An Approach to Artificial Intelligence
T.J.M. Bench-Capon

33. Integrated Project Support Environments: The Aspect Project
Edited by Alan W. Brown

34. Object-Oriented Languages
G. Masini, A. Napoli, D. Colnet, D. Léonard and K. Tombre

35. An Introduction to Programming with Specifications:
A Mathematical Approach
R. Kubiak, R. Rudsiński and S. Sokołowski

36. Knowledge-Based Systems and Legal Applications
Edited by T.J.M. Bench-Capon